THRESHOLD CONCEPTS WITHIN THE DISCIPLINES

EDUCATIONAL FUTURES
RETHINKING THEORY AND PRACTICE
Volume 16

Scope
This series maps the emergent field of educational futures. It will commission books on the futures of education in relation to the question of globalisation and knowledge economy. It seeks authors who can demonstrate their understanding of discourses of the knowledge and learning economies. It aspires to build a consistent approach to educational futures in terms of traditional methods, including scenario planning and foresight, as well as imaginative narratives, and it will examine examples of futures research in education, pedagogical experiments, new utopian thinking, and educational policy futures with a strong accent on actual policies and examples.

Threshold Concepts within the Disciplines

Edited by

Ray Land
University of Strathclyde, UK

Jan H.F. Meyer
University of Durham, UK

and

Jan Smith
University of Strathclyde, UK

SENSE PUBLISHERS
ROTTERDAM / TAIPEI

A C.I.P. record for this book is available from the Library of Congress.

ISBN 978-90-8790-267-4 (paperback)
ISBN 978-90-8790-268-1 (hardback)

Published by: Sense Publishers,
P.O. Box 21858, 3001 AW Rotterdam, The Netherlands
http://www.sensepublishers.com

Cover photograph: © 2008 R. Land, 'Alhambra'

Printed on acid-free paper

TABLE OF CONTENTS

RAY LAND, JAN H.F. MEYER AND JAN SMITH

EDITORS' PREFACE

Imagine that you are a raw potato – a Desirée potato. We don't know what it feels like to be such a raw potato, nor are we entirely confident that it is appropriate to consider the subjectivity of such a vegetable but, in terms of your chemical composition, we might imagine an ontological horizon defined in terms of being starchy, watery, and sugary. You are about to enter a state of liminality on the way to becoming a *roast* potato. Aspects of the journey thus far have been troublesome. You have lost your red skin. Your delectable yellow creamy flesh has been exposed. You have been parboiled to get rid of some of your starch. Your outer surface has been roughened. You don't know it, but there is still more trouble ahead. That first glimpse of other potatoes in the hot fat may be the first sign of what things may look like 'on the other side' of the portal. You are not yet a roast potato, and you do not know what it is like to *be* a roast potato. And in the preliminary stages of getting to where you are now you could have entertained other options. Such as keeping your skin on for a start. As a peeled, parboiled potato you still have options. You can, for example, be transformed into mash or something more exotic like *soufflé di patate.* With a bit of creative luck, you might even assume the mantle of *pommes boulangère* or *gratin dauphinoise*. But, once you hit the fat that's pretty much it. You are beginning to cross the portal that is the heat induced process of caramelisation: an irreversible chemical process that will transfigure your identity. You will look, feel, smell, and taste different. You will have entered a new space: the world of caramelised roast potatoes.

Sadly the potato has no self-determination, no control over experiences which might either encourage or discourage an understanding of a threshold concept, and we will leave it to its destiny at the point of caramelisation. But there is a serious side to this imaginary journey. As Glynis Cousin points out in Chapter 19 of this volume, threshold concept theory addresses 'the kind of complicated learner transitions learners undergo'. Generating a supportive learning environment to sustain learners whilst they negotiate such transitions involves, she says, 'a deep appreciation of a dialectic between knowing and being.'

> …mastery simultaneously changes what we know and who we are. Learning is a form of identity work. (Cousin, Chapter 19, p. 264)

In the period since the notion of threshold concepts was first presented at the 10th Improving Student Learning Conference in Brussels in 2002, the main characteristics of this conceptual framework have remained constant, and relatively straightforward. The basic idea underpinning this field of enquiry is that, probably in all disciplines, there are conceptual gateways or 'portals' that must be passed through, however difficult that passage might be, to arrive at important new understandings. This was expressed in the seminal paper on thresholds as follows:

> A threshold concept can be considered as akin to a portal, opening up a new and previously inaccessible way of thinking about something. It represents a transformed way of understanding, or interpreting, or viewing something without which the learner cannot progress. As a consequence of comprehending a threshold concept there may thus be a transformed internal view of subject matter, subject landscape, or even world view. This transformation may be sudden or it may be protracted over a considerable period of time, with the transition to understanding proving troublesome. Such a transformed view or landscape may represent how people 'think' in a particular discipline, or how they perceive, apprehend, or experience particular phenomena within that discipline (or more generally). (Meyer and Land, 2003, p. 412).

In attempting to characterise such conceptual gateways it was suggested in the earlier work that they are *transformative* (occasioning a significant shift in the perception of a subject), *integrative* (exposing the previously hidden inter-relatedness of something) and likely to be, in varying degrees, *irreversible* (unlikely to be forgotten, or unlearned only through considerable effort), and frequently *troublesome*, for a variety of reasons. Discussions with practitioners in a range of disciplines and institutions led us to conclude that a threshold concept can of itself inherently represent what Perkins (1999) referred to as *troublesome knowledge* – knowledge that is 'alien', or counter-intuitive, ritualised, inert, tacit or even intellectually absurd at face value. It increasingly appears that a threshold concept may on its own constitute, or in its application lead to, such troublesome knowledge. This volume will analyse further the different ways in which knowledge can prove troublesome for students (and teachers) and will draw attention to the implications of this for the curriculum. Threshold concepts also tend to be *bounded* in that they serve as boundary-markers for the conceptual spaces that constitute disciplinary terrain. Later work (Meyer and Land, 2005) indicated the *discursive* nature of threshold concepts and further potential sources of troublesomeness arising both from language and from the ontological dimension of such threshold concepts. As we gain new knowledge, we are changed by it, and these shifts are manifested in a changed use of language.

For students who find the learning of certain concepts difficult, we have characterised such spaces as akin to states of 'liminality' which tend to be transformative in function, and usually involve an individual or group being altered from one state into another. As a result of such transformation the learner acquires new knowledge and subsequently a new status and identity within the community of practice. However, this state of 'liminality', the space of transformation, can also become a suspended state, or 'stuck place', in which understanding approximates to a kind of 'mimicry' or lack of authenticity (Meyer and Land, 2003). Insights gained by learners as they cross thresholds can be exhilarating but might also be unsettling, requiring an uncomfortable shift in identity. Paradoxically this may be experienced as a sense of loss as an earlier, more secure stance of familiar knowing has to be abandoned as new and unfamiliar knowledge is encountered. A further complication might be the operation of an 'underlying game' or 'episteme' (Perkins 2006) which requires the learner to comprehend the often tacit games of enquiry or ways of thinking and practising (WTP) inherent within specific disciplinary knowledge practices.

Transformation can be protracted, over considerable periods of time, and involve *oscillation* between states, often with temporary regression to earlier status. It would appear, however, that once the state of liminality is entered, though there may be temporary regression, there can be no ultimate full return to the pre-liminal state. There would seem to be no re-winding of the transformative process.

Threshold Concepts have thus emerged as a set of transferable or portable ideas across disciplinary contexts, which offer new insights into teaching and learning, and as a theoretical framework which is both explanatory and 'actionable' (capable of translation into action). The significance of the framework provided by threshold concepts lies in its explanatory potential to locate troublesome aspects of disciplinary knowledge within transitions across conceptual thresholds and hence to assist teachers in identifying appropriate ways of modifying or redesigning curricula to enable their students to negotiate such transitions more successfully. It is principally an analytical framework for trying to understand how students learn, where the barriers to their learning lie, be they epistemological or ontological, and what appropriate pedagogical adjustments or modifications might overcome such difficulties.

It draws eclectically on a number of theoretical perspectives, some from learning theory, and some from other disciplines. It can be seen to some extent as a form of social constructivism; our colleague David Perkins at Harvard has drawn attention to the connection between threshold concepts and his own work on troublesome knowledge and, more recently, on dispositional knowledge. The approach reflects a 'conceptual change' model of learning. It addresses discipline-based learning and Perkins has referred to it elsewhere as a 'theory of difficulty' (Perkins, 2007). Threshold Concepts also, in its analysis of how learner identities undergo transformation as new knowledge is encountered, has affinities with social learning theory, particularly the work of Wenger (1998) on communities of practice, who in turn draws on Vygotsky's (1978) notion of a zone of proximal development. Many of the chapters in this volume show a particular interest in how students enter disciplinary communities of practice and acquire the knowledge practices and particular identities, or ways of being, needed to enter them.

Threshold concepts draw on, but also challenges in some ways, the phenomenographic tradition of studies of how students approach learning, and how they experience and conceive of learning. Noel Entwistle's chapter in this volume indicates connections between the phenomenographic tradition and threshold concepts. From the outset there has been a close relationship between threshold concepts and the tradition of variation theory associated with Ference Marton, and his colleagues in Sweden and Hong Kong (Marton et al, 2004), though we propose a somewhat different model of variation from Marton's (see Chapter 5 in this volume by Meyer, Land and Davies).

In its notion of 'liminality', which is an important part of our analysis, the framework draws from a different tradition on the social anthropological theory of Victor Turner (1969), the originator of the concept. We also make use of notions of discourse and the discursive formation of subjectivity and disciplinary identity through learning. This draws on certain postmodern cultural theory as well as discourse analysis. The strong emphasis on the ontological dimension of learning – for which the graphic tale, earlier, of the desirée potato's transfiguration into roastedness and caramelisation stands as ready testament – reflects similar emphases and concerns in the philosophy of education, most notably in the influential work of Ron Barnett (Barnett, 2005). At the pragmatic level of attempting to identify the points and sources of conceptual difficulty, disjunction and troublesomeness, the work of Ian Kinchin and David Hay (2005), in turn drawing on the earlier studies at Cornell by Joseph Novak (1990), have proved extremely valuable.

So the framework is a varied, rich and occasionally heady cocktail of ingredients, a kind of conceptual *sangria*. It does not fit neatly into one particular niche or under one convenient label, but we feel that it perhaps does not necessarily need to. We hope that its eclecticism might make it of relevance and interest to a very broad range of practitioners, in all disciplines, and particularly those 'front-line' teachers who are frequently faced with the conceptual difficulties and 'stuck places' so often discussed in this volume, and who often bear the responsibility for course design. We also see the framework as not being restricted solely to learning within the context of higher education but of equal value and portability to all other educational sectors.

The first volume of studies on threshold concepts, *Overcoming Barriers to Student Understanding*, appeared in 2006 (Meyer and Land, 2006). This second book, which has its origins in a lively international symposium on thresholds at Strathclyde University, Glasgow in the autumn of 2006, builds and expands on the first in a number of important ways. It provides much more empirical data concerning the experience of threshold concepts and troublesome knowledge from the students' perspective. The volume also adds to the range of disciplinary contexts in which thresholds have been studied. We have in this volume substantial and compelling findings from subjects as diverse as economics, computer science, different branches of engineering, biology, teacher education, languages, art therapy, and transport and product design. The contexts range from England, Scotland, Wales, Northern Ireland and the Republic of Ireland to Sweden, Australia, Canada and the United States. The book also further develops the theoretical dimension of threshold concepts and reflects a migration of interest into wider spheres such as doctoral study, the professional development of academics as teachers, and issues relating to the methodologies that might prove productive in researching threshold concepts in specific disciplines. In regard to this latter point, there remain interesting issues around how we might best research threshold concepts. There is, as yet, no established methodology, or doctrine, in this regard, and perhaps that is how it should be, given the epistemological diversity of disciplines. This remains, however, an avenue of inquiry meriting further exploration.

The book is divided into three sections to reflect these emphases. Part I, 'Theoretical Perspectives', contains extensions, further elaborations or re-examinations of the original framework. David Perkins opens the volume with a thoughtful analysis of learning in terms of *possessive*, *performative* and *proactive knowledge*, suggesting that 'The notions of proactive knowledge and threshold concepts make natural partners'. He goes on to point out how 'a collection of threshold concepts or an unusually pivotal one can provoke a kind of an epistemic shift, where the very "game" or epistemic enterprise of the discipline can come out looking somewhat different'. Threshold concepts, he argues, have a strong 'reorganising power'. However, he cautions that this can bring with it 'an unfamiliarity that sometimes proves acute and off-putting. You can't rebalance the boat without rocking it.'

In the second chapter Noel Entwistle provides a valuable definition of the features of threshold concepts in relation to influential educational research into student learning over the last three decades. This includes phenomenographic studies of conceptions of learning, and Perry's developmental stages in conceptions of knowledge and learning. He argues that threshold concepts have a natural fit with the second of three distinguishable ways in which students' understanding of a subject can be opened up: through certain basic concepts in the early stages of a course, through integrative threshold concepts within the discipline, and through acquiring the distinctive ways of thinking and practising (WTP) characteristic of the subject. He aligns his conclusions with the empirical work from undergraduate economics presented in the following chapter by Peter Davies and Jean Mangan. They have constructed a model, drawn from the findings of the national *Embedding Threshold Concepts* project based at Staffordshire University, which proposes that transformative learning is better conceived as the acquisition of a *web* of threshold concepts organized into three categories of conceptual change. The first is a *basic* view of *personal conceptual change* (newly met concepts some of which transform understanding of everyday experience through integration of personal experience with ideas from the discipline). The second is *discipline-based conceptual change,* a (threshold) conception involving understanding of other subject discipline ideas (including other threshold concepts) integrated and transformed through acquisition of a theoretical perspective. The third is *procedural conceptual change*, requiring the ability to construct discipline-specific narratives and arguments transformed through acquisition of ways of practising.

Bob McCormick, in Chapter 4, critically re-examines the thresholds framework but from the different angle of Sfard's *acquisition* and *participation metaphors,* noting that the thresholds framework tends to mix these metaphors, sometimes seeing knowledge 'as an object, independent of knowers and what they do with the knowledge' but elsewhere drawing on the language of participation with notions such as communities of practice, tacit knowledge, academic territories, and, central to the participation metaphor, the 'transformation of personal identity'. Meyer, Land and Davies follow this in Chapter 5 with a further contribution to the original conceptual framework, suggesting that variation is a key component to the understanding of both how and where students might encounter conceptual difficulty. They provide indications as to how such variation might be assessed – at *pre-liminal*, *liminal*, *post-liminal* and *sub-liminal* stages of the learning trajectory – and consider how the use of variation within pedagogical practice (eg through illustrative example) can help students acquire new conceptual understanding. However the use of variation with some forms of troublesome knowledge (e.g. complex number in mathematics) is not always straightforward.

Maggi Savin-Baden's chapter closes the theoretical section by making a case that threshold concepts should be located in 'a broader conceptualisation of students' disjunction', with a greater emphasis on the relationship between learner identities and threshold concepts than there has been in the research literature heretofore. She concludes that the notion of 'learning spaces' and 'liquid learning' (after Bauman 2000) might be more useful for the construction of a model of transitional learning. Such an approach would allow, furthermore, 'for the recognition of the cyclical nature of learning'.

The central and largest section of the book, 'Disciplinary Contexts', draws on empirical studies undertaken across a range of subject areas. Observing the conceptual difficulties of 'operationally challenged' first year electronic engineering students struggling to come to terms with Java programming, Mick Flanagan and Jan Smith (Chapter 7) identify the 'nested' nature of the troublesome concepts facing this group. They identify the source of that troublesomeness, and any pedagogical resolution of it, within the semiotic complexities of language itself.

In a multi-national study (Chapter 8) Carol Zander, Robert McCartney and Kate Sanders from the USA, Jonas Boustedt, Anna Eckerdal, and Jan Erik Moström from Sweden, and Mark Ratcliffe from the UK used informal interviews and questionnaires to obtain data from teachers, and scripted, structured interviews to obtain data from students, to identify threshold concepts in computer science and to investigate how students might understand these concepts. 'Object-oriented programming' and 'memory/pointers' emerged as early candidates for thresholds, but their study also raises several broader issues with regard to future empirical studies of threshold concepts, such as at what point in a student's learning is data most profitably to be gathered, and what exactly does it mean for a concept to be *integrative?* As these researchers ask 'Is it integrative only if it integrates concepts the student already knows? Or can a concept be integrative if it connects a number of things that are only learned later?'

Also undertaking inquiry within computer science Dermot Shinners-Kennedy (Chapter 9) identifies 'state' as a further threshold concept. He sees this as exemplifying a 'simplicity and everydayness' that might characterise many threshold concepts. Everyday activities, he suggests, 'have a huge number of important concepts associated with them but they are rich with troublesome knowledge. Because they are so automated and compressed we find it difficult to extract the component concepts'. In addition to the sources of troublesomeness identified within the thresholds framework he identifies further problems associated with 'layered knowledge' and 'knowledge in the world'.

Within engineering Caroline Baillie and Anne Johnson (Chapter 10) draw on the findings of a large-scale Canadian study. They used in-depth interviews, course artifacts and student evaluation feedback to identify professional 'ways of thinking and practising' as an engineer as an attitudinal threshold that many students found troublesome. A major source of this appears to be fear of uncertainty. 'Students of engineering enjoy the precision of maths and physics that they learned in high school and find uncertainty in real messy human problems difficult to deal with'. They identify two 'pathways through barriers' which might offer practical ways forward for engineering students.

In electrical engineering Anna-Karin Carstensen and Jonte Bernhard (Chapter 11) studied video recordings of lab-work with Swedish students to develop a way to identify troublesome aspects of any given concept. They considered troublesome concepts in the learning of electrical circuits and control theory, such as frequency response. They describe how their use of variation theory opened up new dimensions in the understanding of learning sequences. In particular they found that certain concepts, such as the Bode Plot in circuitry, can function like a specialist 'key' that opens up the disciplinary portal of understanding. Moreover teaching a 'key' concept, according to this definition, does not just open up that particular concept, but also *the learning of other concepts related to it*. This led to an observed improvement in the scores achieved by students on a test following the course.

In the subject of economics, a discipline in which there has now been considerable research undertaken into threshold concepts, Martin Shanahan, Gigi Foster and Jan Meyer (Chapter 12) gathered data from a first-year microeconomics course at the University of South Australia. They grouped multiple choice and examination questions to reflect the three categories of conceptual change proposed by Davies and Mangan in Chapter 3 of this volume. Their aim was to explore whether the web of threshold concepts proposed by Davies and Mangan can be 'made visible' by quantitative analytical means. More particularly they wished to determine how the Davies and Mangan categories of threshold concepts, as revealed through students' multiple choice responses early in the course, correlated with their final examination marks. They conclude that there is 'sufficient evidence of statistical association' to support the contention that students' prior acquisition of an interrelated web of threshold concepts can affect their performance in standard economics examinations. Moreover they contend 'that properly-constructed multiple choice questions are capable of capturing variation in students' acquisition of threshold concepts, and that evidence of such variation can inform the pedagogy of threshold concepts'.

Also in the discipline of economics Andrew Ashwin (Chapter 13) is concerned to examine the experience of conceptual difficulty amongst the many students who encounter economics before undergraduate level. Examining the understanding of a rise in oil prices with students in the 14-19 age group, he employed the Biggs and Collis (1982) SOLO taxonomy initially 'because it was anticipated that it would more accurately reflect the quality of the learning outcome with respect to understanding and assessing threshold concept acquisition'. His findings identify a need for a 'transformed understanding of a subject' in the years before entrance to higher education. A focus on the idea of *thinking in the subject* is, he suggests, more useful than a primary focus on knowledge and content, if we wish to avoid ritualised knowledge and 'grade chasing'. He favours using the idea of a web of concepts (cf, Davies and Mangan, Chapter 3 of this volume) to gain an understanding of a discipline, where concepts have a degree of inter-relationship between them. 'To understand one concept one might require some understanding of another, and moreover an ability to recognise the relationship between the two'. Such qualitative understanding, he argues, would emphasise the ability to be able to recognise and interpret economic concepts and phenomena in a wide range of different contexts. Moreover, to 'see the similarities in the critical attributes that the concepts possess, and be able to relate these to the approach to a problem … would be seen as constituting *economic thinking*' at this important stage of learning.

Biology, suggests Charlotte Taylor (Chapter 14), is seen as being 'a more wide-ranging discipline than others, particularly in the sciences, since it encompasses a wide range of specialist fields'. Building on her earlier studies she undertakes a series of interviews with both teachers and graduates to explore the complexity of her discipline and attempt to identify the most salient areas of troublesome knowledge as well as the potential thresholds in biology. Both of these groups, she reports, identified a number of areas of biology which might be identified as candidates for threshold concepts, and these areas seem to be principally concerned with the *complexity, dynamics* and *variability* to be found in biological systems. 'The area of molecular biology was seen by many as particularly troublesome as it involved concepts which were constantly changing as new discoveries are made. Graduates are keenly aware of their new position at the cutting edge in science, and the inherent problems and challenges in this area'. These boundaries, she argues, have to be constantly re-assessed and the new knowledge and thinking integrated into the view of the discipline.

In the world of teacher education 'Knowledge and understanding are transformed in unpredictable ways for beginning teachers'. Researching in the context of a Scottish mentoring programme Moya Cove, Julie McAdam and James McGonigal (Chapter 15) recognise that the early establishment of classroom norms of behaviour, and gaining a personal sense of organisation and effectiveness within classroom life, can be a particularly troublesome and daunting prospect for novice teachers. As these researchers point out:

> Learning to confidently walk the social and pedagogical boundaries between firmness, direction and supportive engagement with young learners may well be a threshold concept that eases the pursuit of many other classroom aims.

As they listen to these beginning teachers' experiences and reflections they come to identify a sense of where ten recognised threshold concepts had begun to alter the students' awareness of teaching and learning. This to some extent offers a simpler prospect than the current twenty-two benchmark statements and ten transferable skills in the government professional standards, which still remain complex for beginners to comprehend. The researchers thus draw a tentative conclusion that 'Threshold concepts might therefore assist in developing student teachers' confidence about their progression through the teacher education experience, and its often puzzling jargon'.

The remaining contributions to this central section of the book highlight the diversity of disciplinary contexts in which the application of threshold concepts is finding resonance. Marina Orsini-Jones, in her chapter on language learning (Chapter 16), investigates the troublesome concept of *rank scale* in the learning of grammar. She implemented a carefully constructed programme of support which involved the following: doubling the time allocated to explaining grammar in general, changed assessment practices, provision of more samples of grammatical analysis, more collaborative practice workshops to complement lectures, the use of supportive virtual learning environments and the encouragement of meta-reflection through students' learning journals. As a result some of the students who had managed to grasp the rank scale concept:

> became very aware that there was an extra dimension to grammar analysis which was new to them and that had opened new doors of linguistic understanding. The realisation that the *rank scale* unlocked the hidden architecture of a sentence *transformed* their perception of language learning and language analysis. Some students also stated that grasping the *rank scale* concept had helped them in analysing sentences in all the languages they were studying. They were now able to transfer the concept and this was enabling them to see grammar links that they had not seen before.

However, as the author goes on to report, the *integrative* nature of this concept and its *irreversibility* came under discussion when it emerged that certain students seemed able to understand and apply rank scale in one language (e.g. German) but not in another (e.g. English). This raises the intriguing question of whether this particular threshold concept can only be transferred within the same language and not across different languages, unless there is a chronological dimension to the acquisition of this understanding, requiring perhaps 'the crossing of more thresholds' in order for some students to see the connections between languages.

In a very different context, that of art therapy with cancer patients, Caryl Sibbett and William Thompson (Chapter 17) explain how 'Knowledge can be troublesome not just cognitively, but also emotionally, attitudinally, bodily and inter-personally or institutionally and socially.' They propose the generative idea of *nettlesome knowledge* which 'comprises elements of knowledge that are deemed taboo in that they are defended against, repressed or ignored because if they were grasped they might 'sting' and thus evoke a feared intense emotional and *embodied* response. The sting of nettlesome knowledge can make us uncomfortable and so it can be stigmatised.' The nettlesome aspects of cancer suffering may be excluded in that they are deemed taboo and hence *unthinkable, unspeakable, unhearable, unseeable* and *untouchable*. Liminal states themselves (of which cancer itself is a potent example) were also found in this study to be associated with taboo for both the health professionals, the therapists and their clients. The authors go on to explain, through an analysis of the nature and complexities of play, how arts-based learning can successfully bring the unspeakable and unhearable into view and hence into reflection and therapy, with significant accompanying shifts in identity.

The tacit nature of visual design knowledge comes under scrutiny in the study of automotive and product design students by Jane Osmond, Andrew Turner and Ray Land (Chapter 18). They point out how the course they have been observing in a longitudinal four year study offers more than the accumulation of skills and information, and is viewed as 'a process of becoming – in this case becoming a certain kind of creative and critically minded design practitioner. Through this transformative practice a professional identity is formed, and, through the desire to become accepted within the community of creative design practitioners, learning can become a source of motivation, meaningfulness and personal and social energy'. The researchers have identified the development of spatial awareness as an important threshold concept that is both necessary to visual design and at the heart of this process of professional formation. However, the empirical data from their interviews with both design staff and students highlighted the troublesome nature of *tacit* and implicit understandings in the teaching of spatial awareness in design contexts. Moreover threshold concepts seem to be entangled with a much wider pattern of practice and enquiry, a set of games (reminiscent of Perkins' 'underlying episteme') that are played with the concepts, and which in turn can provide a further source of troublesomeness for the novice. The data they are gaining is being used to assess the relative advantages and limitations of the currently adopted *atelier* method as a learning environment for the development of spatial awareness and other related concepts, and to identify pedagogical modifications to this approach where appropriate.

The final section, 'Pedagogical Directions', indicates ways in which the threshold concepts framework is beginning to 'migrate' into wider areas of educational practice and policy. Glynis Cousin (Chapter 19), reviewing changing emphases in learning theory in recent decades, detects in the thresholds framework a turning away from what has been termed 'the mortification of the teacherly self', (McShane, 2006) which appears to have been an unintended consequence of student-centred approaches. She queries the 'dismantling and outlawing' of teacher-centredness in favour of student-centredness, and wonders whether a well-intentioned 'counter-position meant as a heuristic device' has been turned into 'a source of moralising'. She suggests that it might be time in terms of broader paradigms to swing the pendulum back to teachers, 'not as lone sages on the stage but to strongly position them with their students and educational researchers/developers as partners in an inquiry into disciplinary concerns'. She names such a partnership *transactional curriculum inquiry* and argues that threshold concept research can foster this kind of approach:

because it squarely places subject specialists at the centre of an inquiry into the difficulty of their subject. In this way there is a restoration of dignity for academics and a promising reconfiguration of the research relationships between students, academics, educational researchers and developers.

Vernon Trafford (Chapter 20) carries the thresholds framework into the terrain of doctoral study. In a substantial empirical inquiry into the experience of many doctoral research students he concludes that understanding of the nature and purpose of *conceptual frameworks* acts as a threshold concept in doctorateness. Moreover, successful negotiation of this threshold seems to be a necessary condition of success in doctoral studies. 'The importance of this process', he points out, 'has been shown as a major determinant of how examiners assess the scholarship submitted by candidates'. The cameo accounts he provides from doctoral candidates vividly depict the associated phenomena of liminality and troublesome knowledge as they approach and pass beyond this particular threshold. This passing through the threshold concept to understanding of conceptualisation and doctorateness, he emphasises, is a crucial 'ontological perspective' hitherto underemphasised by supervisors and their candidates.

In the concluding chapter Mia O'Brien, working in the context of Australian higher education, has undertaken a detailed study of the professional development of university teachers and the ways in which the *teaching* of threshold concepts 'implies pedagogical knowledge and thinking that is itself threshold in nature and potentially troublesome'. At present, she argues, 'research on the kinds of pedagogical thinking teachers of threshold concepts undertake is limited, as is our empirical understanding of the transformative nature of this practice for teacher knowledge and expertise'. She questioned teachers in Arts, Health Sciences, Business Studies, Physical Sciences, Psychology and Biological Sciences. She asked them what the threshold concept is in their teaching and why it is important for students to learn it. What is difficult, challenging or problematic about learning this threshold concept? What do they do to support students to learn this concept and why? Her findings reveal that there are three threshold concepts central to university teaching and learning: *threshold concepts as subject matter, as learning, and as teaching.* But while these terms might be well known and soundly articulated within the literature, her data indicates that 'a deep and transformative understanding of these concepts *cannot be taken for granted* within university teaching.' If teaching is to be more effectively directed towards student learning, she concludes, there are two related gaps that university teachers will need to find their way across:

(a) the gap between the assumed and taken for granted epistemological and ontological foundation from which an academic currently views the world, and the capacity to speak objectively about this view from a critical perspective, and (b) the necessity for pedagogical thinking, reasoning and action to be grounded within disciplinary epistemologies and ontology and to locate these centrally within the learning experience of students (often in the absence of a critical curriculum philosophy).

These many diverse studies, undertaken in a wide range of institutions, in various disciplines and in different cultures, would seem to indicate that the threshold concepts model offers a new way of engaging busy academics by encouraging them to resolve students' learning problems from *within* their discipline. The academic's knowledge and status, to some extent neglected by 'student-centred' approaches, are restored within a more balanced transaction between teacher and learner, occasioning to some extent, perhaps, a swing back of the pendulum. Certainly a significant appeal of the threshold concepts approach seems to be that it allows the academic to help the student negotiate conceptual thresholds from the perspective of their subject, and by using the language of their discipline. Academics tend to identify and take possession of threshold concepts quickly, as they have the specialist knowledge and expertise within their disciplinary discourses. They are not required to bring with them the extra baggage of a separate, and sometimes alien, discourse of 'education'. Conversely, threshold concepts are not shrouded in a doctrine of salvation from stuck places. As reported in the UK educational press recently:

> There are no five easy steps to teach threshold concepts. Rather, they are always analysed and resolved from, and within, specific and situated disciplinary contexts. This is not surprising, given that academics are always keen to discuss the nuanced meanings of their specialism. But identifying the sources of troublesome knowledge that constitutes a barrier to student understanding can prove a powerful way of adapting one's teaching or re-thinking course design issues. (Meyer and Land, 2007 p.14)

We believe strongly, as Glynis Cousin argues in her case for transactional curriculum inquiry, that 'the overwhelming strength of threshold concepts is precisely in the opportunities for co-inquiry it presents between subject experts, students and educational researchers'. This holds out for these key actors a 'pursuit of shared understandings of difficulties and shared ways of mastering them.' The thresholds framework, as one form of transactional inquiry, offers an approach 'which becomes neither student-centred nor teacher-centred but something more active, dynamic and in-between'.

Ray Land, Jan H.F.Meyer and Jan Smith
Glasgow and Durham
January 2008

REFERENCES

Barnett, R.A. (2005). Capturing the universal in the university. *Educational Theory and Practice, 37*(6) 785-797.

Bauman, Z. (2000). *Liquid modernity.* Cambridge: Polity Press

Biggs, J.B. & Collis, K.F. (1982). *Evaluating the quality of learning – The SOLO taxonomy.* New York: Academic Press.

Kinchin, I. & Hay, D. (2005). Using concept maps to optimize the composition of collaborative student groups: A pilot study. *Journal of Advanced Nursing, 51*(2), July, 182-187(6).

Marton, F, Tsui, A. B. M. et al (2004). *Classroom discourse and the space of learning.* Mahwah, NJ: Lawrence Erlbaum.

McShane, K. (2006). *Technologies transforming academics: Academic identity and online teaching,* University of Technology Sydney. Available from: http://www.itl.usyd.edu.au/aboutus/mcshane06_thesis.pdf

Meyer, J.H.F. & Land, R. (2003). Threshold concepts and troublesome knowledge: Linkages to ways of thinking and practising within the disciplines, *Improving student learning − Ten years on,* OCSLD, Oxford, pp. 412-424.

Meyer, J.H.F. & Land, R. (2005). Threshold concepts and troublesome knowledge (2): Epistemological considerations and a conceptual framework for teaching and learning. *Higher Education, 49*(3), April, 373-388.

Meyer, J.H.F. & Land, R. (Eds) (2006). *Overcoming barriers to student understanding: Threshold concepts and troublesome knowledge.* London and New York: Routledge.

Meyer, J.H.F. & Land, R. (2007). Stop the conveyor belt, I want to get off. *Times Higher Education Supplement,* August 17th, p. 14.

Novak, J. D. (1990). Concept maps and Vee diagrams: Two metacognitive tools for science and mathematics education. *Instructional Science, 19,* 29-52.

Perkins, D. (1999). The many faces of constructivism. *Educational Leadership, 57*(3), 6-11.

Perkins, D. N. (2006). Constructivism and troublesome knowledge. In J. H. F. Meyer & R. Land (Eds.), *Overcoming barriers to student understanding: Threshold concepts and troublesome knowledge.* London: Routledge.

Perkins, D. N. (2007). Theories of difficulty. In N. J. Entwistle & P. D. Tomlinson (Eds.), *British Journal of Educational Psychology* Monograph Series II, Number 4 − Student learning and university teaching (pp. 31-48). Leicester: British Psychological Society.

Turner, V. (1969). *The ritual process: Structure and anti-structure.* London: Routledge and Kegan Paul.

Vygotsky, L. S. (1978). *Mind and society: The development of higher mental processes.* Cambridge, MA: Harvard University Press.

Wenger, E. (1998). *Communities of practice: Learning, meaning and identity.* Cambridge: Cambridge University Press.

PART I: THEORETICAL PERSPECTIVES

DAVID PERKINS

1. BEYOND UNDERSTANDING

INTRODUCTION

What is knowledge? I found this fundamental epistemological question on my mind again when a number of months ago I asked for a few volunteers from a group to characterise something they understood really well. Among several good responses, one especially stood out. A gentleman stood up and reported on his understanding of Ohm's law.

He recounted how he had first encountered Ohm's law during formal studies of physics. Later on, someone he knew had explained to him that the same basic principles could be applied more broadly, for instance to the behaviour of heating systems. Then, more years later, he found himself with a puzzle about the layout of his own home heating system. The conduits were not providing the degree of throughput he desired. To be sure, heating ducts are not exactly electrical wires, the various impediments to the flow of hot air not exactly electrical resistance, but nonetheless he put Ohm's law to work to design an arrangement of ducts that might provide superior performance. And they did!

Whether his application was entirely technically correct is not so much the point. It was good enough to be useful. Not only did the fellow display substantial understanding of Ohm's law, he also demonstrated alertness to new opportunities to apply it and an energetic stretch to put it to work in an unfamiliar area. One might say that his knowledge of Ohm's law was not just active but *proactive*.

This small-scale example of the nimble use of knowledge might remind us of iconic models from the past. Leonardo da Vinci was notoriously a questing soul, exploring themes and making contributions across the arts, architecture, anatomy, physics, engineering, and military affairs. For a contemporary figure, Richard Feynman displayed a bold curiosity regarding all sorts of things in addition to quantum theory throughout his life. Such paragons help to sustain a vision of how vitally knowledge can function. However, there is no need to set the bar so high. We should also cherish the small generative connections that help to make sense of a complicated world and help to make it better ... like applying Ohm's law to heating ducts.

With connections small and large in the foreground, it is argued here that learning will only be truly effective when the conception of knowledge underlying it has a proactive character. Proactive knowledge goes beyond understanding to prepare the learner for the alert and lively use of knowledge. A key step in the argument connects proactive knowledge to the idea of threshold concepts in the

R. Land, J.H.F. Meyer & J. Smith (Eds.), Threshold Concepts within the Disciplines, 3-19.

disciplines in two ways. On the one hand, instructional attention to threshold concepts seems likely to foster proactive knowledge. On the other, the concept of proactive knowledge has something of a threshold character, with the potential to reorganise in significant ways how we think about teaching and learning.

POSSESSIVE, PERFORMATIVE AND PROACTIVE KNOWLEDGE

What is knowledge? Knowledge is information, or at least that seems to be the tacit view behind a good deal of learning. According to this *possessive conception*, knowledge is money in the cognitive bank – favourite phone numbers, today's Dow Jones, the dates of important historical events, the whereabouts of the nearest multiplex cinema, how to claim a particular exemption on your income tax. Certainly such knowledge can be handy, but it does not reach very far towards enlightenment or empowerment or a responsible life.

Of course the possessive view is not the only conception of knowledge with currency. Many educators, psychologists, philosophers and others have advocated a richer conception of knowledge, knowledge as understanding. A particular way of looking at that is helpful here, a *performative view* that interprets understanding as a matter of flexible thinking and action (Perkins, 1998; Wiske, 1998). The performative conception foregrounds not just how much knowledge you have but how much you can do with what you have. Performance depends on possession – you have to have it in order to think with it – but goes beyond possession – how well you understand something depends on whether you can reason with it, make predictions, offer critiques, build something, invent something. Back to Ohm's law, if you can recite Ohm's law and apply it to thoroughly routine problems, that demonstrates only knowledge as possession. However, if you can apply Ohm's law to novel problems within electronics, or outside such as to heating ducts, that demonstrates knowledge as flexible performance.

Educators generally see knowledge-as-understanding as an adequate corrective to the possessive conception. However the example of Ohm's law and heating ducts warns that this may not be enough. What's most striking about it is its proactive character – not just knowledge possessed or even knowledge performed but knowledge proactively deployed. Just as performative knowledge includes but goes beyond possessive knowledge, so proactive knowledge includes but goes beyond performative knowledge. For the fellow with the heating puzzle, there was no textbook with a surprise extra-credit problem on heating ducts at the end of the chapter. The fellow made his own connection. For the kind of learning we want, important as understanding is, we need to step beyond understanding.

WHAT KIND OF KNOWLEDGE WHEN

What is knowledge? Another lesson about the nature of knowledge came my way a few months ago during a dinner table conversation about cholesterol. The topic was the relative cholesterol content of different foods and how much it mattered, but at one point we all sat back and asked ourselves how much we really knew about cholesterol. The answer: not much. However, the sketchy and superficial story we did have was rather handy for some practical self-management. Let's face it: a high percentage of the knowledge that gets every one of us through every day is "cholesterol knowledge" – relatively superficial possessive knowledge.

So what kind of knowledge do we need when? When we want to find our way to the bank, do a quick routine arithmetic calculation, make a deposit, and then head home, we are well served by a loose bundle of rather superficial facts and routines. Possessive knowledge does the job.

When we need real understanding, often we still do not need proactive knowledge. Performative knowledge is good enough because the circumstances assert a direct demand. A source we are reading or someone with whom we are conversing uses concepts we understand like the tragedy of the commons or Darwin's theory of evolution, so we can follow the argument and argue back. When we are negotiating a loan at a bank, the bank representative reminds us of the significance of compound interest. The world speaks to us with a loud voice and reminds us of what we know and understand.

However the world often speaks with a softer voice. Knowledge needs to function proactively if it is to function at all. For instance, it is relatively easy not to notice the moment or not to care enough to bother when:

- Politicians make exaggerated statements that might violate other things we already know about the topic.
- Ethical issues arise in small ways during everyday activities – matters of ethnic slurs, fair treatment, intellectual property, and the like.
- National or foreign events occur that would be illuminated by comparison with historical episodes we know about, if only we made the connection.
- Everyday interactions would benefit from better handling informed by ideas about stereotyping, reactance, attribution, and so on from social psychology we have studied, if only we saw the link.
- Medical decisions, insurance decisions, or purchase decisions would benefit from some very simple principles of statistics and probability, if only we thought to apply what we know.

It is not hard to add to this list. John Dewey was one ardent advocate of education for the alert and active use of knowledge. As he wryly remarked in his *Democracy and Education,* "Only in education, never in the life of farmer, sailor, merchant, physician, or laboratory experimenter, does knowledge mean primarily a store of information aloof from doing" (Dewey, 1916, ch. 14). In the complex contemporary world, the mobilisation of formally acquired knowledge beyond classroom settings is becoming ever more of an urgent and neglected priority. Levy and Murnane (2004; Murnane & Levy, 1996), exploring how education prepares learners for today's world of work, emphasise the importance of expert thinking and complex communication skills that in effect activate knowledge. In a synthesis of ideas about citizenship, Haste (2004) notes remarkably low correlations between what people know about areas relevant to citizenship and their actual engagement.

Eraut (1994) is severe in his examination of the degree to which professional education actually prepares graduates for effective functioning in an intricate and demanding information society.

In his visionary *The End of Education*, Neil Postman (1995) emphasises how grand narratives such as "spaceship earth" are needed to weave together diverse disciplines and prepare graduates for active participation in modern culture. Gardner's (2000) *The Disciplined Mind* looks to the three overarching themes of the true, the good, and the beautiful for an education that speaks deeply and honestly to both academic disciplines and today's world. One might even turn to *Consilience*, E. O. Wilson's (1998) epic plea for integrating knowledge, in which he argues that the Balkanisation of knowledge into disconnected disciplines misses one of the great opportunities and indeed necessities of a maturing civilisation. These lively visions of what knowledge can and should be contrast starkly with the silt of education deposited in many young learners' minds. In the words of Alfred North Whitehead (1929), the knowledge is simply "inert."

THE COMPARATIVE ANATOMY OF KNOWLEDGE

What is knowledge? The attitudes and behaviour of different students and teachers reflect different tacit answers to this question. There's nothing new about that. So how does the possessive-performative-proactive distinction compare with prior analyses? Without attempting an extended survey, one touchstone is surely William Perry's (1970) well-known account of the varied epistemological positions found among college students and also others. Perry proposed that students' sophistication develops through a number of phases. Least mature is a stance towards knowledge as answers: the facts and routines are there and it is our role as students to learn them. Through various levels, this leads towards recognition that some answers are contested, but one can reason within the parameters of a discipline to find answers suitable to particular contexts. All this leads through other gradations to Perry's most mature position. We need at least a provisional commitment to one or another framework, leavened by an appreciation that it is subject to challenge from other viewpoints and to ongoing reconstruction.

It is not difficult to align possessive and performative knowledge with Perry's scheme (see Table 1). The focus on facts, memorising, and straightforward application suits well the possessive conception. When students recognise that they can reason within disciplines and contexts, knowledge takes on a more active form, the performative conception. The later positions in Perry's scheme are perhaps a little more difficult to place. They could be understood simply as yet more sophisticated versions of performative understanding, the doing one does with knowledge becoming increasingly nuanced. On the other hand, the flexible thoughtful commitment characteristic of Perry's final position certainly constitutes something of a proactive stance towards knowledge and its use.

Table 1: A synthesis of existing frameworks of student learning

	Possessive	Performative	Proactive
Conception of knowledge, Perry	Absolute & multiple perspectives	Provisional & evidence and reasoning	Personal reasoned perspective
Conception of learning, Säljö	Facts, memorising, applying	Understanding	Seeing things in a different way
Approaches to learning, Entwistle	Surface	Strategic, Deep	Deep
Symptom	Delivery on demand	Performance on demand	Opportunistic deployment
Spirit	Utilitarian	Sense-making	Inquiry and creativity
Challenge	Hard to retain and apply	Hard to understand	Hard to keep alive and use actively

For another touchstone, Säljö (1979) identified a range of mindsets towards learning. On the reductive end is acquiring, reproducing, and applying factual information. Beyond that come more enlightened conceptions of learning, understanding the meaning for oneself and seeing things in different ways. As with Perry's scheme, Säljö's framework aligns readily with possessive and performative knowledge. Possessive knowledge corresponds to the first cluster and performative knowledge to the second. As suggested in Table 1, seeing things in a different way captures at least something of the spirit of proactive knowledge.

Yet another perspective on approaches to learning began with a broad distinction drawn between surface and deep approaches (Marton & Säljö, 1976; Marton, Hounsell, & Entwistle, 1997). Later research revealed another important variant, a strategic approach to studying (Entwistle & Ramsden, 1983). Entwistle (2003) characterises the three approaches in terms of their fundamental agendas. The surface approach aims to cope minimally with academic demands, adopting a focus on facts and routines that often reflects a fear of failure. The strategic approach aims at recognition of good performance through grades and other markers, with a focus on managing one's work well. The deep approach aims at understanding the ideas for oneself, drawing on intrinsic motivation to fuel a focus on systematised understanding of concepts, claims, and evidence.

Turning again to the possessive-performative-proactive distinction, the surface approach clearly fosters possessive knowledge. Built into the strategic approach is

7

a kind of limited understanding, whatever is necessary to score well in the academic context. But that is usually a far cry from the breadth of understanding called for by Gardner's (2000) the true, the good, and the beautiful or Postman's (1995) grand narratives. The strategic approach is proactive in a sense but not in our sense, proactive about doing well and looking good in the classroom. In contrast, the intrinsic motivation of the deep approach is more likely to cultivate truly proactive knowledge.

Although there is a rough fit between these frameworks and the possessive-performative-proactive triad, in some ways full bore proactive knowledge goes beyond what is strictly entailed by the top levels of the frameworks from Perry, Säljö, and Marton/Entwistle. The Perry framework focuses on the *grounds* of knowledge, how we know what we know. In contrast, the possessive-performative-proactive scheme focuses as much on the *uses* of knowledge -- recalling and applying it (possessive), reasoning with it flexibly (performative), and mapping it far and wide (proactive). The Säljö and Marton/Entwistle frameworks pointedly characterise stances towards learning in an academic context but with uncertain implications about the fate of knowledge beyond. In contrast, proactive knowledge emphasises what we do with what we know not only within but outside settings of formal study.

Besides comparing with other schemes, it's worth exploring some distinctions among possessive, performative, and proactive knowledge. For one, how do we know what kind of knowledge we have (*symptom* row of Table 1)? For the possessive conception, the primary symptom is delivery on demand. Can you recite Ohm's law? Can you apply it to a simple standard circuit? With the performative conception, the primary symptom is flexible performances that demonstrate understanding: Can you apply Ohm's law to predict how this novel circuit will behave or to design a circuit? Someone may lay out the challenge directly, or it may simply come up in a highly salient way, as when an electrical engineer faces the task of designing a circuit to specifications. Even the heating duct problem, if posed point-blank with the tip to apply Ohm's law, still sits in the performative category.

In contrast with these, the primary symptom of proactive knowledge is opportunistic deployment. A circumstance arises that could easily be missed, the person notices it, and follows through. Voilà, better heating ducts!

Not surprisingly, rather different attitudes mark the three kinds of knowledge (*spirit* row of Table 1). The spirit of possessive knowledge seems utilitarian, a matter of very direct retrieval and application in a routine way to get things done. As noted earlier with the cholesterol example, most of what we do has something of this character. The shift from possessive knowledge to performative knowledge involves a transition from a utilitarian to a sense-making spirit. Understanding rather than just getting something done now occupies the foreground. The further shift to proactive knowledge invokes yet another mindset, a disposition towards inquiry and creativity.

For a final three-way contrast, the different kinds of knowledge pose different characteristic challenges (last row of Table 1). What is troublesome about possessive knowledge? – its volume, so much to know and apply with a kind of honed routine skill. We become acutely conscious of the problem of volume when orienting to new environments or studying a second language. In contrast, the characteristic performative challenge is one of understanding. The ideas seem bewildering, evasive, counterintuitive. And in further contrast with that, the characteristic challenge of proactive knowledge is lively connection-making across diverse contexts (on troublesome knowledge generally, see Perkins, 2006, 2007).

THE DISPOSITIONAL CHARACTER OF PROACTIVE KNOWLEDGE

The general idea of dispositions is well illustrated by everyday dispositional terms for qualities of mind such as open-mindedness versus closed mindedness, curiosity versus disinterest, or sceptical versus credulous. Qualities like these have to do less with knowledge or ability than with what might be called mindset. They concern not what people are able to do but what they are inclined to do. The open-minded person *could* turn away from other viewpoints but tends to consider them. The closed-minded person *could* ponder other viewpoints but tends to dismiss them. Considerable evidence exists for the role of dispositions of various sorts in thinking, learning, and social judgement (e.g. Cacioppo, Petty, Feinstein, & Jarvis, 1996; Dweck, 2000; Dweck & Bempechat, 1980; Gehlbach, 2004; Kruglanski & Webster, 1996; Stanovich & West, 1997).

Although dispositions are often interpreted simply as a matter of sustained attitudes or motivations, research by my colleagues and I urges attention to both alertness and attitudes (Perkins & Ritchhart, 2004; Perkins & Tishman, 2001; Perkins, Tishman, Ritchhart, Donis, & Andrade, 2000). Effective deployment of a particular pattern of thinking or disciplinary practice requires (1) *alertness* to occasions, (2) a positive *attitude* toward its potential relevance, and of course (3) possession of it and the *ability* to apply it. For instance, an open-minded person has to notice situations when other views are or even might be in play (alertness), take them seriously (attitude), and think them through (ability).

All that said, quotidian and technical conceptions of cognitive performance tend to be strongly abilities-centric. The importance of both alertness and attitude gets forgotten. People undermine themselves by figuring they do not have enough intelligence, which they view as a fixed resource (e.g. Dweck, 2000; Dweck & Bempechat, 1980). Formal studies of thinking and intelligence tend to foreground abilities over other aspects of intelligent engagement with the world (e.g. Dai & Sternberg, 2004; Perkins, 1995; Perkins & Ritchhart, 2004). Classroom interventions targeting cognitive skills emphasise building up repertoires of strategies much more so than fostering proactive attitudes and motivation. To take stock of the abilities-centric trend, see such overviews as Chipman, Segal, & Glaser, 1985; Grotzer & Perkins, 2000; Nickerson, Perkins, & Smith, 1985; Perkins, 1995; Resnick, 1987; Ritchhart & Perkins, 2005; Segal, Chipman, & Glaser, 1985.

Although an abilities-centric stance dominates both folk psychology and considerable academic psychology, shortfalls in cognitive performance can just as easily reflect alertness and attitude. It's one thing to know in principle about the deceptiveness of advertising but quite another to keep up your guard in real situations. It's one thing to know in principle about politicians' manipulations of facts but another to care about and pick up such shell games on the fly. It's one thing to know that decision-makers often fixate on choosing between the apparent options and another thing to remind oneself to look beyond the given or obvious options in personal decision making.

A series of studies reported by Perkins, Tishman, Ritchhart, Donis, & Andrade (2000) demonstrates how dramatic this difference can be. We investigated how students ranging from 5th to 9th grade responded to vignettes about people thinking in everyday situations. We wanted to know whether the participants would detect some rather straightforward instances of hasty, narrow, or unimaginative thinking, and whether they could rethink the situations better themselves. When asked in an open-ended way what they made of the thinking in the stories, only about 10% of the time did the students notice a possible shortfall in the first place, and only about half the time did they respond to specific suggestions that something might be amiss. However, when asked point blank to offer better solutions, virtually all were readily able to do so. At least on these tasks, what limited performance was least of all ability, somewhat attitude, but overwhelmingly sensitivity to situations. The students were "problem blind."

Essentially the same three-way analysis applies to any cognitive resource, including relatively specific systems of knowledge such as Ohm's law. There too, flexible use in realistic situations requires alertness to occasion, a positive attitude towards following through, and of course the knowledge and ability to follow through. These ingredients are necessary and sufficient for proactive knowledge. Proactive knowledge is in effect a dispositional conception of knowledge.

One might view proactive knowledge as a rich mode of mental representation involving semi-specialised processes melded with relevant information (Perkins & Salomon, 1989). Such a representation is rich with pattern recognition "hooks" that help activate it in diverse circumstances. Such a representation is cognitively "hot" rather than "cool," promoting its energetic deployment. To gain a better sense of these characteristics, it's helpful to look to another area of research, transfer of learning.

TRANSFER WITH A TWIST

Two cognitive illusions trouble the way we often treat teaching and learning. The first and certainly the most destructive concerns the possessive conception of knowledge. It's not that the possessive mindset doesn't care about understanding; of course it does. Rather, the illusion is that possession will pretty much produce understanding. The performative conception of knowledge hosts another cognitive illusion. It's not that the performative mindset doesn't care about the use of knowledge far and wide; of course it does. Rather, the illusion is that performative knowledge will generate application far and wide.

Behind the first illusion is a neglected challenge of initial learning. The knowledge was never learned with any depth in the first place. Behind the second illusion is a neglected challenge of where the knowledge goes from there. The knowledge was not acquired in a way that would foster what learning theorists call transfer of learning. Transfer of learning means acquiring knowledge in one context and putting it to use in another. When we apply knowledge we have learned in the formal setting of the classroom to another unit or another subject or to practical settings beyond the classroom, this is transfer. When, having learned to drive a car, we rent a small truck for a move and find that we can drive it pretty well, this is transfer. Our opening example of applying Ohm's law to the design of the heating system is a case of transfer that bridges very different contexts and disciplines, what is generally called "far transfer."

The principal lesson from a century of studies of transfer raises a red flag for educators everywhere: Transfer often comes hard. During the first decades of the 20th century, the pioneer scholar of learning E. L. Thorndike conducted the first notable research in this area. Investigating the widespread belief that the study of Latin "trained the mind," he found that it did not. Students with plenty of Latin did no better in other disciplines than those less classically educated (Thorndike, 1923; Thorndike & Woodworth, 1901).

The parade of largely negative findings about transfer of learning has continued ever since. Knowledge demonstrably acquired and understood in one setting commonly lies fallow in another where it has relevance (e.g. Detterman & Sternberg, 1992; Salomon & Perkins, 1989). In one notable paper, Bransford, Franks, Vye, and Sherwood (1989) discussed the problem of "inert knowledge" (Whitehead, 1929). The authors reported an experiment where some students studied information about nutrition, water as defining the standard of density, airplanes that operated on solar power, and related matters. Their goal was to master the knowledge in a conventional didactic way. Later, the students faced the challenge of planning an expedition in a desert. They certainly understood the knowledge and retained it, as demonstrated by direct testing, but they made very little use of it despite its high relevance.

There is a positive side to this thread of inquiry as well: Transfer is not a lost cause. Transfer falters largely because typical learning experiences do not foster it. Returning to the research just mentioned, Bransford et al. (1989) included another group of students who encountered the same information within a problem-based learning structure: pondering plans for a journey through a South American jungle. Later presented with the challenge of planning the desert trek, the students found many applications for what they had learned earlier.

Salomon and Perkins (1989), in an analysis of the puzzles and prospects of transfer, identified two general mechanisms of transfer of learning: the "high road" of reflective abstraction and deliberate connection making and the "low road" of spontaneous activation of patterns rehearsed in a variety of applications. When instruction fostered one or the other or both, transfer was much more likely. This helps to explain the predominantly negative pattern of findings. Most instruction neither promotes reflective abstraction and connection making nor provides practice in a deliberately disparate collection of cases. But it could!

Proactive knowledge is a transfer-rich view of knowledge. However, proactive knowledge is transfer with a twist. The relationship to the body of research on transfer is more complex than it might seem at first. The kind of transfer called for by proactive knowledge actually differs in several ways from how transfer is usually studied in formal research. First of all, the dispositional character of proactive knowledge means that the desired transfer has strong emotional and motivational dimensions. In contrast, the emphasis in studies of transfer tends to be doggedly cognitive, hardly looking at all at subjects' engagement with the content.

Second, proactive knowledge involves transfer under especially challenging cueing conditions, where it's not clear that any focused response is called for at all. Nothing demands that you assume an alert problem solving stance when you listen to a politician's speech or view a television ad or order burgers at a fast food joint. In contrast, typical investigations of transfer pose explicit tasks. Subjects know they are supposed to solve a problem. The experimenter's question is whether they will apply some specific content of interest they learned before or simply wing it.

Although responsive to subtle cues, proactive knowledge is less daunting in another respect, "far transfer." This term refers to transfer across domains, for instance applying Ohm's law to heating ducts. This actually is an exceptional case of proactive knowledge, albeit a welcome and dramatic one. The central business of proactive knowledge is not so much analogical application to remote domains as it is direct application in weakly cued circumstances.

Finally, studies of transfer normally are carried out in situations with minimum competition for the subjects' attention. The subject is sitting in a laboratory or a classroom with a task to undertake, in contrast with navigating a tentative way through a complex world with all sorts of distractions. It is just there, though, that proactive knowledge needs to earn its name.

THRESHOLD CONCEPTS FOR PROACTIVE KNOWLEDGE

The notions of proactive knowledge and threshold concepts (Meyer & Land, 2006a, b, c) make natural partners. In the metaphor of Meyer and Land (2006a), threshold concepts open up a portal in a domain, affording access to a newly integrative way of thinking about whole swathes of its territory. A collection of threshold concepts or an unusually pivotal one can provoke a kind of an epistemic shift, where the very "game" or epistemic enterprise of the discipline can come out looking somewhat different (Collins & Ferguson, 1993; Meyer & Land, 2006b; Perkins, 1997; Schwab, 1978). Three examples from Meyer and Land (2006a) representing diverse disciplines are *opportunity cost* from economics, *limits* from mathematics, and *signification* from literary and cultural studies. Opportunity cost, for instance, helps learners to recognise that making a choice has an often unrecognised cost. Committing attention and resources to one option generally deprives another of them. A cost of doing X instead of Y is whatever you forego from neglecting Y, a powerful way of bringing into the foreground the intrinsic dilemma of choice in a context of limited resources where you can't "have it all."

The idea of threshold concepts carries an important pedagogical message: where we can find likely threshold concepts, we would do well to organise learning around them (Meyer & Land, 2006a). But there is a cost, in fact an opportunity cost but one generally worth paying. Threshold concepts are likely to be troublesome (Meyer & Land, 2006b; Perkins, 2006). Their reorganising power brings with it an unfamiliarity that sometimes proves acute and off-putting. You can't rebalance the boat without rocking it.

Turning back to the proactive knowledge connection, well-cultivated threshold concepts seem likely to foster proactive knowledge. Recall here the three ingredients of proactive knowledge: ability to apply the knowledge with understanding, serious energetic engagement with the knowledge, and alertness to where it applies. Organising instruction around threshold concepts should contribute to all three. First of all, the keystone character of threshold concepts puts the learner in a better position to think with the knowledge system in question, a clear asset to application. Secondly, knowledge structured around threshold concepts becomes richer and more meaningful, a contribution to engagement.

As to alertness, threshold concepts in many cases introduce cognitive hooks by means of which the learner can recognise relevant applications more readily. For instance, the idea of opportunity cost not only enables a certain kind of technical analysis but also projects a vivid informal generalised narrative. We encounter opportunities in the world, choice points that we might seize or not. However, choice of one path may have a cost in other paths neglected. This common sense story connects with the world much better than any technical rendition.

Or consider the concept of limits from mathematics. Students are often baffled by the epsilon-delta technical definition of limit. However, that formalisation sits on top of an everyday conception of limit, something approaching something else but never quite getting there (Perkins, 2006). It is this informal conception that provides the natural basis for the recognition of potential applications.

Nothing says that every threshold concept has to come with both a technical and an informal face. However, this appears to be quite common, perhaps because the centrality of threshold concepts leads to colloquial forms of expression to facilitate communication within and across disciplines. In any case, when the informal faces are there, threshold concepts help to enable the kind of wide ranging recognition called for by proactive knowledge.

PROACTIVE KNOWLEDGE AS A THRESHOLD CONCEPT

The partnership between threshold concepts and proactive knowledge takes another turn as well. Besides threshold concepts fostering proactive knowledge, the idea of proactive knowledge has something of a threshold character for how we think about teaching and learning. It draws our attention to how learning often falls short and characterises the nature of the gap. In keeping with the idea of an epistemic shift, proactive knowledge suggests that our everyday sense of what knowledge is and how it works lacks an important dimension.

Typical settings of learning foreground a learning architecture that might be called *performance on demand*. Learners are asked directly and straightforwardly to do specific things. The doing in question may have a possessive character—state Ohm's law, name the three principal tenets of the theory of evolution, summarise the basic plot of *King Lear*. Better, the demanded doing may have a performative character – predict the behaviour of this circuit using Ohm's law, explain how giraffes might have come by their long necks using principles of natural selection, find and explain partial analogues of King Lear in political history.

But demand is demand. It does not serve proactive knowledge very well. Proactive knowledge requires an active alert questing mindset. Performance on demand gives little opportunity for freeform noticing and self-initiated engagement to occur and offers few structures that encourage it. The demand structure of typical institutional learning favours extrinsic motivation over intrinsic motivation, even though this does not serve achievement as well and seems likely not to foster sensitivity to occasion and self-initiated engagement (e.g. Lepper & Greene, 1978; Lepper, Corpus, & Iyengar, 2005).

Educating for proactive knowledge calls for a threshold-like shift from a culture of demand to a culture of opportunity. In a culture of opportunity, what learners do – the range of choice, the contexts of application, the spectrum of motives and feelings involved, and many other aspects – becomes more open and ranges more widely.

Here are some of the shifts of emphasis that might mark a learning culture of opportunity. There is nothing utterly novel in the following list, but learning that we would generally view as enlightened commonly lacks many of these features.

- *From very other-directed to significantly self-directed.* Learners will not develop proactive knowledge if they are always told what to do with what they are learning. A pedagogy for proactive knowledge asks learners to face frequent choice points and to search for connections rather than have them served up, fostering self-managed exploration, reflective decision-making, and personal responsibility. But not so much of this that the quest becomes bewildering and aversive!
- *From extrinsic motivation to intrinsic motivation.* Instruction should reduce the saliency of extrinsic motivators—heavy pressures for grades for example—and foreground the intrinsic interest, personal dimensions, the teacher's own passionate involvement, and so on. The sorts of choice points noted above also should enhance intrinsic motivation. This does *not* mean that extrinsic motivation has no place.
- *From cool to hot cognition.* Formal learning experiences tend to be cognitively cool. They emphasise a methodical approach, meticulous attention, and so on. A measure of this is fine, but overdone it tends to drain learning experiences of their zest and momentum.

- *From prototypical examples to include diverse and marginal examples and close counterexamples.* Even thoughtful instruction commonly focuses on prototypical examples, not giving a sense of the range of variation or how some putative cases "just miss."
- *From learning about to learning to do.* Even in reasonably constructivist settings of learning students often are still basically "learning about"—say learning about Darwinian theory and the evidence for it, discussing its nuances, critiquing it, and so forth. A step beyond this is to learn to think fluently within Darwinian theory. Instructional paradigms such as problem-based learning and project-based learning foreground learning to do.
- *From learning the pieces to "whole game" learning.* A good deal of learning, even learning for understanding, takes things by bits and pieces rather. It matters whether one studies algebra as a symbol manipulation game or more holistically as a modelling process. It matters whether one studies poetry for its ingenious tropes and other elements of craft or, recalling the threshold concept of signification, for its larger significations about the human condition.
- *From designing to specifications to designing the specifications.* Learning tasks sometimes have a design character—make a plan for this, propose a solution to that. Often rather strict specifications are given. The agenda of proactive knowledge is better served by engaging the learner in formulating some of the specifications or interpreting rather open-ended specifications.
- *From problem solving to problem finding, problem defining.* By and large, instructional tasks tend to focus on solving problems defined by the teacher or text. However, with some guidelines, learners can be encouraged to find and define their own problems some of the time.
- *From learning here and there to learning here, there, and elsewhere.* Academic work tends to occur only in the lecture hall and in the student's typical work setting. The characteristic intellectual setting is the particular class and topic in its technicalities. Activities that broaden out the physical and intellectual contexts are likely to foster proactive knowledge.

With all this in mind, it's important to preserve what is good about performance on demand. There is no real opportunity in a free-for-all. An effective culture of opportunity rather than eliminating performance on demand loosens its hold with more passion, openness, and options.

AGAINST EXCELLENCE

Excellence in learning is the Holy Grail, so we hear from many an ardent educator. But the emphasis on excellence makes for a double irony, first since we fall so far from achieving it and second because it may be altogether the wrong focus. You see, the excellence pursued is typically excellence with possessive and performative knowledge, the kind of excellence that aces the test or the term project. There is an alternative. Imagine an education that invests not so much in performative excellence as in proactive competence.

To be sure, mere competence sounds like a lesser ambition than excellence, but that depends on what we are ambitious *for*. In the world beyond the classroom, proactive competence generally serves learners better than performative excellence. You are better off with proactive knowledge of a few threshold concepts about probability and statistics than with simply performative knowledge of a much more elaborate arsenal, because your more sophisticated knowledge is not very likely to get used -- the problem of inert knowledge again.

Raising our eyes to larger issues and recalling again Postman's (1995) grand narratives and Wilson's (1998) plea for consilience, the world would be a better place if more people energetically integrated merely competent knowledge from diverse sources on such fronts as political, economic, and ecological responsibility. Turning to John Dewey again, this time to his *Experience and Education:* "The central problem of an education based upon experience is to select the kind of present experiences that live fruitfully and creatively in subsequent experiences" (Dewey, 1938/1997, p. 28). By "subsequent," Dewey surely does not have in mind tests and term papers.

Pedagogues appalled by this argument against excellence may find relief in a further point: The case bears somewhat more on studies outside of students' ultimate professional direction than it does on studies squarely in the centre. While proactive knowledge has tremendous importance for a disciplinary focus, far more total learning time is available there towards grabbing the twin rings of performative and proactive excellence. Also, as students advance in a disciplinary focus, they are likely to encounter something closer to a learning culture of opportunity than students just studying "the basics."

That said, I venture that students would be better off with a culture of opportunity early on, whether they make the area their central commitment or not, and that often advanced disciplinary studies do not actually bring students into apprenticeship with the kinds of complex problem solving and patterns of application that they would encounter in professional life (Eraut, 1994). So I'm reluctant to let education in a disciplinary speciality entirely off the hook.

It's all about opportunity costs! Yes, we would like to have both performative and proactive knowledge in the fullest measure. But a culture of demand versus a culture of opportunity is a broad choice involving different investments. When limited resources make the tradeoff real, what is the better option? To answer that question, we only have to remember that education should prepare learners for encounters with a complicated and challenging world that does not reliably tell them what they should do.

ACKNOWLEDGEMENTS

Many of the ideas in this chapter were worked out jointly with my colleague Shari Tishman. Conversations with two other colleagues, Noel Entwistle and Robert Swartz, helped to refine them. The Spencer Foundation is thanked for sponsoring a recent synthesis of research on dispositions, developed by Shari Tishman and myself. The work on dispositions draws on the dispositions research group at Project Zero of the Harvard Graduate School of Education, including currently Mark Church, Patricia Palmer, Ron Ritchhart, Shari Tishman, and Terri Turner, along with a number of other colleagues who in various sites across a small and informal network have helped to advance it. I also thank the Stiftelsen Carpe Vitam Foundation and the Abe and Vera Dorevitch Foundation for their support of our inquiries. The positions taken in this chapter are of course not necessarily those of these agencies or individuals.

REFERENCES

Bransford, J. D., Franks, J. J., Vye, N. J., & Sherwood, R. D. (1989). New approaches to instruction: Because wisdom can't be told. In S. Vosniadou & A. Ortony (Eds.), *Similarity and analogical reasoning* (pp. 470-497). New York: Cambridge University Press.

Cacioppo, J. T., Petty, R. E., Feinstein, J. A., & Jarvis, W. B. G. (1996). Dispositional differences in cognitive motivation: The life and times of individuals varying in need for cognition. *Psychological Bulletin, 119*(2), 197-253.

Chipman, S. F., Segal, J. W., & Glaser, R. (Eds.) (1985). *Thinking and learning skills, Volume 2: Research and open questions.* Hillsdale, New Jersey: Lawrence Erlbaum Associates.

Collins, A., & Ferguson, W. (1993). Epistemic forms and epistemic games: Structures and strategies to guide inquiry. *Educational Psychologist, 28*(1), 25-42.

Dai, D. Y., & Sternberg, R. J. (Eds.) (2004). *Motivation, emotion, and cognition: Integrative perspectives on intellectual functioning and development.* Mawah, NJ: Erlbaum.

Detterman, D., & Sternberg, R. (Eds.) (1992). *Transfer on trial.* Norwood, NJ: Ablex.

Dewey, J. (1916). *Democracy and education: An introduction to the philosophy of education.* New York: The Macmillan company (online version accessed January 2007, http://xroads.virginia.edu/~HYPER2/Dewey/header.html).

Dewey, J. (1938/1997). Experience and Education. New York: Touchstone.

Dweck, C. S. (2000). *Self-theories: Their role in motivation, personality, and development.* Philadelphia, PA: Psychology Press.

Dweck, C. S., & Bempechat, J. (1980). Children's theories of intelligence: Consequences for learning. In S. G. Paris, G. M. Olson, & H. W. Stevenson (Eds.), *Learning and motivation in the classroom* (pp. 239-256). Hillsdale, NJ: Lawrence Erlbaum Associates.

Entwistle, N. J. & Ramsden, P. (1983). *Understanding Student Learning.* London: Croom Helm.

Entwistle, N. J. (2003). Enhancing teaching-learning environments to encourage deep learning. In E. De Corte (Ed.), *Excellence in higher education* (pp. 83-96). London: Portland Press.

Eraut, M. (1994). *Developing professional knowledge and competence.* London: Falmer Press.

Gardner, H. (2000). *The disciplined mind : beyond facts and standardized tests, the K-12 education that every child deserves.* New York: Penguin Books.

Gehlbach, H. (2004). Social perspective taking: A facilitating aptitude for conflict resolution, historical empathy, and social studies achievement. *Theory and Research in Social Education. 32*(1), 39-55.

Grotzer, T. A. & Perkins, D. N. (2000). Teaching intelligence: A performance conception. In R. J. Sternberg (Ed.), *Handbook of intelligence* (pp. 492-515). New York: Cambridge University Press.

Haste, H. (2004). Constructing the citizen. *Political Psychology, 25*(3), 413-439.

Kruglanski, A., & Webster, D. (1996). Motivated closing of the mind: "Seizing" and "freezing." *Psychological Review, 103*(2), 263-283.

Lepper, M. R. & Greene, D. (Eds.) (1978). *The hidden costs of reward: New perspectives on the psychology of human motivation.* Hillsdale, NJ: Erlbaum.

Lepper, M., Corpus, J., & Iyengar, S. (2005). Intrinsic and extrinsic motivational orientations in the classroom: Age differences and academic correlates. *Journal of Educational Psychology, 97*(2), 184-196.

Levy, F. & Murnane R. (2004). *The new division of labor: How computers are creating the new job market*. Princeton, NJ: Princeton University Press.

Marton, F., & Säljö, R. (1976). On qualitative differences in learning. I. Outcome and process. *British Journal of Educational Psychology, 46*, 4-11.

Marton, F., Hounsell, D. J., & Entwistle, N. J. (Eds.) (1997), *The Experience of Learning* (2nd Ed.). Edinburgh: Scottish Academic Press.

Meyer, J. H. F. & Land, R. (2006a). Threshold concepts and troublesome knowledge: An introduction. In J. H. F. Meyer & R. Land (Eds.), *Overcoming barriers to student understanding: Threshold concepts and troublesome knowledge* (pp. 3-18). London: Routledge.

Meyer, J. H. F. & Land, R. (2006b). Threshold concepts and troublesome knowledge: Issues of liminality. In J. H. F. Meyer & R. Land (Eds.), *Overcoming barriers to student understanding: Threshold concepts and troublesome knowledge* (pp. 19-32). London: Routledge.

Meyer, J. H. F. & Land, R. (Eds.) (2006c). *Overcoming barriers to student understanding: Threshold concepts and troublesome knowledge*. London: Routledge.

Murnane, R. J. & Levy, F. (1996). *Teaching the new basic skills: principles for educating children to thrive in a changing economy*. New York: The Free Press.

Nickerson, R., Perkins, D. N., & Smith, E. (1985). *The teaching of thinking*. Hillsdale, New Jersey: Lawrence Erlbaum Associates.

Perkins, D. N. (1995). *Outsmarting IQ: The emerging science of learnable intelligence*. New York: The Free Press.

Perkins, D. N. (1997). Epistemic games. *International Journal of Educational Research, 27*(1), 49-61.

Perkins, D. N. (1998). What is understanding? In Wiske, M. S. (Ed.), *Teaching for understanding: Linking research with practice* (pp. 39-57). San Francisco, CA: Jossey-Bass.

Perkins, D. N. (2006). Constructivism and troublesome knowledge. In J. H. F. Meyer & R. Land (Eds.), *Overcoming barriers to student understanding: Threshold concepts and troublesome knowledge* (pp. 33-47). London: Routledge.

Perkins, D. N. (2007). Theories of difficulty. In N. Entwistle & Peter Tomlinson (Eds.), *Student learning and university teaching*. British Journal of Educational Psychology Monograph Series II: Psychological Aspects of Education – Current Trends (pp. 31-48). Leicester, UK: British Psychological Society.

Perkins, D. N. & Ritchhart, R. (2004). When is good thinking? In D. Y. Dai & R. J. Sternberg (Eds.), *Motivation, emotion, and cognition: Integrative perspectives on intellectual functioning and development* (pp. 351-384). Mawah, NJ: Erlbaum.

Perkins, D. N., & Salomon, G. (1989). Are cognitive skills context bound? *Educational Researcher, 18*(1), 16-25.

Perkins, D. N., Tishman, S., Ritchhart, R., Donis, K., & Andrade. A. (2000). Intelligence in the wild: A dispositional view of intellectual traits. *Educational Psychology Review, 12*(3), 269-293.

Perkins. D. N. & Tishman, S. (2001). Dispositional aspects of intelligence. In S. Messick & J. M. Collis (Eds.), *Intelligence and personality: Bridging the gap in theory and measurement* (pp. 233-257). Maweh, NJ: Erlbaum.

Perry, W. (1970). *Forms of intellectual and ethical development in the college years*. New York: Holt, Rinehart and Winston.

Postman, N. (1995). *The end of education : redefining the value of school* (1st ed.). New York: Knopf.

Resnick, L. B. (1987). *Education and learning to think*. Washington, DC: National Academy Press.

Ritchhart, R. & Perkins, D.N. (2005). Learning to think: The challenges of teaching thinking. K. Holyoak & R. Morrison (Eds.), *Cambridge handbook of thinking and reasoning* (pp. 775-802). New York: Cambridge University Press.

Säljö, R. (1979). *Learning in the learner's perspective. I. Some common-sense conceptions*. (Report 76). Gothenburg: University of Gothenburg, Department of Education.

Salomon, G. & Perkins, D. N. (1989). Rocky roads to transfer: Rethinking mechanisms of a neglected phenomenon. *Educational Psychologist, 24*(2), 113-142.

Schwab, J. J. (1978). Education and the structure of the disciplines. In I. Westbury & N. J. Wilkof (Eds.), *Science, Curriculum, and Liberal Education* (pp. 229-272). Chicago: University of Chicago Press.

Segal, J. W., Chipman, S. F., & Glaser, R. (Eds.). (1985). *Thinking and learning skills, Volume 1: Relating instruction to research.* Hillsdale, NJ: Lawrence Erlbaum Associates.

Stanovich, K. E. & West, R. F. (1997). Reasoning independently of prior belief and individual differences in actively open-minded thinking. *Journal of Educational Psychology, 89*(2), 342-357.

Thorndike, E. L. (1923). The influence of first year Latin upon the ability to read English. *School Sociology, 17,* 165-168.

Thorndike, E. L. & Woodworth, R. S. (1901). The influence of improvement in one mental function upon the efficiency of other functions. *Psychological Review, 8,* 247-261.

Whitehead, A. N. (1929). *The aims of education and other essays.* New York: Simon & Schuster.

Wilson, E. O. (1998). *Consilience.* New York: Knopf.

Wiske, M. S. (Ed.) (1998). *Teaching for understanding: Linking research with practice.* San Francisco, CA: Jossey-Bass.

AFFILIATION

David Perkins
Graduate School of Education
Harvard University

NOEL ENTWISTLE

2. THRESHOLD CONCEPTS AND TRANSFORMATIVE WAYS OF THINKING WITHIN RESEARCH INTO HIGHER EDUCATION

INTRODUCTION

This chapter explores the nature of threshold concepts and transformative ways of thinking, initially against the general background of previous research and then, specifically, in relation to concepts used in research into teaching and learning in higher education. Two key concepts used in the literature are Perry's ideas on the development of *epistemological beliefs* or conceptions of knowledge (Perry, 1970, 1988), and the categories used by Säljö and others to differentiate between *conceptions of learning* (Säljö, 1979, 1982). These two descriptions not only parallel each other in describing important changes in students' ideas about the subject matter they are studying, they also show important thresholds, or pivotal positions, at which students' understanding is transformed. Sophisticated conceptions of learning are associated with deep approaches to learning, but the relational nature of approaches means that the threshold only increases the likelihood that a deep approach will be used. Approach to learning has, however, become a threshold concept for university teachers in opening up their thinking about how their own teaching can best support students' understanding, and even the notion of *threshold concept* itself seems to serve a similar function in thinking about the teaching of specific disciplines. The chapter concludes by looking again at the defining features of threshold concepts in relation to the research discussed in the paper, accepting the idea there are three distinguishable ways in which students' understanding of the subject can be opened up; through certain basic concepts in the early stages of a course, through integrative threshold concepts, and through acquiring the distinctive ways of thinking characteristic of the subject.

THE NATURE OF THRESHOLD CONCEPTS

The idea of threshold concepts emerged through discussions with university teachers of Economics as part of the ETL project (2005), a major investigation into teaching and learning in four contrasting subject areas. Among the array of concepts to which students are introduced within undergraduate degree courses, some seemed to have powerful influences on students' subsequent learning. Most of these were seen by staff and students alike as *troublesome knowledge* (Perkins,

R. Land, J.H.F. Meyer & J. Smith (Eds.), Threshold Concepts within the Disciplines, 21–35.

2006), proving difficult both to teach and to learn, but once understood they had an important transformative effect on students' understanding. Meyer and Land (2003) described these as 'threshold concepts', with the notion of 'opportunity cost' in Economics being a particularly clear example.

> A threshold concept can be considered as akin to a portal, opening up a new and previously inaccessible way of thinking about something. It represents a transformed way of understanding, or interpreting, or viewing something without which the learner cannot progress. As a consequence of comprehending a threshold concept, there may thus be a transformed internal view of subject matter, subject landscape, or even world view. (Meyer & Land, 2003, p. 1)

Subsequent discussions with staff and other researchers refined the description of threshold concepts further by recognising that, as 'conceptual gateways' into more advanced ways of thinking about topics and subject areas, they are by definition *transformative*, but they are also typically:

> *irreversible* (unlikely to be forgotten, or unlearned only through considerable effort) and *integrative* (exposing the previous hidden interrelatedness of something) ... it was also suggested that that the new 'conceptual space' opened up by such transfigured thought is in turn *bounded*, possessing terminal frontiers, bordering with thresholds into new conceptual spaces. (Meyer & Land, 2005, pp. 373-374)

The defining features of threshold concepts are, however, still being discussed, and for the purposes of this paper, our focus will be mainly on their transformative and integrative properties.

Any new concept introduced into the research arena has to be examined carefully to ensure that it is adding something important to what we know already. As a result, the notion of *threshold concept* has already come under considerable scrutiny (Meyer & Land, 2006). Here, the findings emerging from one particular project (Davies & Mangan, 2007) will be used to provide a framework for the rest of the chapter.

The 'Embedding Threshold Concepts' project is seeking to clarify the nature of threshold concepts within Economics and also develop materials to support student learning. It involves collaborative work with teachers in four universities. Initial discussions with staff suggested that it was quite difficult for them to grasp the essential transformative property of threshold concepts, with the term often being confused with the more commonly used idea of *key concepts*. From the evidence collected from both staff and students, it is now possible to recognise three different kinds of transformative thresholds in learning.

In the early stages of Economics degree courses, students have to understand how the meaning of the terms used in the academic study of Economics clarifies everyday thinking about the subject – distinctions between 'price' and 'cost', for example – and in the process they develop the basic conceptual raw material of academic discourse in Economics. These simple concepts transform students' interpretation of everyday Economics and so clarify their thinking, but they do not have the integrative power expected of threshold concepts.

The second form of transformation involves concepts that not only transform thinking but are also integrative, bringing together several of the basic concepts. The transformative property is created through grasping crucial interrelationships between the basic concepts; 'opportunity cost' seems to come into this category. But if students are to enter fully into the academic discourse, they also have to see how to handle economic problems by reducing the complexity of situations through considering what would happen 'other things being equal'. They also have to learn how to interpret graphs, understand the function of models, and use the statistical and linguistic tools that allow academic reasoning to be developed and presented to others. And this is the third form of threshold identified by Davies and Mangan.

These three types of threshold will prove useful in looking at concepts and ways of thinking that have been widely used in research into higher education, but first we need to look briefly at earlier research into the nature of conceptions and understanding.

CONCEPTIONS AND UNDERSTANDINGS

There is, of course, a vast literature already available on conceptual change, particularly within the fields of cognitive and educational psychology (see, for example, Schnotz, Vosniadou, & Carretero, 1999). From a psychological perspective, conceptions are seen as developing by extracting and integrating similarities and differences among varied experiences of a concept (Ausubel, Novak, & Hanesian, 1978). Marton (2007) and Marton and Tsui (2004) has been developing a pedagogical theory of learning which elaborates these descriptions by seeing learning as depending on the *discernment* of the critical features of concepts, brought about through seeing the *variation* that is involved in those aspects. Discernment can then lead to an integration of those features into the *simultaneous* fusion that is experienced as understanding, or the opening up of the subject through grasping a threshold concept. As Marton (2007) explains:

> Our theory begins by exploring the nature of the awareness involved in coming to see a phenomenon or topic in an importantly new way, and leads to questions about what we need to do in order to learn how to handle new situations in more powerful ways. If we are to be able to handle a situation in a more powerful way, we must first *see* it in a powerful way, that is discern its critical features and then take those aspects into account by integrating them together into our thinking simultaneously, thus seeing them holistically. And to discern those critical features, we must have experienced a certain pattern of variation and invariance in the object of learning. A medical student, for example, has to listen to the hearts of many different patients before any sense can be made of the differences heard, while to say anything interesting about the taste of a certain wine, we must first have tasted many different wines. (p. 20)

23

One recent theme in the research on conceptual change is the implications of the co-existence of differing conceptions of the same concept within a person's memory (Halldén *et al.*, 2002*)*. An Economics student may, for example, recognise the distinction between, say, 'price' and 'cost' and yet revert to the everyday equivalence of the terms when asked to explain an everyday economic event (Dahlgen, 1997). Students have to learn not only the technical meaning of the terms but also be able to recognise in what situations they should be used (Entwistle, 2006). So, conceptions seem to be constructed within long-term memory as a web of connections bringing together differing semantic aspects, such as defining features and illuminating examples, but with related contextual aspects – the situations to which the concepts relate.

The research on conceptual change tends to focus on isolated concepts, but in higher education we are also concerned about how students bring together groups of concepts so as to understand topics or theories. A series of interview studies looking at this experience among university students preparing for final examinations throws more light on the processes and feelings involved (Entwistle & Entwistle, 1992, 2003). In these interviews, the students emphasised that understanding involved relating ideas in their mind that also aroused feelings of coherence and connectedness. While students described a feeling of wholeness in their understanding, they also recognised that it was 'provisional'. They recognised that it was complete only in relation to the material they had covered and to the specific demands of the course on which they were to be examined.

I: How do you know that you understand something?

S: Well, with past experience you can relate it to something... But sometimes, when it's all clicked into place, later on you discover that it's not necessarily clicked into the right places, so you could have a feeling that you understand, but [it's not quite right]

I: And how do you know when you don't understand?

S: Because it just doesn't connect, because you can't make logical connections between the bits ... You just don't feel at ease with whatever it is you are meant to be doing, you're confused ... [When you understand] you do definitely get a feeling that the penny's dropped, it just all clicks into place ... If you don't understand it's just everything floating about and you can't get everything into place, like jigsaw pieces, you know, suddenly connect and you can see the whole picture.

I: So what happens ... when you come across some other ideas or some other evidence?

S: That doesn't necessarily mean you did not understand it: you only understood it *up to a point*. There is always more to be added ... Yes, you have one theory, and then you add on the reaction to that theory; there might (then) be another one to add to that – so you keep (on) adding.

This extract illustrates how different facets of a topic come together simultaneously – 'click into place' – to create a satisfyingly complete picture, along with a feeling of confidence that the understanding can be used to provide adequate explanations that fulfil present requirements.

In the situation investigated in this series of studies, it is not a specific concept or theory that is responsible for the insight arrived at, but rather the students' attempts to make sense of topics for themselves. In the process, students who were carrying out their exam revision in a thorough way, using a 'deep strategic' approach, often reported sensing their understanding as an integrated whole, almost as an 'entity' which they could, in a sense, see. These entities were described by Entwistle and Marton (1994) as *knowledge objects,* and they had characteristics which involved 'opening up the subject', even if it was generally not through a specific 'gateway'. Table 1 indicates the characteristic features of knowledge objects, based on a subsequent analysis (Entwistle & Entwistle, 2003).

Table 1. Features of 'knowledge objects' as experienced in preparing for examinations

– Awareness of a tightly integrated body of knowledge
  A structured understanding developed through summary notes

– Visualising the structure in a quasi-sensory way
  A pattern created to establish a memorable representation

– Awareness of unfocused aspects of knowledge
  Details available for providing convincing evidence

– Guiding explanations of the understanding reached
  Logical pathways used for linking steps in an argument

We are still awaiting the detailed exploration of experiences of acquiring threshold concepts in a variety of subject areas, but it would be surprising if some of the experiences of the transformations in thinking about the subject created by grasping threshold concepts were not similar to those found in the studies of knowledge objects (Entwistle, 2006). It will be interesting, however, to see what difference is made by the framework for understanding being provided within the syllabus, instead of being worked out by the student more or less independently. By linking students' personal understandings directly to specific understanding targets, differences between students should also become easier to interpret.

THRESHOLDS WITHIN CONCEPTIONS OF KNOWLEDGE AND LEARNING

While there is burgeoning research into the nature of threshold concepts in several different subject areas, as demonstrated by the range of the chapters within this volume, previous studies of student learning have also described important thresholds which lead to crucial transformations of thinking. Such conceptual change can be found, for example, in the work of Perry (1970) on conceptions of knowledge, and Säljö (1979) on conceptions of learning.

Perry identified important steps in epistemological development as students' *conceptions of knowledge* changed, and these changes were found to open up the student's thinking in important ways. He identified a recurring developmental pattern in students' beliefs about knowledge over the course of their student life. He described nine positions (or views) which are typically clustered into five sequential groups or stages (see top of Figure 1), ranging from a certainty that all knowledge is either right or wrong (*dualism*), to acknowledgement that there are many ways of looking at a situation (*multiplicity*), to awareness of knowledge as provisional, and then to a realisation that knowledge depends on interpretations of evidence with a variety of possible conclusions being drawn from it (*relativism*). This progression leads eventually to a readiness to make a personal stand on issues, based on justifiable interpretations of evidence, while accepting that all knowledge and ideas are ultimately relative (*personal commitment*). Perry saw the gradual emergence of relativism as a crucial transition that allowed students increasingly to enter into academic discourse. As one of the students commented:

> The more I work here, the more I feel that what I'm trying to do is to become what you might call a detached observer of ... any situation ... One who can ... detach himself emotionally ... and look at various sides of a problem in an objective, empirical kind of way – look at the pros and cons of a situation and then try to ... analyze and formulate a judgement ... bringing into consideration ... what the other person would feel and why he would feel so. (Perry 1970, p. 126)

Perry (1988) himself stressed the importance of this pivotal position in his scheme, and wrote enthusiastically about the different view of learning that emerged at that point.

> (Relativism) has taken us over a watershed, a critical traverse in our Pilgrim's Progress... In crossing the ridge of the divide, ... (students) see before (them) a perspective in which the relation of learner to knowledge is radically transformed. In this new context, 'Authority', formerly a source and dispenser of all knowing, (becomes)... a resource, a mentor, a model ... (Students) are no longer receptacles but the primary agents responsible for their own learning ... (Perry 1988, p.156)

Perry did not see the developmental process as irreversible, however. Indeed, students regularly regressed back towards dualism, sometimes due to the difficulty of handing the idea of relativism, and at other times because the experience of relativism threatened their own strongly held beliefs. This could be seen as similar to the experience of *liminality* found with threshold concepts (Meyer & Land, 2005).

In his exploration of the nature of *conceptions of learning*, Säljö (1979) identified a series of distinguishable categories of description that have subsequently been seen as indicating another developmental progression (see bottom of Figure 1). The first two conceptions describe the learning implied by the majority of quiz shows, which depends on remembering factual information, usually by rote learning. Within this conception, learning is seen as the process of accumulating the separate 'pieces' of knowledge provided, ready-made, by a teacher or other source, and then reproducing them on demand The third category marks the beginning of a qualitative change, as information is seen as having a purpose beyond acquisition: it also has to be applied.

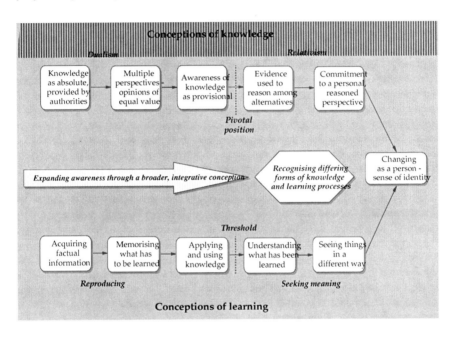

Figure 1. Developmental stages in conceptions of knowledge and learning

The progression reaches an important threshold when learning becomes equated with understanding. As people begin to see learning as involving the effort to make sense of ideas for themselves by relating it to their previous knowledge and experience, information becomes transformed into personal meaning. Beyond that, learning involves seeing things in an importantly different light, and so becomes fully transformative of understanding (Marton & Tsui, 2004). Finally, people may begin to experience learning as transformative in a broader sense, namely changing them as a person (Marton, Dall'Alba, & Beaty, 1993). While this final stage seems to be present in both developmental schemes, Perry links this to moral development, but it could also be seen as a change in the students' sense of their own identity.

Säljö found that people with advanced conceptions of learning became more aware of the different purposes for which alternative processes of learning could be used. Subsequent research indicated that they are also able to regulate their learning processes more consciously, and so adopt those most appropriate to specific tasks (Vermunt, 1998, 2007). They may become aware, for example, that the two main learning processes – rote and meaningful learning (Ausubel, Novak, & Hanesian, 1978) – are both valuable, but for importantly different purposes and at different stages in learning a subject. This awareness can be seen as an emergent property of the development process at university; students acquire a metacognitive view of how knowledge is developed and how academic ideas are best acquired. And this broader overview has important consequences for students' approaches to learning. It helps them to take advantage, within a teaching-learning environment, of those activities that have been designed to encourage and support a deep approach (Entwistle & Peterson, 2005).

In Perry's and Säljö's categories, we have descriptions of crucial transitions in students' thinking which parallel each other quite closely. It seems unlikely that the actual thinking processes involved are as distinct as the separate conceptualisations perhaps imply; rather, these processes are interconnected as students become more aware of the nature of academic knowledge and of how their learning might be better adapted to developing those forms of knowledge. This implies a shift in focus – from the task itself to the process of learning.

Our consideration of the work on conceptions of knowledge and learning was carried out to show how a threshold might be the result of a series of transformations in how students make sense of their university experience. The nature of the changes described indicates that we are not dealing with any specific threshold concept, but rather with the broadest level of transformation identified by Davies and Mangan (2007), describing ways of thinking which help students to think about the subject as novice professionals. In our recently completed ETL project across four contrasting subject areas we found that university teachers were able to indicate what they *really* wanted their students to learn, and we came to see these as their essential high-level aims.

> The ETL team coined the phrase *ways of thinking and practising* in a subject area (WTP) to describe the richness, depth and breadth of what students might learn through engagement with a given subject area in a specific context. This might include, for example, coming to terms with particular understandings, forms of discourse, values or ways of acting which are regarded as central to graduate-level mastery of a discipline or subject area. (McCune & Hounsell, 2005, p. 257)

Although the pattern of development shown in Figure 1 indicates the existence of crucial thresholds, and ones that have been generally accepted in the literature, there is an important difference from the transformations that are expected from subject-specific thresholds. This opening up of the subject is not tied directly to any specific concept or theory within a course, and students may pass through this threshold without any conscious recognition of an enhanced understanding. The process seems to be both gradual and, for the most part, subconscious. Students themselves are unlikely to be aware of the existence of their conceptions of knowledge and learning; these are constructs created by a researcher to describe important features found within interviews to other researchers and to teachers. The content-based concepts are, in contrast, the direct focus of the students' learning, and so the thresholds, and the consequences for future learning, can be directly experienced. The broadest level of threshold identified by Davies and Mangan seems to involve an appreciation of how evidence is found and used within the discipline, which is closely similar to one aspect of 'relativistic thinking'. The other aspect of relativism relates to the nature of knowledge in general terms, and so avoids the bounds created by any particular subject area; and that is also true of sophisticated conceptions of learning.

THRESHOLD CONCEPTS IN ACADEMIC DEVELOPMENT

The starting point for what has come to be called 'student learning research' (Biggs, 2003) was the original work of Marton and his team in Gothenburg in the mid-1970s, which led to the distinction between deep and surface *approaches to learning* (see Marton & Säljö, 1997). They also pointed out that such processes depended not only on the students' differing intentions but also on the content of the learning task and context within which it was set. Conceptions of learning are empirically related to approaches to learning, but as students with a sophisticated conception recognise that there are different learning processes to adopt for different purposes, they will not use deep approaches all the time. So, while conceptions of learning involve a threshold, approaches to learning do not seem to act, in themselves, in this way for students. The distinction can, however, act powerfully as a threshold concept for university teachers.

The extensive work on teaching-learning environments has unravelled some of the most important influences on deep approaches and high quality learning outcomes (Biggs, 2003; Entwistle, Nisbet, & Bromage, 2005; Meyer, 1991; Richardson, 2007; Vermunt, 2007), and has also found contrasting views of teaching (Prosser & Trigwell, 1999) which parallel the distinctions between deep and surface, and are to some extent related to them. Staff may see their role mainly as one of transmitting information or, alternatively, they may concentrate on encouraging conceptual change. But, like approaches to learning, approaches to teaching are relational, depending on the students and the stage in the degree course. Nevertheless, the strongest lever for change in staff conceptions is the ability to see teaching from the students' perspective, which allows a more sophisticated view of the relationship between teaching and learning to emerge.

Many of the courses now being taught as initial training for lecturers stress this perspective, often leading inexperienced staff towards crucial insights into the relationship between teaching and learning. These staff may come to recognise that their influence as teachers goes beyond making the subject accessible; they are also influencing how students think about the subject and, importantly, also affecting how they think about the nature of learning in general. This insight can fundamentally affect the outlook of teachers, and so qualifies as a powerful threshold concept. Indeed, it has been used effectively in this way by various

29

academic developers (Biggs, 2003; Prosser & Trigwell, 1999). As Meyer (2005) explains, such an approach to academic development can:

> empower newly appointed university teachers to begin the process of developing a mental model or conceptual framework ... in a form that can initially serve, and be further developed, as a basis for professional practice ... [This] framework ... is ... essentially defined by the 'student experience of learning' research literature. The threshold concept ... – the transformative gateway to the reconceptualisation of practice – is *variation in student learning*. The aim is for colleagues to reconstitute aspects of generic theory within their own disciplines in terms of some of the classic patterns ... in student learning engagement. In doing so, and in reflecting on their own gathered evidence, the theoretically underpinned focus ... of professional practice shifts from that of teaching to that of *learning* and teaching. (pp. 360-361)

While this notion of variation in student learning may serve as a trigger for seeing teaching and learning in a different way, teaching-learning environments are complex interacting systems that university teachers only gradually come to understand in ways that can fully transform their thinking. It is presumably an appreciation of this complexity within a framework such as that shown as Figure 2, which may act as a threshold into a whole new way of thinking about the nature of teaching and learning in higher education. This conceptual map shows student characteristics at the top, with influences of the teaching-learning environment being arranged across the bottom (based on the findings from the ETL project, 2005). Each of the boxes in this diagram can be opened up in the way suggested for 'teaching that develops skills and understanding', but that would prevent the diagram acting as a (somewhat) simplifying map linking together some of the main influences on the quality of student learning. (For more details about a similar model, see Entwistle, 2007.)

In looking for other threshold concepts in academic development, an intriguing possibility has been recognised in the development project undertaken by Davies and Mangan and their collaborators. Introducing Economics lecturers to the notion of threshold concepts seems to open up their thinking about the nature of knowledge in Economics, and show how the subject can be presented to students in more interesting and effective ways. In other words the threshold concept itself is acting as a threshold concept in thinking about teaching and learning.

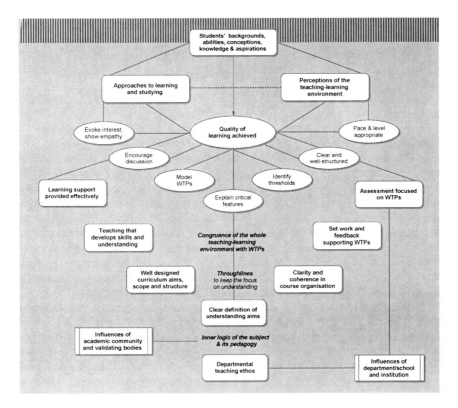

Figure 2. Interactions between influences on the quality of student learning

Marton (2007) sees his own pedagogical theory of learning as having a similar effect, and he has also found that encouraging teachers to work together in thinking about the forms of variation, which are important in a particular topic, has a powerfully beneficial effect on the quality of both teaching and learning. And this also seems to be true of discussions of threshold concepts.

> When university teachers start looking at their colleagues' ways of dealing with the same content that they themselves have taught, and when ways of dealing with content become a topic of conversation for them, then an important step towards the improvement of university teaching and learning will have been taken. (Marton, 2007, p. 28)

DISCUSSION AND CONCLUSIONS

The main purpose of this paper was to discover whether some of the concepts used in educational research are threshold concepts, and in the process to help to clarify the transformative nature of thresholds. It seems clear that there are differing transformative thresholds, only one of which fits the definition of a threshold concept. Defining features of a threshold concept indicate that it must relate to a specific and important aspect of a syllabus, and that it also must be capable of opening up the subject in important ways through integrating other, lower-level concepts.

Drawing on the distinctions made by Davies and Mangan (2007), basic concepts that help students initially to see the subject in a different way are not integrative and so not threshold concepts as such, although they can act as transformative thresholds for individual students. The term *threshold concept* represents the second category identified by Davies and Mangan, as it opens up the subject through the integration of other concepts. The final category of threshold is too broad to be called a concept; it seems better to describe it as a disciplinarily specific *way of thinking*, but it still does serve as an important transformative threshold for students. It is unlikely, however, to be experienced as a single event, as can happen with a threshold concept, but rather as a growing awareness of the nature of the discipline as a whole, along with the steady build up of professionally relevant knowledge and skills. Conceptions of knowledge and learning represent thresholds of this broader kind, as do the frameworks linking approaches to learning to teaching-learning environments for university teachers.

So far, much of the research into threshold concepts has focused on identifying them within a syllabus and from the teacher's perspective but, if we are to understand the transformative function of thresholds of various kinds, we must find out a great deal more about how they are experienced by students. Staff have described how threshold concepts integrate lower-level concepts and so serve as a portal which opens up the subject in important ways. But how do students experience these concepts? How many of them experience the transformation in their thinking which the threshold concepts offer? Once the concepts have been introduced, what other work is necessary by the individual student to recognise the transformatory power of the concept? The answers to these questions would have to come from a thorough analysis of interviews with students about their experiences of learning specific concepts, in which the students' understanding of them is systematically probed through the progressive deepening in questioning that encourages students to explore their own understanding, as in the earlier research into the experience of understanding (Entwistle & Entwistle, 1992, 2003).

The earlier research into students' experiences of understanding and of their experiences of 'knowledge objects' indicates what may be involved in grasping threshold concepts and seeing the connections with other parts of the syllabus which flow from those understandings. Research into conceptual change, and into epistemological development, provides another example showing that concepts in students' minds may well have an unstable early existence. We need to discover to what extent *liminality* (Meyer & Land, 2005) occurs and whether this, and the claim of irreversibility, is supported empirically across a variety of subject areas. Such extension of the work on threshold concepts through research into the students' experience of them will allow our understanding of the nature of both threshold concepts and transformative ways of thinking to be substantially improved.

The other development needed is, of course, to see how best to teach for transformations in student learning, and studies are already beginning to point the way (Meyer & Land, 2006). The research of Marton (2007), working with school-teachers to help students discern critical features, suggests one approach to teaching threshold concepts, while Perkins' (2007) exploration of *theories of difficulty* suggests other ways forward. He argues that staff can be aware of areas of the curriculum that regularly prove troublesome, and yet fail to act on these danger signs. Even when recognising the need for action, any change in teaching may simply take the form of spending more time in teaching those topics, but without any real understanding of what is causing the difficulty. Perkins argues that what staff need to do is to 'teach smarter'; in other words, they need to explore the reasons for any observed difficulty carefully before deciding on a course of action. Much current teaching, while often 'pretty good',

> always leaves a residue of persistent trouble spots … For *really* good pedagogy, we need to [have] a theory of difficulty that identifies the trouble spots in that particular content, strives to explain them, and points toward adjustments in the teaching-learning process to help with them. Thus, theories of difficulty become … a natural front for teachers learning about their students and their own craft, and a natural part of the considerable research on teaching and learning and human development. (Perkins, 2007, p. 44)

Concentrating on threshold concepts within a syllabus, in itself, is unlikely to lead to much improvement in students' understanding: the reasons for current difficulties have to be explored and used to guide changes in pedagogy. Moreover, although the potential that threshold concepts apparently have for transforming student understanding offers great promise for university teachers, staff will still need to be mindful of the many other sources of difficulty that Perkins, and others, have outlined.

REFERENCES

Ausubel, D. P., Novak, J. S., & Hanesian, H. (1978). *Educational psychology: A cognitive view.* New York: Holt, Rinehart & Winston.

Biggs, J. B. (2003). *Teaching for quality learning at university* (2nd edition). Buckingham: Open University Press/Society for Research into Higher Education.

Davies, P. & Mangan, J. (2007). Threshold concepts and the integration of understanding in economics. *Studies in Higher Education, 32,* 6.

Entwistle, A. C. & Entwistle, N. J. (1992). Experiences of understanding in revising for degree examinations. *Learning and Instruction, 2,* 1-22.

Entwistle, N. J. (2006). Knowledge objects: Contextualised personal understandings constructed for specific purposes. Paper presented at the EARLI SIG on Conceptual Change in Stockholm, 14-17 June, 2006.

Entwistle, N. J. (2007). Research into student learning and university teaching. In N. J. Entwistle & P. D. Tomlinson (Eds.), British Journal of Educational Psychology Monograph Series II, Number 4 – *Student learning and university teaching* (pp. 1-18). Leicester: British Psychological Society.

Entwistle, N. J. & Entwistle, D. M. (2003). Preparing for examinations: The interplay of memorising and understanding, and the development of knowledge objects. *Higher Education Research and Development, 22*, 19-42.

Entwistle, N. J. & Marton, F. (1994). Knowledge objects: understandings constituted through intensive academic study. *British Journal of Educational Psychology, 64*, 161-178.

Entwistle, Nisbet & Bromage (2005). Teaching-learning environments and student learning in electronic engineering. In L. Verschaffel, E. De Corte, G. Kanselaar, & M. Valcke (Vol. Eds.), *Powerful environments for promoting deep conceptual and strategic learning* (pp. 175-198). *Studia Paedagogica New Series 41*. Leuven, Belgium: Leuven University Press.

Entwistle, N. J. & Peterson, E. R. (2004). Conceptions of learning and knowledge in higher education: relationships with study behaviour and influences of learning environments. *International Journal of Educational Research, 41*, 407-428.

ETL Project (ESRC-TLRP). (2005). Subject reports on Biological Sciences, Economics, Electronic Engineering, and History are available online at http://www.tla.ed.ac.uk/etl/publications.html

Halldén, O., Petersson, G., Scheja, M., Erlen, K., Haglund, L., Österlind, K., & Stenlund, A. (2002). Situating the concept of conceptual change. In M. Limon & L. Mason (Eds.), *Reconsidering conceptual change: Issues in theory and practice* (pp. 137-148). Dordrecht: Kluwer.

Marton, F. (2007). Towards a pedagogical theory of learning. In N. J. Entwistle & P. D. Tomlinson (Eds.), British Journal of Educational Psychology Monograph Series II, Number 4 – *Student learning and university teaching* (pp. 19-30). Leicester: British Psychological Society.

Marton, F. & Säljö, R. (1997). Approaches to learning. In F. Marton, D. J. Hounsell, & Entwistle, N. J. (Eds.), *The experience of learning: implications for teaching and learning in higher education.* Available online at http://www.tla.ed.ac.uk/resources/EOL.html

Marton, F. & Tsui, A. B. M. (2004). *Classroom discourse and the space of learning.* Mahwah, NJ: Lawrence Erlbaum.

McCune, V. & Hounsell, D. (2005) The development of students' ways of thinking and practising in three final-year biology courses. *Higher Education, 49*, 255-289.

Meyer, J. H. F. (1991). Study orchestration: the manifestation, interpretation and consequences of contextualised approaches to studying. *Higher Education, 22*, 297-316.

Meyer, J. H. F. (2005). Closing the gap between educational research and educational development: A model of engagement. In C. Rust (Ed.), *Improving student learning 12 – Diversity and inclusivity* (pp. 360-376). OCSLD, Oxford Brookes University, Oxford.

Meyer, J. H. F., & Land, R. (2003). Threshold concepts and troublesome knowledge (1): linkages to ways of thinking and practising within the disciplines. Paper presented to the 10th Conference of the European Association for Research on Learning and Instruction (EARLI), Padova, Italy, August 26-30, 2003.

Meyer, J. H. F., & Land, R. (2005). Threshold concepts and troublesome knowledge: Epistemological considerations and a conceptual framework. *Higher Education, 49*, 373-388.

Meyer, J. H. F., & Land, R. (Eds.) (2006). *Overcoming barriers to student understanding: threshold concepts and troublesome knowledge.* London: Routledge.

Perkins, D. N. (2006). Constructivism and troublesome knowledge. In J. H. F. Meyer & R. Land (Eds.), *Overcoming barriers to student understanding: Threshold concepts and troublesome knowledge.* London: Routledge.

Perkins, D. N. (2007). Theories of difficulty. In N. J. Entwistle & P. D. Tomlinson, (Eds.), British Journal of Educational Psychology Monograph Series II, Number 4 – *Student learning and university teaching* (pp 31-48). Leicester: British Psychological Society.

Perry, W. G. (1970). *Forms of intellectual and ethical development in the college years: A scheme.* New York: Holt, Rinehart and Winston.

Perry, W. G. (1988). Different worlds in the same classroom. In P. Ramsden (Ed.), *Improving learning: New perspectives* (pp. 145-161). London: Kogan Page.

Prosser, M. & Trigwell, K. (1999). *Understanding learning and teaching: the experience of higher education*. Buckingham: Open University Press.

Richardson, J. T. E. (2007). Variations in student learning and perceptions of academic quality. In N. J. Entwistle & P. D. Tomlinson, (Eds.), British Journal of Educational Psychology Monograph Series II, Number 4 – *Student learning and university teaching* (pp 61-71). Leicester: British Psychological Society.

Schnotz, W., Vosniadou, S., & Carretero, M. (Eds.) (1999). *New perspectives on conceptual change*. Oxford: Pergamon.

Säljö, R. (1979). *Learning in the learner's perspective. I. Some common-sense conceptions* (Report 76). Gothenburg: University of Gothenburg, Department of Education.

Säljö, R. (1982). *Learning and understanding*. Gothenburg: Acta Universitatis Gothoburgensis.

Vermunt, J. D. (1998). The regulation of constructive learning processes. *British Journal of Educational Psychology, 68*, 149-171.

Vermunt, J. D. (2007*). The power of teaching-learning environments to influence student learning*. In N. J. Entwistle & P. D. Tomlinson (Eds.), British Journal of Educational Psychology Monograph Series II, Number 4 – *Student learning and university teaching* (pp. 72-89). Leicester: British Psychological Society.

AFFILIATION

Noel Entwistle
University of Edinburgh

PETER DAVIES & JEAN MANGAN

3. EMBEDDING THRESHOLD CONCEPTS: FROM THEORY TO PEDAGOGICAL PRINCIPLES TO LEARNING ACTIVITIES

INTRODUCTION

If the theory of threshold concepts (Meyer & Land, 2003) is to be useful in guiding teaching and improving student performance, it must be translated into principles that can inform the design of teaching and the curriculum. The aim of this chapter is to consider these principles and explore various types of learning activities that aim to embed threshold concepts in economics teaching by putting these principles into practice.

The problem that is being addressed here is expressed by Frank (1998, p. 14) in the following terms: 'When the dust settles, most students leave the introductory course never having fully grasped the essence of microeconomics. Thus, the opportunity cost concept, so utterly central to our understanding of what it means to think like an economist, is but one among hundreds of other concepts that go by in a blur.' Threshold concepts provide a way of describing the desirable overall learning outcome for students: they have learned to think and practice in the manner of scholars of a discipline, using a coherently structured body of ideas and procedures to analyse problems as they are defined by that discipline. In the words of one economics lecturer quoted by Meyer and Land (2006, p. 15): 'We want our students to start to think about problems, issues. You get them to formulate, if not explicitly at least implicitly, some kind of formal analytical structure or model that simplifies things but then allows someone to think through a problem in a very structured way.' The structure of thinking is particularly important in a discipline such as economics which is currently defined in a very integrated manner with fairly sharp boundaries (Reimann, 2005). It is not surprising in these circumstances to find that there are significant 'learning spillovers' between the major sub-parts of the discipline (Guest and Vecchio, 2003).

However, currently, undergraduate students of economics have little experience of being asked to 'formulate an analytical structure'. Empirical research (Becker & Watts, 1998; Reimann, 2005) indicates that there is little variation in students' experience of learning of undergraduate economics either in the USA or the UK. In the UK their experience consists of fast-paced lectures accompanied by tutorials. Information is transmitted in lecturers and then consolidated and applied in

R. Land, J.H.F. Meyer & J. Smith (Eds.), Threshold Concepts within the Disciplines, 37–50.

tutorials. A survey by Guest and Duhs (2002) in Australia also found that students believed they experienced too much transmission of content and not enough opportunity to apply ideas. In this 'theory-first' (McCormick & Vidler, 1994) approach to teaching and learning analytical structures are not formulated by students, they are taken as given. A typical outcome of this approach is the one described by Frank. Students 'acquire' a set of concepts but this has little impact on the way that they experience economic phenomena.

There is already a strong literature suggesting ways in which this problem can be remedied by engaging students with the subject matter of economics in ways that go well beyond 'chalk and talk' (e.g. Becker & Watts, 1998; Becker et al., 2006; Davies, 2004). The approaches to teaching and learning suggested in this chapter have some similarities with ideas that may be found in the existing literature. However, threshold concepts provide a way of understanding learning in economics that not only offers a coherent rationale for organising teaching in some ways rather than others but also offers a productive stimulus for generating some new ideas about the kind of teaching which is more likely to be effective. Since 2004 the 'embedding threshold concepts in first-year undergraduate economics' (ETC) project[1] has been developing this rationale and designing, using and evaluating teaching and learning activities on the basis of this rationale.

In the next section we explain how the theory of threshold concepts has led the project to propose several pedagogical principles for learning activities. In Section 3 we exemplify the types of activity that have been developed by the project and comment on evidence from the use of these activities with students. This evidence is drawn from initial trials with undergraduate students at four universities in England. In Section 4 we discuss some general issues in the design of these activities and some implications for future practice and research.

RELATING THEORY TO PEDAGOGICAL PRINCIPLES

Davies and Mangan (2007) use a table (here reproduced as Table 1) to show some differences between the conceptual change involved in the acquisition of threshold concepts and conceptual change in the acquisition of basic concepts. The latter term is used here to refer to the way in which a discipline classifies phenomena to create an order that is susceptible to the modes of analysis deployed in the discipline.

We base our initial identification of pedagogical implications of this schema on some ideas from variation theory (Pang & Marton, 2003, 2005).[2] Any phenomenon may be understood in qualitatively different ways and each way of understanding highlights some features of that phenomenon and may also presume particular relationships between those features. A feature of a phenomenon may be one of its properties or it may be a characteristic of the context within which the phenomenon is located. The pedagogic principle derived from variation theory is that the teacher should draw the learner's attention to simultaneous variation in the features of a phenomenon that are critical to the desired conception.

Table 1. Definition and exemplification of three types of conceptual change

Type of conceptual change	Type of transformation and integration	Examples in economics
1. Basic	Newly met concepts some of which transform understanding of everyday experience through integration of personal experience with ideas from discipline.	Distinctions between price/cost; income/wealth (stocks/flows); nominal/real values; investment/saving. Real money balances, natural rate of unemployment.
2.Discipline Threshold concepts	Understanding of other subject discipline ideas (including other threshold concepts) integrated and transformed through acquisition of theoretical perspective	Interaction between markets, welfare economics, opportunity cost
3. Procedural (in the case of economics: how are models of the economy constructed and evaluated)	Ability to construct discipline specific narratives and arguments transformed through acquisition of ways of practising.	Comparative statics (equilibrium, ceteris paribus), time (short-term, long-term, expectations), elasticity

How does this principle apply to the 'basic concepts' identified in Table 1? The first row in Table 1 includes conceptual change in which there is discrimination between phenomena that were previously regarded as a single phenomenon. For example, 'money' and 'income' are often used interchangeably in everyday language. Similarly, no distinction is made in everyday language between the idea of a 'stock' of money (e.g. the total amount of notes, coin and bank deposits) and a 'flow' of money being exchanged for other things. Experience of money in everyday life and conversation does not highlight variation in features (particularly those associated with the total amount of money in a society) that lead to the discernment that income, the stock of money and the flow of money are distinct phenomena. The distinction between 'income' and 'money' is necessary to prepare the ground for the distinction between the supply and the demand for money. Some features of the phenomenon 'demand for money' are presented in Figure 1.

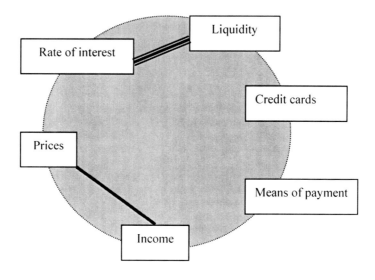

Figure 1. Some features of the phenomenon of the demand for money

Each of the features identified in Figure 1 is commonly referred to in textbook explanations of the demand for money (see for instance Begg *et al.*, 2005, pp. 396-397; Mankiw & Taylor, 2006, pp. 611-612). Some features, which may be highlighted in students' experience (e.g. credit cards), may not be pertinent to the conception of the demand for money which the discipline assumes. Other features, such as liquidity, may not be highlighted in students' everyday experience. Variation theory suggests that learners should experience simultaneous variation in each of those features that are critical to the target conception of the phenomenon. However, there is a complicating factor. These features are not independent of each other. In the case of prices and income the relationship is a simple ratio, since many textbook representations focus on the effect on the demand for money of a change in money income relative to prices in order to present the argument in terms of the effect of 'real income'. In the case of interest rates and liquidity the relationship is more complex and specific to the discipline. Individuals may hold their wealth in the form of money or interest bearing savings. The advantage of holding money is that it provides liquidity, but the opportunity cost of holding money is the interest that is foregone by doing so. Simultaneous variation in the features 'rate of interest' and liquidity' is insufficient to force an interpretation of this relationship in terms of opportunity cost. This interpretation is dependent on bringing a superordinate or threshold concept to bear upon the conception. This distinctive way of integrating concepts in a discipline is evident even more strongly in more complex models that students encounter later in their studies.

For example, the IS/LM model depicts *interaction between markets* (a discipline threshold concept, Row 2 in Table 1) in presenting a conception of the overall level of economic activity. The phenomenon of the demand for money (Figure 1) becomes a feature of the phenomenon 'overall level of activity in the economy'. In Figure 2 we concentrate on the features of this phenomenon that are highlighted by the conception in the 'IS/LM' model. The phenomenon is represented by the grey circle which is given specific form by the features that are highlighted in the boxes around its perimeter. The conception of the demand for money that is embedded in Figure 2 has two critical features: interest and income and it is the deeper level of theory presented in Figure 2 that provides the context for conceptualising the demand for money in these terms.

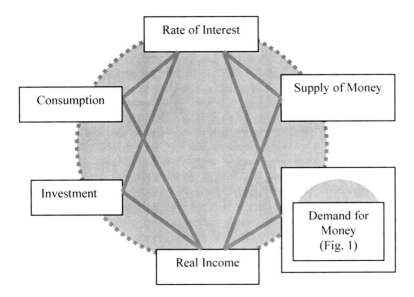

Figure 2. Features of the 'overall level activity in the economy' as conceived in the 'IS/LM' model

The relationships between the features in Figure 2 are more complex than those in Figure 1. They are generated by the use of the modelling procedures (Table 1, Row 3) of *equilibrium, ceteris paribus and elasticity* in the context of the discipline threshold of interaction between markets (Table 1, Row 3). Discernment of simultaneous variation in each of the critical features is not sufficient to understand the conception of the economy that is represented here. Once a conception of the level of activity in the economy in terms of the IS/LM model has been established, new light is shed on the more basic conceptions (such as the demand for money) that act as critical features in understanding the more complex phenomenon. The threshold concept of interaction between markets, when understood through the procedural concepts that are necessary to operationalise this concept, acts as a 'keystone' binding conceptions together.

We can now outline the key pedagogical issues in supporting students' acquisition of discipline threshold concepts. First a threshold concept acts as a keystone bringing form and robustness where previously there was a collection of ideas, in this case enabling the learner to extend their use of the demand and supply framework from analysis of one market to the effects of inter-market interactions on equilibrium price and output in different markets.

Second, the conception of 'demand for money' which is a critical feature of the conception of overall activity in the economy in Figure 2 is removed from direct experience and can only be experienced hypothetically. Comparative static analysis is the procedural device developed by the discipline to make this hypothetical experience possible. Third, the relationships between the features in Figure 2 are directed by the procedural thresholds in Row 3 of Table 1. That is, the dimensions become visible through the use of the procedures. Understanding the discipline threshold requires an awareness of how, and why, it is generated through the use of the procedural thresholds. In the terms used by McCune and Hounsell (2005) row 3 in Table 1 refers to the 'way of practising' in the discipline and Row 2 in Table 1 refers to the 'way of thinking' in the discipline. Fourth, since the acquisition of threshold concepts transforms understanding of previously acquired subject knowledge, students need to be ready to accept that at each stage in their learning that their understanding is provisional. This problem becomes most intense when the acquisition of a new threshold concept transforms understanding of a previously acquired threshold concept: an inevitable outcome if threshold concepts work together in a web to define the way of thinking and practising in a subject. In the words of Entwistle (2007, p124) 'In developing their conceptions, students experience the limitations suggested by Meno's paradox: an adequate conception often requires a student to create links with a broader conceptualisation of the topic, which has to be built from the very ideas that the student has yet to understand.'

To address these problems we propose four principles:

– *Highlight variation to ensure there is a sufficient foundation of basic concepts to make it possible to work towards acquisition of the threshold concepts:* This addresses the first problem by providing the learner with a base of conceptions that may be open to re-working through subsequent teaching and learning.
– *Expose the way in which scholars in the discipline use procedural thresholds by highlighting variation in the use of key procedures:* this addresses the third problem that an understanding of the way procedures are used in the discipline is essential to an understanding of the threshold concepts.

42

- *Help students to integrate their understanding through using key procedures in re-working their understanding of previously acquired concepts in the light of threshold concepts:* this addresses the first, second and third problems by treating the acquisition of new concepts as bound up with the re-working of previously acquired ways of thinking. It helps students to think of their learning in terms of building a coherent structure (Bransford *et al.*, 2000).
- *Help students to regard their understanding as provisional and to tolerate uncertainty:* this addresses the first and fourth problems. Students have to learn 'incomplete' conceptions in order to make more 'complete' conceptions accessible to them.

PEDAGOGICAL PRINCIPLES EXEMPLIFIED

To put these principles into practice the 'Embedding Threshold Concepts in Undergraduate Economics' project has developed three types of activity: 'reflective exercises', 'problem-focused exercises' and 'threshold network exercises'.[3] In this section we describe each type of activity and explain how they aim to address the pedagogical principles. We draw upon evidence gathered through trialling the activities in four universities during the academic year 2005/2006. Through this trialling we sought to identify unforeseen issues in the design of the activities and the demands on students and lecturers. We also aimed to gather evidence that would confirm or conflict with our design principles. We did not at this stage aim to collect test data on students' achievements. The average prior achievement of students varied significantly across the four institutions. A further source of variation lay in whether students were studying economics or another subject (such as Business Studies) as their main discipline. We have not so far found any significant relationship between prior achievement and the ways in which students have responded to these exercises. Data were also gathered in the form of evaluations from staff and in a small number of instances we also gathered data through in-depth interviews with students who had recently completed an exercise. Our interpretation of these data was informed by the comments of the project's external evaluators and colleagues from each of the partner institutions in the project.

Reflective Exercises

Our 'reflective exercises' begin by posing an applied question in economics (for example, 'What are the economic arguments on whether a football club should sell an important player?'). The phrasing of the question was intended to make it accessible to students, so that it is possible to conceive of an answer being provided on the basis of 'everyday knowledge' which might be contrasted with an answer that might be given by an economist. The first part of the exercise aims to get students to recognise alternative ways of framing an answer to the problem. If students meet a problem that is already framed by the concepts and procedures of a discipline they miss the opportunity to see how and why scholars frame the problem in this way. The 'framing' part of this activity addresses principles 1 and 2: *Highlighting variation to ensure a sufficient foundation of basic concepts* and *exposing the way in which scholars use procedural thresholds.* Part of the framing activity for an exercise on money is reproduced here as Table 2. Students are asked to tick however many of the statements they think appropriate.

Table 2. Part of the framing activity for a Reflective Exercise on Money

a	As a student, when you graduate and get a job your income will rise and you will demand more money in order to spend more.
b	For many students their money demand is their student loan.
c	Income is what we get paid over a certain period of time, over week, month or per term, whereas money is what we have in notes and coins or in the bank at a particular point in time.
d	The quantity of money is the amount of notes and coins issued.
e	The quantity of money is the amount of notes and coins in circulation and certain types of bank deposits.
f	What I have in notes and coins and in my bank account today is my income.
g	What I have in notes and coins and in my bank account today is my money balances.

Table 3. The proportion of students selecting different options in Framing Questions for the activity 'Money – just another good?'

Question	Percentage of students selecting each of the options available for each question						
	a	b	c	d	e	f	g
A	100	0	20	20			
B	0	60	0	40	20	70	100
C	60	0	40	80	10	10	
D	0	0	80	60	70		
E	19	89	3	0	0	35	16

The choice of items here is intended to highlight features that are critical to the discrimination of economic phenomena: e.g. money and income, stocks and flows. Another part of the framing activity is concerned with the recognition of the role of threshold concepts(s) that are important in the integration in highlighted in Principle 3, in this example the focus is on opportunity cost. Table 3 shows the percentage of students selecting each of the options in the framing questions for the activity 'Money – just another good?' The percentages add up to more than one hundred in each row because students could choose as many options as they wished. Options which scored close to 0 or 100 showed little or no variation across the cohort of students and a number of these options were removed from later versions of the activity. Evidence from lecturers' observations and subsequent interviews with students indicated that students' engagement with this part of the activity was high.

Students were then able to compare the way they were framing the problem with the way in which an economist might frame the problem. We provided feedback that sought to expose the reasoning behind the way in which an economist might frame the problem. Students were then presented with a variation on the initial question and asked to provide a coherent overall response to the problem, drawing on the feedback they have received. It is at this point that students are asked to integrate their understanding addressing Principle 3 *Help students to integrate their understanding through using key procedures in re-working their understanding of previously acquired concepts in the light of threshold concepts.*

However, it was not evident that the second half of the exercise was sufficiently supporting students' ability to re-work and integrate their thinking. This could reflect the time that lecturers allowed for students to complete the activity, the conception of teaching held by lecturers and the conception of learning held by students. The activities were included in standard one hour slots and in a number of instances lecturers aimed to complete the activity using only part of this time. The belief that teaching consists in transmitting information remains widespread and this belief generates a pressure on lecturers to make sure that sufficient content has been covered in their teaching sessions. When the activities were used within a standard lecture slot in a large lecture theatre the problems with engagement in the second half of the activity were most noticeable and quite likely due to students' expectations of the large lecture format.

Nevertheless, there must be some doubt as to whether the current design of the activities provides sufficient support for students' re-working and integration of their thinking. In some cases this may because we need additional framing in the first part of the exercise. This can be illustrated through an activity that focused on the possible gains from trade. A number of students who framed the problem in the way that might be expected from an economist, nevertheless failed to integrate their understanding of the discipline in developing their answer to the final problem in the exercise. This required an understanding of the idea of comparative advantage in terms of opportunity cost and few students were able to demonstrate this kind of understanding. For example one student who was interviewed believed that they had understood the comparative advantage principle, but then proceeded to explain the principle purely in terms of absolute advantage. As part of our review of these activities we have added 'framing' on this aspect.

One difficulty that we encountered in the design of these exercises was how to phrase the feedback in a way that avoided lapsing into a presentation of the 'textbook answer'. The danger here was that students might interpret such exercises as keeping the 'right answer' hidden until part way through, and thus, perhaps, encouraging a strategy of waiting till the 'right answer' was presented in a form that they would then try to memorised. To counteract this problem, feedback is being revised to cast it more in terms of a narrative which might express an economist's thoughts as they framed the problem, recognising the difficulties they faced in the task.

Problem Focused Exercises

The title of this type of exercise reflects a debt to problem based learning, but no intention to rigorously follow PBL principles. Our problem focused exercises require less substantial initial data, less time and more structured 'scaffolding' for students than would be expected in a PBL activity.[4] Crucially, the accompanying tasks identify the phenomenon which will form the focus of the learning rather than leaving this identification to the learners as would be normal in a PBL activity.[5] It has some similarities with the use of case studies as advocated by Carlson and Velenchik (2006). An important common thread in each of these examples is the value of cases that students believe are relevant to their interests in order to motivate initial engagement (Siegfried and Sanderson 1998, Watts 1998).

In one problem-focused exercise students were asked to suggest explanations for a difference between the price of music downloads in two countries. Students were given a short piece of text to prompt their thinking. In this text a representative for Apple refers to differences between 'the economic model' in each country and the cost of providing the service. The final paragraph suggests that if there were no barriers to mobility of customers between the markets then the price difference would disappear. The task for students is to identify that these explanations are suggested in the text and then to begin to interpret and critically examine these possible explanations. Our problem-focused activities assume that students cannot carry out these steps without 'scaffolding' that draws their attention to variation in possible theoretical explanations (Principles 1 and 2). In the example, students are given different theoretical constructions that could explain a difference in price between two markets. These theoretical constructions show different relationships between the features of the phenomenon: price, cost, demand and output. To complete the task students have to consider which of these explanations is most appropriate given the evidence they have about the context. This is followed by a second task in which asks students to relate different diagrams to different interpretations of the data. This use of variation (Principles 1 and 2) is the first way in which these exercises are distinguished from other problem-based approaches to learning.

The final task in these problem focused exercises aims to address Principle 3 (*helping students to integrate their understanding*) by guiding students' reflection on the way they have attempted to analyse this problem. In the particular example on music downloads students are asked to choose one out of four named concepts that they could manage without in their analysis of the problem. The chosen concepts are either procedural or discipline thresholds (Table 1). This idea owes something to a suggestion by Hansen (1998, p. 89).

One of the issues that we have encountered in the design of these activities is how much integration to encourage. Evidence generated in the first stage of the project (Davies and Mangan 2007) showed that a key difference between lecturers' and students' analysis of economic problems lay in the number of different economic ideas which were brought coherently to bear upon the problem. However, the design of an exercise to support students' learning needs to be sensitive to their readiness: how many ideas are they currently capable of bringing together? Diagrams in economics are used to 'bring ideas together' but this may be lost on students who learn diagrams as fixed entities to be deployed in given circumstances rather than the expression of a particular set of ideas in a particular context. Principles 1, 2 and 3 provide a useful guide for the design of an exercise, but professional judgement is still required as to adjust the demand of an exercise according to students' readiness.

Threshold Network Exercises

Our third type of activity mainly targets Principle 3 (*Helping students to integrate their understanding*). The exercises give a short applied problem and a list of concepts that might be used to make sense of the problem. Students are asked to choose which concepts (including procedural or discipline thresholds concepts) they will use and provide an account of how using these concepts together generates a good analysis of the problem. The aim is to encourage students to appreciate the web of concepts. Coming to an understanding of the power of these concepts in a wider range of problems may deepen the students understanding in earlier applications. Students are again given feedback describing how an economist might carry out the task that has been set for them.

DISCUSSION

Our development of activities for teaching and learning has progressed alongside development of the idea of 'threshold concepts' and the relationships between this idea and other aspects of the theory of learning. Developments in our understanding of the relationship between threshold concepts and variation theory have been particularly influential in our thinking about the design of activities for teaching and learning. However, the process of trying to develop practice has also prompted reflection on the idea of threshold concepts and the implication of this idea for pedagogic principles. Consequently, what we have presented here is work in progress. We are very conscious, for example, that our activities have not directly addressed one of the four pedagogic principles (*Helping students to regard their understanding as provisional and to tolerate uncertainty*) and that our evidence on the problem focused and threshold network exercises is limited as many of these have only been recently developed.

We have also observed that the both stages of the reflective exercises have not been equally popular with lecturers and students. We can speculate as to the reasons for this, but at present we are not able to offer systematic evidence to shed light on the issue. It could be that principles 1 and 2, which are emphasised strongly in the first stage of the Reflective Exercises, are more pertinent to lecturers' intentions in the first year of undergraduate courses. The aim of integration may be seen as a task for levels 2 and 3. However, it might equally be the case that insufficient support for integrating understanding and re-working of prior knowledge is provided in the exercises. The aim may be possible if the implementation in the activities was better. Given the importance of integration and developing the structure of understanding to the whole 'threshold concepts approach' this is an important issue for further work. It may be that further work will help to clarify the pedagogical principles that have been suggested here.

Nevertheless, we do believe that these examples show (1) that when the insights of variation theory are combined with those from threshold concepts they can be used to develop a coherent analysis of the problems facing learners and (2) that it is possible to derive pedagogical principles from the idea of threshold concepts and that activities that are devised on the basis of these principles are distinctive when compared to other approaches to teaching and learning which at first sight are quite similar.

In the coming academic year we will be carrying out investigations that examine the whole of the learning experience, including the use seminar groups who use our activities and those who do not on the same module. We were already of the view that it is important in embedding to consider assessment, since assessment is the main student driver. This view was reinforced in several ways by our experience during the year and we will be developing assessment tools and strategies and this will enable us to start assessing the overall impact on the learning process. We also found our interviews with students useful in this context and in the coming year we will be carrying out interviews focused directly on the student responses to particular parts of our material in the period immediately following their use to conduct a detailed analysis of the variation in students' understanding. We have also discussed the use of web CT in our project group to provide feedback tailored to the particular student's replies. The use of this medium does also have other advantages such as allowing the staged build up of models that may aid student's understanding. However, it does have the disadvantage of being seen as an 'optional extra' both by students and staff, unless clearly built into a programme (by for instance making it clear that it relates to the assessment in some way).

NOTES

[1] The Embedding Threshold Concepts in First-Year Undergraduate Economics Project is based at Staffordshire University, UK. The project is funded by the Higher Education Funding Council for England and the Department for Employment and Learning (DEL) under the Fund for the Development of Teaching and Learning and it involves a partnership with Coventry, Durham and West of England Universities. We are grateful to Noel Entwistle and Steve Hodkinson and also the members of the project team for their support in developing the ideas presented in this chapter.
[2] We recognise an issue here in the use of the words concept and conception. We aim to show how we resolve this through our subsequent exposition using figures 1 and 2.
[3] Examples of these exercises can be seen on the project web site to be found at http://www.staffs.ac.uk/thresholdconcepts
[4] The Buck Institute for Education in California has been very active in developing problem-based learning in economics. Their web site can be found at http://www.bie.org/ and a related site at http://www.pbl-econ.org/ See also Maxwell and Bellisimo (2003) Problem Based Economics, Overview, Buck Institute for Education.
[5] This forms a substantial part of the seven stage PBL structure advocated at the University of Maastricht. (See http://www.unimaas.nl/pbl/)

REFERENCES

Becker, W. E. & Watts, M. (1998). *Teaching economics to undergraduates: Alternatives to chalk and talk.* Cheltenham, UK: Edward Elgar.

Becker, W. E., Watts, M., & Becker, S. R. (2006). *Teaching economics: More alternative to chalk and talk.* Cheltenham, UK: Edward Elgar.

Begg, D., Dornbusch, R., & Fischer, S. (2005). *Economics,* 8th Edition. Maidenhead: McGraw-Hill.

Bransford, J. D., Brown, A. L., & Cocking R. R. (Eds.) (2000). *How people learn, brain, mind, experience and school, commission on behavioral and social sciences and education.* Washington: National Academy Press.

Carlson, J. A. & Velenchik, A. (2006). Using the case method in the classroom. In W. E. Becker, M. Watts, & S. R. Becker (Eds.), *Teaching economics: More alternatives to chalk and talk.* Cheltenham: Edward Elgar.

Davies, P. (Ed.) (2004). *The handbook for economics lecturers: Teaching.* Bristol: Economics Network of the Higher Education Academy. http://www.economicsnetwork.ac.uk/handbook/

Davies, P. & Mangan, J. (2007). Threshold concepts and the integration of understanding in economics. *Studies in Higher Education, 32*(6) in press.

Entwistle, N. (2007). Conceptions of learning and the experience of understanding; Thresholds, contextual influences and knowledge objects. In S. Vosniadou, A. Baltas, & Z. Vamvakoussi (Eds.), *Reframing the conceptual change approach in learning and instruction.* Oxford: Elsevier.

Frank, R.H. (1998). Some thoughts on the micro principles course. In W.B. Walstad & P. Saunders (Eds.), *Teaching Undergraduate Economics: A Handbook for Instructors.* Boston, MA: Irwin/ McGraw-Hill.

Guest, R. & Duhs, A. (2002). Economics teaching in Australian Universities: Rewards and outcomes. *The Economic Record, 78,*(241), 147-160.

Guest, R. & Vecchio, N. (2003). Are there learning spillovers in introductory macroeconomics, *International Review of Economic Education, 1*(1), 36-60.

Hansen, W. L. (1998). Integrating the practice of writing into economics education. In W. E. Becker & M. Watts (Eds.), *Teaching economics to undergraduates: Alternatives to chalk and talk.* Cheltenham, UK: Edward Elgar.

Mankiw, N. G. & Taylor, M. P. (2006). *Economics.* London: Thomson Learning.

McCormick, B., Vidler, C., & Thomas, L. (1994). *Teaching and learning the new economics.* London: Heinemann.

McCune, V. & Hounsell, D. (2005). The development of students' ways of thinking and practising in three final year biology courses. *Higher Education, 49*(3), 255-316.

Meyer, J. H. F. & Land, R. (2003). Threshold concepts and troublesome knowledge: linkages to ways of thinking and practising within the disciplines. In C. Rust (Ed.), *Improving student learning. Improving student learning theory and practice — 10 years on.* Oxford: OCSLD.

Meyer, J. H. F. & Land, R. (2006). Threshold concepts: an introduction. In J. H. F. Meyer & R. Land (Eds.), *Overcoming barriers to student understanding: threshold concepts and troublesome knowledge.* London and New York: Routledge.

Pang, M. & Marton, F. (2003). Beyond "lesson study": Comparing two ways of facilitating the grasp of some economic concepts. *Instructional Science, 31*(3), 175-194.

Pang, M. & Marton, F. (2005). Learning theory as teaching resource: Enhancing students' understanding of economic concepts. *Instructional Science, 33*(2), 159-191.

Reimann, N. (2005). First–year teaching environments in economics. *International Review of Economics Education, 3*(1), 9-35.

Siegfiried, J. J, & Sanderson, A. R. (1998). Using sports to teach economics. In W. E. Becker & M. Watts (Eds.), *Teaching economics to undergraduates: alternatives to chalk and talk.* Cheltenham: Edward Elgar.

Watts, M. (1998). Using literature and drama in undergraduate economics courses. In W. E. Becker & M. Watts (Eds.), *Teaching economics to undergraduates: Alternatives to chalk and talk.* Cheltenham: Edward Elgar.

AFFILIATIONS

Peter Davies and Jean Mangan
Institute for Education Policy Research
Staffordshire University, UK

ROBERT MCCORMICK

4. THRESHOLD CONCEPTS AND TROUBLESOME KNOWLEDGE

Some Reflections on the Nature of Learning and Knowledge

INTRODUCTION

The seminal paper on threshold concepts by Meyer & Land (2003) represents an interesting and unusual analysis of knowledge across disciplines, which raises profound questions about the nature of knowledge and learning. The fact that different disciplines have different views of knowledge (something I will examine later), may or may not be related to their different views of learning, but it is these latter views I want to examine as a basis for looking again at the way Meyer and Land construe their empirical data.

This paper will argue that different views of learning will determine how 'threshold concepts' and 'troublesome knowledge' are conceived and that each view has different implications for pedagogic responses, some not altogether helpful to those trying to educate students in higher education!

GROUND CLEARING ON VIEWS OF LEARNING AND KNOWLEDGE[1]

First it is important to be clear about what views of learning I am referring to in the introduction above. Here I take the contrasting metaphors put forward by Sfard (1998), the acquisition and the participation metaphors, which between them roughly characterise the major controversy over theories of learning.[2] The *acquisition metaphor* (AM) is the kind of stance that 'cognitive constructivists' take, where learning is seen as an individual construction process (in the head), which for example will result from there existing a cognitive conflict between how a learner construes or conceptualises something and the evidence that they are confronted with.[3] To some extent this is what Perkins (1999) is referring to in seeing troublesome knowledge as being 'counter-intuitive'; it does not match the conceptualisation the learner has and cognitive conflict is needed to shift the learner (all concepts have this property to some extent). This view of learning thus sees knowledge as an object (e.g. a concept) that has to be acquired by students (by active means) and that the resulting conceptual framework for the discipline is reproduced within students' heads and the more understanding they have, the more

R. Land, J.H.F. Meyer & J. Smith (Eds.), Threshold Concepts within the Disciplines. 51–58.

their frameworks will replicate that of the expert in the subject. Subjects that lay out clear conceptual relationships and hierarchical relationships are implicitly taking this AM view of knowledge and thus of learning.

As I want to focus on the implications of the *participation metaphor* (PM), this will be elaborated upon more than the AM view. PM, in contrast to AM, takes a more social view of knowledge construction and sees learning as 'learning to participate' in a 'practice', characterised by Lave & Wenger (1991), and more substantially defined by Wenger (1998) as participation in a 'community of practice'. Thus knowledge is not an object but is knowing how to participate in the community's practices. One important implication of this is that learning is 'becoming', creating an 'identity'. Becoming knowledgeable in mathematics is not only learning the procedures and techniques of mathematicians, but exhibiting their values and norms (e.g. of when a proof is convincing or of what constitutes an elegant solution). Meyer & Land (2003) indicate some of these ideas in their paper. There are also ideas of shared construction of knowledge, which are more relevant to pedagogy than to some of the discussion of threshold concepts, so for the moment I will put this aside. There is an important extension to this social view in ideas of situated cognition (which not all who take a PM perspective may accept); the knowledge that is learned is bound to the physical, historical and social context of the situation within which it is learned. This gives an explanation for inert knowledge; it is knowledge that may be, for the student, bound up with the classroom context within which it is learned and is entirely inert in the world outside and cannot be used. Students who learn about batteries and bulbs in a physics classroom may, for example, think it is impossible to connect up a circuit without there being a 'bulb holder' (McCormick, 1999)!

In part this view relates to the worlds that students inhabit and those of teachers at either school or university level. The science academic will inhabit an everyday world of, say, chemistry, and expect the students to similarly inhabit this, but also try to convince them that this chemistry is relevant to their everyday life. Lave (1988) considered everyday mathematics (in the supermarket) and compared it with 'school mathematics', showing that shoppers were able to handle shopping mathematics that was equivalent to school mathematics, but when faced with the equivalent school mathematics problems they performed much worse.[4] Thus in wanting a learner to be able to use school/college mathematics in the world outside (or indeed any subject), there is an assumption that the 'abstract' form encountered in school or college can be transferred to this everyday world. Those who take a situated view argue that school mathematics for the learner is just another context, and that often the knowledge is inert and may only be useful within the college context.[5]

REFLECTIONS ON THE VIEWS OF MEYER AND LAND

As I indicated earlier, Meyer and Land (2003) show elements of both of these metaphors, though they understandably do not acknowledge them. At one point they, as it were, 'mix' their metaphors. They take an apparently AM approach usually when they talk of threshold concepts in science and mathematics, where the concepts are quite definite ('complex number', 'limit', p. 2; 'gravity' as a building block, p. 4). Or in notions of there being an independent 'conceptual space', p. 5; indeed towards the end noting that in subjects like mathematics, physics and medicine there is a 'body of knowledge' (p. 9). These characterisations see knowledge as an object, independent of knowers and what they do with the knowledge. But elsewhere they also use the language of PM with the familiar idea of 'community of practice'; for example, when they talk of tacit knowledge (p. 7), 'academic territories' (p. 5) and, central to the PM, 'transformation of personal identity' as a characteristic of a threshold concept. The discussions of what I took to be transitions into new worlds, when they discussed Adam and Eve (p. 4), took the idea even further. Perhaps most profound was the discussion of music, which went beyond the specific cultures of academic subjects and brought into play the culturally acquired knowledge of tuning systems whose development is almost entirely through participation in the culture (whether as a performer or listener). A mixed metaphor is indicated in the contrast of the discussion of boundaries of 'conceptual space' (knowledge as object) being the demarcation of academic territories (p. 5), where knowledge is related to a group of knowers and what they do.

None of this is to say that Meyer and Land are being unhelpfully inconsistent or that their informants are showing a wide range of similarly inconsistent views of knowledge, though there are evidently subject differences in the relationships to AM and PM. Indeed Sfard (1998) argues that it is often the case that we shift metaphors to cope with different situations. In doing so she is taking a view of the two metaphors that does not see them in competition, but not all theorists do so, and for debating purposes I will adopt the exclusive view of the PM.

VIEWING THRESHOLD CONCEPTS FROM A PARTICIPATION PERSPECTIVE

Let me now take this situated view as part of the PM in general and make some reflections on the points made by Meyer and Land (2003) by examining some examples of their analysis. For effect I will push their examples and my use of the PM to the limit, and they could rightly object to my account!

Cooking

Even in terms of an AM perspective this example causes me problems. If we take the idea of concepts in a subject being threshold to *that* subject, there is no extension that such concepts have the same power in other subjects (a point implicitly acknowledged by them in their contrast of the discourse of social and

53

economic policy between economists and non-economists; p. 4). In the cooking example there is to my knowledge only one master chef, Blumenthal (2006),[6] who used science as part of his cooking practices, and this science is bio-chemistry. Further he had to spend considerable time in the kitchen developing these science ideas specifically in the context of cooking. Thus thinking of this from a point of view of the PM, and communities of practice, it is not in my view tenable to put forward a 'threshold concept' from one practice (academic physics), and assume it is threshold in another practice. The everyday practices of the two communities in this case are quite different and it is going too far to assume that the 'concepts' are equally enlightening and hence 'threshold' to each.

Students and Threshold Concepts

If we go back to the higher education classroom and assume that the academic subject specialist is trying to bring students into a subject community i.e. make them knowledgeable about that subject (the 'transformation of personal identity' Meyer and Land refer to, p. 4), then a threshold concept must be seen in terms of the practices of the community. As noted in their discussion of ritual knowledge (p. 6), students don't see these larger practices, but rather a set of routines and procedures (even if some of them are based around concepts). There are some examples of where higher education teachers have indeed tried to turn their classrooms into communities. Schoenfeld (1996) ran his undergraduate mathematics classroom as if it were a community of mathematicians and he would present problems, some which he had not tried to solve before, and ask students to convince each other (not just looking to him for what were correct answers). This is high-risk stuff, but it is a pedagogic implication of the PM view of learning![7]

However, within this view lies for me a completely intractable problem when the subject is not in itself the main focus of the teaching. I have in mind the 'service' function of subjects in degree programmes, for example mathematics and science for engineers, or statistics for physical or social scientists. If we take the view that the mathematics specialist, say, is trying to develop the mathematical identity of the engineer, then this may be a problem in terms of a clash of identities or at least competing ones. It also underlines an issue about the nature of the 'mathematics' that is used and how it is conceived by mathematicians and, in this case, engineers. The conceptual structure, and the whole notion of what it means to be mathematical, is likely to be different for the mathematics specialist than it is for the engineer. Let me give one example from my electronics colleagues at the Open University (see McCormick, 1999). All electronics engineers learn about second order differential equations, which, among other things, are used in designing (alternating current) electronic circuits. They tend to use, however, a derivative Niquist diagram that more closely models the various components in the circuit that relate to the various parts of the diagram rather than the constants etc., within the differential equation.[8] This is a phenomenon that others have noted where the knowledge expert's use is more closely linked to the devices and elements of the systems etc., they are dealing with (what Gott, 1988, called 'device' knowledge).

There may be no doubt that underlying the engineer's use of science or mathematics is the abstraction that the mathematician or scientist holds central to their particular perspective on their subjects, but in terms of the everyday work of others like engineers who are 'using' this knowledge, it is likely that they will work with a different conception. As with the food example, this makes the idea of a threshold concept in mathematics for an engineering student problematic.

Students' Everyday Worlds

As if the situation were not complicated enough, students, even in a mathematics classroom where their intention is to learn to become mathematicians, are likely to formulate their identity according to other pressures. History classrooms, for example, reflect not the community of practice of historians, but the community of practice of students 'learning' history. This latter community will be formed from the everyday practices that educational institutions set for students including routines of class attendance, assignment submission, examination requirements and the whole culture of performance that provides the setting for modern higher education. So a student might see the identity they want to develop as being a 'successful student', requiring them be alert to all the assessment clues, handing work in on time, being attentive etc. Alternatively there will be those who see themselves as getting the best value for money for their fees and the highest performance for the minimum work, or those that see the tuition side of university as a side show and are more intent on union work, counter-culture activity, or just plain idleness! It would be possible to construct any number of these identities that are part of the students' becoming, none of which have much bearing on the practices into which a subject specialist will be trying to enculturate the students.

These three issues (use of physics in cooking, the service function of a subject and students' everyday worlds) do not, as I said, offer an easy view of a pedagogic approach that might be the outcome of an analysis of the situation from the PM perspective. But, if there is a hint of truth in them, it certainly makes the idea of how to 'transform personal identity', as part of coming to terms with threshold concepts, somewhat complex!

SOME ASIDES

Although I have considered the main elements of the idea of threshold concepts, there are a few other ideas of Meyer and Land (2003) which I would like to address. These issues also derive from taking a PM perspective.

Inert Knowledge

I have already made the point about how a PM perspective views inert knowledge, which from the students' point of view means that they see the ideas taught in the history and social studies classes as bound by the context of these two 'classrooms'; their knowledge is context-specific. One of the things that some cognitive constructivists and situated learning theorists agree upon is the importance of bridging the contexts and helping students to read the context and to be able to use the 'abstract' knowledge that is supposed to be context-free. But this means taking the context seriously, and not using it as a way of 'dressing up' the underlying abstraction.

Alien Knowledge

This notion relates to how much the student has entered the everyday world of the subject specialist and understands what practices are important in it. Thus the problem that students have with Newton's laws, for example, relates to the fact that in the everyday world of most people, friction *is* present and so objects don't continue in the same line of motion if there is no force acting on them as they do in an apparently 'theoretical world' (Meyer & Land, 2003, p. 7)! Students will be asked to come out of this 'theoretical world' and apply the ideas where there is friction and quickly it all becomes very complex. A beam being acted on by forces in an applied mathematics course or a physics lesson apparently has no mass (at some levels of analysis), but then suddenly in the technology classroom it does and a student is supposed to have some idea of how it might perform in a mechanism.[9]

Tacit Knowledge

Meyer and Land (2003) already provide us with the analysis of this in terms of a PM perspective as they talk of it being shared within a community of practice (p. 7). But what is important here is that such knowledge is learned through taking part in the practices of the community and so again these must form the centre of the learning experience. This takes us back to the kinds of things that Schoenfeld (1996) was advocating, which I described earlier.

Subject Differences

At a number of points I have indicated how different subjects have different views of knowledge, and this is striking in the Meyer and Land (2003) analysis. I also queried whether this could be attributed to different views of learning, and lacking any empirical data, I would have to leave it as a query. It may be that it reflects more general positivist, interpretivist or post-modern perspectives to knowledge and the enquiry that surrounds them. This apparently is the case in their discussion of 'troublesome language' (p. 9). However, it seems to me to be an important empirical exploration to examine the extent to which there are systematic differences in views of learning among the subjects, or whether the differences reflect individual orientations that vary as much within, as across, subjects.

CONCLUDING COMMENTS

As I said at the outset, I do not seek to undermine or refute the discussion by Meyer and Land (2003) on threshold concepts and troublesome knowledge, rather to explore these ideas through a different lens. Sometimes this coincides with their analysis and sometimes not. Whatever perspective to learning is taken, the pedagogic implications are not straightforward, and there has to be serious questions asked as to what can be achieved in the contemporary higher education system, especially as it increasingly responds to the 'student as customer' tune.

NOTES

[1] These views are presented in a simplified form and do not represent the full richness of each.

[2] These controversies were debated in the *Educational Researcher* from the late 1990s: Anderson *et al.*, 1996, 1998, 2000; Cobb, 1994; Cobb & Bowers, 1999; Greeno 1997.

[3] This does not imply that there is no role for others in this process, only that the construction is individual.

[4] There are a number of other such studies e.g. Nunes *et al.* (1993).

[5] As indicated earlier this view is controversial as the references in Note 2 indicate.

[6] See a commentary by *Chemistry World*: http://www.rsc.org/chemistryworld/Issues/2005/May/Cookedtoperfection.asp (checked 8 August 2007).

[7] There are some useful frameworks for how such a classroom might look, though there are precious few implementations that have been published; in any case most of this work is at school level (e.g. Brown *et al.*, 1989).

[8] There is also the problem that computers have introduced numerical methods for solving the differential equations, and in any case most engineers work with computer-aided circuit design that requires the engineer to specify inputs and outputs and the computer does the detailed work. (But that's another story!)

[9] I have shown how, in relatively simple mechanisms that students of 11-12 years' old might design and build, the physics of its performance would soon defeat the average mathematics teacher let alone the students (McCormick, 1999)!

REFERENCES

Anderson, J. R., Greeno, J. G., Reder, L. M., & Simon, H. A. (2000). Perspectives on learning, thinking, and activity. *Educational Researcher, 29*(4), 11-13.

Anderson, J. R., Reder, L. M., & Simon, H. A. (1996). Situated learning and education. *Educational Researcher, 25*(4), 5-11.

Anderson, J. R., Reder, L. M., & Simon, H. A. (1998). Situative versus cognitive perspectives: form versus substance. *Educational Researcher, 26*(1), 18-21.

Blumenthal. H. (2006). *In Search of Perfection: reinventing kitchen classics.* New York: Bloomsbury.

Brown, J. S., Collins, A., & Duguid, P. (1989). Situated cognition and the culture of learning. *Educational Researcher, 18*(1), 32-41.

Cobb, P. & Bowers, J. (1999). Cognitive and situated learning: perspectives in theory and practice. *Educational Researcher, 28*(2), 4-15.

Cobb, P. (1994). Where is the mind? *Educational Researcher, 23*(7), 13-20.

Gott, S. H. (1988). Apprenticeship instruction for real-world tasks: the coordination of procedures mental models and strategies. In E. Z. Rothkopf (Ed.), *Review of research in education 15 1988-89* (pp. 97-169). Washington DC: American Educational Research Association.

Greeno, J. G. (1997). On claims that answer the wrong question. *Educational Researcher, 26*(1), 5-17.

Lave, J. (1988). *Cognition in practice: mind, mathematics and culture in everyday life.* Cambridge: Cambridge University Press.

Lave, J. & Wenger, E. (1991). *Situated learning: Legitimate peripheral participation.* Cambridge: Cambridge University Press.

McCormick, R. (1999). Practical knowledge: A view from the snooker table. In R. McCormick & C. Paechter (Eds.), *Learning and knowledge* (pp. 112-135). London: Paul Chapman.

Meyer, J. H. F. & Land, R. (2003). *Threshold concepts and troublesome knowledge: Linkages to ways of thinking and practising within the disciplines.* Enhancing Teaching-Learning Environments in Undergraduate Courses Project, Occasional Report 4. Edinburgh: University of Edinburgh School of Education.

Nunes, R., Schliemann, A. D., & Carraher, D. W. (1993). *Street mathematics and school mathematics.* Cambridge: Cambridge University Press.

Perkins, D. (1999). The many faces of constructivism. *Educational Leadership, 57*(3), 6-11.

Schoenfeld, A. (1996). In fostering communities of inquiry, must it matter that the teacher knows the answer? *For the Learning of Mathematics, 14*(1), 44-55.

Sfard, A. (1998). On two metaphors for learning and the dangers of choosing just one. *Educational Researcher, 27*(2), 4-13.

Wenger, E. (1998). *Communities of practice: Learning, meaning and identity.* Cambridge: Cambridge University Press.

AFFILIATION

Robert McCormick
Faculty of Education and Language Studies
The Open University

JAN H. F. MEYER, RAY LAND, & PETER DAVIES

5. THRESHOLD CONCEPTS AND TROUBLESOME KNOWLEDGE (4)

Issues of Variation and Variability

INTRODUCTION: VARIATION AND DISCERNMENT

A long standing tradition (Dienes, 1959, 1960) in pedagogical theory has asserted the importance of focusing learners' attention on variation in critical features[1] of phenomena they are trying to understand. This tradition has been given renewed vigour through the development of variation theory by theorists in the phenomenographic tradition (Marton & Booth, 1997; Marton & Trigwell, 2000; Fazey & Marton 2002). In this chapter we aim to show that reviewing the idea of variation from the perspective of threshold concepts yields insights on learning that are of particular importance within higher education. These insights arise in large measure from relinquishing the insistence within variation theory that learning is 'a change in an individual's way of experiencing something' (Runesson, 1999 p.1). To that extent, the interpretation of variation from the perspective of threshold concepts may be seen as a more general position.

There are several features that are common to each of these perspectives on variation and it may be helpful to stress these at the outset: (1) each phenomenon has several features, (2) these features may be physical properties (or definitional features) of the phenomenon or associations between the phenomenon and particular physical or social environments, (3) a phenomenon may be understood in different ways and each different way of understanding focuses on a sub-set of features of the phenomenon that are critical to that way of understanding it and, (4) a way of understanding may focus on only one feature of the phenomenon. Threshold concepts introduce a distinctive perspective through their emphasis on the *social features* in the second point.

In developing our argument we first summarise the theories of variation proposed by Dienes and by phenomenographers. We use the example of understanding complex numbers to suggest some limits to the application of variation theory as currently expounded. We then aim to show how the framework provided by threshold concepts is able to take account of cases such as the understanding of complex numbers and go on to discuss how threshold concepts suggest four modes of variation that are of particular importance to the progress of learning.

R. Land, J.H.F. Meyer & J. Smith (Eds.), Threshold Concepts within the Disciplines, 59–74.

THEORIES OF VARIATION: DIENES AND PHENOMENOGRAPHY

In 1959 the eminent mathematics educator and psychologist Z. P. Dienes formulated a theory of 'mathematics learning' that stressed the importance of making learners aware of variation in those dimensions of a phenomenon that are critical to the particular way of understanding the phenomenon that the teacher wants them to acquire. The essence of his theory is that (in mathematics) there is an inherent structure that can be revealed by exposing the learner to variation. More formally in his own initial words:

> *Hypothesis A.* Visual, tactile and muscular images must be formed to create perceptual equivalents of a concept. *From the common essence of these will be abstracted the conceptual structure.* This suggests that the more varied the perceptual models, the easier the acquisition of the concept. It is when we have had dealings with a variety of perceptual equivalents of a concept that we discover the purely conceptual structure *by seeing that there is something in common to all the perceptual equivalents.* It is thus that a really mathematical insight is achieved …. (emphasis added) (Dienes, 1959, p. 16)

In a more formalised exposition of his theory he distinguished between four pedagogical 'principles', the third and fourth of which are of particular relevance here:

> 3. *Mathematical Variability Principle.* Concepts involving variables should be learnt by experiences involving the largest possible number of variables.

> 4. *Perceptual variability principle.* To allow as much scope as possible for individual variations in concept-formation, as well as to induce children to gather the mathematical essence of an abstraction, the same conceptual structure should be presented in the form of as many perceptual equivalents as possible. (Dienes, 1960, p. 44).

He cites as an example the case of a parallelogram:

> To give the maximum amount of experience, structured so as to encourage the growth of the concept, it seems *a priori* desirable that *all* possible variables should be made to vary while keeping the concept intact. For example, with the concept of a parallelogram we can vary the shape by varying the angles and the lengths of the opposite sides; we can vary the position, as long as we keep the opposite sides parallel. Clearly a set of congruent parallelograms placed in the same position would not be a suitable set of experiences for the growth of the concept. (Dienes, 1960, pp. 42-43.)

In the terms used in our introduction, Dienes suggests that simultaneous variation in each of the critical features of the phenomenon is needed to help the learner to acquire the conception of a parallelogram. His third and fourth principles are more frequently cited in subsequent work (e.g. Behr *et al.*, 1980) that has aimed to elucidate his ideas. In his third principle (mathematical variability) he uses the term 'variable' rather than feature and his suggestion that the 'largest number of variables' should be involved is interpreted here in terms of 'as many of the features that are critical for the conception as practicably possible'. His fourth principle (perceptual variability) asserts that learning is more likely if the phenomenon is presented in a variety of physical forms.

Continuity between the ideas of Dienes and more recent formulation of variation theory in the phenomenographic tradition can be illustrated through an example taken from Runesson's (1999, pp. 316-317) account of how to support the development of pupils' understanding of a square:

> When focussing on the angles, the teacher compares the picture of the square with one of a rhombus. She points to the angles in the rhombus and contrasts them with the angles in the square. By doing so, she exposes a variation in the size of the angle. She opens up for a variation in that dimension. A right angle can then be experienced by the pupils as one value in the dimension "angle size". Correspondingly she can vary other aspects of the square and thus open up for other dimensions of variation: the length of the sides, the number of sides, different squares (i.e. the length of the sides of the squares are different) etc. She can also focus on other aspects of squares, such as the occurrences of squares in everyday life, pointing out that the flooring material is made up of square shapes, the chessboard has 64 squares, the six sides of a dice are squares etc. By doing this, she opens up a dimension of variation of different squares.

In this account we can see use being made of Dienes' 'mathematical variability principle' (references to angles, length of sides, number of sides) and his 'perceptual variability principle' (comparison of squares in two and three dimensions and in different physical settings). The teacher's role in focusing awareness of variation in critical elements of the phenomenon is common to both accounts of variation, although simultaneity is less obvious in Runesson's description of practice. More recently Runesson (2006, p. 400) has provided an account of supporting the development of a pupil's understanding of graphs in which she emphasises the importance of simultaneity:

> Taking the situation with Ellen as an example, different aspects of what she was learning came to the forefront of her attention, whereas others did not. Initially, she did not pay attention to the speed of the motion. Only the change of position in relation to the tower was the focus of her attention; that is, position was a discerned aspect. However, a few minutes later, when she tried to achieve a steeper curve, she noticed how fast she was moving also. Now she discerned the position and the speed at the same time. When noticing position and speed simultaneously, she experienced the relation between a change of position and the graphical representation in a new way and acted accordingly. In summary, when more discerned aspects were at the forefront of her attention and discerned at the same time, her way of experiencing the relation of her movements and the graphical representation changed.

Phenomenography provides a more general basis for variation theory in two ways. It extends variation theory to all phenomena, not just the mathematical phenomena with which Dienes was concerned and, more substantially, it provides a deeper rationale for the relationship between variation, experience, and learning. Nonetheless, some difficulties are thrown up by the developing exposition of this account of learning. Runesson (2006, p. 402) goes on to state:

> So the discernment of height, which is an aspect or a dimension of the individual, takes an experienced variation of that particular dimension. A discerned aspect or a feature of an experienced object is thus discerned as a dimension of variation.

Dimension, aspect and feature are used interchangeably here, whilst 'aspect' is used in a different sense by Marton and Booth (1997) and 'dimension' is used in a different sense elsewhere by Runesson (2006) and in other accounts of Variation Theory such as Pang (2003). We prefer the term 'feature' in this chapter to avoid the potential confusion that may otherwise arise. More fundamentally, Phenomenography asserts two aspects of the relationship between variation, experience and learning.

First, 'learning is seen as a change in an individual's way of experiencing something ... It amounts to becoming capable of discerning certain aspects of a phenomenon and being capable of holding them in focal awareness (attending to them) simultaneously' (Fazey & Marton, 2002, p. 237). This capability is an ontological status, an expression of what it means to learn. What *is* learnt is relational: a relationship between the individual and the phenomenon within a particular contextual frame of reference. Observations by learners are always bounded, as they are necessarily perceived from a particular certain vantage point. There are inevitably different ways of sensing the same phenomenon.

Second, there is an assertion of causation, identifying the necessary conditions for learning to occur. In the view of Marton and Trigwell (2000, p. 381):

> There is no learning without discernment. And there is no discernment without variation. If good teaching is about making learning possible, how do good teachers help students experience variation? ... We argue that they constitute a space of learning which contains those aspects[2] of the object of learning that are subject to variation simultaneously. For learning to occur, whether it be in the formal learning contexts established by these teachers, or in the less formal contexts of participation in social practices, there must necessarily be a certain pattern of variation present to experience, and this pattern must be experienced.

At any one time, a learner cannot simultaneously give equal attention to every conceivable detail of a phenomenon (Gurwitsch, 1964). So, at any instant, some features will come to the fore as figure (with 'focal awareness' or attention) and others will recede to the background. Features in the background will co-exist but will not be directly focused upon. However when some new situation arises, the structure of awareness can change dramatically. Something that was very peripheral has the potential to become very central. So the state of variation is always dynamic. Experience of colours is cited as a good example. In order to 'experience a colour' (for example, blue), *other* colours must have been experienced otherwise there would be no knowledge of what 'blue' is. Colours would have no meaning. This 'experienced variation' is a crucial point in terms of the pedagogy of variation theory.

We might offer two further observations. In relation to the notion of perceptual equivalents, Zolan, Strome and Innes (2004) provide further examples of what is in effect an application of the theory of variability that owes no conceptual debt to phenomenography. In Biology one encounters the concepts of *mitosis* and *meiosis*. These concepts represent complex process of cell division and gene regulation that are fundamental to an understanding of genetics (Taylor, 2006). Zolan *et al.* (2004 p.24) have developed a 'hands-on modelling' pedagogy for overcoming conceptual 'bottlenecks' that involves coloured pipe cleaners and beads. Students are required to manipulate these objects 'to illustrate a process.' Also involved is the development of mental 'dynamic cartoons' posited by the authors (pp. 22-23) to represent an aspect of how professional scientists would overcome "the challenges that limit our students' learning".

It is also interesting to speculate on the degree of correspondence between variation theory and Saussurean linguistic theory. Variation theory in the phenomenographic tradition seems to constitute an educational application of Saussurean structuralism in linguistics (Sanders, 2004) in terms of the way in which individual words (*parole*) come to have operational meaning within a language (*langue*). More specifically this comes about through the way in which words come to have specific meaning by not meaning what every other word in a language means, that is through variability of definition. For the speaker of a language, knowing how to use the language meaningfully, and in utterances which are often unique (never having been constructed in that form by any other speaker), there would seem to be a necessity for experienced variation and for simultaneous variation in those features critical to a conception. When some new situation arises, which is almost constantly in the use of a language, the structure of awareness and hence meaning can change dramatically, so the state of variation is again always dynamic.

ON THE LIMITATIONS OF VARIATION THEORY

In the previous section we noted that current variation theory asserts two relationships between variation, learning, and experience. However, we relinquish the assertion of causation, that experience of variation is a *necessary* pre-condition of *all* learning. The importance of this distinction can be illustrated by the possible interpretations of a statement by Pang and Marton (2005). In their discussion (p. 163) of how children 'understand numbers', they state that in discerning 'many-ness' the child

> *must* have experienced variation in that aspect. They *cannot* experience the 'seven-ness' of seven, for instance, without experiencing the 'six-ness' of six and the 'eight-ness' of eight'. The same is true for experiencing the 'sequential' aspect of numbers. (emphasis added)

In terms of ontological status (that learning is a change in the way a phenomenon is experienced) this argument is unproblematic. A child who is not able to differentiate seven-ness from six-ness cannot be said to have learnt 'seven'. However, the statement appears to conflate this status with a prior condition of experiencing variation ('must have experienced') and it is this apparent conflation that we explore in this section. The argument is developed through two cases in which we can say that an individual experiences a phenomenon *without* prior experience of variation.

The first case is semantic. In so far as humans are born with innate capabilities these are not the product of experience of prior variation. For example, Butterworth (1999 p. 107) asserts that people are born with an 'an inner core of ability for categorizing small collections of objects in terms of their numerosities'. This capacity for infants to categorise the world in terms of 'numbers of things' (up to four) exists because there is an area of the brain (the inferior parietal lobule) that contains a posited genetically programmed 'number module' which differentiates between the sizes of numbers and what those sizes mean. Whilst we might reasonably exclude innate characteristics from 'learning', their existence highlights the importance of distinguishing between ways of experiencing the world and the way in which a new way of experiencing the world is acquired.

The second case is more substantial. Since a conception of a phenomenon is composed of a pattern of relationships between critical features of that phenomenon we might consider possible variation in the type of critical feature and possible variation in the type of pattern of relationships. In the example of a conception of a deer given by Marton and Booth (1997) the critical features are physical features of the beast that distinguish it from its context and from other beasts and the relationship between those critical features is additive: the beast is the sum of its parts. On the other hand Pang and Marton (2005) provide an example of understanding the phenomenon of 'price' in the context of learning economics. Their target conception of 'price' has critical features that are hypothetical (what *would be* supplied and what *would be* demanded in particular circumstances) and the relationships between the critical features are functional in a mathematical sense and *not* unidirectional. A change in price will lead to a change in demand and a change in demand will lead to a change in price. Observable patterns of the critical features of the phenomenon that are produced by real or simulated market outcomes (amount supplied, amount demanded, price etc.) can be interpreted in different ways. When all of the critical features are allowed to vary the pattern of variation that can be experienced *does not* force one interpretation. A key aspect of the social context of understanding phenomena is that academic disciplines have developed procedures for overcoming such problems through underpinning theories which *legitimate* one interpretation rather than another.

The fundamental point here is that each feature of a phenomenon and each posited relationship between features of a phenomenon is itself a conception.[3] Conceptions of less complex or less composite phenomena become, in turn, critical dimensions of more complex and generalised phenomena. A particular conception of a phenomenon may arise not only from experience of variation in its critical features, but from the interpretation that is given to that variation by a superordinate conception. In some cases the principle of variation may break down entirely when a superordinate conception is not open to variation.

This is the case with complex numbers, and it is emphasised that the discussion here is vicariously from the perspective of the novice student encountering the concept for the first time, and not that of the expert. In mathematics a complex number, which is troublesomely not a 'number' in the conventional sense of the word, is defined as a real number (a number as conventionally used in everyday experiences) plus another entity i that is multiplied by another real number. In symbolic terms, if z is a complex number, then $z=x+iy$, where x and y are real numbers and $i=\sqrt{-1}$ (that is, $i^2=-1$). A complex number thus has a *real* and an *imaginary* part. The imaginary part of a complex number (iy) is troublesomely defined for the novice (and even more so for the lay reader!) in terms of an *abstract*, apparently *absurd*, and *dimensionless* entity (i: the square root of minus one). An additionally troublesome thing about complex numbers is that they can be used in calculations in an 'imaginary' world to yield results that are meaningful in the real world.

As an 'object of learning' there is only one feature of i that can be brought into 'focal awareness', namely, its definition. There are no features of 'i-ness' in terms of 'abstractness' or (to the novice) apparent 'absurdness' that can be varied or held constant to aid the discernment of i. There can also be no variation in i in a mathematical sense because i is a constant. At the next level of conceptual difficulty, in what is again an apparently absurd operation, i is multiplied by a real number y to yield an abstract entity (iy) which *can* vary according to y. However it makes no sense to talk about variation in the 'iy-ness' of iy as an aid to its discernment, nor does it make any sense to talk about the '($x+iy$)-ness' of $x+iy$ (or, more compactly, the 'z-ness' of z) because complex numbers have no natural ordering. Although they can be represented by orthogonal co-ordinates on a plane, one dimension of which is real, and the other imaginary (although plotted on a real number axis), this co-ordinate representation of a point that can vary in position on an imaginary plane does not help discernment either. One could conceivably contrive a feature of variation, for example along the lines that a complex number is a real number (so far so good, at least we are dealing with a number) to which is added a real (and literally) number of i's, but this is redundant reasoning. Thus, for the novice, the *definition* of a complex number represents an abstract and apparent 'absurdity' in terms of one critical feature and it is difficult to see how, as a pedagogic strategy, one can create variation in this feature to aid its discernment.

On a more technical note it is worth commenting that the history of complex number shows two phases which may mirror a division in the manner in which complex numbers present themselves as a threshold today. The concept of a complex number gradually emerged over three centuries, with considerable dispute, but once Hamilton (1837) expressed it essentially in the above form with prescribed rules of manipulation, the whole panoply of complex analysis, and the application of the complex number to the solution of mathematical and engineering problems, developed within a few decades. Novice students of mathematics may still face the strangeness that bedevilled its development, but students of engineering are faced, essentially, with *complex analysis*. The distinction here is that between the discrete concept of complex number and its embodiment in complex analysis. This does not mean that the latter students do not face thresholds in which the complex number is a key element, as illustrated by the work of Carstensen and Bernhard on the Laplace transform in circuit theory (see Chapter 11 of this volume), and that of Flanagan, Taylor and Meyer (work in progress) on reactive power in transmission line theory. The point here is that the application of complex analysis to real world problems is amenable to variation. Such variation can aid in the discernment of a particular analytical approach and, in doing so, aid in the discernment of complex number as something as real (if not more so) as real numbers but this is a different argument to that presented in the preceding paragraph.

It should be noted further that the use of the term 'absurdity' in this context does not imply, in a dismissive or trivialising sense, that which is silly or ridiculous. Rather it is a multivalent term which denotes what is uncertain, irrational and lacking in causality. It has connotations perhaps more in keeping with the serious use of the term in literature or theatre, and as represented in the philosophy of the absurd proposed by Camus (1991) and earlier avant-garde manifestations such as Dadaist theory. Here, the philosophical, artistic or literary counterpart of *i* often involves the rendering fluid of seeming certainties such as time, place and identity. These increasingly are represented as ambiguous and unpredictable. The Theatre of the Absurd (Esslin, 2001), for example, tends to stress the impermanence of values, and invalidates previous dramatic conventions to emphasis the precariousness and arbitrariness of existence. 'Indeed, it was anti-theatre. It was surreal, illogical, conflictless and plotless. The dialogue seemed total gobbledygook. Not unexpectedly, the Theatre of the Absurd first met with incomprehension and rejection' (Culik, 2000, p. 1). The sense of estrangement and detachment engendered by such work remains similarly troubling when encountered by today's students and for this reason the pedagogical challenges of bringing such elusive and ill-defined objects of learning into focal awareness are deemed to be portable to other disciplinary contexts.

VARIATION ON VARIATION: THE THRESHOLD CONCEPTS FRAMEWORK

Following on from the discussion about complex number above, a more generative perspective on variation is opened up by asking the question 'How do students vary in the development of their understanding or not of a threshold concept?' (The presence of a threshold concept within a disciplinary context is taken as a given). Meyer and Land (2003 p. 412) introduced the notion of a *threshold concept*[4] in terms of a visual-spatial metaphor as being:

> akin to a portal, opening up a new and previously inaccessible way of thinking about something. It represents a transformed way of understanding, or interpreting, or viewing something without which the learner cannot progress. As a consequence of comprehending a threshold concept there may

thus be a transformed internal view of subject matter, subject landscape, or even world view. This transformation may be sudden or it may be protracted over a considerable period of time, with the transition to understanding proving troublesome. Such a transformed view or landscape may represent how people 'think' in a particular discipline, or how they perceive, apprehend, or experience particular phenomena within that discipline (or more generally).

Threshold concepts are likely to be *transformative* (occasioning a significant shift in the perception of a subject, or part thereof), *irreversible* (unlikely to be forgotten, or unlearned only through considerable effort), *integrative* (exposing the previously hidden interrelatedness of something) and *troublesome* (in a number of possible senses after, and building on, the work of Perkins (1999). Language will also play a significant role in understanding threshold concepts in that they are located within the specific discourses of disciplines (Meyer & Land, 2006).

This argument implies that describing conceptions as a relationship between an individual and a phenomenon is insufficient to capture the full extent of learning. To some extent a new way of understanding a phenomenon socially re-positions a learner. This social re-positioning is far more important when they acquire a transformative and integrating threshold concept than when they acquire, for example, the concept of 'deer'. Sharing a way of thinking with others allows access to communities, but it may also reduce acceptance or capacity to participate in another community. Insofar as learners perceive these social implications of learning they may be more or less willing to approach a threshold in their thinking.

It is in the nature of disciplinary thought, or the possibility of identifying a community of scholars, that the threshold concepts which are deployed by those scholars stand in distinct relationships to each other (Davies & Mangan, 2007). They may complement each other, forming a web of inter-related threshold concepts, operating together to provide an episteme ('way of knowing'), or 'underlying game' (Perkins, 2006). Alternatively, in distinct subsets, they may define contrasting schools of thought within a disciplinary community. In either case, developing an understanding of a previously unfamiliar threshold concept involves further transformation in understanding of threshold concepts with which the learner is already familiar. An individual may, for example, move from one school of thought to another within a discipline, re-working their previous understanding of the discipline.

The importance of social relationships (and thereby the learner's sense of identity) in the understanding threshold concepts opens up new sources of variation that do not come into view until the concept of learning is seen as a relationship between the individual, the phenomenon, *and others*. We consider these sources of variation further on, but first we pause to illustrate the nature of threshold concepts.

FOUR MODES OF VARIATION

In the light of this analytical framework we would argue that, in student learning terms, there is posited *variation*[5] in four progressive stages of the journey towards and through the portal, and possibly simultaneously at the level of the underlying episteme. More specifically, and again appealing to the visual-spatial metaphor, there is a distinction between:

1. Variation in the extent of the learner's awareness and understanding of an underlying game or episteme – a 'way of knowing' – which may be a crucial determinant of progression (epistemological or ontological) within a conceptual domain. Such tacit understanding might exist or develop *in the absence* of any formalised knowledge of the concept itself; it might, for the learner, represent a 'natural way of thinking'. Variation in such tacit understanding constitutes a mode of *subliminal* variation.

2. Variation in how the portal initially 'comes into view', that is, how it is initially perceived or apprehended, and with what mindset it may therefore be approached or withdrawn from. We refer to this mode of variation as *preliminal variation.*

3. Variation in how the portal, that is the liminal space itself, is entered, occupied, negotiated and made sense of, passed through or not. This mode we characterise as *liminal variation.*

4. Variation in the point and state of exit into a new conceptual space, and the epistemological and ontological terrain encountered from that point onwards. This mode constitutes *postliminal variation* indicating the trajectory of future learning.

We maintain that these modal distinctions offer an important set of dimensions *of variation* for teachers wishing to identify at which points, and in what ways, individual students might experience conceptual difficulty and experience barriers to their understanding. Used as a set of analytical lenses we argue further that these modes of variation can inform course design and redesign. These modes also represent a conceptual basis for developing *new methods of assessment.*

For example, in returning to the example of a complex number, the threshold concepts framework initially invites a consideration of how individuals vary in terms of the 'underlying game' of dealing with purely abstract and apparently absurd entities (*subliminal* variation). The argument here is that the underlying game, the tacit episteme, is the comfortable 'natural' capacity to *think* in purely abstract terms, to manipulate entities that have no frame of reference in the experience of the 'real' world. For complex number the tacit episteme may simply be a natural acceptance of the need to define a new set of 'numbers' to solve an equation like $x^2+1=0$.

How a complex number 'comes into view' is in turn, and in this case, a matter of non-negotiable definitional (and arguably troublesome) knowledge the acceptance (or not) of which is part of the *preliminal* variation. This preliminal aspect of variation will incorporate any perceived troublesomeness that such an initial view may present. Variation in the preliminal stage of the journey is essentially concerned with how the portal of the threshold concept 'comes into view', what it 'looks like', how it 'appears'. Inevitably presage and the existing discursive forces operating to construct one's existing subjectivity will to some extent determine what will be seen by the learner and what will not be seen; that is, what will be discursively occluded or precluded. There is likely to be variation in impressions of the form and structure of the portal rather than in terms of what these features represent in a transformational ontological sense (the *liminal* aspect).

On the other hand, externalising variation in the 'underlying game' aspect of the journey to the portal assumes a methodology for engaging students with a tacit grasp of something yet to be encountered. One way of exploring variation in such an engagement is via a *proxy* for the threshold concept (cf. Reimann & Jackson, 2006 for an example). An interesting technical question arises here in terms of whether one can actually achieve this through phenomenographic methodology when the 'phenomenon' has not yet been experienced.

We argue that, for some students, threshold concepts may 'come into view' as simply an unproblematic or natural way of formalising something that is already intuitively familiar, or that may have been experienced in a particular way. A student, for example, may be comfortable in terms of everyday experience with the basic ideas that choice involves sacrifice, and that the value placed on the sacrifice represents a way of comparing choices (in terms of what has been 'given up'). Such a student may embrace the definition of *opportunity cost*[6] (a threshold concept in economics) as simply a comfortable formalisation of something already experienced that now has a precise and unambiguous meaning. But to a student without a tacit understanding of choice and sacrifice the definition may be counterintuitive and alien, just as say, in literary or cultural study, where a student unused to decoding different levels of textual meaning may find the notion of *irony* troublesome. Indeed it may not come into view at all. In similar vein, a student comfortable with the idea of one thing getting forever closer to another thing but never actually reaching it, might embrace the definition of a *limit of a function*[7] in pure mathematics as a precise formalisation of something that immediately has obvious and unambiguous meaning. But to a student without a notion of 'the underlying game' the symbolic definition, and the word 'limit' itself, may represent impassable obstacles to understanding (see Meyer & Land, 2006, chapter 2, for a further elaboration of these points).

Variation in entering a new conceptual space is well illustrated in the following two extracts. The first is taken from Andrew Wiles' (1997) commentary on his long journey in seeking to prove Fermat's Last Theorem:

> Perhaps I can best describe my experience of doing Mathematics in terms of a journey through a dark unexplored mansion. You enter the first room of the mansion and it's completely dark. You stumble around bumping into the furniture, but gradually you learn where each piece of furniture is. Finally, after six months or so, you find the light switch, you turn it on, and suddenly it's all illuminated. You can see exactly where you were. Then you move into the next room and spend another six months in the dark. So each of these breakthroughs, while sometimes they're momentary, sometimes over a period of a day or two, they are the culmination of – and couldn't exist without – the many months of stumbling around in the dark that proceed them.

The second is from a commentary on the impact of the proof:

> There's an important psychological repercussion which is that people are now able to forge ahead on other problems that they were too timid to work on before. *The landscape is different*, in that you know that all elliptic equations are modular and therefore when you prove a theorem for elliptic equations you're also attacking modular forms and vice versa. *You have a different perspective* of what's going on and you feel less intimidated by the idea of working with modular forms because basically you're now working with elliptic equations. (Emphasis added). (Ribet, quoted in Singh (1998, p. 304).

THE ENGAGEMENT OF THRESHOLD CONCEPTS WITH VARIATION THEORY

The pedagogy of variation theory emphasises that the role of the teacher is to *create* the variation[8] in critical features of the 'object of learning' that students are exposed to. The dimensionality of this variation, as related to features of the phenomenon, needs to be developed as a conscious act of teaching and orchestrated in a manner that allows the students to *simultaneously* experience such features as they are able to. The teacher makes conscious decisions about what to vary and what not to vary, but whether there is an implicit underlying logic present in this process remains unclear. To proceed in good faith, we would again emphasise the distinction between the modes of variation mentioned above and, in particular, variation in the preliminal, and liminal, stages in respectively approaching and understanding a threshold concept. The term 'approach' is being used in a navigational sense; something is 'in sight' – how do you get there, by what route and strategy, and so on. There are also notions of 'stuck places', mimicry, and obstacles, that need to be negotiated within the liminal state (see Meyer & Land, 2006).

There is clearly an opportunity for *exposure* to variation in the preliminal stage that can be orchestrated by the teacher. The point here, from the threshold concept framework, is that the repertoire of that exposure must be fundamentally shaped by *knowledge on the part of the teacher* of the preliminal variation, its possible dimensionality, and likely implications. Pace (2004, p. 15) for example discusses the existence of what he calls a 'bottleneck' for students of history in terms of the 'ability to distinguish between essential and nonessential features of a historical narrative...' Students get stuck in acquiring this crucial aspect of being able *to think like an historian*. The problem is that text *per se* does not usually convey the required distinction between what is important, or not, within it. Historians are able to organise a text by interrogating it in terms of bringing questions to it that require an answer, by filtering out its central thesis and subsidiary arguments, in distinguishing between these arguments and their supporting evidence, and so on. In order to help students through this bottleneck Pace advocates, as a pedagogic principle, the creation of variation into the appearance of critical features of the text by deliberately manipulating the font size to distinguish between the essential, the non essential, and the redundant.

So there is an obvious resonance here with the application of variation theory (even within its self-imposed limitations) progressing from a phenomenographic approach to identifying, and formalising, the structure of similarities and differences in students' experience of some phenomenon. But this approach presupposes that the phenomenon has, or is being, experienced. We would seek to know also how, and by what logic, does one either *respond* to variation or *create* variation where it does not exist.

According to variation theory, 'a way of seeing' can be defined in terms of critical features that must be discerned and focussed on simultaneously (Pang and Marton, 2005). If we insert the words 'things differently' after 'way of seeing' in the preceding sentence, then we have part of the essence of a threshold concept stated in the language of variation theory. But this is a narrow formalisation that restricts rather than expands the portal metaphor because within variation theory there appears to be no possible retreat from the assertive position that discernment requires the presence of variation. There is much evidence that individuals vary in the way that they experience various phenomena. Marton and Booth (1997) relate this variation (individual differences) in experience 'to differences in ability to discern critical aspects of the phenomenon in question'.

In contrast, the threshold concepts framework is more *eclectic*; it admits *empirical sources* of variation firstly in students' and teachers' experiences that emanate outside, as well as within, the phenomenographic approach (but without any conceptual debt in terms of imposed logical connectedness or hierarchical structure). Sources of variation resulting from the full spectrum of qualitative research approaches (for example, narrative, grounded theory) are thus admitted, as are sources suggested by statistical models such as 'dissonance' in student learning. To these sources are added variational aspects of well established frameworks of epistemological difficulties within the disciplines such as in mathematics (see Brousseau, 1983, 1997).

CONCLUSION

This chapter has contrasted two contemporary, and powerful conceptual frameworks that seek to improve the quality of student learning through particular processes of teaching. These frameworks, namely threshold concepts and variation theory, share a pedagogical principle that teaching is a reflexive process of exposing and addressing patterns of variation in student learning. Both of these frameworks share a central focus on variation in student learning. Within the threshold concepts framework this focus is on learning episodes anchored in the understanding of transformative concepts. A distinction is made between how such transformative concepts are initially apprehended (or discerned or 'come into view') and then engaged with and comprehended (or not), where such engagement leads the learner in terms of future trajectories of learning, and the degrees of engagement with influential underlying games or epistemes. Variation theory emphasises 'critical' variation in learning, underpinned by an axiom that without variation there can be no discernment of a particular phenomenon (the object of learning). Both frameworks introduce particular ways of thinking about 'variation' in how students learn, and both share the very practical challenge of using a knowledge of this variation to inform and reconceptualise teaching practice including assessment. Where variation theory concentrates upon issues of variability in terms of the teacher's presentation of the object of learning, threshold concepts theory offers four modes of variation – subliminal, preliminal, liminal, and postliminal – in terms of the way that teachers might need to factor pedagogical principles into the design and redesign of courses.

In order to answer questions of conceptual difficulty or 'stuckness' we require the existence of *variation* within an *a priori* expectation of possibly conceptual discreteness in terms of the four posited modes of variation as already argued. There is a further expectation that the variation, even within this conceptually discrete partitioning, will exhibit a further underlying *dimensionality*. Such dimensionality results from the selection of certain analytical procedures above others that produce data structures within which individual differences *are preserved*. There is then the question of how the data and how its methodology of production can be operationalised or rendered *actionable* by teachers into purposeful design activity. Nonetheless we would argue that consideration of variation through these four modes of variation opens up an intriguing new research agenda for the development of tools of estimation and analysis that might do much to alleviate the conceptual difficulty experienced by individual students and overcome the recurrent barriers to understanding that have been identified within specific disciplinary settings.

ACKNOWLEDGEMENTS

The ideas in this chapter relating to variation theory and to complex number benefited from conversations with colleagues Jonte Bernhard of Linköping University and Anna-Karin Carstensen of Jönköping University. Thanks are also due to Mick Flanagan of University College London who helped to refine our thinking. The positions taken in this chapter are of course not necessarily those of these individuals.

NOTES

[1] Our use of the term 'feature' here follows Marton and Pong (2005) p.337. Marton and Pong use the term 'element' and sometimes the term 'feature' to refer to a characteristic of a phenomenon which may or may not be highlighted by a particular conception of that phenomenon. This idea is, to some extent prefigured by Stones (1992) who refers to characteristics that are highlighted in a conception as 'criterial attributes', although his theory of learning is different from that used by Marton and Pong.
[2] In the terminology preferred in this chapter it would be more appropriate to use the word 'feature' instead of 'aspect'. 'Aspect' is used elsewhere by phenomenographers (e.g. Marton and Booth 1997, p 88) to refer to aspects of experiencing something: the 'structural aspect' and the 'referential aspect'.
[3] An observation that may also be found in Stones (1992).
[4] This term is also used in artificial intelligence but there is no overlap in terms of definition or conceptual interpretation.
[5] Variation is defined here as the extent or degree to which individuals vary; that is, variation is essentially about individual differences. It is assumed that such variation is amenable to observation and estimation in a measurable sense of dispersion (quantitative or qualitative).

[6] *Opportunity cost* is typically defined as 'the next best but rejected alternative when making a choice'. The term itself has nothing to do with 'opportunity' other than in a possible contrived sense, and very little to do with 'cost' in an everyday consumer sense buying something.

[7] A function f(x) is said to tend to the limit L as x tends to a if, for any $\varepsilon > 0$, $\exists$ $\delta > 0$ such that $|f(x)-L| < \varepsilon$ whenever $0 < |x-a| < \delta$. Under these circumstances the formalisation of the limit is written as: $\lim_{x \to a} f(x) = L$. And the troublesome aspect is that f(a) need not be defined. In simple English, literally translated, a function of x is said to tend to the limit L if, for any small positive number called epsilon (ε), there exists another number called delta (δ), such that the modulus (absolute value) of the difference between f of x and L is less than epsilon whenever the modulus of the difference between x and a lies between zero and delta. The simple English version is not a particularly helpful way of seeing the concept of a limit of a function 'coming into view'. An even simpler English version that conveys no sense of the classical 'epsilon – delta' mathematical formalisation is that the function can be made as close to L as we like by making x sufficiently close to a. For those who have difficulty with the abstract 'epsilon – delta' formalisation, the limit of a function can also be illustrated geometrically but as a pedagogic device this approach suffers from a lack of generalisability.

[8] Variation is not defined here in terms of individual differences as in endnote 6 above, but in terms of (variation in) different views of the critical features of the object of learning.

REFERENCES

Behr, M., Post, T., Silver, E., & Mierkiewicz, D. (1980). Theoretical Foundations for Instructional Research on Rational Numbers. In R. Karplus (Ed.), *Proceedings of Fourth Annual Conference of International Group for Psychology of Mathematics Education*. Berkeley, CA: Lawrence Hall of Science.

Brousseau, G. (1983). Les obstacles epistemologiques et les problemes en mathematiques. *Recherches en didactique des mathematiques, 4*(2), 65-198.

Brousseau, G. (1997). *Theory of didactical situations in mathematics*. Dordrecht: Kluwer Academic Publishers.

Butterworth, B. (1999). *The mathematical brain*. Macmillan.

Camus, A. (1991). *The myth of Sisyphus and other essays*. London: Vintage.

Culik, J. (2000). *The theatre of the absurd: The west and the east*. Available at: http://www.arts.gla.ac.uk/Slavonic/Absurd.htm

Davies, P. & Mangan, J. (2007). Threshold concepts and the integration of understanding in economics. *Studies in Higher Education. 32*(6), in press.

Dienes, Z. P. (1959). The growth of mathematical concepts in children through experience. *Educational Research, 2*(1), 9-28.

Dienes, Z. P. (1960). *Building up mathematics*. London: Hutchinson Educational.

Esslin, M. (2001). *The theatre of the absurd*. London: Methuen Drama.

Fazey, J. A. & Marton, F. (2002). Understanding the space of experiential variation. *Active Learning in Higher Education 3*, 234-250.

Gurwitsch, A. (1964). *The field of consciousness*. Pittsburgh, PA: Duquesne University Press.

Hamilton, W.R (1837). Theory of conjugate functions, Or algebraic couples; With a preliminary and elementary Essay on algebra as the Science of pure time. In *Transactions of the Royal Irish Academy*, vol. 17, part 1, pp. 293-422.

Marton, F. & Booth, S. (1997). *Learning and awareness*. Mahwah, NJ: Lawrence Erlbaum.

Marton, F. & Pong, W-Y. (2005). On the unit of description in phenomenography. *Higher Education Research and Development, 24*(4), 335-348.

Marton, F. & Trigwell, K. (2000). Variatio Est Mater Studiorum. *Higher Education Research & Development,* 19(3), 381-395.

Meyer, J. H. F. & Land, R. (2003). Threshold concepts and troublesome knowledge: linkages to ways of thinking and practising within the disciplines. In C. Rust (Ed.), *Improving student learning. Improving student learning theory and practice − 10 years on*. Oxford: OCSLD.

Meyer, J. H. F. & Land R. (Eds.) (2006). *Overcoming barriers to student understanding: Threshold concepts and troublesome knowledge*. London and New York: Routledge.

Pace, D. (2004). Decoding the reading of history: An example of the process. In D. Pace & J. Middendorf (Eds.), *Decoding the disciplines: Helping students learn disciplinary ways of thinking*. New Directions for Teaching and Learning, no. 98. San Francisco: Jossey-Bass.

Pang, M. F. (2003). Two faces of variation: continuity in the phenomenographic tradition. *Scandinavian Journal of Educational Research, 47*(2), 145-156.

Pang, M. & Marton, F. (2005). Learning theory as teaching resource: Enhancing students' understanding of economic concepts. *Instructional Science, 33*, 159-191.

Perkins, D. (1999). The many faces of constructivism. *Educational Leadership, 57*(3), 6-11.

Perkins, D (2006). Constructivism and troublesome knowledge. In J. H. F. Meyer & R. Land (Eds.), *Overcoming barriers to student understanding: Threshold concepts and troublesome knowledge*. London and New York: Routledge.

Reimann, N. & Jackson, I. (2006). Threshold concepts in economics: A case study. In J. H. F. Meyer & R. Land (Eds.), *Overcoming barriers to student understanding: Threshold concepts and troublesome knowledge*. London and New York: Routledge.

Runesson, U. (1999). *Variationens pedagogik. Skilda sätt att behandla ett matematiskt innehåll*. [*The pedagogy of variation: Different ways of handling a mathematical topic*]. Göteborg: Acta Universitatis Gothoburgensis.

Runesson, U. (2006). What is it possible to learn? On variation as a necessary condition for learning. *Scandinavian Journal of Educational Research, 50*(4), 397-410.

Sanders, C. (Ed.) (2004). *The Cambridge companion to Saussure*. Cambridge: Cambridge University Press.

Singh, S. (1998). *Fermat's last theorem*. London: Fourth Estate Limited.

Stones, E. (1992). *Quality teaching: A sample of cases*. London: Routledge.

Taylor, C. (2006). Threshold concepts in biology: Do they fit the definition? In J. H. F. Meyer & R. Land (Eds.) *Overcoming barriers to student understanding: Threshold concepts and troublesome knowledge*. London and New York: Routledge.

Wiles, A. (1997). Extract from an interview downloaded from http://www.pbs.org/wgbh/nova/transcripts/2414proof.html on 20th July, 2006.

Zolan, M., Strome, S., & Innes, R. (2004). Decoding genetics and molecular biology: Sharing the movies in our heads. In D. Pace & J. Middendorf (Eds.), *Decoding the disciplines: Helping students learn disciplinary ways of thinking*. New Directions for Teaching and Learning, no. 98. San Francisco: Jossey-Bass

AFFILIATIONS

Jan H.F. Meyer
School of Education
University of Durham

Ray Land
Centre for Academic Practice and Learning Enhancement
University of Strathclyde, Glasgow

Peter Davies
Institute for Education Policy Research
Staffordshire University

MAGGI SAVIN-BADEN

6. LIQUID LEARNING AND TROUBLESOME SPACES: JOURNEYS FROM THE THRESHOLD?

INTRODUCTION

This chapter will argue that the notion of threshold concepts is an important component of the picture of student stuck-ness when learning in higher education. However, it will be suggested that threshold concepts may be one of several issues that are catalysts for disjunction and that as yet such catalysts have been explored little. For example, new learning experiences, threats to identity, discipline-based pedagogy, pedagogical signatures and troublesome language can all be catalysts to disjunction. Thus this chapter will suggest that threshold concepts should be located in a broader conceptualisation of students' disjunction. It will begin by suggesting that although the terms 'concepts' might be seen as both cognitively and ontologically positioned there still need to be a greater emphasis on the relationship between learner identities and threshold concepts than there is in some of the current research literature to date. For example, the difficulty with the notion of locating ideas of troublesomeness around 'knowledge' 'concepts' or 'theories of difficulty' seem to somewhat dislocate the concerns from the identities and biographies of learners and teachers. Further, Davies (2006) has argued that threshold concepts can be located, noticed and identified as generalizable concepts that can necessarily be embedded inn curriculum structure. Yet to argue for such a position immediately implies that threshold concepts are dislocated from learner identities. Therefore, this chapter will suggest that the notion of 'learning spaces' and 'liquid learning' and a model of transitional learning *might* be more useful, holistic and encompassing than 'threshold concepts', 'disjunction' or 'stuckness', since 'learning spaces' allows for the recognition of the cyclical nature of learning, learner stances, learner identities learning contexts and teacher approaches.

LEARNING SPACES

The concept of learning spaces captures the idea that there are diverse forms of spaces within the life and life world of academics and students where opportunities to reflect and review their own learning position occur. The notion of life-world is based on both Husserl (1937/70) and Habermas (1989) and represents the idea that as human beings we have a culturally transmitted stock of taken-for granted perspectives and interpretations that are organized in a communicative way. Thus,

R. Land, J.H.F. Meyer & J. Smith (Eds.), Threshold Concepts within the Disciplines, 75–88.

challenges to students' life-world(s) may be at odds with, or bear little relationship to, their current meaning systems.

In learning spaces, staff and students often recognise that their perceptions of learning, teaching, knowledge and learner identity are being challenged and realise that they have to make a decision about their response to such challenges. Often the decisions and responses made by the learner mean the learning space is a positive experience. Yet learning spaces are invariably undervalued by university leadership and industrious colleagues and not recognised as being important in our media populated culture. Learning spaces are often places of transition, and sometimes transformation, where the individual experiences some kind of shift or reorientation in their life world. Engagement in learning spaces does not necessarily result in the displacement of identity (in the sense of a shift causing such a sense of disjunction that it results in costs personally and pedagogically, and hence has a life cost), but rather a shift in identity or role perception, so that issues and concerns are seen and heard in new and different ways. Learning spaces thus might also be seen as liminal in nature in that they can be seen as betwixt and between states that generally occur because of the particular need for an individual to gain or create a learning space.

'Transitional learning spaces' can be liberating places, where knowledge is suddenly understood, easily applied and becomes wholly connected. However, such spaces are not always like this. In this paper a model of 'transitional learning spaces' will be presented that illustrates the relationship between catalysts to disjunction, encounters with liminal spaces and the possible options that learners take in dealing with disjunction. Further, staff and students may experience inherent difficulties about learning particular ideas or concepts in certain ways because there is little connection with their learner identity. Whilst some might argue that this lack of connection relates to 'learning styles,' instead it will be suggested that learning stances, which recognise the importance of identity in learning, might be a more useful description than learning style. Moreover, it will be suggested that locating learning bridges and positioning oneself in learning spaces may be the most effective means of overcoming stuck-ness and moving over a threshold. However, it will be acknowledged that being within a learning space does not necessarily guarantee movement over the threshold since movement may be cyclical, resulting in movement towards further disjunction or a return to being in some form of preliminal or liminal space.

LIQUID LEARNING

Troublesome spaces are places where 'stuckness' or 'disjunction' occurs. For both academics and students, becoming stuck in learning is often seen as deeply problematic rather than as being useful and transformative. Such transformative spaces are often 'liquid' in nature, so perhaps the learning in such spaces should be termed 'liquid learning'. Thus rather than the current system of a series of often distantly related modules in undergraduate programmes it might be more effective to centre the curriculum on uncertainty and liquidity rather than content. Therefore, liquid learning would focus on diverse forms of problem scenarios that could be taken in any order, or be sequenced, but the focus would be on the problem-orientatedness of knowledge rather than a notion of solid content. The current forms of ordering and containment inherent in current curricula seem to reflect a more modern than post-modern stance to learning, of perhaps 'solid modernity'. Bauman (2000) suggests that in the age of solid modernity there was a sense that accidents and sudden or surprising events were seen as temporary irritants, since it was still possible to achieve a fully rational perfect world. Thus, solid modernity was characterised by slow change, where structures were seen as being tough and unbreakable. Bauman has argued that we have moved into liquid modernity, the state of living in constant change characterised by ambivalence and uncertainty. To live in the liquid modern we need to act under the conditions of uncertainty, risk and shifting trust. Liquid learning on the other hand is characterised by emancipation, reflexivity and flexibility, so that knowledge and knowledge boundaries are contestable and always on the move. This kind of learning tends to occur in action learning sets, creative project groups, and some forms of problem-based and scenario-based learning. However, what is important about liquid learning is that it is constantly changing. There is a tendency, for example, to move to innovative forms of learning, which allow for emancipation and criticality to emerge, but over time, these often become increasingly solid spaces as the need to maintain and control overtakes the original desire for liquidity. Reverting to solid learning stances may result from organisational, institutional, peer or student pressure; yet, it might also be because liquid learning is inherently risky and taxing. Thus, catalysts to troublesome spaces *include:*

- Modes of knowledge
- Disciplinary difficulty (including signature pedagogies)
- New learning experiences
- Prior learning experiences that have previously been difficult
- Threats to identity
- Threshold concepts
- Scaffolding learning
- Troublesome power

However only one of these catalysts will be discussed here: Modes of knowledge.

MODES OF KNOWLEDGE

Knowledge has been defined in a whole host of ways. Gibbons *et al.* (1994) have argued for Mode 1 and Mode 2 knowledge. Mode 1 knowledge is propositional knowledge that is produced within academe separate from its use and the academy is considered the traditional environment for the generation of Mode 1 knowledge. Mode 2 knowledge is knowledge that transcends disciplines and is produced in, and validated through, the world of work. Knowing in this mode demands the integration of skills and abilities in order to act in a particular context. Whilst this division has been popular and useful to many, it does to some extent reflect some of the problems Ryle's (1949) notion of *knowing that* and *knowing how*, which operates on the basis of Cartesian dualism. Although Mode1 and Mode 2 knowledge are more complex and their position is better argued than that of Ryle, the problem with both of these stances is in the boundary spaces between the two forms of knowledge. Barnett (2004), however, argues for Mode 3 knowledge, whereby one recognises that knowing is the position of realising and producing epistemological gaps. Such knowing produces uncertainty because 'No matter how creative and imaginative our knowledge designs it always eludes our epistemological attempts to capture it' (Barnett, 2004, p. 252).

What is missing from the arguments and formations of knowledge and knowing is not only the way in which the spaces between these forms of knowledge are managed, but also what it is that enables students and staff to make the connections between all of them. It might be suggested that the missing links here are disregarded forms of knowledge. For example, Cockburn (1998) suggests that knowing when to keep your mouth shut and the virtues of tact are forms of knowing that are required in many professions but are not forms of knowing that are made explicit in the academy. Disregarded forms of knowledge then might be termed Mode 4 knowledge since it transcends and overlays Mode 1, 2 and Mode 3 knowledge, forming a bridge across the space between them. However, Mode 4 knowledge is also a mode in its own right, since it involves not only realising and producing epistemological gaps but also realising the ways in which these gaps, like knowledge and knowing, also have hierarchical uncertainty. Gaps, like knowledge, have hierarchical positions and this makes both the gaps and the knowledge, and the knowing and the knower eminently uncertain and liquid. The modes are set out in Table 1 below.

Table 1. Modes of knowledge

Mode 1	Propositional knowledge that is produced within academe separate from its use and the academy is considered the traditional environment for the generation of this form of knowledge.
Mode 2	Knowledge that transcends disciplines and is produced in, and validated through, the world of work.
Mode 3	Knowing in and with uncertainty, a sense of recognising epistemological gaps that increase uncertainty
Mode 4	Disregarded knowledge, spaces in which uncertainly and gaps are recognised along with the realisation of the relative importance of gaps between different knowledge and different knowledge hierarchies
Mode 5	Holding diverse knowledges with uncertainties

The concept of disregarded knowledge encompasses knowledge often equated with emotional intelligence, such as when and how to use self-promotion, when to keep silent and when to intervene, but also Haraway's (1991) concept of responsible knowledge – the need to take responsibility for the position from which we speak. Disregarded knowledge is neglected because it lacks status in academic life and is just that – disregarded. Furthermore, Taylor et al (2001: 59) suggest that what is required is an expanded notion of knowledge and reason, so that the current narrow definitions of both of these concepts no longer dominate. For example, Midgley (1994) has remarked that epistemology has neglected a whole area of knowledge, that of knowing people.

> ... pressure to prepare students for employment often conflict with the desire to develop their critical faculties and to encourage them not only to participate in the production of knowledge, but to believe, too, that if they want to, they can change things. (Taylor *et al.*, 2002, p. 66)

Further, Haggis (2004) argues for a new conceptualisation of knowledge which she terms as learning that is social and relational, yet I would suggest that what she portrays using the voices of her participants is in fact disregarded knowledge because it is about the idea of being able to function 'skilfully in a practical world'.

> People talk about giving, sharing, learning from each other, learning how to be sensitive to their children, and learning how to make things go smoothly in social situations. There is also a kind of learning that seems to be about *functioning skilfully in a practical world* ... Others talk about problem-solving and common sense, verbal and relational skill (as opposed to a fear of writing), and make jokes about academics who can't do basic practical tasks ... people talk of finding out, reaching up, learning how to rise above tragedy, developing lateral thinking, taking away prejudice, getting answers, understanding, expanding the mind, and experiencing joy. (Haggis, 2004, p. 347)

However, Mode 5 knowledge might be a position whereby one holds a number of modes together in a complex and dynamic way. The position here is essentially one of treasuring stuckness and sitting with chaos. It is a post tacit and pre realisation phase and thus it has a liminal quality about it. It is a position of realisation that emerges in a place of stuckness and is a mode of knowledge whereby one realises that living with and in uncertainty is not a place to be reached or gained, but instead a place of transformation, a position of complex and dynamic chaos where one learns to value stuckness in ways not previously understood. Further, Perkins' work is also useful here in understanding the impact of diverse forms of knowledge, and how this is often covert and therefore misunderstood by students and often disregarded by staff (Perkins, 1999).

A MODEL OF TRANSITIONAL LEARNING SPACES

This model has grown out of my own concerns about the relationship between disjunction and threshold concepts and in particular the (over) generalizability of such concepts. I would argue that all learning is necessarily biographical and contextually related. Thus, this model can only relate to and be shaped by individuals in relation to their own stances as learners.

The model is to be seen as a liquid learning space in which a series of 'learnings' occur. The starting point is a catalyst to change which results in disjunction and movement into a liminal space, one such catalyst might be threshold concept. However, once through a liminal space the journey continues, over a learning bridge into engagement and on to a position of transition or transformation, to a place of proactive learning.

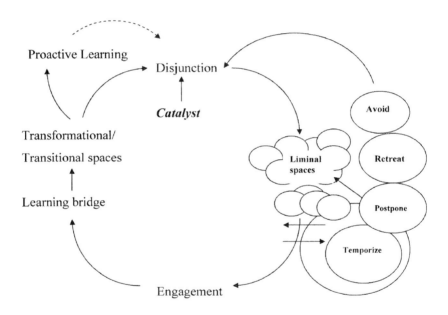

Figure 1. A model of transitional learning spaces

A Troublesome Journey ...

This model of transitional learning spaces begins with the suggestion that there are catalysts which result in students (and staff) encountering disjunction and that this is the beginning of a journey towards transition, transformation and proactive learning.

Disjunctive Spaces

Many staff and students have described disjunction as being a little bit like hitting a brick wall in learning and they have used various strategies to try to deal with it. It has similarities with troublesome knowledge in that it often feels alien and counter intuitive. However, *it does not always* feel like hitting a brick wall. There is often a sense of vague stuckness, a feeling of confusion or an idea that one has come across some difficulty or troublesomeness but what that is, is not entirely clear. It is similar to troublesome knowledge because until disjunction is experienced in a learning environment it is difficult to explain, particularly in terms of students feeling fragmented. After someone has first encountered disjunction they enter a liminal space. However, it might be that there are different types of disjunction or levels of disjunction, and that these might result in movement into different kinds of liminal spaces.

Disjunction is not only a form of troublesome knowledge but also a 'space' or 'position' reached through the realisation that the knowledge is troublesome. Disjunction might therefore be seen as a 'troublesome learning space' that emerges when forms of active learning (such as problem-based learning) are used that prompt students to engage with procedural and personal knowledge. Alternatively, disjunction can be seen as the kind of place that students might reach after they have encountered a threshold concept that they have not managed to breach.

Students deal with disjunction in a number of different ways that means that the conflict, ambiguity and incoherence experienced by individual students cannot be defined by distinctive characteristics, but there are some general trends. What seems to be apparent is that disjunction is dealt with by students, in one of five ways, through forms of decision making that are conscious and/or unconscious. Thus, students may opt to *retreat* from disjunction, to *postpone* dealing with it, to *temporize* and thus choose not to make a decision about how to manage it, to find some means to *avoid* it and thus create greater disjunction in the long term, or to *engage* with it and move to a greater or lesser sense of integration. Retreat and avoidance can be on the edge of liminality, or within liminality where a position of turning back may occur. Temporization and postponement tends to be in the liminal space and the students may stay there for some time before engaging.

Liminal Spaces

Disjunction leaves the learner in a liminal state, characterised by a stripping away of old identities, an oscillation between states and personal transformation. Liminal spaces are thus suspended states and serve as a transformative function, as someone moves from one state or position to another. Engaging with liminal spaces may involve choice but in the case of troublesome spaces they are often more likely to be 'stuck places' (Ellsworth, 1997). Yet this conception of stuck places would seem to imply that stuckness is a place one travels to – whereas disjunction is often a position one seems to find oneself in, often somewhat unexpectedly. There is little (if any) preparation and it may be because of this that disjunction is the place where people are before they reach a liminal space, prompted by a threshold concept or a new learning experience. Thus having overcome the shock of the disjunction they find they begin to re-examine their position, and in so doing see the terrain that they then choose to move through towards a liminal space.

Meyer and Land (2006) argue for preliminal variation but it would seem that what occurs for students is not just 'variation' but different ways of managing the disjunction being experienced. For example, Meyer and Land (2006) believe preliminal variation is a means of distinguishing between 'variation in students'' 'tacit' understanding (or lack thereof) of a threshold concept'. This, they argue, means that it may be possible to understand why some students approach and manage threshold concepts while others cannot. Yet it might not just be about students' ability to manage the threshold concept but also their reaction to it. However, I suggest that liminal spaces may be temporary *and* permanent, but there are still questions to be asked about what occurs in liminal spaces and the kinds of identities that emerge in such spaces. In his biography Mandela speaks of his Xhosa rite of passage where after the circumcision ceremony in which he was declared a man, he returned to the hut:

> We were now *abakwetha*, initiates into the world of manhood. We were looked after by an *amakhankatha*, or guardian, who explained the rules we had to follow if we were to enter manhood properly. (Mandela, 1994, p. 33)

Mandela then describes a series of rituals and ceremonies which were the rules he had to follow. Clearly the position in which Mandela found himself after circumcision was a liminal space. Although he had been declared a man, there was this space in which he was located for a time before he could then enter manhood properly. However, it would seem that the route out of a liminal space tends to be a learning bridge.

A REFLECTIVE PAUSE: MOVING OUT OF LIMINALITY

There is a point in the model where movement occurs away from the liminal space into engagement, but little so far has been discussed about the ways of doing so. This section discusses such involvement and also introduces questions about the extent to which liminality is sanctioned as a form of social control, before moving on to discuss learning bridges and the remainder of the model.

Stuck places are not only transient places but also places where it is possible to see that what one believed to be truths and ways of being are now contingent and provisional. Thus, living with/in liminal identities means expecting resilience and constant renewal is to be a life companion. Therefore, possible ways out of liminal states include:

– Embracing dilemmas

There is a tendency in higher education, globally, to either ignore dilemmas, to attempt to resolve them quickly or to rationalise the situation, often blaming someone else for the difficulty. Yet to sit with the dilemmas often results in greater self-understanding and a means of moving forward which may not have initially presented itself. O'Reilly (1989) has argued that there are risks involved in moving from experience that is incoherent to making public statements about one's self. For example, experience is often incoherent and in speaking of experience to others (publicly) is to risk sounding as if our experience is meaningless, contradictory and multiple (which it probably is).

– Learning to live with tensions and moving between tensions iteratively

To embrace dilemmas means also to live not only with tensions, but also sometimes in a constant state of tension. To move between possibilities offers the opportunity to be open to new ways of thinking, of engaging with different and diverse forms of information and of considering different personal and pedagogical stances.

– Living with open boundaries

To live with open boundaries is to assume, always, that life and learning is unfinished, unresolved, irresolvable and unknowable. Open boundaries are therefore necessary problematic but engaging with them means that continuous identity modification becomes a state of being.

– Valuing doubt

Whilst doubt is something that is usually seen as negative, here it is suggested that doubt is a means of moving away from a liminal space. Instead of trying to eliminate doubt in learning and in knowledge creation it is better to realise it and value it so that both staff and students see both doubt and uncertainly as central principles of learning.

– Acknowledging the importance of third spaces

The notion of the 'third space' (Gutiérrez, *et al.,* 1999, pp. 286-287) captures the idea that there are 'particular discursive spaces … in which alternative and competing discourses and positioning transform conflict and difference into rich zones of collaboration and learning'. These spaces tend to be polycontextual, multivoiced and multiscripted. Although the research by Gutiérrez *et al* related to children learning across languages and cultures, the notion of third spaces is helpful in locating and understanding the languages, discourses and cultures implicit within disciplinary pedagogies. By enabling students and new staff to comprehend and negotiate a third space can help them to move away from a liminal space. Such negotiation will involve engaging with official and unofficial spaces allowing parallels to be drawn between hybrid genres, knowledges, humour and official and unofficial worlds.

However, perhaps the main catalyst for moving out of a liminal space in learning is a greater self understanding, a sense of understanding ones story better and 'in relation' to other stories, theories or texts. Yet such movement is not unproblematic, particularly if it is seen to be transgressive.

SOCIALLY SANCTIONED LIMINALITY AND TRANSGRESSIVE FORMS OF LIMINALITY

It would appear that some forms of formulations of liminality are more acceptable than others. For example, the rituals and associated liminality Turner describes seem to be those that are socially sanctioned and to seek to maintain the status quo:

Both these types of ritual [i.e. status elevation and reversal] reinforce structure. In the first, the system of social position is not challenged. The gaps between the positions, the interstices, are necessary to the structure. If there were no intervals, there would be no structure, and it is precisely the gaps that are reaffirmed in this kind of liminality. The structure of the whole equation depends on its negative as well as its positive signs (Turner, 1969, p. 201).

Whether it is entry into a profession through graduation, becoming a married person through a ceremony or changing social status, these are in general socially sanctioned. Thus, an issue that appears to be discussed little in relation to the recent interest in liminality (for example Meyer & Land, 2006, Sibbett, 2006) is the relationship between liminality and ritual in academic contexts. It would seem that although there is some acknowledgment that engaging with threshold concepts relates to the rites of passage of becoming a professional, the rituals associated with these rites of page are somewhat obfuscated. Much of the work on liminality to date has been based on rituals and rites of passage, whether becoming a man, a priest, or a cancer patient.

However, unacceptable forms of liminality also exist and invariably seem to emerge in symbolic expressions that are seen to be disruptive or transgressive. Such forms tend to be oppositional in nature, characterised, for example by not being involved in traditional and often patriarchal ceremonies, as Tambiah argues:

Ritual is a culturally-constructed system of symbolic communication. It is constituted of patterned and ordered sequences of words and acts, often expressed in multiple media, whose content and arrangement are characterised in varying degrees by formality (conventionality), stereotyping (rigidity), condensation (fusion), and redundancy (repetition) (Tambiah, 1985, p. 128).

Thus movements away from liminal spaces tend to be celebrated differently and are often seen as being eccentric, for example choosing not to graduate following a PhD but instead to make a quilt with friends, or carrying out a peace ceremony at home to celebrate the resolution of a difficult and troublesome conflict. Such rituals or symbolic expression are therefore often hidden or have been moved into hidden spaces. As a result, these rituals are often marginal and seen as subversive since they ate seen to stand against rites of passage, rituals and liminality as a form of social control. Thus, it might be that liminality could be seen as ultimately hegemonic because it is used to maintain rituals and the status quo – or might it be that it is the ritualising practices that bring about liminality which in themselves are necessarily hegemonic.

The place and spaces of ritual and ritualisation are often conflictual spaces, but it is not entirely clear what the place of conflict is in ritual and liminal spaces – Turner, for example seems to suggest that rituals are a means of 'containing' conflict. It might be that threshold concepts themselves are becoming hegemonic in higher education. For example, if a student does not engage with the threshold concepts embedded within the curriculum along with the (new) rituals associated with them students may risk transgressing the rituals and social practices of the discipline. Thus, 'embedding' threshold concepts in curricula in an epistemic may be problematic. This is because to embed concepts might not only result in disregarding the importance of learner identities but also may be seen as creating or affirming a dominant narrative and as a means of ritualising disciplinary practice. Thus it might not be possible to 'become' an engineer, lawyer or economist unless the student has passed over a number of given knowledge thresholds.

RETURNING TO THE MODEL

Learning Bridges

Learning bridges vary in their structure and appearance, as well as their perceived relevance to students. Broadly speaking, learning bridges are mechanisms that help to link or connect different past and present positions in ways that enable shifts to be made – whether transitional or transformative. Thus, learning bridges include:

- Developing a new epistemological position
- The realisation of Mode 3, 4 or 5 Knowledge
- The honing of critique
- Reviewing prior experiences of learning
- Legitimating experience

However, learning bridges are discussed in detail elsewhere (Savin-Baden, 2007). Instead, it is important to consider the position in which one is located after a learning bridge, that of transitional and transformational learning spaces.

Transitional and Transformational Learning Spaces

Transitional spaces are shifts in learner experience caused by a challenge to the person's life-world that occur in particular areas of students' lives, at different times and in distinct ways. The notion of transitions carries with it the idea of movement from one place to another and with it the necessity of taking up a new position in a different place. Leaving the position and entering the transitions may also be fraught with difficulties that may result in further disjunction for the student. Thus, transitions can often be difficult and disturbing and yet simultaneously be areas where personal change takes place. Transformational spaces are spaces where a sense of coming into oneself occurs – there is a sense of identity construction, of self-realisation and of seeing the world anew. The difference between transitional and transformational spaces is that in a transitional space there is a sense of shifting from one place to another, whereas in a transformational space there is a sense of life-shifts, of knowing the world differently in contexts in which they live, work and learn.

Proactive Learning, The Beginning and the End of the Spiral

The notion of proactive learning is one that requires a new stance, a different vision, an active leap away from previous perspectives. This conception of knowing is the higher order form of knowing suggested by Perkins (2006a), who has argued for three conceptions of knowing:

1. Retention and application: characterised by ritual type activity such as driving to work;

2. Understanding: the ability to perform what you know and thus to be able to think with what you know about, for example being able to explain causality in history;

3. Active and adventurous; a proactive conception of knowledge which requires creativity and the ability to see things differently. This is an approach that requires a leap away from bounded understanding.

Whilst much of the learning that occurs in this model is transitional, the possibilities for transformational learning occur when a leap is made beyond understanding knowledge to engaging with it actively. To engage students in proactive learning I would suggest requires engagement with liquid learning and problem situations, which prompt students to consider their stances, identities, and moral positions. Yet in liquid learning threshold concepts cannot be delineated. Instead, threshold concepts are not 'concepts' per se, they are troublesome spaces that emerge in the life world of the learner that are connected to their biographies and identities as a learners.

CONCLUSION

This chapter has argued that there is more work to be done around the notion of threshold concepts in the disciplines and perhaps this model of transitional learning begins some of that work Thus this is my attempt to 'engage' with the disjunction prompted by the notion of threshold concepts (which in itself is a threshold concept). Yet I find too that I remain in a liquid learning state, just as perhaps one of Faulks' characters, Sonia, was at the end of his novel:

There were questions to which her husband and brother had bent their minds – had sent themselves as good as mad trying to answer; but it seemed to Sonia at that moment, drenched and tired as she was, that, perhaps for quite simple reasons connected to the limits of their ability to reason, human beings could live out their whole life long without ever knowing what sort of creatures they really were. Perhaps it did not matter; perhaps what was important was to find serenity in not knowing. (Faulks, 2005, p. 609)

REFERENCES

Barnett, R. (2004). Learning for an unknown future. *Higher Education Research and Development, 23*(3), 247-260.

Bauman, Z. (2000). *Liquid modernity*. Cambridge: Polity Press.

Cockburn, C. (1998). *The space between us. Negotiating gender and national identities in conflict*. London: Zed Books.

Cousin, G (2006). Threshold concepts, troublesome knowledge and emotional capital: An exploration into learning about others. In J. H. F. Meyer & R. Land (Eds.), *Overcoming barriers to student understanding: Threshold concepts and troublesome knowledge*. Abingdon: RoutledgeFalmer.

Davies, P. (2006). Threshold concepts. How can we recognize them? In J. H. F. Meyer & R. Land (Eds.), *Overcoming barriers to student understanding: Threshold concepts and troublesome knowledge*. Abingdon: RoutledgeFalmer

Ellsworth, E. (1997). Teaching positions: Difference, pedagogy and the power of address. New York: Teachers College Press

Faulks, S. (2005). *Human traces*. London: Vintage.

Gibbons, M., Limoges, C., Nowotny, H., Schwarzman, S., Scott, P., & Trow, M. (1994). *The new production of knowledge: The dynamics of science and research in contemporary societies*. London: Sage.

Gutiérrez, K., Baquedano-Lopez, P., & Tejeda, C. (1999). Rethinking diversity: Hybridity and hybrid language practices in the third space. *Mind, Culture, & Activity: An International Journal, 6*(4), 286-303.

Habermas, J. (1989). *The Theory of Communicative Action, Vol. 2*. Cambridge: Polity.

Haggis, T. (2004). Meaning, identity and 'motivation': Expanding what matters in understanding learning in higher education? *Studies in Higher Education, 29*(3), 335-352.

Haraway, D. (1991). *Simians, cyborgs, and women: The reinvention of nature*. London: Routledge

Husserl, E. (1937/70). *The crisis of the European sciences and transcendental phenomenology*. Trans. D. Carr. Evanston, IL: Northwestern University Press.

Mandela, N. (1994). *The long walk to freedom*. London: Abacus

Meyer, J. H. F. & Land, R. (2006). Threshold concepts and troublesome knowledge: issues of liminality. In J. H. F. Meyer & R. Land (Eds.), *Overcoming barriers to student understanding: Threshold concepts and troublesome knowledge*. Abingdon: RoutledgeFalmer.

Midgley, M. (1997). Visions of embattled science. In R. Barnett & A. Griffin (Eds.), *The end of knowledge in higher education*. London: Cassell

Perkins, D. (1999). The many faces of constructivism, *Educational Leadership, 57* (3) 6-11.

Perkins, D. (2006a). Beyond understanding. Keynote paper presented to Threshold Concepts in the Disciplines Symposium, University of Strathclyde, 30th August.

Perkins, D. (2006b). Constructivism and troublesome knowledge. In J. H. F. Meyer & R. Land (Eds.), *Overcoming barriers to student understanding: Threshold concepts and troublesome knowledge.* Abingdon: RoutledgeFalmer.

O'Reilly, D. (1989). On being an educational fantasy engineer: Incoherence, the individual and independent study. In S.Weil & I. McGill (Eds.), *Making sense of experimental learning: Diversity in theory and practice.* Buckingham: Open University Press/SRHE .

Ryle, G. (1947). *The concept of mind.* Harmondsworth: Penguin (reprinted 1968).

Savin-Baden, M. (2007). *Learning spaces: Creating opportunities for knowledge creation in academic life.* Maidenhead: McGraw Hill.

Sibbett, C. (2006). Nettlesome knowledge, liminality and the taboo in cancer and art therapy experiences. Paper presented to Threshold Concepts in the Disciplines Symposium, University of Strathclyde, 30th August -1st September.

Tambiah, S. J. (1985). *Culture, thought and social action: An anthropological perspective.* Cambridge, MA: Harvard University Press.

Taylor, R., Barr, J., & Steele, T. (2000). *For a radical higher education. After postmodernism.* Buckingham: SRHE and Open University Press.

Turner, V. (1969). *The ritual process: Structure and anti-structure.* London: Routledge.

AFFILIATION

Maggi Savin-Baden
Coventry University, UK

PART II: DISCIPLINARY CONTEXTS

MICHAEL THOMAS FLANAGAN & JAN SMITH

7. FROM PLAYING TO UNDERSTANDING

The Transformative Potential of Discourse Versus Syntax in Learning to Program

INTRODUCTION: THE GAMES STUDENTS NEED TO PLAY

First year electronic engineering students are no exception to their contemporaries in their addiction to computer games. However, their mastery of these lucrative products of object-oriented programming (OOP) does not readily translate into an understanding of OOP when presented as a formal first year course. One of the fascinations of teaching programming is that, whilst many students learn to program without apparent difficulty, a significant proportion finds the activity extremely troublesome. This observation may be compounded for students of electronic engineering, where threshold concepts (Meyer and Land, 2003, 2005) may be 'nested' in the curriculum. Such potential thresholds may lie in the concepts of OOP, in the exemplifiers dictated by electronic engineering syllabi or in the linguistics of a computer language itself. Implications for teaching and curriculum redesign vary significantly across this spectrum. In this context, students' problems appear to arise from two sources: firstly, the form of the programming language which, to paraphrase Andersen (1990), parasitises English but cannot be read as English, an overwhelming threshold conception, or secondly, more localised threshold concepts inherent in OOP itself, such as abstract classes and interfaces. Consequently we have adopted a three-fold schema to discuss these potentially troublesome concepts (Figure 1).

The focus in this chapter is on our third stream: students who find that the language itself is a threshold, and cannot make sense of the game's rule book. These are our operationally challenged students (Smith, 2006). This stream will be discussed in the context of a linguistic challenge. The more localised thresholds associated with the first two streams will be discussed elsewhere.

CONCEPTUAL AND OPERATIONAL CHALLENGES

An analysis of both common mistakes and of the examination questions successfully completed by conceptually and operationally challenged students suggests the problem is deeper than a simple failure to appreciate the role of the individual components of the algorithm, e.g. data structures, data manipulation instructions, conditional expressions, control structures, etc. The language itself appears troublesome, and what they face is a translation problem. The students are highly qualified and many in the conceptually and operationally challenged

R. Land, J.H.F. Meyer & J. Smith (Eds.), Threshold Concepts within the Disciplines, 91–103.

streams are among our most successful students in other courses. The motivation of the bulk of such students appears strong, as indicated by their high attendance rate and continuing determined efforts to complete each programming exercise over two years.

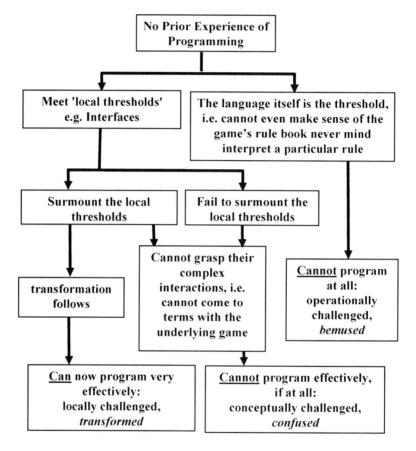

Figure 1: Threefold schema of computer language learning problems

In hypothesising that this situation is a language problem we have looked at our chosen language, Java. In common with most computer languages, it is based on a context-free grammar and, in its formal specification (Gosling et al., 2004), its authors describe its lexical and syntactical structures in such terms. This facilitates its specification, its implementation and, more generally, the discussion and resolution of such problems as undecidability. It has also been said that the common base of context-free grammars 'has also been critical in making it readily possible for people to learn such languages' (Wolfram, 2002). However, close observation of the common mistakes of the operationally challenged stream suggests that we may more fruitfully borrow from a different tradition in semiotics and linguistics in attempting to analyse the problem. In coding such components as conditional expressions, iterative loops and variable declarations, student errors bear a resemblance to linguistic problems in natural languages as discussed in terms of the semiotic concept of the markedness of oppositional pairs (true/false, public/private) and of synonym definition (if/whether) (Chandler, 2002; Tobin, 1990; Battistella, 1996).

THE THEORY OF MARKEDNESS

every single constituent of any linguistic system is built on an opposition of two logical contradictories: the presence of an attribute ("markedness") in contraposition to its absence ("unmarkedness") (Jakobson, cited in Chandler, 2002, p. 110)

Markedness is now regarded as linguistically central (Trask, 1999). Table 1 summarises the differences between the marked and unmarked forms in such natural language relationships. The marked signifier is generally the more complex and the one most likely to present problems in learning.

Table 1. The marking relationship (after Stross, 2005)

Unmarked	Marked
Greater frequency of use within language (dominant form)	Lesser frequency of use
May not be overtly marked	Will be overtly marked
The implied in an implicational relationship	The implier in an implicational relationship
Less complex morphologically	More complex
Appears in neutralized context	Does not appear in neutralized context
Early child acquisition	Late acquisition, more difficult
Usually first added and last lost in language change	Last added and first lost

The dominance of the unmarked over the marked is often expressed as the number of occurrences of the unmarked form as a percentage of all occurrences of both within a significant example of the language (Chandler, 2002, pp. 110-115). Our corpora for comparison are the world wide web and Flanagan's Java library (see Table 2).

The true/false pair is only weakly asymmetric in Java and the students neither perceive the concept of a Boolean pair as difficult nor do they actually find it so. However when we come to the keywords public and private, public is highly dominant and although operationally challenged students have few problems with public, they certainly find the marked sign, private, problematic. They do not, however, self-identify this as a problem. In Java, public signifies that the following variable has no restrictions on its access, i.e. no special methods have to be written to assign a value to it or to obtain its value - the neutral form. The keyword, private, signifies that the following variable does require such methods to be incorporated into the class in which the private variables are declared. The public/private problem becomes much more troublesome for operationally challenged students when extended to include the even more asymmetric public/protected pair. Protected is a keyword signifying that such special methods are needed as for the private keyword, unless the variable it referred to benefits from object-oriented concept of inheritance, i.e. an even more cognitively complex signifier.

Table 2. A comparison of dominance within markedness between English and Java. The percentage figure is the dominance of the unmarked form as a percentage of both forms

Sign pairs in English	Occurrence on www June 2006	Sign pairs in Java	Occurrence in Java library	Student perceived level of difficulty	Observed student level of difficulty
true / false	1.2 billion / 0.4 billion [75 %]	true / false	1082 / 918 [54 %]	low	low
public / private	5.2 billion / 1.9 billion [73 %]	public / private	2959 / 756 [80%]	moderate	high
public / protected	5.2 billion / 0.6 billion [90 %]	public / protected	2959 / 223 [93%]	moderate	very high
		absent implied signifier / static	~4000 / 1000 [~80 %]	low	very high
		float/ Float	283 / 24 [91 %]	moderate	very high
		double/ Double	4163 / 365 [92%]	moderate	high

Computer languages that do not have a need for a private signifier do not have a designated public one reinforcing the semiotic analogy that we are adopting as this resonates with Derrida's oppositional logic of binarism in which neither term makes sense without the other (Derrida, 1976).

Difficulties with these issues stand out in operationally challenged students' exercises and exams. Variables, on their first use, must not only be preceded by a keyword signifying its accessibility but must be preceded by a keyword indicating its type, i.e. integer, floating point number, alphabetic character. To locally challenged students, such declarations are logical if somewhat annoying, but to conceptually and operationally challenged students who we suspect are looking at Java as they would look at English, or mathematics at best, such declarations are problematic. They would not declare each word as noun, verb, adjective or whatever, on first using it in an essay and they would not declare numbers as integer or floating point in a mathematical calculation.

Thimbleby's (1999) Critique of Java suggests that:

> there are two quite different sorts of serious problems facing the Java programmer, **barriers**, which are explicit limitations to desired expressiveness, and **traps**, which are unknown and unexpected problems. Typically, a barrier reveals itself as a compile time error, or in the programmer being unable to find any way to conveniently express themselves. A trap, however, is much more dangerous: typically, a program fails for an unknown reason, and the reason is not visible in the program itself.

He exemplifies barriers with the rules dictating where statements importing packages (pre-existing collections of Java classes) must occur. Thimbleby discusses this in terms 'of the design choice having a negative effect on the explanation of Java (and, by implication, on the learnability of the language)'. In our experience this does translate, in operationally challenged students' programs, to the incorrect placing of this statement: they place it where first needed rather than at a prior position dictated by the Java rules. Thimbleby's barriers tend to match the mistakes made by our operationally challenged students, his traps tend to match locally challenged student errors.

The next simple oppositional pair in Table 2 'absent implied signifier'/static, is highly asymmetric, causes immense problems for operationally challenged students but again elicits few comments in questionnaires. The key word static precedes a method that is general, e.g. a mathematical function such as sine. Its opposite, the absent implied keyword, indicates an 'instance' method, that is a method that can only be associated with an instance of a specific software object, e.g. the method that opens a window (the instance of an object) in a computer's browser. In object oriented programming, it makes sense that the unmarked signifier is the one most naturally associated with an object, so natural as to not even warrant a keyword. However, the natural unmarked English opposite of static, at least for engineers, is not 'instance', 'per-object' or 'non-static', all terms used to denote the absent signifier in program documentation and textbooks, it is the word dynamic (70% dominant). This is reflected in the incorrect discussion answers of most operationally challenged and many conceptually challenged students where dynamic is commonly and explicitly offered as the opposite to static and implicitly, if somewhat incoherently, in their attempts at programming.

Keyword and variable names may start with or without an initial capitalised letter but the two forms are not interchangeable. The keyword float (91% dominant) signifies that the following variable is a simple floating point number which is referred to as a primitive data type. The word Float signifies the following variable is an instance of an object that contains a floating point number but possesses other properties as well. The float/Float pair exemplifies the alien difference between a natural language and a symbolic language and the interactive complexity of the latter. In English the failure to capitalise the initial letter of a proper noun may raise an eyebrow but have few other consequences. In Java, failure to recognise the difference between a float variable and a Float variable can be very serious. It could, for instance, lead to the drawing of fallacious conclusions in equality testing. If we test whether two identical primitive data types are equal the response will be yes (true). However if we test whether two Float objects with identical properties, i.e. containing the same floating point number, are equal, the answer is no (false). The equality check, in the case of objects, checks that their identities – in effect, their locations within the computer memory – are the same, but does not seek to identify their contents.

THE PROBLEM OF PROGRAM CONTROL AND SYNONYMOUS OPERATIONS

The conceptually and operationally challenged students also commonly find problems with two sets of pair statements that may appear as synonyms but cannot always be treated as such. These are the if and switch statements and the for and while statements. What, for the locally challenged students, represent problem-free and useful statements allowing control over the flow of their programs become, for conceptually and especially operationally challenged students, statements that, though not initially perceived as problematic, typically result in blocks of coding which start as one form, e.g. an if statement, but drift through nonsense code to end as the other half of the pair, e.g. a switch statement. The resonance here is with the work of Tobin (1990) in which he discusses the lexical and grammatical problem of the difference between if and whether in English. He believes that the highly asymmetric choice of the use of if or whether is not arbitrary but motivated by a subtle semantic distinction which revolves around the way in which they are perceived within continuous or discontinuous space. The marked member, whether, presents possibilities that occupy a continuous abstract internal space whereas the unmarked member, if, offers no such semantic integrality. The unmarked form offers possibilities perceived as general and the marked form offers the cognitively more difficult process of perceiving the possibilities as part of an integral set.

Table 3 compares these English and Java pairs showing similar dominance in analogous Java 'synonyms' and we note that alongside existing if/switch problems, our operationally challenged students show a similar habit in conflating the coding of the for and while statements.

The above markedness analysis strengthens the proposition that some students are reading code as they would natural language. In attempting to gain insight into this misreading it is worth pursuing the 'semiotic analogy' a little further. The markedness analysis suggests that students are interpreting computer syntax as a sequence of triadic Peircean signs whereas the earlier, and from the point of view of natural language, less adequate Saussurian dyadic signs would be more appropriate. Umberto Eco's conception of the closed and open text presents an interesting point at which a reader of an English text and a reader of programming code may be contrasted. Eco's "model readers" on reading an "open text" make up their own mind at many key points in the text, reassessing previous moves from this vantage point (Eco, 1979; Cobley & Jansz, 1997). His "average readers" on reading a "closed text" are offered occasions on which they can make up their own mind but the range of possible interpretations is limited and ruled by a quite rigid logic. Sadly, for those students who appear to be emulating Eco's "average reader" a computer program, to extend Eco, is a 'totally closed text' in which the many opportunities at each point in the narrative are not present, the rules are absolute and all-embracing. "

Table 3. A comparison of dominance within markedness between two English conditional conjunctions and two pairs of Java program flow control statements

Sign pair in English	Occurrence on www June 2006	Sign pair in Java	Occurrence in Java library	Student perceived level of difficulty	Observed student level of difficulty
if / whether	7.1 billion / 0.9 billion [89 %]	if else / switch	884 / 64 [93 %]	moderate	high
		for / while	1714 / 194 [90 %]	moderate	high

The frustration that arises when students unwittingly read program code as natural language commonly leads to requests along the lines of: 'can we have some notes, like some other courses, which we can learn the subject by rote'. In other words, the students want us to facilitate their mimicry. On being refused, the request changes to one for some kind of template that would convert rote learning 'mimicry' into 'programming'. It is a measure of their real frustration and brings to mind Andersen's (1990) comment on comparing computer and natural languages whilst discussing the human-computer interface:

Complete descriptions of natural semiotic systems rarely exist, and in any event their expressions cannot generate the object signs through a causal chain, although folklore has often dreamed of that kind of sign: they are called spells.

Some operationally challenged students, when really dispirited, would like a 'spell' but would settle for mimicry as second best.

In this chapter we have exemplified the usefulness of a markedness analysis in defining those aspects of programming, that when taken in their totality, present the operationally challenged student with an overwhelming threshold conception which may equate to what Perkins (2006, p. 42) terms 'an underlying episteme':

As used here, epistemes are manners of justifying, explaining, solving problems, conducting enquiries, and designing and validating various kinds of products or outcomes.

Frustrated and unable to access this fundamental episteme, the operationally challenged students then, in trying to solve their programming errors, compound their troubles by further mis-identifying their source.

METAPHORS AND MISTAKES

Dijkstra (1989) recognised the problem of the overall complexity of programming as a barrier to learning but sadly expressed it in terms of a rejection of metaphor and imagination that most now, we believe, would see as unhelpful (Travers, 1996). However, in this, he did raise the problem of the use of language with an instructive example:

> We could, for instance, begin with cleaning up our language by no longer calling a bug a bug but by calling it an error. It is much more honest because it squarely puts the blame where it belongs, viz. with the programmer who made the error.

Our students have major problems interpreting error messages but we do not believe that this is simply a problem of an inappropriate metaphor. It may be a small component of the problem – we all prefer to think that the other person/machine is at fault. However changing *bug* to *error* will not significantly alter the relationship between the student and the computer. Students do not need anthropomorphic prompts to believe errors lie with a faulty machine but their response to error messages does bring firmly into consideration the student-computer interface. The response to error messages, especially that of the conceptually and operationally challenged students, is initially not to blame the machine but often one of perplexity, even paralysis. They will stare uncomprehendingly at what to experienced programmers is a clear well documented error message or set of messages. This response is one of total failure of signification. A typical error message is shown in Figure 2 with added explanatory boxes (the student would see the message without the boxes).

Maybe the failure of signification is a combination of, to non-experts in Java, unfamiliar signs (exception instead of error, symbol to signify the name of a variable, method, or class, the use of the object oriented dot convention instead of a standard English phrase with spaces between words, thread - concept met but not developed in most introductory engineering courses), a juxtaposition of signs, some present coincidently (the computer name, both the operating window line number and the Java code line number) and, possibly, an overall visual appearance that suggests an abstract iconic sign when none exists.

Student response once the 'paralysis barrier' is surmounted is even more instructive. The multiplicity of errors that are often generated reinforces their transference of the origin of their errors to the machine - "I cannot possibly have made so many mistakes". This highlights a difference between a native language and a computer program and occasionally can lead to a transformation in the students' understanding of programming. Make a mistake in speaking such as using a wrong tense, the incorrect sentence will sound odd but the sense of the conversation will probably not suffer greatly. A corresponding error in Java, e.g. an incorrect variable declaration, may not only prevent compilation but generate a cascade of error messages as the subsequent code may no longer be interpretable by the compiler even though it contains no syntactic errors. Students are advised that they should always correct the error indicated in the first occurring message and then recompile the program - with luck the remaining error messages will evaporate. The operationally challenged students, by and large, do not do so - time and time again they obsessively work through the complete error message list. However, a few students have commented that the 'error message evaporation' sparked an appreciation of the interactive complexity of a program and that consequently such exercises of first constructing a flow chart directing them through this complexity were no longer seen as unnecessary.

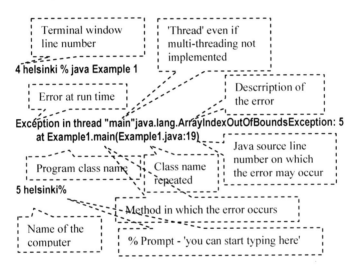

Figure 2. Typical Java error message

More recently Christian Holmboe (2002, 2005) has also concluded that teaching object-oriented design should be treated as a linguistic exercise. He starts with the early Wittgenstein and his language game. This is a fruitful area for those interested in object-oriented design as there are many analogies between the formal definitions of object-oriented design (OMG, 2001) and the postulates on objects within the Tractatus (Wittgenstein, 1921). Holmboe importantly contrasts the specification and learning of object orientation with the 'early Wittgenstein' and the 'late Wittgenstein' stressing Wittgenstein's realisation that language and meaning were constructed in social practices rather than from logical reasoning. His conclusion that 'the logically perfect language of class diagrams are not as close to natural thinking as may have been intended' is highly relevant to teaching languages such as Java. His statement that 'it can be shown that students of data modelling struggle with the pragmatics of their prior linguistic experience when trying to fit their experiential world into categories and classes' gels well with the conclusions we are drawing, at least for our operationally challenged students. However, we believe them not to be peculiar to object-oriented languages, but to be generally true of high level languages as revealed by a more basic semiotic analysis, although object-oriented design does greatly compound the problems.

THE SEMIOTICS OF PROGRAMMING AS A THRESHOLD

Transformative Aspects

In contrast to the locally challenged and conceptually challenged streams, whose localised thresholds arise out of the compounding of specific OOP troublesome concepts, e.g. interfaces, with identified troublesome concepts in the applied physics underpinning the computing exercises, e.g. complex numbers or electric fields, for the operationally challenged students the language itself is the overwhelming threshold. Those that do cross this threshold, though they may still have to meet the more localised thresholds, in coming to terms with the interactive complexity of programming languages undergo a transformation that facilitates an understanding not only of the local structures, such as the control statements discussed above, but can now grasp many of the structures that underpin computer languages at a deeper level, e.g. methods, object-oriented classes.

Integrative Aspects

The transformative aspect that leads on to an ability to grasp the underpinning structures such as methods and classes facilitates the integration of such concepts into more all embracing key procedures such as the instantiation (creation in software) of an object.

Discursive Aspects

Electronic engineering students at UCL are expected to attain a high level of programming knowledge and skills. However computer science is not their discipline and consequently they do not benefit, as do computer science students, from being in an environment that facilitates their embracing of the ethos of the curriculum, a possible factor in the differing ways computer science and non-computer science students negotiate the liminal space of this overwhelming threshold. Nonetheless, there are common features and we have, as have some computer science departments (Hanks, 2006), moved from requiring students to work singly to work as pairs or threesomes. We have additionally moved to a more project based approach. We have repeatedly seen students who having grasped a local threshold concept themselves enthusiastically and volubly attempt to lift their partners over the same threshold.

Bounded Aspects

The identification of the bounded nature of the more localised compounded thresholds does present some problems but this is not true of the overwhelming linguistic threshold. The notion of boundedness may best be illustrated by the use of specialist terminology that acquires a meaning in one subject that clashes with everyday usage. One such as example, commonly perplexing our students, relating to computing, is the term 'deprecate'. Whilst common usage imbues this word with negative connotations, in computing it simply means to let an aspect of programming gently wither away, e.g. the retention of an outdated method by its replacement for many revisions and updates of a programming language. The concept of deprecation, then, is bounded by its context of use. This example reinforces our semiotic approach and further examples could be drawn from several of the markedness examples discussed above.

Reconstitutive Aspects

The locally challenged students generally identify the localised compounded thresholds that they meet irrespective of whether they surmount such thresholds. The operationally challenged students do not even correctly identify their troublesome concepts as outlined in Tables 2 and 3 until they surmount the overwhelming threshold. Then, both they and their class facilitators can recognise the transformation demonstrating a shift in learner subjectivity. Our experience of observing such a transformation is that it is *irreversible* and the *troublesome*, *incoherent* and *alien* aspects (Perkins, 2006) have been discussed in the markedness examples presented above.

IMPLICATIONS FOR TEACHING PROGRAMMING IN ENGINEERING CONTEXTS

Our analysis of operationally challenged students suggests that we should introduce the language game formally to such students. Indeed Holmboe has begun to introduce the language game to his object-oriented design students including readings from Wittgenstein but he is addressing a more mature and main stream computing class. However we believe that a gentler introduction would work with engineering students and evidence of the validity of such an approach may be gained from a second year course which includes an introduction to fuzzy logic controllers. Fuzzy logic would, at first sight, appear a likely candidate as a threshold concept for engineering students. It aims to turn imprecise – fuzzy – statements into the formalism of set theory and program code. This is such a strange progression for engineering students that the formalism of the method is preceded by a discussion of language as we use in it everyday life and how we might reduce it to a set of rules that may then be implemented digitally. This precipitates a very interesting discussion and fuzzy logic not only causes very few problems in the course but is the most popular topic as judged by the statistics of the optional questions answered in the examinations.

The direction of much of the discussion that informs the teaching of programming in computer science – such as which language to teach first, whether a knowledge of computer architecture is an essential prerequisite, etc. – is relevant to our concerns, but we believe the linguistic and 'nested' nature of troublesome concepts for engineering students cuts across these dichotomies. Consequently, further research into the tipping points of our three streams is required to enable the design of exercises addressing threshold concepts and these may differ quite significantly for the three streams. The above analysis has been matched by analyses of the other two streams leading to a clear appreciation of the nature of the compounded local thresholds but we have yet to achieve a meaningful synthesis across this spectrum. We have, as yet, a poor grasp of how the semiotic problems impact on the incorporation of grasped local thresholds into the overall threshold conception. Work is in progress on this synthesis.

REFERENCES

Andersen, P. B. (1990). *A theory of computer semiotics, semiotic approaches to construction and assessment of computer systems*. Cambridge: Cambridge University Press.

Battistella, E. L. (1996). *The logic of markedness*. Oxford: Oxford University Press.

Chandler, D. (2002). *Semiotics: The basics*. Abingdon: Routledge.

Cobley, P. & Jansz, L. (1997). *Introduction to semiotics*. Royston, UK: Icon Books.

Derrida, J. (1976). *Of grammatolgy* (transl. G. C. Spivak). Baltimore, MD: John Hopkins University Press.

Dijkstra, E. W. (1989). On the cruelty of really teaching computing science. *CACM, 32*(12), 1398-1404.

Eco, U. (1979). *The role of the reader: Explorations in the semiotics of texts*. Advances in Semiotics. Indiana University Press.

Flanagan, M. T., *Michael Thomas Flanagan's Java scientific library*. Retrieved on 10 June 2006 from the World Wide Web: http://www.ee.ucl.ac.uk/~mflanaga/java

Gosling J., Joy B., Steele G., & Bracha G. (2004). *The Java™ language specification*, third edition, Boston: Addison-Wesley. On-line version: http://java.sun.com/docs/books/jls/download/langspec-3.0.pdf

Hanks, B. (2006). Student attitudes toward pair programming. In *Proceedings of the 11th annual SIGCSE Conference on Innovation and Technology in Computer Science Education*, Bologna, 2006.

Holmboe, C. (2002). Revitalising old thoughts: Class diagrams in light of the early Wittgenstein. In J. Kuljis, L. Baldwin, & R. Scoble (Eds.), *Proc. PPIG 14*, 14th Workshop of the Psychology of Programming Interest Group, Brunel University, June 2002, pp. 196-203.

Holmboe, C. (2005). The linguistics of object-oriented design: Implications for teaching, Annual Joint Conference Integrating Technology into Computer Science Education, in *Proceedings of the 10th Annual SIGCSE Conference on Innovation and Technology in Computer Science Education*, Caparica, Portugal, pp. 188-192.

Meyer, J. H. F. & Land, R. (2003). Threshold concepts and troublesome knowledge: linkages to ways of thinking and practising within the disciplines. In Rust, C. (Ed.), *Proceedings of the 2002 10th*

International Symposium on Improving Student Learning Theory and Practice – 10 years on (pp. 412-424). Oxford: Oxford Centre for Staff and Learning Development.

Meyer, J. H. F. & Land, R. (2005). Threshold concepts and troublesome knowledge (2): Epistemological considerations and a conceptual framework for teaching and learning. *Higher Education, 49*(3), 373-388.

OMG. (2001). *Unified modelling language specification v1.4.* Needham, MA: OMG ObjectManagement Group. [OMG web page: http://www.omg.org/]

Perkins, D. (2006). Constructivism and troublesome knowledge. In Meyer, J. H. F. & Land, R. (Eds.), *Overcoming barriers to student understanding: Threshold concepts and troublesome knowledge.* London and New York: Routledge

Smith, J. (2006). Lost in translation: staff and students negotiating liminal spaces. SEDA Spring Conference 2006: Advancing Evidence-Informed Practice in HE Learning, Teaching and Educational Development, 8-9 June 2006.

Stross, B. (2005). Introduction to graduate linguistic anthropology course. Retrieved on 10 June 2006 from the World Wide Web: http://www.utexas.edu/courses/stross/ant392n_files/marking.htm

Thimbleby, H. W. (1999). A critique of Java. *Softw., Pract. Exper. 29*(5), 457-478. On-line version: Thimbleby, H. W. (1998). A critique of Java, Retrieved on 10 June 2006 from the World Wide Web: http://www.uclic.ucl.ac.uk/harold/srf/javaspae.html.

Tobin, Y. (1990). *Semiotics and linguistics.* London and New York: Longman.

Trask, R. L. (1999). *Key concepts in language and linguistics.* London: Routledge.

Travers, M. D. (1996). Programming with agents: New metaphors for thinking about computation. PhD Thesis, Massachusetts Institute of Technology. On-line version: http://alumni.media.mit.edu/~mt/diss/index.html.

Wittgenstein, L. (1921). *Tractatus logico-philosophicus* (transl. C. K. Ogden). London: Routledge.

Wolfram, S. (2002). *A new kind of science.* Wolfram Media.

AFFILIATIONS

Michael Thomas Flanagan
Department of Electronic & Electrical Engineering
University College London

Jan Smith
Centre for Academic Practice & Learning Enhancement
University of Strathclyde

CAROL ZANDER, JONAS BOUSTEDT, ANNA ECKERDAL,
ROBERT MCCARTNEY, JAN ERIK MOSTRÖM, MARK RATCLIFFE
& KATE SANDERS

8. THRESHOLD CONCEPTS IN COMPUTER SCIENCE: A MULTI-NATIONAL EMPIRICAL INVESTIGATION

INTRODUCTION

Computer science is a complex, highly technical, and rapidly changing field. In addition, it is a new subject: we have had relatively few years to study the ways in which students learn and how to help them most effectively. Meyer and Land (2003, 2005) have proposed using 'Threshold Concepts' as a way of characterising particular concepts that might be used to organise and focus the educational process. The idea has the potential to help us focus on those concepts that are most likely to block students' learning progress (Davies, 2003).

This chapter describes an ongoing project aimed at empirically identifying threshold concepts in computer science. In a multi-national, multi-institutional study, we have gathered data from both educators and students. The paper outlines our experiences with various experimental techniques, issues raised, and results to date.

Directly below, we discuss work in computing curricula that examines, from varying perspectives, the core concepts in computing; this work provides some specific places to begin looking for threshold concepts. We then describe the techniques we have used to gather data about potential threshold concepts from the perspective of both instructors and students. The results of a preliminary analysis of the data are presented, including the identification of two threshold concepts in computing with some associated evidence. Finally, we present our preliminary conclusions and discuss the future directions of this research effort.

CORE COMPUTING CONCEPTS FROM THE COMPUTER SCIENCE LITERATURE

It is reasonable to assume that any threshold concept in computing should be represented in the 'core' concepts in the discipline. Although there was no work on threshold concepts in computer science when we started, there was a body of work on the computer science curriculum that identified the core concepts. Three areas that apply fairly directly to threshold concepts are the 'Breadth-first' approaches to introductory computer science, the 'Fundamental ideas' approach to organizing computer science concepts, and the curriculum guidelines published by the professional societies.

R. Land, J.H.F. Meyer & J. Smith (Eds.), Threshold Concepts within the Disciplines, 105–118.
© 2008 Sense Publishers. All rights reserved.

Breadth-first Introductory Computer-Science Courses

The breadth-first approach to teaching computer science is based on the idea that all of the important concepts in the computing curriculum should be introduced early, so students start their education with an overview of the field. This overview is generally organised around a set of 'important' concepts. The particular concepts to cover vary from author to author but can include decision trees, number representation, patterns, divide-and-conquer, recursion, the Church-Turing thesis, the von Neumann architecture, time complexity, intractability, types and values, classes and objects, design, encapsulation, inheritance, polymorphism, program correctness, iteration, conceptual and formal models, levels of abstraction, reuse, and tradeoffs (Biermann, 1990; Brookshear, 2005; Schneider & Gersting, 1998; Evans, 1996).

The main criteria for these concepts is that they be core concepts in computer science, and that they can be presented in the context of an introductory course. While most computer scientists would agree on the general importance of these concepts, they are probably not all threshold concepts. A concept such as 'divide and conquer,' for example, integrates many areas of computer science, but it does not appear to be troublesome for students to understand. Similarly, the idea of reuse is an easy one to grasp, even though it may be harder to implement consistently. The concepts on the breadth-first courses' lists may not be transformative, and some of them are probably all too easy to forget. Which, if any, of them qualify as threshold concepts is a question for empirical investigation.

Fundamental Ideas

Schwill (1994) has proposed organizing the computing curriculum around another set of core concepts, the 'Fundamental Ideas', a set of ideas that are central to the discipline. This follows from the work of Bruner (1960), who proposed that science-based teaching should be organised around the structure of the subject, as expressed by its fundamental ideas. These are ideas with broad applicability that can be taught at multiple levels within the curriculum, from early to advanced, at increasingly sophisticated levels.

Drawing on work applying Fundamental Ideas to mathematics, Schwill proposes four criteria for these ideas in computer science (paraphrasing):

Horizontal criterion The idea is applicable or observable in multiple ways and multiple areas of computer science; it organises and integrates multiple phenomena.

Vertical criterion The idea can be taught at every intellectual level, at different levels of sophistication.

Criterion of time The idea is clearly observable in the history of computer science, and will be relevant for a long time.

Criterion of sense The idea also has meaning in everyday life, and can be described in ordinary language.

These criteria can be used to organise and relate subjects in computer science. The idea is that when new concepts are presented, they are related to the appropriate Fundamental Ideas that the students know, thus providing context. Moreover, relating new concepts to these ideas should further develop the ideas, so the learning process can be seen as gradually gaining a greater understanding of these Fundamental Ideas.

There is some overlap between Fundamental Ideas and Threshold Concepts. Both are integrative, and both include topics that should be understood by any competent computing professional. But the Fundamental Ideas are likely *not* transformative, in that they are gradually developed from common-sense understanding of everyday phenomena. Threshold concepts, on the other hand, may not be teachable at every level.

Overall, these approaches seem to be orthogonal. Threshold concepts are based on transformative events, while Fundamental Ideas are based on long-term development. It seems likely that any given threshold concept could be described in terms of the related Fundamental Ideas, and that there are threshold concepts that appear at points in the development of a given Fundamental Idea. Threshold concepts identify the troublesome points in a student's development, while Fundamental Ideas identify different ongoing threads in this process which may or may not have such troublesome points.

Curriculum Standards

As with most disciplines, there are defined standards for computer science undergraduate degree programmes. *Computing Curricula 2001* (Joint Task Force on Computing Curricula, 2001), developed by the two largest computing professional organisations in North America, gives detailed descriptions of the sorts of courses that a degree programme should include, and describes the 'body of knowledge' in discrete chunks.

There are a couple of impediments to using these 'Knowledge units', however. The main problem is the number: the Joint Task Force report defines 63 core 'units' (organised into 13 topic areas), and each of these is made up of a number of 'topics' (generally 3-5). For example, *Functions and parameter passing*, a candidate threshold concept, is one of six topics under the core unit *Fundamental programming constructs*. Another problem is that the knowledge units are arranged hierarchically so that they match up with traditional course areas, but closely related topics may not be close within this structure. For example, Call-by-value vs. Call-by-reference is a topic under *Abstraction mechanisms*, but is closely related to the aforementioned *Functions and parameter passing*.

The lists of concepts produced from Breadth-first concepts, Fundamental Ideas, and curriculum standards provide a reasonable starting point in identifying threshold concepts. There is general agreement that these are important within the discipline, and the organisations of these schemes suggest certain relationships between concepts. Most of the candidate threshold concepts that we identify from the interview and questionnaire data are represented in some fashion on each of these lists. In common with Mead *et al.* (2006), we believe 'the issue of cognitive difficulties with learning computer science concepts is not clearly addressed.'

More information about how threshold concepts relate to the computer science literature can be found in Eckerdal *et al.* (2006). The paper considers threshold concepts as compared with a constructivists approach to learning, how mental models are used, student misconceptions and learning, how a breadth-first approach can be applied, and organising the computing curriculum around *Fundamental Ideas.*

DATA GATHERING AND ANALYSIS

We gathered data from both instructors and students in computer science using a variety of techniques. In this section, we consider first techniques used to gather data from instructors, with a brief analysis, and then techniques used to gather data from students and the techniques used to analyse that data.

The Instructors: Informal Interviews and Surveys

We collected data from computer science instructors at two international conferences of computer science educators. In June 2005, in Portugal, at the Conference on Innovation and Technology in Computer Science Education, we interviewed 36 instructors from nine countries and asked for suggestions of concepts that meet the criteria for a threshold concept. Our interviews with the instructors were unstructured, done in a fairly conversational style with one researcher asking questions and another taking written notes.

From these, we learned several interesting things. First, the idea of threshold concepts is compelling: nearly everyone we spoke with was immediately interested. In total 33 concepts were suggested, with the most popular being: levels of abstraction; pointers; the distinction between classes, objects, and instances; recursion and induction; procedural abstraction; and polymorphism. Second, while some concepts came up again and again, there was no universal consensus, possibly reflecting the current state of computer science education. For example, in the most recent guidelines for computer science curricula mentioned in the previous section, they suggest six possible approaches to the introductory sequencing of courses (Joint Task Force on Computing Curricula, 2001).

In November 2005, we gave a poster and had discussions with researchers at the Koli Calling 2005 Conference on Computer Science Education in Finland (McCartney & Sanders, 2005) and used a questionnaire and interviews to gather data more systematically from conference participants.

Preliminary analysis indicates that these results are similar to those collected in Portugal, but more carefully tied to the defining characteristics of threshold concepts--not surprising, given the structure of the questionnaire. It was also apparent that instructors focus on 'difficult to learn' more than any other aspect of the concepts they discuss.

The Students: Semi-Structured Interviews

Given the tentative list of concepts derived from instructors and the literature, we thus began to investigate the question of whether these − or any other − concepts are experienced by students as thresholds.

We considered using a grid with possible threshold concepts and the five requirements along the axes. The intention was to give the grid to students together with an explanation of the requirements of a threshold concept. The students would fill in the grid by checking the requirements they considered fulfilled for each of the concepts listed. We planned to look for patterns and similarities in the students' answers that could support the assumption that some of the concepts are perceived as threshold concepts by the students. However, our first tests showed filling in the grid to be both time-consuming and cumbersome. We also considered mind-maps or concept-maps but decided that they would not, at this stage, provide us with the desired information.

Instead of using the grid or concept-maps, we decided on a series of semi-structured interviews (Kvale, 1996). We chose to interview graduating students, since they were more likely than novices to have mastered the relevant concepts, and to have done so long enough ago to have some perspective. So far we have completed 16 interviews with students at seven institutions in a total of three countries, ranging from 20 minutes to over an hour long. The base questions used in these interviews are given in Appendix 1.

When interviewing instructors in Portugal we found that many interviewees focused on the troublesome aspect, while not considering the other criteria. To avoid this tendency to accentuate one requirement we decided not to give the students any definition of threshold concepts or even mention the term. Instead we chose to elicit this information by constructing structured interview questions that addressed each of the requirements.

We did begin by addressing the troublesome criterion, asking the students for a list of troublesome concepts ('things' they remembered were problematic to learn). From this list, we selected one concept to pursue in depth, however, and addressed the other criteria in that context. The interviewers agreed in advance on a list of five threshold concept candidates, developed from the previous interviews with instructors and from the literature. If the student mentioned one of those, that concept was chosen. Otherwise, one of the other concepts mentioned by the student was pursued.

The aim of this deeper investigation was twofold. It enabled us to gather evidence as to whether the specific concept met the requirements for threshold concepts (see Questions 8-15, Appendix 1). In addition, it gave us data for a deeper analysis (Marton & Booth, 1997) of graduating students' understanding of central concepts (see Questions 6-7, Appendix 1).

For analysis, the recorded interviews were transcribed verbatim. Interviews conducted in Swedish were translated into English by the interviewer. Each interview was marked with the concept that had been discussed in depth and the concepts that had been discussed in more than one interview were chosen as threshold concept 'candidates'. The corresponding interviews were analysed in order to find out if the threshold concepts requirements were met.

While we obtained valuable data about computer science threshold concepts from these interviews, we also made some observations about the technique and the nature of empirical investigation of threshold concepts that would likely apply in other domains as well. For example, the timing of the interview is an issue. If a substantial amount of time has passed since the research participant (whether student or instructor) learned the concept, we may be able to reasonably conclude that the concept is *irreversible* or unforgettable. At this point, however, *troublesome* and *transformative* are more difficult to investigate. The student may have forgotten that there was a problem at all or may be unable to describe clearly what made the concept troublesome, and may not remember what his or her understanding was before mastering the concept.

Conversely, if an interview is conducted while the student is still grappling with a particular concept, or when he or she has very recently mastered it, the *troublesome* and *transformative* criteria are easier to investigate, but *irreversible* is harder. Such interviewees may be able to describe their problems vividly, but it is impossible to tell whether, if and when they master the concept, they will then forget it.

THRESHOLD CONCEPTS IN COMPUTER SCIENCE

Two threshold concepts were identified in the analysis of the interviews with the graduating students: object-oriented programming (OOP) and memory/pointers. This section gives short explanations of each concept for readers not familiar with them and relevant excerpts from the interviews indicating that the concept meets the requirements for a threshold concept.

Object-Oriented Programming

Ideally, the graduates of computer science programmes should be able to produce high quality software that is correct, efficient, reusable, extensible, and easy to use. Object-oriented programming languages support these goals (Meyer, 1988; Hamilton & Pooch, 1995) and, as a result, they have become the dominant type of programming language worldwide, both in industry and in the classroom (Roberts, 2004a).

Much has been reported on the experiences of teaching and learning object-oriented programming (Thomas *et al.*, 2004; Chen & Morris, 2005). Unfortunately, despite its promise of real benefits to industry, object-oriented programming is experienced as difficult both to teach (Roberts, 2004b; Kolling, 1999) and to learn (Lahtinen *et al.*, 2005).

Students find basic object-orientation *troublesome* to learn. Eckerdal and Thuné (2005) interviewed first-year students who had just finished their first programming course on their understanding of some object-oriented concepts. Many students stated that they found the concepts troublesome to understand despite great effort to learn them.

Luker (1994) argues that learning the object-oriented paradigm, 'requires nothing less than [a] complete change of the world view,' indicating that it is a *transformative* experience. Luker and Eckerdal and Thuné further discuss how object-oriented programming *integrates* concepts within the paradigm.

The interviews performed with graduating students give further evidence of object-oriented programming as a threshold concept. One student discussed object-oriented programming as *troublesome* to learn when asked about something where he or she were stuck at first but which then became clearer:

Student8: Stuck at first − I would have to say the initial object-oriented programming. Knowing how classes communicate, how you communicate between classes and really understanding how objects work; that was basically, once I grasped it, it was fine.

The researcher performing the interview asks the student about the *integrativeness* of object-oriented programming later in the interview by asking how the understanding has affected the understanding of other computer science concepts:

Student8: Well, for instance, the class we did for software engineering, what we did right now, the server that I wrote, each client that connects to the server, I thought of it almost as an object, which it is basically. And then that client connection would be held on to while waiting for other connections. And then there'd be this huge array of connections. And then, I mean, that wasn't that difficult for me to grasp that concept just because we'd kind of went over it in class, but I just think understanding object-oriented programming helped me to understand that there was this group of objects, group of threads, group of clients, whatever.

Interviewer: That they were all working together?

Student8: That we're all working together, exactly. And understanding object-oriented programming, I think, made that easy to learn; easy to understand it.

This student learned about OOP, later learned about a more advanced topic, multi-threaded programming, and perceived a real connection at a fairly abstract level.

Another student also indicated that object-oriented programming is troublesome to learn when asked if there was something that was difficult to understand but later was suddenly understood:

Student6: No, it's almost everything I think! Ehhh, hum, ehhh ... object oriented programming was one thing for example that took a long time before ... it clicked. Why and how it should be used.

The researcher later asks the same student if object-oriented programming is *irreversible*.

Student6: Yes, I need to review sometimes, [...], often it's just syntactical details, [...] basic stuff is there, I've mainly used Java so, sure I'm a little bit stuck in those tracks but I can usually bring everything with me and just transfer it to C++ for example, [...]

Interviewer: The big stuff is there so to speak.

Student6: Yes, [...] I can forget, to make some mistakes in the beginning but as long as I've once known and done it correct some time then it usually comes back

The student explains that some syntactic details might be forgotten in a specific object-oriented programming language, but 'the basic stuff is there' (the object oriented paradigm) and 'it usually comes back', implying object-oriented programming is *irreversible.*

The quote also shows the close relation between the *irreversible* and the *integrative* aspects of this threshold concept. The student explains that he or she can use the knowledge gained from one language and transfer it to another language.

Later in the interview the researcher discusses the *transformative* aspect of learning object-oriented programming by asking how the student to describe the difference between how problems are looked at before and after finding a solution:

Student6: Yes, it's like day and night, before I came here I had ... I couldn't ... abstract the problems on, well to a very small extent perhaps, but today it's ... I can identify the problems usually in a very short time, unless it's very complex and difficult to understand but today I only see small sub-problems and ... usually simple solutions to them. Before it was just one large program that ... I solved sequentially in some way and the programs looked like that ...

Discussing the same topic the interviewer later asks about the role OOP has played in problem solving:

Student6: It simplifies it, even if I don't use an OO language the OOP way of thinking can help a lot in ... in some way ... well, you can give a lot of data, you can give it some kind object status even if it doesn't have its own methods etc. ...

The student explains that he or she looks at programming in a completely new way after learning object-oriented programming. The knowledge has *transformed* how the student looks at problems.

Memory and Pointers

A second concept identified as a potential threshold concept was memory/pointers. When computers execute a program, they temporarily store information 'in memory' similar in concept to how letters are put into mailboxes or pigeonholes at an office. Just as each pigeonhole has a label with a name, each position in computer memory has a unique address. For example, the age of, say, Tim Andersson, is stored at address 139.

But the addresses themselves are data and can also be stored somewhere. So for example, the address 139 where the age of Tim Andersson is stored could itself be stored at address 271. In that case, the address 271 is called a 'pointer.' This distinction − between data and data that refers to other data − is widely accepted to be difficult for students. Four of the instructors from whom we gathered data volunteered memory/pointers as a possible threshold concept.

That the concept of memory and pointers can be *troublesome* is illustrated by the following excerpt:

> Student13: And so when you implement pointers and see then you're like okay I need to figure out how I modify that and it affects the memory. And then if I reference the memory I get what back. And then you start passing the arguments. And you have to understand passing by reference or passing by value. And a lot of those were definitely big hurdles right in the beginning because I didn't − it was just − I guess too theoretical of a concept for me to really put in practical sense. I got through it by brute force and just forcing it and studying it and a lot of application. Like seeing subtle differences with examples. Seeing one example where you'll reference and one example you'll call by value and show the actual different results you get by doing it from reference versus value. And why you do it and why you ... another.

The student describes the difficulties in understanding how pointers work in general and together with parameter passing (call by reference means that a pointer to the actual value is sent to the called function/procedure).

Another student confirmed that pointers can be troublesome:

> Student3: I know that pointers are something that a lot of students have trouble with. And I think that probably talk to a lot of other students and find out how they're doing them, how are they approaching them. And have they figured them out. [...]

> And I think once you've realised that a pointer is just pointing to a place in memory, it's just pointing to a location, that's all it is. Then I think everything will flow from that. Yeah, because you realise then that the object itself is just a place in memory too.

> Interviewer: So before you weren't even thinking about memory so much.

Student3: Exactly. I didn't at all. Like in Java, I didn't think about memory nearly so much. I mean I knew that certainly memory was allocated, that memory was allocated with its variables and attributes and that kind of stuff. But I didn't ... when I was writing a program, I didn't ever think about what was happening underneath. Especially garbage collection.

Not only can we see that this student found pointers troublesome, but also that they are integrative and *transformative*. Once the student understood how memory and pointers work he or she was able to use this knowledge to explain how objects and references are implemented, thus getting an improved understanding of how Java works.

In another part of the interview the same student described how the understanding of pointers has helped in other subjects:

Student3: Well, as I was saying in the hardware class and in Operating Systems, we definitely discussed pointers and I used it both conceptually and also in, well not in Operating Systems, but in the hardware class in assembly language, we definitely used pointers.

We definitely were dereferencing all the time in assembly language, so when we were, for example, writing to an address register, we would have to dereference it in order to get at the address to find out what was going on at that particular address in memory. So, definitely I used it again and again.

The clearest statement that the concept of pointers is irreversible comes from an interview with another student:

Interviewer: Was your understanding – the understanding that you gained – is this something that you had to keep reviewing to keep remembering? Or is this something that once you had it, you had it?

Student13: The syntax I would have to review, guaranteed. The syntax is – it's a little – it's syntax. But the basic idea of passing by reference or value; no, once I understood that I – every time it's mentioned I immediately know and understand – I can see a picture – a diagram in my head of what I'm supposed to do. What--how the effect will work. So the concept was not lost at all.

CONCLUSIONS AND FUTURE WORK

The main contributions so far from our project to the field of research into threshold concepts are techniques for empirically investigating threshold concepts and some observations regarding issues raised during this investigation.

We used both informal interviews and questionnaires to obtain data from instructors and scripted, structured interviews to obtain data from students. We considered using grids and concept maps. The grid we initially designed was too cumbersome and time-consuming to fill out. These tools may be more useful in the future as we focus our list of possible threshold concepts.

Two main ideas guided the design of the student-interview script. The first was to investigate Threshold Concepts from the students' perspective by asking questions that would reveal if each of the criteria was met. The second was to investigate how students understand these concepts, and from this to be able to draw conclusions to improve teaching and learning. This part of the work is still in its infancy.

These interviews provide evidence to support the claim that threshold concepts exist in Computer Science. Specifically, they suggest that object-oriented programming and memory/pointers are both threshold concepts. Especially in the case of object-oriented programming, further investigation is needed, however: the actual threshold concept may be a more specific topic within the one identified.

Our investigations also raised several broader issues with regard to empirical studies of threshold concepts:

- At what point in a student's learning should data be gathered? If too early, there is no way to tell if the concept will later be forgotten; if too late, the Student may not remember that there was a problem, or may not be able to remember how he or she perceived the subject before mastering the concept.
- What exactly does it mean for a concept to be *integrative?* Is it integrative only if it integrates concepts the student already knows? Or can a concept be integrative if it connects a number of things that are only learned later?

As a tentative solution to the first issue, we plan to interview students at various points in their programmes. By asking novices about the concepts we have already tentatively identified − object-oriented programming and memory/pointers − we can strengthen our understanding of those thresholds and how they are perceived by students. In addition, we plan to ask novices more open-ended questions, to identify possible threshold concepts whose difficulty the seniors may have already forgotten.

Much analysis also remains to be done on the data we have already gathered. For example, we have only looked closely at a couple of candidate threshold concepts. Several other candidates were mentioned, and even a single interview may provide substantial interesting data.

APPENDIX 1. SCRIPT FOR SEMI-STRUCTURED INTERVIEWS (INTERVIEWER ADDS ADDITIONAL AND FOLLOW-UP QUESTIONS AS APPROPRIATE)

Student Interview

An introduction to the study is described followed by the questions:

1. Could you tell me about something where you were stuck at first but then became clearer? *(Student answers <X>)*

The rest of this session will now focus on <X>.

2. Can I start by asking you to tell me your understanding of <X>?

3. Assume that you were explaining <X> to someone just learning this material, how would you do it?

4. Tell me your thoughts, your reactions, before during and after the process of dealing with <X>.

5. Can you tell me what helped you understand <X>?

6. Can you describe how you perceived/experienced <X> while you were stuck and how you perceived/experienced it afterwards?

7. Based on your experience, what advice would you give to help other students who might be struggling with <X>?

8. Please tell me what other things you need to understand in order to gain a good understanding of <X>.

9. Can you tell me how your understanding of <X> has affected your understanding of other things?

10. Was your understanding of <X> something that you had to keep reviewing or having learned it once were you OK with it?

11. Describe how and in what context you have used <X> since you learned it?

12. Is there something more you want to tell me about <X>?

13. To finish the interview, can you tell me whether there are any other things where you were stuck at first but then became clearer? I promise I won't ask you about them in detail!

REFERENCES

Biermann, Alan. (1990). *Great ideas in computer science: A gentle introduction.* Cambridge, MA: MIT Press.
Brookshear, J. Glenn. (2005). *Computer science: An overview* (8th edition). Boston, MA: Addison Wesley.
Bruner, J. S. (1960). *The process of education.* Cambridge, MA: Harvard University Press.
Chen, S. & Morris, S. (2005). Iconic programming for flowcharts, java, turing, etc. In *Proceedings of the 10th Annual SIGCSE Conference on Innovation and Technology in Computer Science Education (ITiCSE)* (pp. 104-107). Caparica, Portugal.
Davies, Peter. (2003). Threshold concepts: How can we recognise them. Paper presented at EARLI Conference, Padova. Available from:

http://www.staffs.ac.uk/schools/business/iepr/docs/etcworkingpaper(1).doc. [Last accessed 29/06/07]

Eckerdal, Anna, McCartney, Robert, Moström, Jan Erik, Ratcliffe, Mark, Sanders, Kate, & Zander, Carol. (2006). Putting threshold concepts into context in computer science education. In *Proceedings of the 11th Annual SIGCSE Conference on Innovation and Technology in Computer Science Education (ITiCSE)* (pp. 103-107). Bologna, Italy.

Eckerdal, Anna & Thuné, Michael. (2005). Novice java programmers' conceptions of 'object' and 'class', and variation theory. In *Proceedings of the 10th Annual SIGCSE Conference on Innovation and Technology in Computer Science Education (ITiCSE)* (pp. 89-93). Caparica, Portugal.

Evans, M. (1996) A new emphasis & pedagogy for a CS1 course. SIGCSE Bulletin, 28(3), 12-16.

Hamilton, J. A. & Pooch, U. W. (1995). A survey of object-oriented methodologies. In *Proceedings of the conference on TRI-Ada'95: Ada's role in global markets: Solutions for a changing complex world* (pp. 226-234). Anaheim, CA.

Joint Task Force on Computing Curricula. (2001). Computing curriculum 2001, computer science volume. Technical report, IEEE Computer Society and Association for Computing Machinery. Available from http://www.sigcse.org/cc2001/. [Last accessed 29/06/07]

Kölling, M. (1999). The problem of teaching object-oriented programming, Part 1: Languages. *Journal of Object-Oriented Programming, 11*(8), 8-15.

Kvale, S. (1996). *InterViews: An introduction to qualitative research interviewing.* Thousand Oaks, CA: Sage.

Lahtinen, Essi, Ala-Mutka, Kirsti, & Järvinen, Hannu-Matti. (2005). Early programming: A study of the difficulties of novice programmers. In *Proceedings of the 10th Annual SIGCSE conference on Innovation and Technology in Computer Science Education (ITiCSE)* (pp. 14-18). Caparica, Portugal.

Luker, P. A. (1994). There's more to OOP than syntax. *SIGCSE Bulletin, 26*(1), 56–60.

Marton, F. & Booth, S. (1997). *Learning and awareness.* Mahwah, NJ: Lawrence Erlbaum Associates.

McCartney, Robert, & Sanders, Kate. (2005). What are the 'threshold concepts' in computer science? In T. Salakoski & T. Mäntylä (Eds.), *Proceedings of the Koli Calling 2005 Conference on Computer Science Education* (p. 185). Koli, Finland.

Mead, J., Gray, S., Hamer, J., James, R., Sorva, J., Clair, C. S., & Thomas, L. (2006). A cognitive approach to identifying measurable milestones for programming skill acquisition. *SIGCSE Bulletin, 38*(4), 182-194.

Meyer, B. (1988). *Object-oriented software construction.* International Series in Computer Science. Upper Saddle River, NJ: Prentice Hall.

Meyer, Jan & Land, Ray. (2003). Threshold concepts and troublesome knowledge: Linkages to ways of thinking and practising within the disciplines. ETL Project Occasional Report 4. Available from http://www.ed.ac.uk/etl/docs/ETLreport4.pdf. [Last accessed 29/06/07]

Meyer, Jan & Land, Ray. (2005). Threshold concepts and troublesome knowledge (2): Epistemological considerations and a conceptual framework for teaching and learning. *Higher Education, 49*, 373-388.

Roberts, Eric. (2004a). The dream of a common language: The search for simplicity and stability in computer science education. *SIGCSE Bulletin, 36*(1), 115–119.

Roberts, Eric. (2004b). Resources to support the use of java in introductory computer science. In *Proceedings of the 35th SIGCSE Technical Symposium on Computer Science Education* (pp. 233-234). Norfolk, VA.

Schneider, G. Michael & Gersting, Judith L. (1998). *An invitation to computer science* (8th edition). Belmont, CA: Brooks/Cole.

Schwill, Andreas. (1994). Fundamental ideas of computer science. *Bulletin European Assoc. for Theoretical Computer Science, 53*, 274-295.

Thomas, Lynda, Ratcliffe, Mark, & Thomasson, Benjy (2004). Scaffolding with object diagrams in first year programming classes: Some unexpected results. In *Proceedings of the 35th SIGCSE Technical Symposium on Computer Science Education* (pp. 250-254). Norfolk, VA.

AFFILIATIONS

Carol Zander
Computing and Software Systems
University of Washington, Bothell

Jonas Boustedt
Department of Mathematics, Natural, and Computer Science
University of Gävle

Anna Eckerdal
Department of Information Technology
Uppsala University

Robert McCartney
Department of Computer Science and Engineering
University of Connecticut

Jan Erik Moström
Department of Computing Science
Umeå University

Mark Ratcliffe
Valtech UK
London, UK

Kate Sanders
Department of Mathematics and Computer Science
Rhode Island College

DERMOT SHINNERS-KENNEDY

9. THE EVERYDAYNESS OF THRESHOLD CONCEPTS

State as an Example from Computer Science

INTRODUCTION

The definition of a threshold concept requires a qualifying concept to have an irreversible effect that integrates a body of knowledge and transforms our way of viewing it. These requirements tend to encourage us to look for significant concepts, particularly because they have to transform, and the notion of transformation seems to carry with it an intuitive sense of momentous effect. Significant is an acknowledged metaphor for big and there is a danger that our search for threshold concepts may be influenced by such a view. For example, impromptu enquiries amongst Computer Science educators about what might be a threshold concept in computing invokes responses that include recursion, polymorphism, abstraction and pointers; all topics that would be viewed as advanced components of a computing curriculum. The lure of the big concepts is a common pitfall, as the legendary naturalist David Attenborough (Attenborough, 2005, p. 7) has observed

> We are greatly prejudiced by our size. We find it very difficult to believe that an animal that is many thousand times smaller than ourselves can have anything in anyway comparable to our own motives, or to experience anything that resembles our basic emotions of fear and hunger, let alone aggression or sexual excitement. And until recently science abetted such thoughts. Bees and blowflies, beetles and butterflies were mere automata, mindless robots reacting automatically to the simplest stimuli. To credit them with anything else was unjustified and scientifically disreputable anthropomorphism.

The proposal of state as a threshold concept in computer science nominates a seemingly humble concept. A justification for the proposal is provided later but for now it is worth noting that the choice appears consistent with the proposals that have emanated from other disciplines. For example, the economists have identified opportunity cost; precedent has been offered by the schools of law; and pain by the physiotherapists. All of these concepts are in the conceptual framework of a typical young child. For instance, what child is not vividly aware of the nuances of opportunity cost when faced with the choices arranged around them in a sweet shop? What parent has not been reminded that the pleasure they are currently proposing to deny one child was granted to a sibling on a previous occasion? In

R. Land, J.H.F. Meyer & J. Smith (Eds.), Threshold Concepts within the Disciplines. 119-128.

any environment where children are present 'knocks' will result and consolation and tear-wiping go hand-in-glove. Of course, the instances of these concepts are still rough-edged and lack the sophisticated reasoning that will accompany them when they have been refined and smoothed, but their seedling presence in children of very tender age is astounding nonetheless.

It seems paradoxical that these small or simple concepts could have the ability to irreversibly integrate and transform a body of knowledge that attempts to explain the behaviour of the global economy, the operation of international law or the treatment of back injuries. Notwithstanding this, given their simplicity how could they be 'troublesome'?

EVERYDAYNESS

Across the disciplines, a pattern is evolving in relation to threshold concept identification that appears to favour what might be considered everyday concepts. (Norman, 1989, p. 125) provides a useful explanation of why everydayness is a common characteristic of troublesome knowledge.

> Everyday activities must usually be done relatively quickly, often simultaneously with other activities. Neither time nor mental resources may be available. As a result, everyday activities structure themselves so as to minimize conscious mental activity…These characteristics restrict everyday tasks to those that are shallow (having no need for looking ahead or backing up) and those that are narrow (having few choices at any point, and therefore requiring little planning) … the mental effort required for doing the task is minimized.

We do not reason about everyday tasks. We perfect them to the point of automation. Consequently, we do not recognise or explore in any meaningful way the implications of the concepts packaged in the task. (Minsky, 1986 p. 22) describes this type of knowledge as 'layered knowledge', associated with our maturing skills and abilities which he suggests:

> As time goes on, the layers become increasingly remote until, when we try to speak of them in later life, we find ourselves with little more to say than 'I don't know'.

In a similar vein (Thurston, 1990) talks of 'compressed knowledge' which, in the context of mathematics, he describes as follows

> …you may struggle a long time, step by step, to work through some process or idea from several approaches. But once you really understand it and have the mental perspective to see it as a whole, there is often a tremendous mental compression. You can file it away, recall it quickly and completely when you need it, and use it as just one step in some other mental process.

The layered or compressed nature of everyday knowledge enables us to 'use it as just one step' but this cognitive convenience also makes it inert and a key source of trouble. By way of example, consider the concept of a list, a universally applicable everyday task. Making, modifying, using or discarding a list would be considered a trivial task by almost everyone. However, you can very easily confound someone by asking them to give you an example of an empty list. The concept of an empty list is counter-intuitive for most people. Who would have a list with nothing in it? However, if prompted, most people will accept the concept of an empty To-do list. Similarly, if you ask a group of people to provide you with a list of the people they have murdered you would hope that the list would be empty! Lists are the source of very many conceptual difficulties encountered by students of computing. Ironically, their everyday list handling capabilities are quite sophisticated. Many of the difficulties arise from the possibility of the list being empty, an inert part of their everyday conception of list and so layered or compressed that it is rarely if ever considered a possibility.

KNOWLEDGE IN THE WORLD

Another source of trouble is what (Norman, 1989, p. 54) describes as 'knowledge in the world'. As he explains,

> ... not all of the knowledge required for precise behaviour has to be in the head. It can be distributed – partly in the head, partly in the world, and partly in the constraints of the world.

People visiting a particular city don't have to know all the one-way streets and parking locations to travel safely around the city. They exploit the road signs and other 'knowledge in the world' to make informed decisions about where to go. However, difficulties can arise when the knowledge in the world is not available.

The absence of knowledge in the world can lead to unforeseen conceptual difficulties. For example, Shackleford and Badre (1993) observed that their students were quite capable of calculating the average of a list of numbers but, even after sufficient instruction, were incapable of writing a program to do it. When solving the problem manually (i.e. without using a computer) the students were able to rely on the physical list of numbers included in the statement of the problem. No cognitive resources or effort were expended remembering the numbers in the list or the number of numbers in the list. When a query or difficulty arose, the student could refer back to the physical list (i.e. knowledge in the world) and apply the averaging mechanism (i.e. knowledge in the head) to solve the problem. However, when writing a program to solve the problem most of the students were unable to provide a mechanism to correctly detect the end of the list and compute the average. Thus, their conceptual Achilles heel was not the algorithm to calculate averages but the simple notion of knowing when one has reached the end of a list!

Hendry and Green (1994) asked a group of spreadsheet users to solve the averaging problem. Like the students, when the number of numbers in the list was known the problem was easily solved. When the number of numbers could be varied, none of the subjects could solve the problem. The authors concluded

> Solving this seemingly simple problem is difficult because primitive system-oriented functions are required … These functions have no place in the user's knowledge of how to solve the problem … an advantage of the spreadsheet is that 'it suppresses the inner world' of variables and flow of control and eliminates many of the complexities and 'programming games' associated with conceptually simple operations like adding a list of numbers.

Knowledge in the world can be both a crutch and a captor. When our conceptual framework has been formulated with the benefit of knowledge in the world, it can be difficult to exploit the framework in the absence of that knowledge. Everyday experiences are implicitly 'knowledge in the world' related and consequently are susceptible to this weakness.

STATE AS A THRESHOLD CONCEPT IN COMPUTING

In a computing context the concept of *state* exhibits many of the difficulties associated with threshold concepts. The following sections identify some of those difficulties and document the case for state as a threshold concept in computing.

Troublesomeness

State is pervasive in everyday situations. In spoken language we often hear people (parents especially) advising others (children especially) to look at the state of themselves, their room, their clothes, their hair and so on. We talk about the state of the economy, our personal finances, the road system, school buildings, our rivers and the broader ecosystem. It is impossible to have a discourse about these things without having some values or entities to refer to. For example, we would not be surprised to hear mention of unemployment in the course of a discussion about the economy, or bank balances in the context of someone's personal finances, or greenhouse gas in relation to the ecosystem.

Everyday processes have state characteristics. We monitor the state of food as it roasts, boils, fries or sets. The food has to be brought to the correct state for each phase of the preparation. These state transitions have to be managed and are dependent on the current state. For example, we apply more or less heat depending on the current state to ensure the next required state is reached correctly. In addition, the sequence in which the state changes are arranged is important. It is inconceivable that we would chop an onion and then attempt to remove the outer protective skin or cut a meat joint before roasting it. In sporting events the 'state of play' is recorded using what we call the score. Indeed, when screening the so-called highlights of a sporting event, sports editors restrict the content to occasions when the state changed (i.e. someone scored) or had the potential to change (i.e. near misses). Thus, when we need to review a long process in a short period of time we identify the critical state-changing points and examine the actions at that time to determine how or why the state changed.

We have symbols and rituals for identifying state. For example, females often wear a ring on their ring-finger to acknowledge their betrothed state. Married males and females frequently observe a similar ritual acknowledging their married state. A person's position in a hierarchy is often evident by the uniform and accoutrements they wear or the title by which they are addressed hence the threshold concept status of 'signification' in the study of history. We talk of their status and our reactions and responses are often dependent on what we perceive that status to be.

We have specific language for articulating, recording or comparing state. For example, the state of the stock market may be described as bullish or bearish; security risks can be coded green, blue, yellow, orange or red; food can be raw, rare, medium-rare, well-done or overcooked. Thus associated with each state of interest to us we have a domain of values used for measuring and identifying the possible states. As the examples highlight, the domain of values may be a trivial two-valued set or a more elaborate multi-valued set. Regardless of the simplicity or extravagance of the value domain it is always the case that the current value identifies the current state.

In some situations several values contribute to an amalgamated or aggregated state value. For example, the state of the economy might be measured by reference to the budget deficit, the rate of inflation, the unemployment level and gross domestic product. In these cases, the domain of values can be immense because it is derived from the Cartesian product of the constituent domains. It is impossible to enumerate all of the values in domains like this and they are, effectively, domains with an infinite range of values. Consequently, economic model builders are unable to test their models with every possible combination of values to determine which combination yields a target equilibrium. Like economic models, computer programs are also models of some external reality and they too are affected by the inability to undertake exhaustive testing.

Because of the everydayness of state, few of us think of it in explicit or conscious terms. State is an extremely good example of the type of ritual, tacit and inert knowledge that we have at our disposal. As (Perkins 1999) has illustrated, this type of knowledge is difficult to harness because access to it proves so problematic. This is more a consequence of what was described earlier as the layered or compressed nature of the knowledge than of cognitive slovenliness. Our familiarity causes us to ignore important aspects. For example, users of mobile phones are often oblivious to the fact that the current state of the phone battery, the communication signal or their current credit status need to be recorded and monitored despite the fact that they constantly monitor and alter these things themselves. Generally, when we are monitoring something, say food, we are not conscious of the fact that our next action is determined by the current state or that our actions that change the state are the critical ones.

These issues manifest themselves in computing situations when, for example, students attempt to find errors in their programs. They frequently forget to use an appropriate variable to record the state of important items. They rarely focus on the points in the program where state changes occur and instead become overwhelmed by the tedium of inspecting every statement. They frequently get the sequencing of actions wrong because they assume that simply because they have specified the actions the computer will know what to do. Novice programmers are notoriously bad at what computer scientists describe as program debugging, despite the fact that they have extensive experience of the activity in other contexts.

Linguistic nuance (Meyer & Land, 2005) can also be a source of trouble. For example, the term 'parameter passing' is used by programmers to identify data exchange between the components of a system. One of the problems is that the terminology is misleading because it is grounded in the language of the system software (i.e. compiler) and not the programmer. When the system encounters an information exchange it has to decide how to deal with it, that is, it has to decide how to pass the information from one component to the other. However, this is of no consequence to the programmer who is only interested in what needs to happen to the data once it is received by the component it is being passed to. In everyday situations it is the receiver of the information who determines how it gets used, as the adage 'A secret is something you tell one other person' confirms. The term parameter-passing misses an important aspect of data exchange – data is not passed it is received. For this and other reasons (see below) parameter passing is a notoriously problematic concept for novice programmers.

The centrality of state is also profoundly counter-intuitive (Perkins, 1999) for most novice programmers mainly because, in popular culture, a persistent perception of computers is that they are capable of doing anything. This perception has been fuelled by the ubiquitous presence of computer-type devices with sophisticated features such as still and video cameras, car satellite navigation systems, music players, game machines and televisions. Given that a typical mobile phone has more computing power than the Apollo 11 moon-landing spacecraft had (Ben-Ari, 2005), it is not surprising that many novice programmers are surprised to learn that a computer is capable of only two possible actions. It can

- inspect the state of a process, or
- change the state of a process.

One might argue that viewing a computer from this perspective represents a 'low' or 'machine' level view. However, Turing's seminal work on computability was grounded in such a view. In fact, the simplicity of this view is its strength.

Whilst the simplicity and elegance of this view may be appealing to experts it tends to have a negative effect on beginners. They find it difficult to accept that just two simple operations could be used to create the elaborate systems they experience in their everyday encounters with technology. Once again, their inert and tacit knowledge deserts them. For example, the musicians amongst them will know, but they will not be consciously aware, that the works of Schubert, U2 and The Sex Pistols were created using just eight notes from the music scale. All English speaking students will know that the alphabet contains just twenty six letters yet we are able to enjoy reading Joyce, McGahern and Rowlings and many other authors who exploit and expand our vocabulary and dictionary. Those with even a passing acquaintance with mathematics will have learned that using just ten digits and a handful of arithmetic operators we can undertake almost all of the computations we require. As children most of us witnessed or experienced the unbelievable array of objects that could be created from the incredibly small collection of building blocks provided in Lego building sets. Thus, despite many everyday examples to the contrary we find it difficult to believe that very small toolsets can provide the infrastructure to build very sophisticated and immensely varied artefacts.

Integration

State management is the essence of programming. Every technique and tool in the programmer's repertoire is concerned with supporting versatile and efficient management of the state space. Throughout the history of software design and development, all of the techniques and insights that have had a significant influence on the discipline (e.g. structured programming, object orientation, information hiding) have had state as their focus. The following list, though not exhaustive, highlights the integrative nature of state in the design, development and implementation of computer systems. The conceptual span ranges from the simplest concepts associated with software development to the most advanced.

- Requirements Engineering marks the commencement of a software project. Even at this stage state plays an important role. Requirement Engineers (Maiden, 1998) 'produced the first extensive categorization of requirements engineering problem domains' by categorizing each problem domain using eight dimensions all of which are implicitly or explicitly state based.
- Almost all of the system design techniques in widespread use (i.e. Jackson System Design, Unified Modelling Language and their equivalents) are state based
- Proofs of correctness, pre and post conditions, invariants, formal specifications and related topics, generally viewed as advanced computer science topics, are all inextricably bound to the concept of state. Typically notations specify the initial and goal states and the transition required to reach the goal state. The method used to make the transition is usually not included. Thus, the focus is completely dominated by the states.
- Even in relatively small programs the state space (i.e. the Cartesian product of the domain ranges of the variables used in the program) can be extremely large and potentially infinite. Program design techniques (e.g. structured programming, information hiding, modularisation, objects) are tools for partitioning the state space into cognitively manageable components. Unintentional side effects represent uncontrolled or undetected gaps in the state space management strategy or implementation and are the source of most programming errors.
- State and variables are inextricably linked because state is always realised or represented by a value or a collection of values. Global and local data and the concept of scope are all associated with state as represented by variables.
- Concurrent and/or parallel programming, generally perceived as the most complex of programming tasks, is essentially about protecting shared variables/state from interference.

- Monitors, semaphores and other tools used to control synchronisation in concurrent systems all arise because of the need to manage process state and in particular interleaved process states.
- Many of the concepts associated with object-oriented systems are explicitly state based. For example, mutators or 'sets' control state changes, accessors or 'gets' provide inspection, and constructors establish the initial state. In C++ systems the keywords const and friend can be used to constrain or relax the state properties of an object.

Transformation and Irreversibility

With the exception of trivial problems, programming solutions are built as networks of interacting components. Whereas in the past one might have encountered a 10,000 line monolithic program, present day design techniques are more likely to produce 1000 ten-line program components. Managing the interactions of these components is one of the most critical aspects of the programmer's task because the components manipulate the program state to produce the desired result. Erroneous or inadvertent alterations of the state can be difficult to locate and correct, especially in large or sophisticated component networks.

For components to interact they need to exchange information and, as mentioned earlier, programmers use the term 'parameter passing' to describe this activity. There are only two ways a parameter can be passed, (1) by value (i.e. copy), and (2) by reference. Every programming language adheres to this principle. The terminology may vary slightly from language to language or paradigm to paradigm – for example, logic programs use bound and free variables – but the principle is universally applicable.

How data is passed determines how it can affect the global program state. Data passed by value, can be manipulated but the manipulations cannot change the global state of the program. Manipulations that alter data passed by reference can also alter the global state of the program. Notwithstanding the apparent simplicity of this mechanism, it is persistently reported as problematic despite student's comprehension of related concepts. (As an aside, we note that parameter passing provides yet another example of the integration properties associated with threshold concepts. A component can only inspect or alter the data it receives because that is all the digital device can do and as a consequence that is all the software components that control it can do!)

The principal source of problems associated with parameter passing is that the concept, as an act of pedagogy, is never presented in the context of the affects on the state of the program. Typically, tutors focus on the requirements of the system and how it has to determine the passing style specified in the program and generate the appropriate instructions to achieve it. In that context parameter passing is viewed as a technical difficulty that has to be resolved. Once a mechanism for resolving the problem has been established it is irrelevant how many times it is deployed.

When one takes the approach that parameters are not passed but are in fact received, a more appropriate terminology can be introduced. For example, parameters may be received protected (i.e. program state cannot be altered) or received unprotected/exposed (i.e. program state can be altered).

This approach is also more consistent with the way programming languages specify the exchange mechanism. If a program component needs to be able to alter the state of the data received, then it (i.e. the component) specifies that requirement. If the component simply needs to inspect the state of the data received then it specifies that requirement. Thus, the component receiving the information identifies how it wants to or needs to receive that information.

The state based approach to data exchange is far more logical and consistent than the 'parameter passing' approach. More importantly, it acts as a transforming agent for a number of significant programming concepts. For example, whilst many students can appreciate the utility of decomposing a large problem into a series of smaller component problems they often fail to recognise the crucial importance of partitioning and localising the state changes effected by the components. Exploiting the state based approach motivates and fosters better debugging strategies, provides an explanation and justification for encapsulation, and leads somewhat naturally to the notion of objects and object oriented programming. Anecdotal evidence suggests students schooled in the state based approach are more comfortable with concepts associated with program design, information hiding and compiler techniques.

When considering iteration tutors, and as a consequence students, generally focus on the control-flow properties of the iterative constructs, namely, repetition, test before or after and whether there will be zero or more executions of the statement block. The test is usually referred to as a condition. Tutors are usually very explicit about highlighting the connection between the condition and the provision in the statement block of a suitable mechanism for modifying its result. Despite this, students frequently forget to include such a mechanism and create loops that have no way of terminating (i.e. infinite loops). In addition, students have difficulty establishing the utility of the test before and test after properties and the so-called 'out by one' error occurs frequently.

Iteration is rarely viewed as a repeated state inspection (i.e. as one of the two basic operations identified earlier). From a state perspective, the significance of the initial state is self-evident and by implication the position of the test before or after the statement block exposes the possibility of zero executions or at least one execution. Thus, the test position is not so much a property of the iteration construct and more a consequence of the state-based environment. Similarly, the implications of not altering the state within the statement block are obvious, and identifying which state variables must be altered within the loop body it is a straightforward exercise.

Like the parameter-passing scenario anecdotal evidence suggests that the state based approach to the teaching of iteration is far more successful than the traditional control-flow approach.

CONCLUSIONS

Our search for threshold concepts might be misguided by our cognitive weaknesses. Simply because something is perceived as important or significant does not make it so. Things that bind are usually concealed, or at least not prominent, and facilitating concealment requires binding agents to be small and innocuous (e.g. stitches, mortar, joints). Given that integration is a key feature of threshold concepts, the smaller concepts appear to provide more utility than the more grandiose ones.

Everyday activities have a huge number of important concepts associated with them but they are rich with troublesome knowledge. Because they are so automated and compressed we find it difficult to extract the component concepts. In addition to the troublesome sources identified by Perkins we have added problems associated with 'layered knowledge' and 'knowledge in the world'.

To date most of the concepts proposed as threshold concepts have been distinguished by their everydayness. This exposition of state as a threshold concept in computer science is intended as an exemplar. Other concepts associated with computer science that might qualify as threshold concepts include 'delimiter' and 'offset'. Both embody simplicity and everydayness. Consideration of these aspects of the conceptual map of a discipline may make the search for threshold concepts a little more obvious than previously envisaged.

REFERENCES

Attenborough, D. (2005). *Life in the undergrowth.* London: BBC Books.

Ben-Ari, M. M. (2005). The Concorde doesn't fly anymore. *ACM SIGCSE Bulletin, 37*(1), 196.

Hendry, D.G. & Green, T.R.G. (1994). Creating, comprehending and explaining spreadsheets. *International Journal of Man-Machine Studies, 40*(6), 1033-1065.

Maiden, N. M. H. (1998). Problem domain categories in requirements engineering *International Journal of Human-Computer Studies, 49*(3), 281-304.

Meyer, J. H. F. & Land, R. (2005). Threshold concepts and troublesome knowledge (2): Epistemological considerations and a conceptual framework for teaching and learning. *Higher Education, 49*(3), 373-388.

Minsky, M. (1986). *The society of mind.* New York: Simon and Schuster.

Norman, D. (1989). *The design of everday things.* New York: Doubleday Currency.

Perkins, D. (1999). The many faces of constructivism. *Educational Leadership, 57*(3), 6-11.

Shackelford, R. L. & Badre, A. N. (1993). Why can't smart students solve simple programming problems? *International Journal of Man-Machine Studies, 38*(6), 985-997.

Thurston, W. P. (1990). Mathematical education. *Notices of the AMS, 37*(7), 844-850.

AFFILIATION

Dermot Shinners-Kennedy
Department of Computer Science and Information Systems
University of Limerick

CAROLINE BAILLIE & ANNE JOHNSON

10. A THRESHOLD MODEL FOR ATTITUDES IN FIRST YEAR ENGINEERING STUDENTS

INTRODUCTION

The Professional Skills course taught at Queen's University has been designed to provide students entering Applied Science with a base from which to develop their approaches to learning and to provide an early opportunity to 'think like an engineer.'

Although assessment has demonstrated that the Professional Skills course has achieved its aims of helping students develop the knowledge, skills and the attitudes listed as objectives, feedback and evaluation leave no doubt that the students have difficulty with this course. Most students do well in achievement of knowledge and skill objectives, but achievement of attitudinal objectives remains problematic.

The Professional Skills experience has revealed that students experience some of these professional skills as 'troublesome knowledge' (Perkins, 1999). Meyer and Land (2003a, 2003b) have suggested that troublesome knowledge indicates the existence of a 'threshold,' which they describe as 'akin to a portal, opening up a new and previously inaccessible way of thinking about something.' Associated with a threshold is a central concept, the 'threshold concept.' Crossing the threshold means the threshold concept is attained and the student has 'a transformed internal view of subject matter.' Thresholds must be passed before significant new knowledge can be learned. In this paper we identify professionalism as a threshold by examining students' experience in the Professional Skills course. We present an analysis of student feedback using the Threshold Concepts framework and show that they negotiate professional knowledge in terms of troublesome knowledge. We focus attention on acquisition of attitudinal objectives and discuss strategies for helping students to deal with barriers to achieving these objectives – to cross the threshold.

BACKGROUND: THE PROFESSIONAL SKILLS COURSE AT QUEEN'S

Over six hundred first year Applied Science students participate in the Professional Skills course. The course is facilitated by a course co-ordinator (a senior Applied Science faculty member), four course leaders (faculty from various Applied

R. Land, J.H.F. Meyer & J. Smith (Eds.), Threshold Concepts within the Disciplines, 129–141.

Science disciplines) and 15 multidisciplinary teaching assistants (TAs). The TAs are trained for two days in the pedagogy and content of the course. They are given a guidebook which is the same as the student handbook but with structured lesson guides.

At the beginning of the course, students are put into groups of 20. Each group consists of three teams, each of which comprises six or seven students. These groups work together with a TA for the term.

The course format is radically different from other courses in the Applied Science common first year. It is delivered in two parts, beginning with an intensive week-long module that takes place in the week before classes begin for the term. During this week students engage in supervised activities and exercises as well as being assigned projects. During the course of the twelve week term, the groups continue work on their projects, employing a combination of self-study and TA-moderated team meetings.

During the first week six/eight groups work in 'pods' in large halls where their TAs facilitate a series of one to two hour interactive exercises. After the first week the same groups meet with their TA once a week to report on progress. Students work in three teams on an overall project with their whole group of 20. This year's project invited students to act as engineers involved in the design and implementation of a nuclear power plant, one team acting on behalf of the plant itself, one team acting on behalf of an environmentalist lobby group and one on behalf of the government and the community. However, the kind of personal development necessary for collaborative work such as this is difficult at age 17-18 (the normal entry age for Canadian students), especially when the students have developed successful survival strategies for high school exams. When many of their other classes in first year appear to be similar to their school experiences in content and pedagogy, the innovative format and non-technical aspects of the content in the Professional Skills course present an intimidating challenge to many students, to their concept of what it means to be an engineer and to how they see themselves as this 'new kind of engineer.'

COURSE OBJECTIVES

The Professional Skills course at Queen's has specific objectives designed to help students develop a number of skills that will be crucial to their success as professional engineers. Specifically, the course objectives state that students will improve their ability to:

– Manage their own learning time
– Work well in teams
– Understand their own roles as team players
– Plan projects efficiently and effectively
– Communicate effectively orally and in writing
– Access information from a variety of sources
– Demonstrate enhanced creative thinking

These objectives describe acquisition of knowledge and skills – what Mezirow (2000) would call epistemic and socio-linguistic habits of mind. The final three course objectives describe changes in attitude or world view – what Mezirow refers to as moral-ethical and philosophical habits of mind:

- Demonstrate sensitivity and inclusiveness towards diversity
- Critique, analyse, and synthesise the many issues with which engineering is concerned, including environmental, liability, and health and safety issues
- Demonstrate enhanced social responsibility

These objectives can also be described as 'emancipatory knowledge' (Habermas, 1971).

COURSE ACTIVITIES – SIMULATING A COMMUNITY

The course activities have chosen to aid students in the development of *Response-Ability* in both their professional and personal capacities. We define 'Response-Ability' as the ability to respond with an enlightened and empathetic sense of the world and of their own responsibility as human beings and as graduate engineers.

The large-scale project model of the Professional Skills course provides a simulation environment that facilitates development of a more complex world view, as students, for example, 'design a sustainable community.' This is essential for achievement of the objective 'demonstrate enhanced social responsibility.' Clearly, demonstration of such enhanced social responsibility requires not merely a semantic understanding of the social responsibility, but a deeper understanding of this concept and what it means to how they view the world. It requires a shift in students' world view. Students come to 'embody' social responsibility.

In their groups, students work on large-scale projects that force them to consider a variety of competing viewpoints. For example, one team of students will develop a pesticide plant or a nuclear power plant. The focal concern of this team will be economics. Another team of students will take on the role of environmental advocacy, researching potential harm or hazards from proposed projects, educating stakeholders about risks, and lobbying against potentially harmful projects. The third team of students will be assigned the role of human rights agency, with the mandate to protect human rights and to examine the social impact of projects such as power and chemical plants. Readings and examination of case studies are the means by which students become informed.

Each group then comprises teams that have very different viewpoints. Each team has the primary task of advancing their cause (building a plant, protecting the environment, safeguarding human rights). As a group, or miniature community, however, the teams must eventually come together to work as a unit. They must discover ways of reconciling their conflicting goals in order to succeed as a group. As they work through the problems of managing the roles of twenty group members over a busy term, they achieve the skills objectives. In reconciling the conflicting positions assigned to each team, they need to achieve the attitudinal objectives of the course.

131

THRESHOLD CONCEPTS AND TROUBLESOME KNOWLEDGE

Troublesome Knowledge

Meyer and Land (2006), building upon the work of Perkins (1999), describe a number of reasons why students have difficulty learning which they categorize as types of *troublesome knowledge*:

– Ritual knowledge
– Tacit knowledge
– Alien knowledge
– Inert knowledge
– Troublesome language
– Conceptually difficult knowledge
– Ways of thinking and practising

Meyer and Land (2006) have suggested that the negotiation of threshold concepts is likely to entail troublesome knowledge. For this study, we explicitly set out to explore if the students were coming up against troublesome knowledge. We wondered if the existence of a threshold might explain the lack of satisfaction expressed by many students.

Interviews confirmed that students experienced many of the types of troublesome knowledge that Meyer and Land discuss. In the section below, we have selected example statements that document students' experience. Categories of knowledge may be described in terms of more than one type of troublesome knowledge. However we have assigned a single category of troublesome knowledge, although certainly there are aspects of more than one type evidenced in many of the statements.

Data Collection

Data was collected in a variety of complementary ways in order to examine the learning process from as many perspectives as possible. We used the same data sources to explore troublesome knowledge.

1. In-depth interviews were conducted with a sample of volunteer participants. Ten students, eight TAs, four course co-ordinators and four first year faculty who were not involved in the Professional Skills course were interviewed. They were asked to reflect upon their experience of the course. These interviews netted fifteen hours of recorded material.
2. Course artifacts were examined: the course materials were scrutinized and the work produced by the 640 students who participated was assessed.
3. Students created and delivered their own course evaluation. During the intensive week, students learned basic principles of evaluation. They were asked to design a mechanism that would elicit the views of their peers. The evaluations they designed most commonly took the form of a short questionnaire comprising two or three questions such as 'What did you like

most about the course?', 'What did you find the hardest to learn?', and 'What would you change for next year?' Students administered the questionnaires to each other within their groups, recorded responses and submitted the notes to the TA at the end of the session. All 640 students took part.

4. Questionnaires designed by Ake Ingerman based on data collection methods 1 and 3 were administered by TAs to all students in the course. 320 completed questionnaires were returned.

5. Students from the University's Engineering Society also designed a tool for evaluation of the whole first year experience and posted it online. Responses were submitted by 101 students. These too, were analysed.

6. At the end of the project term students were asked to take part in a focus group discussion led by the TA about their experiences of learning on the course. Responses from all the evaluations were collected and collated and themes and quotations representing those themes derived. For the most part these were free-form questions and students themselves derived the themes for their responses.

7. Feedback was collected at an interactive plenary session held with all 640 students. This session was videotaped.

Data Analysis

All the above forms of data were analysed to search for the possible sources of troublesome knowledge in the categories defined by Meyer and Land (2003). We also looked for any further areas of troublesome knowledge.

Results and Discussion

A selection of the most representative voices from the interviews is presented here. We begin with those that illustrate achievement of some of the course objectives:

- 'It was different and everybody brainstormed to create solutions.'
- 'I thought the sessions were effective at providing examples of types of situation that we may face in the future. It was challenging at times, forcing us to show opinions and have input.'
- 'I felt challenged. My difficult challenge was getting up and coming to class on time. My TA really pushed my mind this week. He made me realise that engineering encompasses a lot more than I had initially anticipated.'
- 'I was definitely motivated and stimulated to think about topics with views I've never used. I like being in groups using chart paper to discuss and write out our answers. I believe that this week has made me think about issues like social and environmental.'
- 'The approach was very good. By being in a different environment, my mind was stimulated in new ways.'

- 'I liked the case studies because they get everyone involved. I especially liked the acting things because everyone has a part and it makes it more creative.'
- 'The course is far better as a week; there was more time to get to know each other.'
- 'I very much liked the concentrated week of Professional Skills group sessions. It kept us in the right frame of mind.'

Despite many positive responses relating to the course objectives, some students felt that they did not get much from the course. We do not have precise numbers, but we estimate that about 20% of students were dissatisfied. A range of the negative comments is presented here:

- 'Due to the mandatory attendance rule, I have learned what I could have learned in 1 hour in 1 week.'

- 'I did not learn much in this course. The idea behind the course is great. Teamwork and communication skills are absolutely critical to have for any job, but teaching them in one week is next to impossible. These are skills picked up in the workplace and just in life in general.'

- 'It is not effective to learn when students interact in the manner they have during the week of the course. Most students did not take the exercises seriously or did not prepare by reading the assigned work. I learned most by reading the material and answering the 'reflective' questions that I made up as I read.'

It is evident that this kind of learning is challenging for some students. Although they state that the course is boring and unnecessary, it is clear from their comments that students are not engaged or bring with them a fixed attitude that rejects attempts to change their beliefs.

Students perceive some knowledge learned in the Professional Skills course as *ritual*, in that they may accept that they need to know it but do not appreciate the complexity of the knowledge or the reasons why they need to know it. There were many examples of ritual knowledge seen in our data:

1. 'I read the engineer's code of conduct – nothing substantial.'
2. 'To be honest, I have learned things about ethics and liability, however, I don't know if I, now, have a better understanding of those concepts.'
3. 'Values?'
4. 'It's like, learn it and you'll find a use for it later on in life.'
5. 'I found that the skills that we are to learn in this programme have been gone over in high school, therefore this is more of a repeat course.'

Tacit knowledge describes understandings that are often shared within a community of practice but not often explained or exposed to novice and newcomers e.g. a person coming to a new community or country may not pick up on the nuances of different practices that are 'common sense' to old-timers. Some of the concepts learned in the Professional Skills course are inherently difficult because they involve complex relationships. Students learned the principles of the Sustainability Livelihood Approach (SLA) (Carney, 1998). There were many comments that illustrated *tacit knowledge*:

1. 'It was presented well but some of the stuff was very abstract.'
2. 'The second part of chapter 6 – the SLA principles were very abstract and weren't explained well.'
3. 'Chapter 6 – I found the SLA criteria hard to use.'
4. 'SLA – Not very straightforward'

This is an important area of knowledge development if identified by teachers in advance.

For some students, some of the course concepts constituted *alien knowledge* – knowledge that is counter-intuitive to their present understanding. For example, when the properties of objects in motion are discussed, students are often confused by the suggestion that heavier objects will fall at the same rate as lighter objects. Some of the students felt that the material in the Professional Skills course was not relevant because it did not fit their beliefs about what constitutes 'engineering.' There was hostility expressed in some reflections, indicating that first year applied science engineering students have strong opinions about what engineering means. The reflections below illustrate how reluctant students are to consider aspects of engineering that are alien to their understanding and conflict with their beliefs:

1. 'Course wasn't worthwhile because I didn't learn much about engineering and I expected to, this being an engineering course.'
2. [Responding to the question, 'Did you get a better understanding of what it's like to be an engineer?'] – 'No because none of the course was specifically related to being an engineer.'
3. 'I have yet to meet an engineer who writes journals.'
4. 'They just ask ridiculous things of us all the time'

Inert knowledge, that which is seen by the learner as unconnected or irrelevant, is an impediment to learning. Perkins (1999) gives the example of passive vocabulary, words that are understood, but not used. Inert knowledge is troublesome because students need to learn the isolated 'bits' of knowledge before they can be integrated, but it is then often difficult to persuade students to see the whole in a new integrated way. It is conceptually difficult because students have difficulty connecting it to their own world, seeing it as lacking relevance or meaning for them. Examples of inert knowledge were seen in the reflections on the Queen's Professional Skills course:

1. 'I was completely uninterested in nuclear power plants.'
2. 'New technology – didn't seem applicable.'

3. 'Irrelevant topics.'
4. 'Theory is useless and pointless if it is not applied afterwards.'
5. 'I don't think the material you try to cover really conveys meaningful information.'
6. [In answer to the question, 'Would you take a similar course?'] 'No perhaps when it is more applicable and I have practical experience to back it up.'
7. 'I just couldn't visualize it.'
8. 'So I came into this course completely blank-slated and just going into this new notation and new method of thinking was just far, like far, like it was just far-fetched, I mean for lack of a better word.'
9. 'I felt that this course could have had greater impact on me personally and potentially on the group if we had looked at more controversial issues instead of the Kingston transport plan.'

Inert knowledge remains as disconnected, irrelevant pieces until integration is unblocked.

Students may find that language itself presents hurdles. Engineering, like all disciplines, has its own discourse that represents a way of seeing. This foreign discourse can be troubling for the novice, particularly when language has a common meaning as well as a particular meaning within the professional context. An example is 'elasticity,' which in common usage means '*stretchy*,' but in the discourse of material science means 'the property of a material to return to its original size after being stretched.' *Troublesome language* is a barrier to knowledge negotiation because we have no concepts that can exist outside the system of thought and language. It is entirely possible that a concept can be understood one way in one discipline and very differently in another for this reason. For the student entering a new discipline, troublesome language is a frequently encountered barrier as illustrated by these comments:

1. 'The manual uses some fancy buzzwords but they mean nothing and the only purpose they serve is to further confuse the students who are trying to find out what the hell is going on.'
2. 'But looking back, the material was quite simple, but they portrayed it in a very difficult way.'

One of the topics covered in the Professional Skills course was engineering and the law. Students learned about legislation that governs the practice of engineering in the province of Ontario, with particular respect to health, safety and environmental regulations. The following examples show that students found this part of the course difficult because of the language involved:

3. '[want] More simplified language.'
4. 'The textbook seemed to be very choppy and a hard read.'
5. 'The court-setting activity was good but probably a lot of common knowledge to them was not common knowledge to us.'

Acquisition of some types of knowledge is blocked because the knowledge is *conceptually difficult*. Perkins (1999) points out that all fields of study include conceptually difficult knowledge but it is more frequent in mathematics and science. For engineering educators, then, conceptually difficult knowledge is of particular concern since mathematics and science are the foundations of engineering. When students attempt to negotiate conceptually difficult knowledge, they combine their own misconceptions with the new and alien scientific knowledge, creating a barrier that is difficult to penetrate.

In the Professional Skills course, there was relatively little in the way of the knowledge traditionally acknowledged as being conceptually difficult (physics, mathematics). Nonetheless, with many assigned readings that required understanding of these subjects, we did see evidence that conceptually difficult concepts exist within this course:

1. 'My understanding has not improved because I found the book and instructors hard to understand.'
2. 'Lack of a clear solution and vague problem didn't help.'

We have demonstrated above that all forms of troublesome knowledge described by Meyer and Land are present. But the threshold concept appears to be related to *ways of thinking and practising* (Wenger, 1998). Ways of thinking and practising are experienced as troublesome because they involve a shift in thinking. Frank (1998), cited by Meyer and Land (2006), describes the goal of first year Economics as teaching students to 'think like an economist.' Meyer and Land (2006) also describe research by Mears (2005) in which a history teacher explains that 'in taking ownership of the material' in a particular way, her student was 'thinking like an historian.' A further dimension of troublesome knowledge related to attitude has not been discussed specifically by either Perkins or Meyer and Land but might be broadly based within the category *ways of thinking and practising*. This is something we have noticed in student responses and that we would characterise as a *fear of uncertainty*. This is a common concern amongst our students who are very grade-oriented and who are accustomed to right/wrong answers from their maths and science in high school. One student told us his reaction to the course:

'Not enough concrete conclusions drawn at the end of exercises or sessions. This was EXTREMELY frustrating i.e. I don't care what people think about ethics. I want a hard, concrete right or wrong answer/explanation, otherwise the exercises and cases were useless. I gain/come away with learning nothing at all.'

The Professional Skills course is the first in a series of courses that prepares students to work in emerging contexts. For this reason, the teaching model encourages inquiry, providing support and resources rather than directing tasks in a prescriptive manner. This model of teaching and learning is foreign to most students coming from Ontario high schools.

Accordingly, many reflections indicated fear of the unknown as a barrier to engagement. The unknown resides in the knowledge – it is that knowledge that must be formed and applied judiciously in particular contexts. It is the opposite of the knowledge or understanding that can be categorised as the 'concrete right/ wrong' requested above. Although there was evidence of previously identified types of troublesome knowledge within these examples, we have found that the most significant obstacle for many students was their fear of being responsible for their learning. Included here is evidence that students have a narrow view of what constitutes teaching and a belief that they should be told explicitly 'what to learn.'

There was resistance to this teaching model, which encouraged students to take a deeper approach to learning. The anxiety that is expressed in the comments below shows that students fear responsibility for learning, and exhibit reluctance to participate in the activities designed to facilitate learning.

- 'We never understood what was expected.'
- 'The students were unsure of what was expected of them,'
- 'No solid answers'
- 'We did not know how we would be marked so we did not know where to begin'.
- 'I felt incredibly frustrated most of the time, not knowing what was happening or what was supposed to happen.'
- 'Confusing, frustrating… Felt like the course is testing me not teaching me.'
- 'Teaching should be better – more guidance.'
- 'You are marking us on the way we think. Who are you to judge?'
- 'Games! Not effective. Filler times. Why are we paying for games?'

We believe that experiencing real human problems in engineering is disorienting and uncomfortable for students who are anxious about how they will be assessed and want simply to know what the right answer is.

THRESHOLDS IN ENGINEERING

The work by Meyer and Land (2003a) does appear to offer a useful lens through which we can begin to identify the difficulties encountered by students in the Queen's Professional Skills course. From the data, we can identify concepts to be learned as *alien* (counter-intuitive to their own experience of the world*)*, and *inert* (irrelevant to their current needs), in many cases *ritualistic* ('we did this at high school') and against their *tacit* understanding of what engineering is ('I did engineering to avoid reading and writing'). The interdisciplinary work also brings with it *troublesome language* and even though many students are unaware of this, they find the concepts challenging to understand.

We have also identified that the threshold for this course could be described as *ways of thinking and practising* (Wenger, 1998) in engineering.

THE PATHWAYS FORWARD

If we acknowledge that there are blocks to the threshold of developing professional engineering 'attitudes,' we need to consider the ways that are open to us to help students pass through the threshold or jump over the blocks. We identified two pathways through barriers (Baillie, 2002) which might be of assistance at this point:

1. Attitude – humility, empathy, interest

It is known in many different areas of communication theory and psychotherapy that humility, empathy and interest are necessary for learning. It is not possible to gain new knowledge if you believe that you know it all already. Even if something appears to be familiar, it is an attitude of arrogance that will prevent learning anything new from the situation. Popper believes that to gain knowledge we need open-mindedness, imagination and a constant willingness to be corrected (Popper, 1989). For Kepler, it was 'freedom from pride and conceit' (Casper, 1993, p. 373).

2. Conversation – refutations, questions, avoiding avoidances

Attitude is obviously not enough, as a passive recipient can never build knowledge with another person. Feedback is imperative but it is not simply a case of repeating back the knowledge 'given' to them. We are suggesting here that learning develops through 'knowledge negotiation'.

The first of these two is often clearly ignored in our course planning. So, how do successful students navigate their way through these thresholds and how can we help them to do this? Conversation is the key. Most of the work in class involves student conversation, questioning and refutation. Through conversation with each other, with their TAs, with teams presenting opposing viewpoints, ideas are refuted, questions are posed, answers are revealed, and the difficult ideas that could be avoided alone cannot be avoided in the team. In an evaluation, one student wrote:

> I learned about thinking like an engineer. Seeing the larger picture, and how our work, as engineers, impacts society. The ethics section taught me that in the profession of engineering, sometimes safety can be compromised.

Despite our best efforts however, some students still complained that they did not have an opinion on the subject, were not interested in the topic and would prefer a more 'hands-on' project. Part of the challenge of this course is, in fact, to help students *develop* an interest in aspects of engineering that are not covered in other courses. Some students say they came to engineering to avoid these issues.

We see that the students had greater difficulty with learning objectives where their personal values and opinions suddenly became relevant. Whereas students may simply feel that talking about values is difficult, we recognize that they are blocked from learning because empathy and humility are needed to meaningfully engage with others who have different personal beliefs and values. The course structure, however, does not aid in the development of empathy and humility. The weekly meeting with their TA is not enough to 'hold' the anxiety of students when their grades are at stake.

Teamwork requires cooperation as a minimum and attitudes of team members play a significant role in ensuring the success of the team. As they work collaboratively over the week and then the term, students should generally find that their attitudes change. They need to develop greater humility within the group, greater empathy for and interest in the views of others. These changes in attitude that develop during sustained group activity could then create a pathway through the threshold. We suggest that a skilled teacher could 'hold' their anxiety. We suggest that working in smaller groups would allow the teacher or TA to be more alert to attitude, providing the safety net that would allow students to take steps, however tentatively, through the threshold.

We might consider how we can help students to develop a sense of humility and empathy. In other words, how do we help students to unlearn what they think they know in order for them to want to learn the concepts presented in the Professional Skills course? This may be the most important question to consider not only for the future of the Professional Skills course, but for the whole of the first year experience.

CONCLUSION

This paper presents an analysis of the student evaluation data to determine whether troublesome knowledge was present which might be causing the perceived threshold in the Professional Skills course in first year engineering.

We discovered that all forms of troublesome knowledge described by Meyer and Land (2003a) were present and that the Threshold Concepts framework was an extremely useful analytical tool. Furthermore, we were able to gain insight into a threshold to 'ways of thinking and practising' in the discipline of engineering which related to an anxiety to 'get the right answer.' Students of engineering enjoy the precision of maths and physics that they learned in high school and find uncertainty in real messy human problems difficult to deal with. We have offered some suggestions to address these areas of troublesome knowledge and guide students through the threshold. However, more research needs to be done to address the variation around successful ways of entering and passing through the threshold to this component of a professional attitude in engineering.

REFERENCES

Baillie, C. (2002) Negotiating scientific knowledge. In W. Lepenies (Ed.), *Entangled histories and negotiated universals: Centres and peripheries in a changing world* (pp. 32-57). Berlin: Campus Verlag.

Carney, D. (1998). *Sustainable rural livelihoods*. London: Department for International Development, HMSO.

Casper, M. (1993). *Kepler*. New York: Dover Publications.

Meyer, J. H. F. & Land, R. (2006) Threshold concepts and troublesome knowledge: An introduction. In J. H. F. Meyer & R. Land (Eds.), *Overcoming barriers to student understanding: Threshold concepts and troublesome knowledge* (pp 3-18). London and New York: Routledge.

Meyer, J. H. F. & Land, R. (2003a). Threshold concepts and troublesome knowledge (1) linkages to ways of thinking and practising within the disciplines. In C. Rust (Ed.), *Improving student learning theory and practice – 10 years on* (pp. 412-424). Oxford: OCSLD .

Meyer, J. H. F. & Land, R (2003b). Threshold concepts and troublesome knowledge (2) epistemological and ontological considerations and a conceptual framework for teaching and learning. Paper presented at the *10th Biennial Conference of EARLI*, Padova, Italy 26th-30th August 2003.

Mezirow, J. (2000) Learning to think like an adult. In J. Mezirow and Associates (Eds.), *Learning as transformation: Critical perspectives on a theory in progress.* San Francisco: Jossey-Bass.

Perkins, D. (1999). The many faces of constructivism. *Educational Leadership*, 57(3), 6-11.

Popper, K. (1989). *The logic of scientific discovery.* London: Routledge.

Singh, N. & S. Wanmali. *Sustainable livelihoods.* Concept Paper. Retrieved 1 September, 2004, from www.undp.org/sl/Documents/Strategy_ papers/Concept_paper/Concept_of_SL.htm

TALESSI – Teaching And Learning at the Environmental Science Society Interface, www.talessi.ac.uk

AFFILIATIONS

Caroline Baillie
Faculty of Applied Science
Queens University, Kingston, Ontario

Anne Johnson
Faculty of Education
Queens University, Kingston, Ontario

141

ANNA-KARIN CARSTENSEN & JONTE BERNHARD

11. THRESHOLD CONCEPTS AND KEYS TO THE PORTAL OF UNDERSTANDING

Some Examples from Electrical Engineering

INTRODUCTION

For many years research into science education has dealt with misconceptions about single concepts, even though one of the common objectives in physics is to develop an understanding of the relationships. Research into threshold concepts examines related ideas, and is thus opening up a new dimension of our understanding. In our own research we have been examining what we call 'complex concepts', i.e. concepts that make up a holistic system of 'single' interrelated concepts.

In the field of electrical circuits there has been a great deal of research on the understanding of direct current (DC) circuits among pre-university students, but hardly any research on alternating current (AC) circuits. Confusion between concepts such as current, voltage, power and energy has been reported. One possible reason that these are troublesome is that they are highly interdependent, so perhaps they cannot be learned one by one, but have to form an integrated whole.

How then does this relate to research on threshold concepts? How can we recognize threshold concepts? And how can we possibly find a way to approach teaching that facilitates thresholds being crossed?

We suggest that it is necessary to distinguish between ways to identify threshold concepts and ways to identify what needs to be addressed in order to open up learning spaces. We propose to use the term *'key' concepts* for those concepts that open up the 'portal', but not in the sense that the term is often used in some educational contexts, as interchangeable with 'core' concepts, and meaning simply that the concepts are an important part of the prescribed syllabus. Here we use the term as a more precise metaphor to mean that the concept in question acts like a key to *open up* the 'portal' of understanding. We try to explore how a threshold concept may be identified. By studying video recordings of lab-work we have been able to propose a way to identify troublesome aspects of any given concept. We describe how variation theory can be used to open up new dimensions in the learning space, thus finding 'keys' to open up the portal. We have then been able, again by video recordings, to evaluate the new learning sequence.

R. Land, J.H.F. Meyer & J. Smith (Eds.), Threshold Concepts within the Disciplines, 143–154.

RESEARCH REVIEW

A Pilot Study on Bode Plots

A troublesome concept, according to teachers who teach electrical circuits and control theory, is frequency response. This can be explored through interviews with teachers and it will generally be agreed that this is a threshold concept. The subject is explained in most textbooks on electric circuits and control theory. In control theory there are two tools that are used to illustrate frequency response: Bode Plots and Nyquist diagrams. Carstensen and Bernhard (2002) suggest that the Bode plot is a 'key' concept (in the specialist sense in which we have indicated above), but the Nyquist diagram is not. Although both are tools that can be used by an engineer, they are not both good tools for learning. Our pilot study (ibid.) shows that a change in the way that Bode Plots are explained not only facilitates students' learning the plots, but also results in them gaining higher scores on a test following the course. The students even get higher scores on tasks that have not been taught; this suggests that teaching a 'key' concept, according to our definition, does not just open up that particular concept, but also the learning of other concepts related to it. This pilot study suggests that further research needs to be carried out in order to investigate what the characteristics of a concept are when it acts in this way like a key. We also suggest that such 'key' concepts deal with more than one semiotic register, as suggested by Tiberghien (2000): 'A hypothesis on learning is that an individual's understanding of a concept (or, more generally, an idea) develops when relations are established between different semiotic registers associated with that idea.'

The concept of Bode Plots is also one where some students are reluctant to make an effort, partly because they know it will be difficult, and will take a lot of time. This hesitation is referred to in the field of threshold concepts as 'troublesome knowledge' (Perkins, 1999). In the pilot study this was explored by making completion of the first Bode Plot compulsory. The plot had to be brought as a 'ticket' to the lecture on frequency response; this is a very unconventional way to make university students 'do the homework'. It resulted in all students completing the task.

The pilot study suggests that to make learning possible it is necessary to incorporate arrangements that make the students engage in the learning activity, in addition to opening up learning spaces. It is not enough to change only the students' engagement, or to develop teaching sequences informed by research; *one must do both.*

Research on the Conceptual Understanding of Electrical Circuits

Most of the research on students' understanding of electric circuits has focused on the domain of pre-university learners' understanding of DC circuits. According to this body of research (see, for example, Bernhard & Carstensen, 2002; Cohen, Eylon, & Ganiel, 1983; Duit & von Rhöneck, 1997; Shipstone *et al.*, 1988;

Stocklmayer & Treagust, 1996) students tend to confuse concepts such as voltage, current, power and energy. This means that students do not clearly distinguish between these concepts and, typically, confusion follows from not relating them properly to each other, for example:

Current consumption;
Battery as constant *current* supply;
No current – no voltage;
Voltage is a part or a property of current.

Research has also shown that it is very difficult for students to perceive a circuit as a whole system and to understand that local changes in a circuit result in global changes, affecting all voltages and currents. One can observe both:

- *Local reasoning*. Students focus their attention upon a single point in the circuit. A change in the circuit is thought of as only affecting the current and/or voltages in the node or mesh where the change is made.
- *Sequential reasoning*. If something is changed in the circuit the student thinks that this only affects current and/or voltages in elements located after the place where the change was made, not before it.

This has been further investigated by Margarita Holmberg (González Sampayo, 2006), as part of her thesis. She used a questionnaire to investigate engineering students' understanding of some concepts in electrical circuit theory. The work looked at students in three different countries. Her results are similar to those from earlier studies of pre-university students. She found inconsistencies in student reasoning, typically occurring in cases of extreme values (zero or infinite) of voltage, current or resistance.

We argue that the reason behind these results is that students see concepts as isolated 'items' and not as being inter-related.

Linking the Laplace Transform to the Real World

Tiberghien and co-workers (e.g. Tiberghien, 2000; Vince & Tiberghien, 2002) categorize knowledge into two domains: the object/event world and the theory/model world. This dichotomy has proved very effective when analysing and developing lab-instructions. She points out that it is important in education to make explicit the links between the theory/model world and the object/event world (Figure 1).

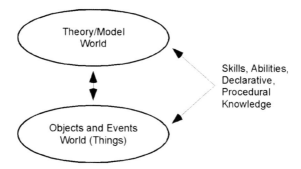

Figure 1. Categorization of knowledge based on a modeling activity (Vince & Tiberghien, 2002, p. 53)

The links that students at university level are supposed to make between the theory/model world and the object/event world are most often links between mathematical models and measurement data, or graphs stemming from mathematical calculations and graphs derived from measurements. Earlier research has shown that these links are not formed spontaneously (Ryegård, 2004; Tiberghien, Veillard, Buty, & Le Maréchal, 1998). In the research by Tiberghien, like our earlier research (see for example Bernhard, Carstensen, & González Sampayo, 2005), it is apparent that students do not even use textbooks or their lecture notes during lab-work. It is, therefore, important to clarify the nature of these links, both in terms of the concepts/relationships in which they are incorporated and the concepts they link. In engineering education the concepts taught are mostly complex, and some links transcend one world while others belong within a single world. In order to map and elucidate these links, and enable them to be highlighted in the lab-instructions, an extended model showing all of the links, and whether they belong to one of the worlds or connect them is required.

We assume that *knowledge is holistic*, but that pieces of knowledge are taught in different sessions, and that if interactions between different parts of the learning objectives are encouraged during lab-sessions (or what we would rather call integrated problem-solving and lab-sessions), relationships between the theory/model world and the object/event world will evolve. The resultant knowledge that the students acquire will be more than the sum of the parts.

We therefore suggest a new model: that of a complex concept (see Figure 2). This builds on Tiberghien's model. The different concepts taught are illustrated by 'islands' of different sizes according to the content of knowledge they represent. The arrows show the links between different concepts. To analyse the links is to find the arrows, to determine which 'islands' the arrows should be drawn between and in what directions the arrows should point. The model may be used for analysis of the intended links, or the links actually made by students, depending on whether the research concerns analysis of 'the intended object of learning' or 'the lived object of learning' (Runesson & Marton, 2002).

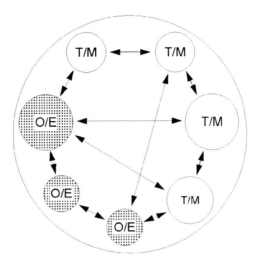

Figure 2. Our suggested new model – Model of learning a complex concept.[1]

The idea behind our model is that knowledge is built both by learning the pieces, i.e. the islands, and by learning the whole, i.e. making explicit links through simultaneous work upon the issues associated with several objects. Some links follow the whole cycle, while others jump across it, thus skipping sequential links. We believe that the links may become established through interaction between different pieces of knowledge as a result of interaction between the theory/model world and the object/event world. The more links that are made, the more complete the knowledge becomes.

In our studies we have found that it is important to determine which links result in the assimilation of more knowledge, and which links appear to be more accessible to students. Some of the links take the form of constructing graphs. To the experts, graphical representations are a single tool, but to novices they are experienced differently depending on whether they are derived from mathematical expressions or from data collection and measurement.

Our method for identifying the troublesome elements was to consider the questions raised during lab-work. This method provides a different insight into what really is troublesome from the commonly used recall interviews. The latter can only highlight what is remembered afterwards; this might not be the same as the real problems encountered. We suggest that this is particularly likely, since those aspects assumed by teachers to be problematic tend to be highlighted during such interviews.

During the analysis of the lab-work, the model of learning a complex concept emerged. The transitions from the real circuit to the differential equation, and on to the Laplace transform, through the inverse transform to the calculated graph, can

147

be considered 'obvious' or 'self-evident', but we have never seen anyone describing 'the object of learning' in such a way before. Therefore we conclude that the circular paradigm is not self-evident, but is perceived in that way because the links between the 'islands' are taken for granted, and are therefore not made explicit during teaching. Teaching often follows the circle as a 'logical order'. Presenting the sub-concepts, but progressing only around the circle will make it difficult to make links between the theory/model world and the object/event world since the routes between the worlds then have to go through two steps (one between the real circuit and the differential equation and the other between the graphs). To make more links across the circle, especially crossing from the theory/model world to the object/event world would open up a more thorough understanding. As an example, the link from the Laplace transform to the calculated graph can be simulated using computers.

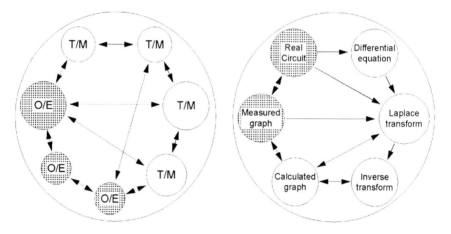

Figure 3. Our model – Model of learning a complex concept – and the model translated into the example of the Transient Lab

The links can be examined by asking two questions: 1) what links do teachers want the students to make, i.e. how can we find a way to teach a specific link (i.e. foster an understanding of the connections between certain concepts)? and 2) what links do students actually make during the lab, i.e. what are they doing or talking about?

An example of how the links can be explored through the students' conversations focuses on Tess and Benny. Tess has been doing all the calculations, and Benny has worked on the simulations. After about 40 minutes they are supposed to wire up the circuit, and they read:

Tess: (Reads from instruction) "Wire up the circuit".
        (Turns her head towards B)

It seems taken for granted what circuit he's talking about.
Benny: Yeah, we'd better read this again.

The gap in understanding may be illustrated by the circle which shows the relationships that the students were intended to learn.

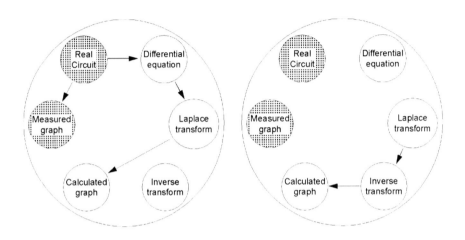

Figure 4. a) Benny's 'lived object of learning' in this first part of the lab session b) Tess' 'lived object of learning' in this first part of the lab session.

In this part of the session, Tess and Benny encountered different 'objects of learning'. At this point, neither of them is thinking about the real circuit, because in order to do so they have to make links back: Benny from the graph and Tess from the mathematics.

The circular model was used to identify the difficulties that the students had when the course was presented in 2002; it was then used to identify which links required extra emphasis. In 2002, learners did not make links between the Laplace transform and the calculated graph. This link would symbolize the direct relationship between the frequency domain and the time domain, an aspect of knowledge that is intended. This link could be made explicit via simulations of the step response using Simulink, where the transfer functions in the Laplace domain can be entered and the result in the time domain can be graphed. Thus it is possible to make the link between the two concepts explicit. In addition, the simulated examples were not just randomly chosen from a textbook, but systematically varied according to the theory of variation (see, for example, Marton & Tsui, 2004; Runesson & Marton, 2002).

To improve the learning outcomes, we manipulated the environment and the learning space: problem-solving and lab sessions were integrated rather than delivered separately, and the learning space was opened through variation.

IMPLICATIONS FOR RESEARCH ON THRESHOLD CONCEPTS AND CONCEPTS ACTING AS 'KEYS'

During the conference on 'Threshold Concepts within the Disciplines' (Glasgow, August 2006), different methods for recognizing threshold concepts where discussed. These included phenomenographic research, teacher and student interviews, analysis of textbooks, and analysis of a concept directly based on the categories that define a threshold concept. Meyer, Land and Davies (2006) focused on appropriate analytical frameworks, and suggested four 'modes of variation': 'sub-liminal', 'pre-liminal', 'liminal' and 'post-liminal variation'. They suggested that these analytical procedures required as inputs either qualitative or quantitative data that are 'procedure compliant.' (See also Chapter 5, this volume.)

One question then is whether results from different data collection methods can be compliant, i.e. if different data sets can be examined using a single suite of analytical tools, categories and theoretical frameworks. Thus, the question arises, should different data sets be analysed by using different tools? If so, are the results directly comparable or complementary?

Below we discuss some of the problems associated with different data collection methods. This is not intended to be a thorough description, but it should serve as an introduction to a discussion on what different methods can contribute.

Some Reported Problems with Interviews as the Data Collection Method

In many papers on threshold concepts (Meyer & Land, 2006) it is suggested that teachers should be interviewed in order to identify troublesome knowledge, and that research into students' understanding should be undertaken in order to find out how they have learned about or experienced the threshold concept. One benefit is that it makes teachers engage in learning in a new way. But, as stated by Davies (2003), this also becomes problematic since teachers may either mention the 'fundamental building blocks' or the things that are already included in their course, and thus confuse what is fundamental to the discipline and what is fundamental to learning. We have identified two additional problems: 1) Teachers often seem to take threshold concepts for granted, and thus they may never be mentioned during such interviews, and 2) they perceive a whole conglomerate of disparate concepts to be troublesome, instead of seeing a single integrated concept as the threshold concept.

When interviewing students there are problems associated with asking the students directly what they consider 'troublesome'. Several reports show that the students' own descriptions of what is difficult do not always agree with those provided by an expert. This is especially so when interviews are conducted with students who are still novices It has been shown that students may not consider something they have yet to understand as being difficult.

What Happens When a Research Method Is Used beyond Its Scope?

Research results can be regarded as models of the real world. No research can describe the whole picture. If one could represent the world as it is, in all its aspects, the result could only be the world itself. Therefore all research aims to find a model that describes a particular aspect of the world. Seen as such, different methods and different theoretical or analytical frameworks open up different dimensions of the world. When one tries to use a model outside its limitations, or a research method beyond its scope, it is likely to fail. One mistake, for example, is to say that phenomenography cannot be used to identify threshold concepts, because concepts are social constructions and phenomenography examines the differences between students' experiences of the real world. To accept that disciplinary knowledge is a social construct implies that it is not constant and has not been defined absolutely. Davies (2003) claims that in phenomenographic studies on 'price and cost', disputes and ambiguities were not identified, nor was the extent of what is currently considered valid knowledge. However, if specialists are interviewed in phenomenographic studies, they may reveal both ambiguities, and the extent of what experts in the field today consider relevant knowledge. Such a study would be an interesting one to carry out in the context of the domain of research. In one such study on the understanding of the 'mole' concept in chemistry, Strömdahl (1996) found a number of differences in conceptions among experts and researchers in chemistry.

Is It Possible to Extend the Scope of a Research Method?

What phenomenography has been successful in doing is to compare teachers' perceptions of 'the learning object', and the students' understanding and experience. 'Learning studies' (Lo, Marton, Pang, & Pong, 2004) is an emerging field of research. Using this approach, teachers and researchers together use the results of phenomenographic studies or teacher experience to design new learning sessions, and evaluate the intended and the enacted 'objects of learning'. One outstanding example has been reported by Wernberg and Holmqvist (2004). It is well known by teachers that learning to tell the time on an analogue clock presents a number of difficulties. There has been no consensus about the best approach. In a 'learning study', however, one teacher suggested that the critical aspect was that the hour hand was all that was needed to tell the time. It was suggested that the minute hand should not be introduced until all learners understood how to read the time using only the former. Once this has been achieved, the minute hand could be introduced as a refinement, giving a more precise measurement of time.

Our research in the field of electric circuit theory and control theory aims to improve education in the same way, by conducting a learning study. We, however, have chosen not to undertake a phenomenographic study. We tried to identify troublesome concepts by means of video recordings, rather than interviews with students. The reason for not undertaking phenomenography is that the data from video recordings of classroom sessions is very rich, (a great deal of data to analyse, as well as long sequences where 'nothing' happens) and thus it is difficult to discern phenomenographic categories (cf. Marton & Säljö, 1997). However, after using our tool to analyse the relationships that students were identifying during the lab-work, it became clear that it was possible to identify phenomenographic categories, but that this was not necessary. The videoed data did not lend itself to phenomenographic studies unless another tool was applied to reduce the amount of data. In contrast, the learning study could be carried out in three steps:

1. Analysis of learning in labs before changes, by means of the model described above;
2. Changing what is possible to learn by using the theory of variation;
3. Analysis of the learning in the new labs.

CONCLUSIONS

The purpose of developing new analytical tools, new models and new concepts in research is to try to describe something better than was previously possible. In our research we have found 'the model of a complex concept', (see figures 2–4) an essential tool for analysing the relationships that are intended and enacted in lab- and problem-solving sessions. Other ways to perform learning studies have also been discussed. Meyer, Land and Davies (Chapter 5, this volume) offer a way to analyse the process of learning or the process of coming to terms with thresholds.

Interviewing teachers is a good way to identify troublesome concepts, such as object orientation in computer science, or learning to tell the time, but video recordings of teaching sessions can help to clarify which constituents of the concept make it difficult to learn. As suggested above, the pilot study on Bode Plots and the study on transient response not only revealed the concepts involved, but also identified the essential relationships between concepts. In addition, it was possible to explore and modify the ways students engaged in their studies. Two important aspects are highlighted by Davies (2006, p. 74): a threshold concept is likely to be troublesome because 'it not only operates at a deep integrating way in the subject, but is also taken for granted by practitioners in a subject and therefore rarely made explicit'. Both of these are revealed through video recordings: the interrelatedness, through the analytical tool used, and the 'taken-for-granted-ness' through the analysis of questions asked in the classroom and the ways that the teacher answers.

Since many concepts being taught are ambiguously defined, and are negotiated as social constructions, Davies (2003) suggests that threshold concepts could be explored 'through a comparison of the reasoning employed by economists and sociologists and through a review of student's thinking about' the threshold concepts. This could, of course, complement what can be discovered by phenomenographic research, where teachers and other experts are interviewed.

Research into 'threshold concepts' thus seems to include three fundamentally different modes of investigation: How do we recognize a threshold concept? In what ways is it difficult and troublesome? And how do we find the critical aspects, i.e. the 'key' characteristic of the concept that will open up the portal?

A key is not the foundation that a building is constructed upon; it is what you use to open the door. 'Core concepts' are the building blocks, fundamental for building a discourse or syllabus, and the 'key' concepts, in our sense, make it possible to enter the building.

NOTES

[1] The shaded circles are analytically attributed to the object/event world and the unshaded circles represent the theory/model world.

REFERENCES

Bernhard, J., & Carstensen, A.-K. (2002). Learning and teaching electrical circuit theory. Paper presented at the PTEE 2002: Physics Teaching in Engineering Education, Leuven.

Bernhard, J., Carstensen, A.-K., & González Sampayo, M. (2005). Connecting the theory/model world to the real/event world — The example integrated lab- and problemsolving sessions in electric circuit theory. Paper presented at the ESERA conference 2005, Barcelona.

Carstensen, A.-K., & Bernhard, J. (2002). Bode Plots not only a tool of engineers, but also a key to facilitate students learning in electrical and control engineering. Paper presented at the PTEE 2002: Physics Teaching in Engineering Education, Leuven.

Cohen, R. A., Eylon, B., & Ganiel, U. (1983). Potential difference and current in simple electric circuits: A study of students' concepts. *American Journal of Physics, 51*, 407-412.

Davies, P. (2003). Threshold concepts: How can we recognise them? Paper presented at the EARLI 2003, Padua.

Davies, P. (2006). Threshold concepts: How can we recognise them? In J. H. F. Meyer & R. Land (Eds.), *Overcoming barriers to student understanding: Threshold concepts and troublesome knowledge* (pp. 70-84). London: Routledge.

Duit, R. & von Rhöneck, C. (1997). Learning and understanding 'key' concepts of electricity. In A. Tiberghien & E. L. Jossem, & J. Borojas (Eds.), *Connecting research in physics education with teacher education.* ICPE.

González Sampayo, M. (2006). Engineering problem solving: The case of the Laplace transform as a difficulty in learning electric circuits and as a tool to solve real world problems. Linköping: Linköping Studies in Science and Technology Dissertation No. 1038.

Lo, M. L., Marton, F., Pang, M. F., & Pong, W. Y. (2004). Toward a pedagogy of learning. In F. Marton & A. B. M. Tsui (Eds.), *Classroom discourse and the space of learning* (pp. 189-225). Mahwah: Lawrence Erlbaum.

Marton, F., & Säljö, R. (1997). Approaches to learning. In F. Marton, D. J. Hounsell, & N. Entwistle (Eds.), *The experience of learning: Implications for teaching and learning in higher education* (2nd edition). Edinburgh: Scottish Academic Press.

Marton, F. & Tsui, A. B. M. (Eds.). (2004). *Classroom discourse and the space of learning.* Mahwaw: Lawrence Erlbaum.

Meyer, J. H. F. & Land, R. (2006). *Overcoming barriers to student understanding: Threshold concepts and troublesome knowledge.* London: Routledge.

Meyer, J.H.F., Land, R., & Davies, P. (2006). Threshold concepts and troublesome knowledge (4): issues of variation and variability. Paper presented at the 'Threshold Concepts within the Disciplines' Symposium, University of Strathclyde, Glasgow, 30th Aug.-1st Sept.

Perkins, D. (1999). The many faces of constructivism. *Educational Leadership, 57*(3), 6-11.

Runesson, U., & Marton, F. (2002). The object of learning and the space variation. In F. Marton & P. Morris (Eds.), *What matters? Discovering critical conditions of classroom learning* (pp. 19-38). Göteborg: Acta Universitatis Gothoburgensis.

Ryegård, Å. (2004). Interaktion mellan teoretiskt och praktiskt lärande – En studie i Elektronikundervisning på högskolenivå (Lic Thesis no 37. In Swedish). Västerås: Mälardalen University.

Shipstone, D. M., von Rhöneck, C., Jung, W., Kärrqvist, C., Dupin, J., Johsua, J., & Licht, P. (1988). A study of students' understanding of electricity in five European countries. *International Journal of Science Education, 10,* 303-316.

Stocklmayer, S. M. & Treagust, D. F. (1996). Images of electricity: How do novices and experts model electric current? *International Journal of Science Education, 18,* 163-178.

Strömdahl, H. (1996). On mole and amount of substance (Göteborg Studies in Educational Sciences 106). Göteborg: Acta Universitatis Gothoburgensis.

Tiberghien, A. (2000). Designing teaching situations in the secondary school. In R. Millar, J. Leach, & J. Osborne (Eds.), *Improving science education: The contribution of research.* Buckingham: Open University Press.

Tiberghien, A., Veillard, L., Buty, C., & Le Maréchal, J.-F. (1998). Analysis of labwork sheets used at the upper secondary school and the first years of university. Working Paper 3, Labwork in Science Education Project. Lyon: Université Lyon 2.

Vince, J., & Tiberghien, A. (2002). Modelling in teaching and learning elementary physics. In P. Brna (Ed.), *The role of communication in learning to model* (pp. 49-68). Mahwah: Lawrence Erlbaum.

Wernberg, A., & Holmqvist, M. (2004). What time is it? Learning study as a method to develop education. Paper presented at the Nordic Educational Research Association 32nd Congress, Reykjavik.

AFFILIATIONS

Anna-Karin Carstensen
School of Engineering, Jönköping University,
National Graduate School in Science and Technology Education and Engineering Education Research Group, Linköping University

Jonte Bernhard
National Graduate School in Science and Technology Education and Engineering Education Research Group, Linköping University

MARTIN P. SHANAHAN, GIGI FOSTER & JAN H.F. MEYER

12. ASSOCIATIONS AMONG PRIOR ACQUISITION OF THRESHOLD CONCEPTS, LEARNING DIMENSIONS, AND EXAMINATION PERFORMANCE IN FIRST-YEAR ECONOMICS

INTRODUCTION

Threshold concepts provide a lens through which to focus on critical, previously neglected aspects of variation in student learning and discipline-specific ways of transformative thinking. Meyer and Land (2006) have posited a conceptual framework for theorising and formalising the *epistemological status* of threshold concepts, as well as the *modes of variation* that may characterise the acquisition of such concepts (Meyer, Land, & Davies, 2008).

Identifying threshold concepts in a discipline, however, is not easy (Davies, 2006). 'Key concepts' as found in a discipline's first-year textbook chapters are not necessarily threshold concepts. In theory, threshold concepts should be transformative, irreversible, integrative, bounded and potentially troublesome (Meyer & Land, 2003). It is unlikely, however, that any single concept will possess all of these characteristics in equal measure – or that a single concept will have the same transformative, irreversible, integrative, bounded and troublesome effect for every individual learner. A seminal paper by Davies and Mangan (2007) advances this debate by questioning whether 'crossing the threshold' of just one concept is a process sufficiently nuanced to identify the variation in learning that occurs in economics (and perhaps in other disciplines).

Within economics, Davies and Mangan (2007) have proposed that transformative learning could be better described by acquisition of a *web* of threshold concepts organized into three categories. The first category of threshold conceptual acquisition is *personal conceptual change*, where a 'naïve or "common-sense" understanding [is] supplanted by a more powerful discipline-based mode of thinking which is associated with specialist language' (p. xxx). This category represents the transformation of everyday experiences via the integration of personal experience with ideas from the discipline. The second category is *discipline-based conceptual change*, which 'integrates and reworks other disciplinary ideas that the learner has previously acquired' (p. xxx). This category represents a transformation that occurs via the acquisition of the discipline's theoretical perspective. Third, Davies and Mangan identify *procedural conceptual change* which '[is] associated with ways of practicing the subject: the discipline specific procedures that are used in the construction of narratives and arguments'

R. Land, J.H.F. Meyer & J. Smith (Eds.), Threshold Concepts within the Disciplines, 155–172.

(p. xxx). There is a necessary and mutual interdependence between personal, discipline and procedural threshold concepts in economics, *all* of which must be acquired in order for the student to gain full mastery of the discipline.

This chapter examines a number of candidate threshold concepts, along with two other explanatory sources of variation, gathered during a first-year microeconomics course at the University of South Australia. Multiple choice and examination questions are grouped to reflect the three categories proposed by Davies and Mangan. We then analyse the relationships among responses in each category and other estimates of students' conceptual thinking – in particular, their approaches to learning. We also examine relationships between levels of and/or growth in conceptual understanding and student success on the final examination.

INSTITUTIONAL CONTEXT, DATA, AND METHODOLOGY

Within the Division of Business at the University of South Australia, all students undertake a core of business-related courses in their first year. A standard single semester microeconomics course, based around an Australian adaptation of the introductory American textbook by McConnell, is one of eight courses taught to fulltime first-year students.

The course introduces a number of core concepts and, with these, threshold concepts within the web of concepts proposed by Davies and Mangan (2007) – for example, 'economic modelling,' 'incentives,' 'opportunity cost,' 'the margin,' 'interaction between markets,' and 'welfare and efficiency.'

One aspect of the course also aims to raise students' meta-learning capacity. Two components of the assessment (in weeks 3 and 13) require students to complete an online discipline-specific version of the Reflections on Learning Inventory (RoLI) (see Meyer and Shanahan (2004) and Meyer (2004)). Students also respond to a series of 40 multiple choice questions designed to test their knowledge of economic principles. And finally, at the end of the semester (week 16) students sit a three-hour written examination. The examination is in three equally weighted parts: a multiple choice section (Section A) constructed to test basic concepts and fundamental retention, a short answer section (Section B) which assesses ability to apply economic principles, and a longer answer section (Section C) designed to reveal deeper levels of understanding.

Each of the 40 multiple choice questions was designed to reveal one of 27 basic conceptual elements considered relevant to an initial understanding of economics. The questions were a combination of questions purpose-written for this exercise (some based on materials from the Embedding Threshold Concepts project at Staffordshire University), and questions taken from the United States-based Test of Economic Literacy. The conceptual elements were then also partitioned into the three categories of conceptual thresholds proposed by Davies and Mangan (Appendix 1).

Multiple choice questions have considerable appeal in detecting variation in students' prior acquisition of conceptual elements, and by inference, threshold concepts. They can be used to examine a variety of levels of understanding, including four of Bloom's (1956) six levels of educational achievement in the cognitive domain. Buckles and Siegfried (2006) furthermore argue (p.51) that '[i]t is not necessary for students to know the specific vocabulary of economics to understand and use fundamental economic concepts correctly. Although we expect students who possess an in-depth understanding to recognize different circumstances in which 'opportunity cost' or comparative advantage can be usefully applied, they do not need to know those terms, but it is likely that they will.' Multiple choice questions may thus capture important variation in students' understanding of threshold concepts while minimizing problems caused by the use of technical language.

In summary, the final data set used in the study reported here includes, for each student: responses to 40 multiple-choice questions at the start and the end of the course, mapped onto 27 conceptual elements, and into three conceptual categories; responses to the 21 learning dimensions embedded in the RoLI (at the start and end of the course) and, finally, raw marks on each of the three sections of the final examination. Estimates of threshold conceptual acquisition and growth in aspects of learning are obtained by taking student-specific differences in the relevant measures across the semester. Gender and age are also included in two regression models predicting final examination performance.

The aim is to explore whether the web of threshold concepts proposed by Davies and Mangan (2007) can be 'made visible' by quantitative analytical means. The research questions are thus: To what extent are students' understandings of the Davies and Mangan categories of threshold concepts, as revealed through their multiple choice responses from week three, correlated with final examination marks in week 16? To what extent are RoLI responses regarding learning dimensions from week three correlated with final examination marks in week 16? Within these two questions, correlations with the three parts of the examination are separately considered. To what extent is threshold concept *acquisition* in each of the three Davies and Mangan categories, calculated as the difference in a student's scores on multiple choice questions between weeks three and 13, correlated with RoLI dimensions at the start of the course? How does threshold concept acquisition relate to changes in RoLI responses over the same period, and to examination performance? In short, we are attempting, using data produced by a repertoire of existing course assessment instrumentation, to identify some of the possible linkages between threshold concepts, learning processes and student outcomes.

FINDINGS

We first examine the statistical association between responses to the initial 40 multiple questions (representing 27 basic conceptual elements) and students' performance on the three parts of the final exam. We aggregate the multiple choice questions into discrete conceptual elements and also separately consider responses to the three parts of the examination.

Table 1 presents some of the more interesting statistical associations. Counter to the focus on 'opportunity cost' in prior research (Shanahan and Meyer, 2006) it is clear that responses to the multiple choice questions on 'opportunity cost' are only significantly associated with Part A of the examination. Responses designed to reveal students' facility with the concept of 'supply and demand' and their appreciation of the 'interrelationship of markets' were significantly associated with all three parts of the final examination. While these raw correlations could be driven by the same (unmeasured) underlying differences between students, they nonetheless support the basic position that a focus on just one threshold concept may be limiting. Table 1 does suggest that successful students may have previously acquired a *range* of conceptual elements at the start of the course, rather than just one or two. Note here that at this stage the multiple choice questions are aggregated into *conventional concepts* and do not reflect the Davies and Mangan (2007) categories. While this is supportive of the case for examining students' understanding of multiple threshold concepts, this evidence is also circumstantial and indirect.

Table 1. *Initial responses to selected multiple choice questions identifying conceptual elements, and their correlation with end-of-semester examination results*

Conceptual element underlying the multiple choice question(s)*	Exam Part A	Exam Part B	Exam Part C
Price and cost (2, 32)	0.184* (503)	0.149 (502)	0.211* (502)
Zero sum game (3, 6)	0.228* (501)	0.183 (500)	0.191 (500)
Opportunity cost (4, 8, 35)	0.227* (495)	0.108 (494)	0.134 (494)
Trade offs (5)	0.240* (503)	0.101 (502)	0.160 (502)
Elasticity (7)	0.215* (504)	0.157 (503)	0.153 (503)
Incentives (12, 15)	0.229* (501)	0.116 (500)	0.141 (500)
Gains from trade (13)	0.222* (504)	0.152 (503)	0.214* (503)
Inter-related markets (16)	0.213* (504)	0.208* (503)	0.192* (503)
Supply and demand (17, 19, 39)	0.289* (503)	0.184* (502)	0.252* (502)
Marginal analysis (18, 38)	0.268* (500)	0.159* (499)	0.138 (499)
Competition (20)	0.274* (503)	0.136 (502)	0.164 (502)
Cost-benefit analysis (22)	0.229* (501)	0.134 (500)	0.118 (500)
Public good (23)	0.235* (501)	0.137 (500)	0.187* (500)
Externality (28)	0.190* (501)	0.163 (500)	0.231* (500)
Comparative advantage (36)	0.225* (499)	0.141 (498)	0.119 (498)
Living standards (40)	**0.182** (502)**	**0.129 (501)**	0.152 (501)

* A numbered subset of the 27 conceptual elements; see Appendix 1 for the complete listing of elements.
** Denotes significance at the one percent level.
Sample sizes provided in parentheses in columns 2-4.

We next aggregate the multiple choice questions into the Davies and Mangan (2007) categories to determine whether aggregation into a *web* of threshold concepts yields greater explanatory power, and examine the variation within the categories. Figures 1, 2 and 3 exhibit the distribution of overall student scores in the three categories: personal, discipline and procedural. (Scores are constructed to map onto a 0-1 interval.) These figures illustrate that, notwithstanding the substantial aggregation, there is considerable variation across students. This is useful, as it suggests that variation in students' prior acquisition of threshold conceptual *categories* could well be associated with examination performance more robustly than the prior acquisition of single conceptual elements.

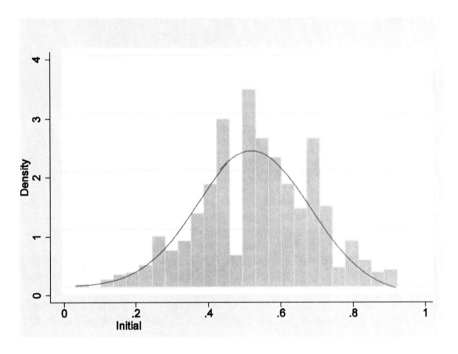

Figure 1. Histogram of the distribution of initial understanding of personal threshold concepts

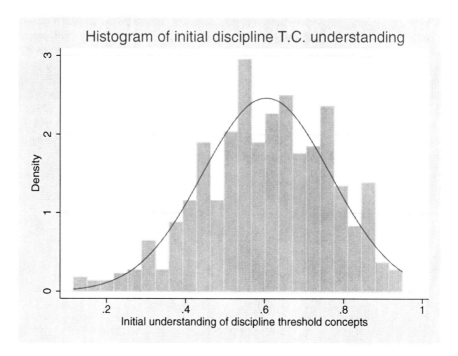

Figure 2. Histogram of the distribution of initial discipline threshold concept understanding

Table 2 presents basic summary statistics on the constructed variables that represent students' initial scores on the three categories of threshold concepts and the change across the semester in these scores. Also included in the table are initial scores on each of the RoLI dimensions, and final examination scores.

The degree of variation reflected in Table 2 is noteworthy; the standard deviation is 25 percent or more of the mean for most of the variables. On average, students do acquire threshold concepts during the course, but the variation in acquisition is relatively large. There is also a relatively high degree of variation in examination marks, and the average mark is just under a pass (a 'pre-moderated' 45 marks out of a possible 100).

Table 3 displays correlations of final examination marks with start-of-semester measures for both threshold concept categories and RoLI dimensions. The pair-wise correlations in Table 3 are calculated using all non-missing observations on the particular pair of variables under consideration. Robustness checks confirm that the choice of sample does not affect the basic pattern of correlations. The sample is, however, limited to students with complete records when regression specifications are estimated later.

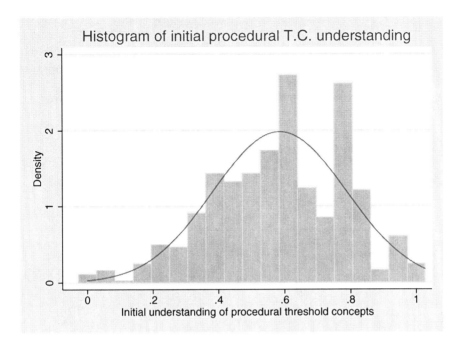

Figure 3. Histogram of distribution of the initial procedural threshold concept understanding

What do we make of these data? It is clear that a student's prior acquisition of threshold concepts is significantly related to that student's examination performance. This is true for all three categories of concepts – personal, discipline, and procedural – and for all parts of the examination, though the strongest correlations with examination results are seen for discipline and procedural concepts. A number of RoLI dimensions are also significantly correlated with final examination performance, though not as strongly, and the overall pattern suggests that those students who score highly on less desirable learning dimensions (such as 'fragmentation') are likely to do worse on the examination, but that the examination performance of students who score better on learning dimensions associated with positive outcomes (such as 'knowing about learning') cannot be predicted as accurately. This observation is consistent with one of the original design intentions of the RoLI; to detect students 'at risk' of failing.

Table 2. Basic summary statistics

Variable	N	Mean	Standard Deviation	Minimum	Maximum
Personal Threshold Concepts (start of semester)	647	0.519	0.163	0	0.917
Discipline Threshold Concepts (start of semester)	623	0.604	0.162	0.115	0.949
Procedural Threshold Concepts (start of semester)	654	0.585	0.201	0	1
Personal Threshold Concepts (change during semester)	458	0.018	0.172	-0.563	0.521
Discipline Threshold Concepts (change during semester)	442	0.018	0.156	-0.538	0.500
Procedural Threshold Concepts (change during semester)	469	0.027	0.207	-0.611	0.778
Learning is fact-based	678	10.87	3.97	0	20
Knowledge objects	678	13.04	3.81	1	20
Memorising as rehearsal	678	10.67	4.09	0	20
Seeing things differently	678	16.30	2.44	7	20
Memorising before understanding	678	9.38	4.71	0	20
Relating ideas	678	14.84	2.81	5	20
Knowledge discrete and factual	678	8.76	3.50	0	20
Memorise after understanding	678	14.47	3.35	1	20
Detail related process	678	8.70	3.49	0	19
Rereading a text	678	13.94	2.62	1	20
Duty as motivation	678	8.03	3.96	0	19
Memorise with understanding	678	13.82	2.73	0	20
Fragmentation	678	7.02	3.42	0	17
Repetition aids understanding	678	13.26	3.95	0	20
Learning by example	678	9.18	4.07	0	20
Knowing about learning	678	16.50	2.22	9	20
Economic misconceptions	678	7.33	3.58	0	19
Economic reasoning	678	12.43	3.05	3	20
Economic activity	678	13.82	2.59	5	20
Price as intrinsic property	678	9.57	4.11	0	20
Price as market outcome	678	13.79	2.74	4	20
Exam – Part A raw marks /33	523	16.97	5.27	3	29
Exam – Part B raw marks /34	524	14.90	7.38	0	32.5
Exam – Part C raw marks /33	524	12.94	6.32	0	29
Exam – Total raw marks /100	524	44.75	16.03	4	86.5

Note: Sample size fluctuations are due to missing data. Space restrictions preclude the inclusion of statistics on students' changes in learning dimensions but these data are available on request.

Table 3. Correlations between scores on initial threshold concepts, initial learning dimensions and final examination

Variable	Whole exam	Exam part A	Exam part B	Exam part C
Personal Threshold Concepts (start of semester)	0.248* N = 489	0.252* N = 492	0.138* N = 491	0.207* N = 491
Discipline Threshold Concepts (start of semester)	0.443* N = 471	0.445* N = 474	0.315* N = 473	0.339* N = 473
Procedural Threshold Concepts (start of semester)	0.411* N = 491	0.409* N = 494	0.270* N = 493	0.327* N = 493
Learning is fact-based	-0.155*	-0.140	-0.132	-0.104
Knowledge objects	-0.083	-0.042	-0.086	-0.049
Memorising as rehearsal	-0.164*	-0.175*	-0.120	-0.109
Seeing things differently	0.039	0.074	0.016	0.019
Memorising before understanding	-0.188*	-0.223*	-0.156	-0.101
Relating ideas	0.057	0.076	0.018	0.057
Knowledge discrete and factual	-0.194*	-0.175*	-0.141	-0.137
Memorise after understanding	-0.047	-0.716	-0.048	-0.002
Detail related process	- 0.178*	-0.185*	-0.135	-0.134
Rereading a text	0.015	0.044	-0.003	0.008
Duty as motivation	-0.148*	-0.138	-0.104	-0.108
Memorise with understanding	0.050	0.091	0.028	0.025
Fragmentation	-0.219*	-0.201*	-0.165	-0.162
Repetition aids understanding	-0.166*	-0.093	-0.149	-0.143
Learning by example	-0.196*	-0.168	-0.183*	-0.133
Knowing about learning	0.050	0.040	0.034	0.049
Economic misconceptions	-0.254*	-0.282*	-0.174*	-0.161
Economic reasoning	0.013	0.047	0.002	-0.002
Economic activity	0.015	0.063	-0.027	-0.001
Price as intrinsic property	-0.266*	-0.276*	-0.178	- 0.189*
Price as market outcome	0.093	0.092	0.053	0.092
N (learning scales)	506	508	508	508

* Denotes significance at the one percent level.

Consistent with earlier work using a different data set (Meyer & Shanahan, 2001; Shanahan & Meyer, 2003), the discipline-specific RoLI dimensions associated with poor examination performance are also significantly negatively correlated with examination performance. The part of the examination most sensitive to high scores on a number of less desirable learning dimensions is the Part A multiple choice section.

Our measurement approach, however, also contains a potential problem. The correlations between students' prior acquisition of threshold concepts measured at the start of the course and their examination performance may be partly driven by similarity in the conceptual content assessed by the two instruments, as opposed to signaling a causal link between initial knowledge and success in *new* learning during the semester. Our focus, however, is the link between students' initial mastery of a web of threshold concepts, and their end-of-semester examination results, regardless of the causal pathway behind this association. Standard first-year economics examinations *should* be assessing concepts that lie at the heart of the discipline, and our prime interest lies in determining whether prior threshold concept acquisition is related to measured student performance in standard educational settings (such as this one). Thus, there is some necessary overlap in the distribution of threshold concept categories in the initial multiple choice test and the final examination (see Appendix 1). Ultimately, the fact that students vary in their initial levels of threshold concept acquisition, and that this variance seems to be correlated with examination success, is broad support for the Davis and Mangan (2007) categories. And, at the very least, this association opens up an avenue for further research. We explore this issue further in the discussion that follows.

The associations between scores on the RoLI dimensions and threshold concept categories at the start of the semester are displayed in Table 4. Many of the significant correlations are negative. These results imply that students with higher scores on less desirable learning dimensions at the start of the course tend initially also to have a poor grasp of threshold concepts – but that students with higher scores on more desirable approaches to learning may not necessarily have a good grasp of threshold concepts. These findings also signal an avenue for future research.

Changes in threshold concept understanding and *changes* in RoLI dimensions are weakly associated with examination performance, although they are related to each other. Table 5 shows the correlation of threshold concept acquisition scores in each of the three concept categories with both final examination marks and changes in RoLI dimensions across the semester. Threshold concept acquisition does not seem to be related to final examination performance, with one exception: a modest, but positive and significant relationship between students' acquisition of discipline-specific threshold concepts and their subsequent performance in Part B of the examination, where they are asked to apply economic concepts. (The pattern of correlations between scores on threshold concept acquisition in the three categories on the one hand, and changes in RoLI dimensions on the other, is also of interest but lies outside the scope of this chapter.)

Table 4. Correlations between scores on initial threshold concept categories and RoLI dimensions

Variable	Personal	Discipline	Procedural
Learning is fact-based	-0.149*	-.204*	-.212*
Knowledge objects	-0.050	-0.085	-0.054
Memorising as rehearsal	-0.177*	-0.170*	-0.252*
Seeing things differently	0.033	0.062	0.079
Memorising before understanding	-0.169*	-0.271*	-0.252*
Relating ideas	0.085	0.136	0.087
Knowledge discrete and factual	-0.141	-0.264*	-0.231
Memorise after understanding	-0.050	-0.058	-0.057
Detail related process	-0.193*	-0.247*	-0.256*
Rereading a text	-0.012	-0.004	0.042
Duty as motivation	-0.163*	-0.282*	-0.219*
Memorise with understanding	0.022	0.061	0.082
Fragmentation	-0.218*	-0.283*	-0.282*
Repetition aids understanding	-0.116	-0.161*	-0.182*
Learning by example	-0.099	-0.218*	-0.183*
Knowing about learning	0.047	0.074	0.047
Economic misconceptions	-0.261*	-0.316*	-0.306*
Economic reasoning	-0.021	0.094	0.043
Economic activity	0.128	0.063	0.106
Price as intrinsic property	-0.233*	-0.313*	-0.315*
Price as market outcome	0.099	0.122	0.099
N	646	622	653

* Denotes significance at the one percent level.

Finally, we present an exploratory first attempt at examining the predictive power of students' grasp of threshold concepts, holding some learning and other factors constant. Two linear regressions to predict final examination marks and a probit model to predict passage (pass/fail) through the examination are estimated, with the results in Appendix 2. The first linear model includes as predictors only scores on threshold concept acquisition and RoLI dimensions at the start of the semester, while the second includes students' gender and age as additional explanatory variables. (Predictions of final examination performance using changes in RoLI dimensions and threshold concept acquisition across the semester resulted in F-values below significant levels and are not presented.) The probit model includes all explanatory variables.

Unsurprisingly, few variables are significant in the two linear models. Nonetheless, there are two variables that are conditionally statistically significant in predicting examination performance in all three specifications: a student's prior acquisition of discipline-based and procedural threshold concepts. (That is

Table 5. Correlations between scores on growth in conceptual measures with growth in RoLI dimensions and final examination

Variable	Personal (growth)	Discipline (growth)	Procedural (growth)
Whole exam	0.057	0.096	-0.023
	N = 410	N = 397	N = 417
Examination part A	0.064	0.092	-0.013
	N = 411	N = 399	N = 419
Examination part B	0.063	0.136*	0.007
	N = 411	N = 398	N = 418
Examination part C	0.011	0.009	-0.055
	N = 411	N = 397	N = 419
Change in:			
Learning is fact-based	-0.010	-0.011	-0.026
Knowledge objects	0.085	0.084	0.101
Memorising as rehearsal	-0.068	-0.023	-0.042
Seeing things differently	0.105	0.077	0.059
Memorising before understanding	0.024	-0.031	-0.092
Relating ideas	0.142	0.105	0.051
Knowledge discrete and factual	-0.007	-0.060	0.019
Memorise after understanding	0.067	0.054	0.039
Detail related process	-0.096	-0.106	-0.093
Rereading a text	0.064	0.067	0.045
Duty as motivation	0.007	-0.013	-0.028
Memorise with understanding	0.104	0.175	0.087
Fragmentation	-0.087	-0.110	-0.148
Repetition aids understanding	-0.011	-0.007	-0.009
Learning by example	0.047	-0.039	-0.070
Knowing about learning	0.183*	0.166	0.155
Economic misconceptions	-0.187*	-0.171	-0.100
Economic reasoning	-0.005	-0.001	-0.036
Economic activity	0.123*	0.092	0.063
Price as intrinsic property	-0.004	-0.125*	-0.132*
Price as market outcome	0.117	0.011	0.071
N (learning scales)	457	442	468

* Denotes significance at the one percent level.

conditional on all the other variables controlled in the model, which the regression approach holds constant.) To a lesser degree, the deep learning process of rereading a text is also significant in both linear regression models. Consistent with earlier research, the probit model also reveals several initial RoLI dimensions to be significantly associated with passage of the final examination: 'knowledge objects,' motivation from a sense of 'duty' to others, and seeing prices as a function of market forces. The sign on most of the other RoLI dimensions is in accord with previous research. Note too that despite the strong raw correlations of these independent variables with examination performance shown in the earlier tables, the overall explanatory power of these models is weak. There are many other factors that influence student success. Nonetheless, these results are more evidence, albeit relatively weak, that discipline-based and procedural threshold concepts may indeed matter. They should, at the very least, be investigated further.

Several graphs further illustrate these associations, and also reveal the comparatively weak but positive association discussed above. The scatter-plot in Figure 4 plots individual students in a space defined on the x-axis by their score in each threshold concept category in the initial multiple-choice test and, on the y-axis, by their score on the final examination. Each student thus appears in the scatterplot as three points; one point for each conceptual category. It is clear that there is in a generally positive relationship between initial scores and final examination performance. The relationship appears stronger for threshold concepts that are discipline-based or procedural. Congruent with earlier results, it appears that while a very low score on threshold concept acquisition (under 0.2 on the scale used) is a good predictor of examination failure, the reverse does not hold: some students with apparently high levels of prior conceptual acquisition as measured at the start of the course nonetheless perform relatively poorly on the final examination.

Finally, to try and present these associations a little more starkly, figure 5 shows the students separated into two groups: those who scored toward the top end of responses to all three categories of threshold concepts (at or above one standard deviation above the mean) and those toward the bottom of the distribution (at or below one standard deviation below the mean). Having selected the students purely on the basis of their position at either end of the distribution of the initial responses, we plot their position in the final examination results. The difference in final examination performance between these two types of students is clear.

The top half of Figure 5 shows the distribution of final examination performance of students from the top of all of the three distributions of threshold concept categories. This histogram spans the full range of examination results, and appears to be roughly normally distributed (considering it includes only 35 students). In contrast, a histogram of examination results for the 11 students at the bottom of all of the three threshold concept distributions, displayed in the bottom half of Figure 5, reveals that only two of these 11 students earned 50% or more on the final examination, and none earned more than 56%. A similar pattern, across a larger number of students, but less stark, was also detected when using students' responses to only two of the conceptual elements covered by the multiple choice questions: 'interrelated markets' and 'supply and demand'. Again the results were consistent with what we know about the importance of prior knowledge in modelling examination performance. While our multiple choice questions may reveal more about prior knowledge than about previously-acquired threshold concepts, this is not necessarily the case. Overall, we think there is enough evidence to warrant further investigation of the importance of previously-acquired threshold concepts.

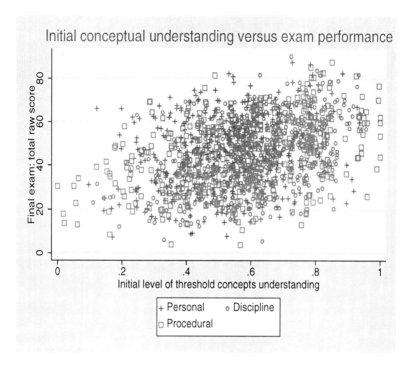

Figure 4. Initial conceptual understanding of threshold concepts verses exam performance.

CONCLUSION

Findings reported here reflect an initial exploration of the argument suggested by Davies and Mangan (2007) that, for both theoretical and empirical purposes, threshold concepts might be better considered in terms of conceptual categories representing a web of concepts, rather than as isolated conceptual elements. In particular, they argue that in the discipline of economics threshold concepts can be categorised as personal, discipline or procedural. This chapter describes a first attempt to operationalise this categorisation on the basis of multiple choice questions. Our initial analysis has focused conservatively on simple statistical associations between student-level threshold concept measures and examination performance, with some attention to learning dimensions.

There is sufficient evidence of statistical associations between scores on threshold concept categories, some RoLI dimensions and examination questions to warrant further investigation. The most robust finding is that students' responses to a categorised range of simple multiple choice questions, designed to reveal their prior acquisition of particular economic concepts, are significantly correlated both conditionally and unconditionally with their final examination results. This finding is buttressed by students exhibiting low scores on prior threshold concept acquisition also tending to exhibit high scores on several less desirable RoLI dimensions – dimensions negatively associated with examination results. In this sample, prior threshold concept acquisition is more robustly related to examination performance than initial learning dimensions.

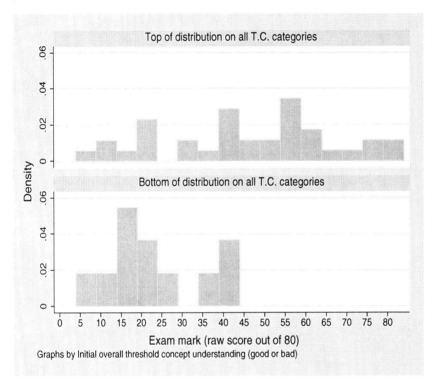

Figure 5. Top and bottom distributions on all threshold concept categories verses exam mark (raw score/80)

We conclude that there is support for the contention that students' prior acquisition of an interrelated web of threshold concepts affects their performance in standard economics examinations. There is certainly need for further research into this topic. Students who enter economics courses without having traversed a set of threshold concepts are likely to do worse in final examinations than those who have already grasped these concepts. Further, in a semester of 13 teaching weeks, there is apparently little opportunity to advance students' understanding of these concepts in a statistically significant manner. Finally, we suggest that properly-constructed multiple choice questions are capable of capturing variation in students' acquisition of threshold concepts, and that evidence of such variation can inform the pedagogy of threshold concepts.

Appendix 1:Categorisation of initial multiple-choice and final exam questions following Davies' and Mangan's (2005a) taxonomy

Category	Davis & Mangan's categories	Concepts covered in MC questions	Initial MC questions	Final Exam questions Part A	Part B	Part C
Personal						
	Price/cost; Income/wealth	Price and cost	2, 32			
	(stocks/flows)	Stock and flow	24,			
	nominal/real	Real v nominal	11,30,31			
	investment/saving	interest	9			
		incentives	12, 15			
		Living standards	40			
		profits	10, 14			
		Economics definition	37	1		
		TOTAL	13/40	1/33		
Discipline	Partial equilibrium	Partial equilibrium	25			
	General equilibrium	Inter-related markets	16	26		
	Welfare economics	Public good	23			
	Opportunity cost	Opportunity cost	4, 8, 35	2		
		Fallacy of composition	27, 29, 33			
		Scientific model	26			
		Zero sum game	3, 6			
		Gains from trade	13			
		Comparative advantage	36			
		Marginality	18, 38	3,14		
		Economic system	1			
		Prod'n possibility Frontier		4		
		Trade-offs	5			
		Markets	21	28	2a,3b, 3c	
		Market Failure		12		
		TOTAL	19/40	7/33	3/8	
Procedural	Comparative statics	Supply and demand	17, 19, 39	5,9,10,13	1	Pt1
	Equilibrium			19		
	Ceteris paribus			6,17		
	Time short/long term			20,22, 31		
	Expectations			21,		
	Elasticity	Elasticity	7	7,8,11,15 ,18		
		Competition	20	24		Pt2
		Cost-benefit	22		5	
		Externalities	28	29,33		Pt4
		Sunk costs	34			
		Behaviour of firms (includes cost decisions)		16,23,25, 27,30,32	2b,3a, 4	Pt3,
		TOTAL	8/40	25/33	5/8	4/4

Appendix 2: Models predicting final examination performance

Independent Variables	(1) Linear regression		(2) Linear regression		(3) Probit model	
Personal	3.905	(5.167)	3.581	(5.171)	-0.049	(0.198)
Discipline	28.315*	(5.732)	27.207*	(5.785)	0.712*	(0.226)
Procedural	14.331*	(4.391)	13.764*	(4.406)	0.688*	(0.175)
Learning is fact-based	-0.142	(0.273)	-0.184	(0.276)	-0.016	(0.011)
Knowledge objects	-0.408	(0.244)	-0.439	(0.246)	-0.023^	(0.010)
Memorising as rehearsal	-0.072	(0.310)	-0.044	(0.311)	0.002	(0.012)
Seeing things differently	0.360	(0.409)	0.385	(0.410)	0.025	(0.016)
Memorising before understanding	0.033	(0.239)	0.042	(0.240)	0.013	(0.009)
Relating ideas	-0.061	(0.337)	-0.038	(0.337)	-0.001	(0.013)
Knowledge discrete and factual	0.133	(0.310)	0.101	(0.311)	0.006	(0.012)
Memorise after understanding	-0.070	(0.270)	-0.041	(0.273)	-0.009	(0.011)
Detail related process	-0.080	(0.292)	-0.075	(0.292)	-0.013	(0.011)
Rereading a text	0.959^	(0.407)	0.910 ^	(0.408)	0.021	(0.016)
Duty as motivation	0.349	(0.237)	0.358	(0.239)	0.022^	(0.009)
Memorise with understanding	-0.215	(0.355)	-0.230	(0.355)	-0.021	(0.014)
Fragmentation	0.185	(0.311)	0.182	(0.311)	0.013	(0.012)
Repetition aids understanding	-0.400	(0.293)	-0.398	(0.293)	-0.021	(0.011)
Learning by example	-0.125	(0.220)	-0.105	(0.224)	-0.005	(0.009)
Knowing about learning	0.378	(0.443)	0.394	(0.444)	0.034	(0.018)
Economic misconceptions	-0.253	(0.277)	-0.198	(0.281)	-0.004	(0.011)
Economic reasoning	-0.128	(0.286)	-0.169	(0.287)	-0.001	(0.011)
Economic activity	-0.312	(0.334)	-0.317	(0.334)	-0.022	(0.013)
Price as intrinsic property	-0.371	(0.229)	-0.373	(0.229)	-0.012	(0.009)
Price as market outcome	0.494	(0.311)	0.403	(0.317)	0.026^	(0.013)
Female	--		-1.706	(1.519)	0.042	(0.058)
Age	--		0.168	(0.154)	0.004	(0.006)
N	373		373		373	
R-squared	0.218		0.219		--	

Note: *   Denotes significance at the one percent level; ^ Denotes significance at the five percent level. Columns (1) and (2) estimate linear regressions predicting raw marks earned on the exam; column (3) fits a probit model to determine the probability of passing the exam. Marginal effects for a one-unit change in each independent variable (not probit coefficients) are shown in column 3. Standard errors are in parentheses.

REFERENCES

Bloom, B. S., Englehardt, M. D., Furst, E. J., Hill, W. H., & Krathwohl, D. R. (Eds.) (1956). *Taxonomy of educational objectives, the classification of educational goals – Handbook I: Cognitive domain*. New York: McKay.

Buckles, S. & Siegfried, J. J. (2006). Using multiple-choice questions to evaluate in-depth learning of economics. *The Journal of Economic Education, 31*(1), 48-57.

Davies, P. (2006). Threshold concepts: How can we recognize them? In J. H. F. Meyer & R. Land (Eds.), *Overcoming barriers to student understanding threshold concepts and troublesome knowledge*. London and New York: Routledge.

Davies, P. & Mangan, J. (2007). Threshold concepts and the integration of understanding in economics. *Studies in Higher Education, 32*(6), in press.

Meyer, J. H. F. (2004). An introduction to the RoLI™. *Innovations in Education and Teaching International, 41*(4), 491-497.

Meyer, J. H. F. & Land, R. (2003). Threshold concepts and troublesome knowledge: linkages to ways of thinking and practising within the disciplines. In C. Rust (Ed.), *Improving student learning. Improving student learning theory and practice – 10 years on*. Oxford: OCSLD.

Meyer, J. H. F. & Land, R. (Eds.) (2006). *Overcoming barriers to student understanding: Threshold concepts and troublesome knowledge*. London and New York: Routledge.

Meyer, J.H.F., Land, R. & Davies, P. (2008). Threshold concepts and troublesome knowledge (4): issues of variation and variability. In R. Land, J. H. F. Meyer, & J. Smith (Eds.), *Threshold concepts within the disciplines*. Rotterdam and Taipei: Sense Publishers.

Meyer, J. H. F. & Shanahan, M. P. (2001). A triangulated approach to the modelling of learning outcomes in first year economics. *Higher Education Research & Development, 20*(2), 127-145.

Meyer, J. H. F. & Shanahan, M. P. (2004). Developing metalearning capacity in students — Actionable theory and practical lessons learned in first-year economics. *Innovations in Education and Teaching International 2004, 41*(4), 443-458.

Shanahan, M. P. & Meyer, J. H. F. (2003). Measuring and responding to variation in aspects of students' economic conceptions and learning engagement in economics. *International Review of Economic Education, 1*(1), 58-84.

Shanahan, M. & Meyer, J. H. F. (2006). The troublesome nature of a threshold concept in economics. In J. H. F. Meyer & R. Land (Eds.), *Overcoming barriers to student understanding: Threshold concepts and troublesome knowledge*. London and New York: Routledge.

AFFILIATIONS

Martin P. Shanahan
Centre for Regulation and Market Analysis
University of South Australia

Gigi Foster
Centre for Regulation and Market Analysis
University of South Australia

Jan H.F. Meyer
Centre for Learning, Teaching, and Research in Higher Education
Durham University and University of South Australia

ANDREW ASHWIN

13. WHAT DO STUDENTS' EXAMINATION ANSWERS REVEAL ABOUT THRESHOLD CONCEPT ACQUISITION IN THE 14–19 AGE GROUPS?

INTRODUCTION

Much of the work on threshold concepts so far has been carried out with undergraduates in higher education. The very nature of these concepts in economics and those in other disciplines might be seen as being one that requires a degree of academic maturity to be able to truly grasp them and enter the 'portal' as referred to by Meyer and Land (2003). There may be some benefit to be gained by the student in coming to terms with a concept through having some experience to bring to bear to help develop understanding.

However, many students encounter economics before undergraduate level. For those involved in the teaching and learning process, the requirement for students to demonstrate an understanding of the subject matter is no less important. The concepts being dealt with are the same and the expectations from the assessment might be similar.

THE ASSESSMENT INSTRUMENTS

The samples of student examination responses used for this exercise are all based around a course entitled Business and Economics (Nuffield) at General Certificate of Secondary Education (GCSE) level. The GCSE course covers two years beginning when a student is aged 14 going into the UK education system at year 10 (ninth grade) and ending at year 11 when the student is 16 (tenth grade).

The assessment objectives (AOs) associated with the course are based on Bloom's taxonomy (Bloom, 1956): knowledge and understanding (AO1), application (AO2), selection and analysis (AO3), and evaluation (AO4). Each assessment objective is weighted at 25%.

For this exercise, however, a different method of assessment was used based on the Structure of Observed Learning Outcomes (SOLO) taxonomy developed by Biggs and Collis (1982). The SOLO taxonomy was used because it was anticipated that it would more accurately reflect the quality of the learning outcome with respect to understanding and assessing threshold concept acquisition.

R. Land, J.H.F. Meyer & J. Smith (Eds.), Threshold Concepts within the Disciplines, 173-184.
© *2008 Sense Publishers. All rights reserved.*

STRUCTURES OF KNOWLEDGE

Structures of knowledge in economics are the constituent parts that make up the understanding of the subject referred to as economics. In part, the subject knowledge we have is brought to us by information, which has been handed down by some external authority. In economics, as with other disciplines, the knowledge and concepts that form the basis of the subject are those which some expert or group of experts has decided is relevant to the subject (Bloom, 1956).

THINKING LIKE AN ECONOMIST

To understand what it means to 'think like an economist', one of the principal features of those who have acquired economics threshold concepts, it is important to have some understanding of what this 'thinking' actually means. Thinking like an economist suggests that there is a way of thinking about economics phenomena that is accepted by practitioners within the subject community. This way of thinking is what separates those within this community from those with an everyday understanding about issues in economics. The approach, methods, conceptual understanding and ways of thinking about the subject help to define what an 'economist' is. This is supported by Polanyi (1958), who suggests that in pursuing a line of study that involves learning and knowledge there will need to be a stage at which individuals achieve equality between themselves in terms of the knowledge possessed by one person and the person who is examining that knowledge.

At one level students might, as emphasised by Marton (1983), have covered certain concepts but have a naïve understanding of them. Their ability to be able to engage in discussion is going to be limited. In short, the ability to 'think like an economist' is dependent on sharing a common understanding of the concepts that form the language of the subject. Some of these concepts will be understood and be used with facility, others might present greater problems because of the abstract, counter-intuitive nature of the concepts and the troublesome knowledge that they represent. It is these latter concepts that represent threshold concepts and which provide the barrier to thinking in the subject.

Polanyi (1958) argues that if we agree with the knowledge that the other person claims to know and with the grounds on which he (*sic*) relies for this knowledge, the critical examination of this knowledge will become a critical reflection of our own knowledge. In developing this understanding both proponents will be involved in discussing and presenting a 'truth'. That truth, according to Polanyi (1958), is dependent on a common system of collateral facts and values accepted by the subject area.

This argument suggests that there is a way of thinking about economics phenomena that could be described as a 'novice' understanding. Rubin (2002) has described these as 'folk economics'; the intuitive economics of untrained persons. Folk economics implies that those taking part in any discussion of an economic issue would not be using the paradigms that the economics community would use in similar discussions. Indeed it can be argued that if 'non-members' of this community were engaged in a discussion with 'members' of the community that non-members might have difficulty understanding and following the logic and the approach of the 'experts' because of a lack of exposure to the concepts, methods and approach that characterise the study of economics. The language and concepts that are used within a subject that forms a community of practice is termed 'boundedness' and is one of the characteristic features of a threshold concept (Meyer and Land, 2003).

THE NATURE OF CONCEPTS

Concepts are objects or ideas that have common attributes. These common attributes are shared by all the members of the category of a concept (Ausubel *et al.*, 1978). For example, the concept 'market' contains a wide range of different members but each have common attributes – a buyer, a seller and a price. In having common attributes, we are able to recognise language communication but may have an imperfect understanding of the concept being discussed. For example, in a discussion of markets, there will be recognition of the fundamental attributes of a market even if the specific market being discussed is not known to one of the parties to that discussion. The concepts that make up economics allow those involved in the study of the subject to be able to recognise communication about them. Some of these concepts will be vital for understanding a particular set of behaviours in economics.

An understanding of a concept such as 'elasticity' will certainly open up a vista of understanding for the student who is able to grasp this important concept. However, the extent to which that understanding can *transform* the landscape will be more dependent on an understanding of a threshold concept – value. An understanding of value will transform how an individual sees the relationship between the implications that derive from elasticity and the reasons why firms are able to 'get away' with charging different prices for the same good or service at different times (for example). The whole issue becomes a different problem with a completely different perspective when the threshold concept of value has been acquired.

ASSESSMENT

The SOLO taxonomy provides descriptions of the structural organisation of knowledge at increasingly more complex levels across modes of learning (Boulton-Lewis, 1998). It was developed to focus on common learning situations – the meaningful learning of existing knowledge. It is not only about assessing the extent to which a student has acquired knowledge, facts, skills, concepts or problem solving strategies, it is about how these are used. It is about how much and how well a learning-application episode has been carried out (Biggs & Collis, 1982). It is posited that the SOLO taxonomy can be used as a means of assessing the extent to which a student 'thinks like an economist' given that there is a description of these characteristics within the SOLO taxonomy.

The taxonomy relates performances of 'understanding' to five levels of outcome:

- *Pre-structural:* characterised by unconnected pieces of information with little or no organisation or coherence.
- *Unistructural:* characterised by the making of simple connections between obviously related information and concepts but with no understanding of importance associated with the connection.
- *Multistructural:* a number of connections might be made between different concepts and terms within the subject but with a lack of understanding of their relevance in the big picture.
- *Relational:* The parts are understood in the whole and the student demonstrates an understanding and appreciation of the relative importance of the parts in relation to the whole.
- *Extended abstract:* The ability to be able to make connections not only within the boundaries of the subject but beyond it and to be able to take this understanding and make generalisations to other contexts.

The different levels of outcome here imply a different degree of understanding in relation to the piece of work given to the student. It is being asserted therefore that the SOLO taxonomy can be one way in which a measure of the degree to which a student can be said to think like an economist can be assessed. If a student's work is placed in the extended abstract level, then it is being assumed that this might be representative of a student who has managed to breach the portal. A move from SOLO level 4 to Level 5 implies an improved ability to be able to see and understand the subject from a variety of different perspectives; to be able to take concepts and methods and relate these to new and different situations and contexts. At this level, the student would have a transformed understanding of the subject.

ASSESSING OUTCOMES

The examples used in this chapter are a small selection of those reviewed to highlight how we might use such an assessment measure to identify *levels* of understanding in student responses to questions on the subject. They have been selected to demonstrate the qualitative nature of these different levels of understanding. The questions in these examples are part of a series of responses on an examination paper that is designed to try to focus on problem solving in business and economics. A series of short pieces of evidence, including written, image and data, set some of the context for the student around which the questions are based.

The context in this case was based around the rise in oil prices between 2003 and 2005, the impact this might have had on different businesses and the opportunities for the use of alternative energy sources as a result. The student is not, at this level of study, expected to have any detailed understanding of the oil industry itself but to use the knowledge and skills in economics and business built up throughout the course to answer the questions. The student responses have been faithfully reproduced – errors included!

Student Response A

Question: *To what extent is the development of wind farms the solution to a country's energy problems?*

The development of wind farms is a great solution to a country's energy problems because it will reduce costs that the company usually has to pay; for example coal and oil. Also, it is friendly to the atmosphere because it will not release carbondioxide or poisonous gases into the air and therefore there will be less problems and fear about global warming.

The money saved by the use of wind farms can be used for other resources or needs, like building more houses beginning new businesses, which will let the country to have more money to be richer. Also the money can be given to charities or other industries which will help a whole country in the ways of reducing the burning of fuels, building more wind farms and other needy sources.

This example begins with a simplistic judgement and goes on to offer some explanation in support. There is some use of terms, for example, the reference to cost but this explanation confuses the effect on a business and the needs of the country as a whole, which is the focus of the question. There is recognition that wind power might be more environmentally friendly. The answer then goes on to suggest that there will be 'money saved' by using wind farms and that this money can be used to provide a variety of other services such as building houses or starting new businesses. There is then a suggestion that this money can be used for charity. The level of understanding here is somewhat confused. It is not clear that the student appreciates the extent to which a wind farm might 'save money' nor who it is that is able to save this money – a business, the government? Equally, the assumption that such savings can be used in the ways suggested implies a naïve understanding of the business and economic environment.

There are a number of concepts and methods appropriate to the subject touched upon in the answer. There is some understanding of how funds can be used for investment (although that term is not used) and some limited analysis is attempted. Despite this there is no significance identified between the concepts and methods involved. There is a simple procedure explained which, it could be argued, is largely the result of a series of learned responses that took place during the study of the course. The understanding of how these responses fit with the overall subject and the topic concerned is lost. This is given as an example of a unistructural response. There are simple connections made throughout the piece, for example, the effect on costs, the environment and how money saved could be used elsewhere. The information, which a student following this subject would be expected to be familiar with, is made clear but the relationships between this information are only demonstrated at a basic and obvious level. There is little

177

understanding of the significance, extent or importance of the connections made; they are merely given without qualification.

Student Response B

Wind farms are just a part of the solution to a country's energy problems. Wind farms and other sources of renewable energy such as solar power and hydroelectric power stations, cost a lot to set up but are quite cheap to run and provide free and clean energy.

However, the output of energy is less reliable than traditional forms such as oil and coal. For example, wind farms produce very little or no electricity if there is no wind. Also it's often difficult to find areas suitable for wind farms or solar power or hydroelectric power stations. If demand for energy is still increasing, these sources of energy may not be able to supply as much as is needed which could make it as expensive as oil. However, oil and other finite resources are limited in supply so new solutions are crucial. Overall, I think wind farms and other renewable resources are a large part of the solution, but even once in place there may continue to be shortages if demand continues to increase.

This is a response to the same question by a different student. It also starts with a judgement. It then offers some explanation of the costs and benefits of setting up wind farms and other examples of renewable energy sources. Approaching a problem by looking at the costs and benefits of a decision would be deemed as being an accepted method of thinking in economics. At this level, at least, this is an example of a student exhibiting some characteristics of thinking like an economist.

The answer then moves on to provide some balance in the argument. There is recognition that there are limitations to what wind power can produce, and that the rate at which demand is increasing might outstrip the capacity to supply and as such prices could rise anyway. There is an understanding of the different components of the issue, and these are integrated into a coherent argument. There is evidence that the student has some developed understanding of the topic. The student has placed appropriate terms and concepts into the context and attaches some meaning to these concepts in this context. There is also evidence that the response is not moving beyond the concepts that have been taught. This answer therefore would reflect what we might expect to find in the relational level of the SOLO taxonomy.

The student shows some evidence of understanding the component parts of the question; in addition, this understanding is placed within the context of the whole issue. It is not just a case of seeing wind power as the answer, which is recognised as being part of the solution but also the recognition that if something is not done to curb demand, supply may continue to be outstripped and therefore lead to higher prices similar to that which is happening with oil. This evidence is a clear indication of grasping the relationship between the parts, and of the importance of relating these parts to the whole.

Student Response C

Question: *Some companies use oil directly others indirectly in their business. Assess the extent to which these businesses might be affected by the rise in oil prices.*

Many businesses are affected by this. Obviously those most affected would be those who use oil as a raw material in producing something. The result of this would be an increase in variable costs and either a reduction in profits or an increase in selling price to compensate. Both of these may have similar effects in preventing expansion or reducing market share, however, all similar businesses in the same industry will be affected in the same way. As a result, overall, the effect may be much less, however it depends on circumstances.

Other businesses that may be more greatly affected may be those that sell complimentary products to oil. An example of this would be car manufacturers such as Hummers or similar. The demand for these products may be significantly reduced because of the increase in oil price. However, this again depends on the type of product. If it is an essential product customers may switch to alternatives, however, with Hummers being bought for their added value, the customers may be unlikely to make changes as a result of the increase in prices.

Overall, those businesses which use oil directly would be more affected than those which use it indirectly, however, many businesses are affected in some way by this. The extent to which they are affected depends on a number of things including complimentary products etc.

Response C is from the same paper but a different question. In this answer the student begins with the recognition that businesses most affected will be the ones who use oil directly. The subsequent analysis shows a clear understanding of the way in which this problem could affect such businesses. The next section then seeks to offer some balance by suggesting that all similar businesses will be affected and that the overall effect will be less than it might be if only one business is affected. Such recognition at this level of study is unusual.

The remainder of the answer demonstrates further evidence of a clear understanding not only of the problem involved, but also the extent to which this problem affects different businesses. The discussion about Hummers incorporates an understanding of the difference between 'essential' and 'non-essential' products, value-added and recognition that for people who buy these sorts of vehicles the price of petrol might not be a particularly important factor in their decision to purchase.

The quality of the argument and the range of understanding are very high for this level of study. Throughout the answer, the student is able to draw on a range of business and economics knowledge and understanding to illuminate the argument. The question seeks to target higher order skills of analysis and evaluation and this student shows a considerable degree of ability in this domain. The student not only demonstrates an understanding of the immediate issue, but is also able to make connections between different parts of the subject area not explicitly asked for or implied in the question.

This answer is offered as an example of one which, at this level of study, would sit in level 5 of the SOLO Taxonomy. The response clearly makes connections between different parts of the subject matter including that which is not necessarily implied by the question. The student makes links between the change in oil prices and variable costs, profit and prices (line 3) and between the rise in oil prices and the effect on indirect users of oil (lines 9–10). It also provides some appreciation of the significance of these connections and links the parts to the whole (lines 5–6). In the latter part of the answer, the student is able to hypothesise and make generalised connections outside the context (lines 13–15).

There is an overall impression in the answer that the student recognises the concept of value and can relate it to different situations; there is evidence that the concept of opportunity cost is implicit in the discussion about value added and how some customers might view the impact of higher petrol prices on vehicles that use large amounts fuel.

Other responses from this student, when put together with the example cited above, did provide evidence that there is a pattern suggesting that this student understands a wide variety of issues related to the subject and is able to go beyond the relational level in beginning to conceptualise beyond that which might have been covered in normal lessons.

This student is therefore demonstrating a response that is categorised as extended abstract. By inference, it is also being suggested that this student is thinking along lines that would be seen as being accepted by those in the discipline as an economist. Such a level of understanding does seem to be consistent with an understanding of what threshold concepts within disciplines means in practice.

To make headway in developing the means to qualitatively assess students' work, it will be necessary to have the means by which students can be recognised for *the way they are thinking* and the skills and command of the subject concerned that they are demonstrating. Using a tool like the SOLO Taxonomy moves assessment of understanding away from a 'points' basis to an attempt to look at responses as a whole and find characteristics that fit the different levels of understanding demonstrated and highlighted by the SOLO Taxonomy.

DISCUSSION

Threshold concepts have raised a number of issues that are still to be worked through. There is debate about what constitutes a threshold concept as opposed to a core concept. Are threshold concepts hierarchical, for example? Is it only possible to have a transformed understanding when one has mastered certain concepts? The work by Davies and Mangan (2007) offers a way of seeing a relational structure between concepts within a discipline. Their notion of a web of threshold concepts is a powerful one that moves the debate away from seeing threshold concepts as some form of hierarchical progression within a subject that is only open to a few at higher levels of study. This would suggest that threshold concepts have relevance at all levels of study whether it is in the 14–16 age range as highlighted in this chapter or for undergraduate and postgraduate levels of study.

Threshold concepts might be part of the answer that teachers have been looking for in attempting to improve the level of understanding in students. Threshold concepts help us to focus on finding a definition, in the first instance, to what we mean by learning. This may be a vision of learning that links very closely with that of the characteristics of deep learning – an intention to understand the material, a willingness to interact with the subject content, to exhibit higher order skills in learning, to see the whole yet relate concepts, methods and theories to each other, to relate existing knowledge with new knowledge, to relate concepts to everyday experience and new contexts and to look beyond the subject to help build understanding. This view of learning fundamentally changes behaviour, a behaviour which is now underpinned by a different set of assumptions about reality.

Having defined the learning outcome, teaching and learning, and crucially assessment, can be designed to foster that learning. This chapter could be interpreted as arguing that the SOLO taxonomy is being promoted as the solution to the problem. SOLO, however, gives an illumination into the problem and points towards rather than provides the solution.

In developing methods of assessment we need to be focussing on the need to develop qualitative understanding. At present, certainly in the UK educational system, there is a widespread view that Using the idea of a web of concepts allows us to see an understanding of a discipline, under the assumptions made in the introduction about structures of knowledge, as being concepts that have a degree of inter-relationship between them. To understand one concept one might require some understanding of another, and moreover an ability to recognise the relationship between the two, see the similarities in the critical attributes that the concepts possess, and be able to relate these to the approach to a problem that would be seen as constituting 'economic thinking'.

is the fundamental concern of not only students but also teachers. A new approach to assessment might start to look at developing a means and a measure of assessment that captures the qualitative differences in understanding of students.

This qualitative understanding would emphasise the ability to be able to recognise and interpret economic concepts and phenomena in a wide range of different contexts. The measure of this understanding would have to reliably identify and reflect this interpretation in different student responses. The emphasis would move from knowledge acquisition to knowledge use as a demonstration of the ability to utilise threshold concepts. These threshold concepts would be meshed together in a web of understanding that would characterise a student that was 'thinking like an economist'.

Developing more detailed assessment criteria along the lines of the SOLO taxonomy that could capture these qualitative differences and which was seen as reliable in both the interpretation and regular use of the instrument would be the next stage in the challenge. In many respects, until we get the assessment and the assessment criteria clear we will not be able to foster the sort of learning that has been outlined above.

Using the idea of a web of concepts allows us to see an understanding of a discipline, under the assumptions made in the introduction about structures of knowledge, as being concepts that have a degree of inter-relationship between them. To understand one concept one might require some understanding of another, and moreover an ability to recognise the relationship between the two, see the similarities in the critical attributes that the concepts possess, and be able to relate these to the approach to a problem that would be seen as constituting 'economic thinking'.

The definition of learning as exemplified by the reference to approaches to learning above, when linked to the particular discipline being considered, can be viewed as a manifestation of the requirements to think like an economist. This could be expected whatever the level of study involved. It cannot be expected that there will be some specific stage in a learner's journey where they are suddenly inducted into the 'community' of economists. The aim of any teaching and learning programme should be to encourage this thinking within the subject. The importance of being able to identify examples where students appear to have passed through the portal referred to by Meyer and Land (2003) is as relevant in levels of study at GCSE, for example, as it is for a lecturer dealing with undergraduates. What is required is a common understanding of how to interpret student responses to be able to make such a claim, and to accordingly focus attention on the construction of the curriculum and pedagogy.

In the characteristics of the extended abstract level of the SOLO taxonomy, it is suggested that we have a framework within which to evaluate the quality of student answers, at all levels, and within which to make judgements as to whether a student is able to think like an economist (or other disciplinary expert).

The examples presented do illustrate very clear distinctions between the qualities of responses; most of the examples given are merely snapshots of the total student response across two papers and a portfolio submission. However, in most cases these submissions are typical of the level of response and understanding demonstrated by the students concerned.

There may be some cases where a particular term or concept can be defined accurately by a student otherwise demonstrating confused understanding at a unistructural and multistructural level. In many cases, this is explained by the rote memorisation of the material concerned. When such concepts or terms are placed into a new and different context the student at these performance levels, fail to recognise their significance or make the necessary connections. Such responses are also typical of those found by lecturers in students at undergraduate level.

This is different to the student who is able to demonstrate a greater level of understanding as characterised by the relational and extended abstract levels. If the student demonstrates consistent performance at the extended abstract level then we might be able to conclude that this is an appropriate example of a student demonstrating mastery of threshold concepts and thinking like an economist.

CONCLUSION

The suggestion that student responses should give some indication of their ability to think within a discipline is not original. Finding a way of assessing the extent to which such ability can be measured is something that is still subject to debate. Recent discussions by the Qualifications and Curriculum Authority (QCA) in the UK about changes to the subject criteria for subjects to be examined at Advanced Level referred to the necessity of encouraging students to think in their subject:

...there should be a concentration on the quality of assessment to ensure that it encourages the development of a holistic understanding of the subject. When presented with synoptic assessment, candidates should be asked to think as a historian, mathematician, etc. (QCA, 2006)

We can regard such direction as an important step forward in the move toward improving the quality of learning outcome at all levels towards what can be described as deep learning. Threshold concepts and an understanding of the barriers they can present to students in acquiring deep learning will be an increasingly important feature of this process. In addition, the implications for pedagogy, curriculum design and assessment are all equally important.

Should, for example, students starting GCSE courses or undergraduate studies in subjects like economics be presented with a series of terms and concepts to be learned at the outset and thus place the emphasis on content? Should we simply expose students to a number of different scenarios that have some links with the subject, encourage investigation and exploration of these scenarios to help build familiarity with the critical attributes that are part of the process of conceptual formation as opposed to concept assimilation? (Ausubel *et al.*, 1978). Concept assimilation may form the basis of the pedagogy in many schools and higher education institutions in the UK.

If the focus on content as opposed to understanding is the main criteria then it is likely that we will continue to see more examples of what Perkins (1999) refers to as ritual knowledge. Ritual knowledge is routine and meaningless in character, feeling part of a social or individual ritual rather than having any meaning. It could be argued that an example of ritual learning is where students use concepts without a complete understanding of them. We might point to the way in which students learn concepts in economics but rarely make any connection to the real world they witness and experience every day. In other words, they do not seem to have progressed beyond the threshold and will not 'think in the subject'. Again, teachers and lecturers in schools, colleges and higher education institutions will have experienced such responses.

The importance of threshold concepts and their role in pedagogy is still in its infancy. There is some confusion about what threshold concepts are, mostly confusion with a threshold in understanding, which is quite a different issue and does not necessarily imply a transformed understanding of a subject. The idea of *thinking in the subject* is more useful in guiding our thinking about what we are trying to achieve. At all levels of education it can be argued that there needs to be a focus on encouraging this type of thinking rather than a primary focus on knowledge and content.

To do this, we must apply our fledgling understanding of threshold concepts to pedagogy, curriculum design and the teaching and learning process. Research in the field that focuses on what threshold concepts are within disciplines, and how we might recognise students who demonstrate a transformed understanding give us a powerful direction in which to move the education debate. This chapter offers one suggestion as to a possible way forward.

REFERENCES

Ausubel, D. P., Novak, J. D., & Hanesian, H. (1978). *Educational psychology: A cognitive view*. New York: Holt, Reinhart and Winston.

Biggs, J. & Collis, K. (1982). *Evaluating the quality of learning. The SOLO-taxonomy*. New York: Academic Press.

Bloom B. S. (1956). *Taxonomy of educational objectives. The classification of educational goals. Handbook 1: The cognitive domain*. London: Longman.

Boulton-Lewis, G. (1998). Applying the SOLO taxonomy to learning in higher education. In B. Dart & G. Boulton-Lewis (Eds.), *Teaching and learning in higher education*. Melbourne: ACER.

Davies, P. & Mangan, J. (2007). Threshold concepts and the integration of understanding in economics. *Studies in Higher Education, 32*(6), in press.

Marton, F. (1983). Beyond individual differences. *Educational Psychology 3*(3,4), 289–303

Meyer, J. H. F. & Land, R. (2003). Threshold concepts and troublesome knowledge: Linkages to ways of thinking and practising within the disciplines. In C. Rust (Ed.), *Improving student learning. Improving student learning theory and oractice –10 years on*. Oxford: OCSLD.

Perkins, D. (1999). The constructivist classroom: The many faces of constructivism. *Educational Leadership, 57*(3), 6-11.

Polanyi, M. (1958). *Personal knowledge: Towards a post-critical philosophy*. London: Routledge and Keegan Paul.

Qualifications and Curriculum Authority (2006). QCA Draft Guidance on Synoptic Assessment, March 2006.

Rubin, P. H. (2002). Folk economics. http://ssrn.com/abstract=320940 dated 19th September 2002, last accessed 25th June 2007.

AFFILIATION

Andrew Ashwin
Biz/ed (http://www.bized.co.uk)
Thomson Learning EMEA

CHARLOTTE E. TAYLOR

14. THRESHOLD CONCEPTS, TROUBLESOME KNOWLEDGE AND WAYS OF THINKING AND PRACTISING

Can We Tell the Difference in Biology?

INTRODUCTION: BACKGROUND AND CONTEXT

A discourse on threshold concepts requires discussion of the various characteristics of such concepts within the context of the discipline, and this has been attempted in the field of biology (Taylor, 2006). While clear parallels with other disciplines such as Economics (Davies, 2006) could be recognized in terms of defining possible threshold concepts, apparent differences arose associated with the range of fields within biology. Each discipline is acknowledged as having distinctive ways of thinking and practising in the subject (McCune & Hounsell, 2005), which transcend understanding and use of discipline knowledge, and taken together, describe the community, its way of seeing the world, and the position of its members (Davies, 2006). Such a community is thus bound together by 'the way in which concepts are related and the deep level structure of the subject which gives it coherence and creates a shared way of perceiving that can be left unspoken' (Davies, 2006). Characteristics specific to biology have been documented as including epistemological issues associated with the role of theory in the subject, the use of special techniques, establishing correlations and the concept of quantification (Becher & Trowler, 2001). Biology is also seen as being a more wide ranging discipline than others, particularly in the sciences, since it encompasses a wide range of specialist fields including ecology and environmental biology, through organismal and evolutionary biology, animal and plant physiology, anatomy and taxonomy, and genetics to molecular biology and biotechnology (Taylor, 2006). Biologists themselves are aware of the extent of this range, and acknowledge the way in which concepts in biology may be generalized to fit across this spectrum, as well as the way in which biology interacts with other related disciplines (Becher & Trowler, 2001). These distinct characteristics of the discipline may explain why biologists are identified with concepts involving complexity, dynamics and variability.

EXPERIENCES OF BIOLOGISTS TEACHING IN UNIVERSITIES

Biologists have enthusiastically embraced the ideas encompassed in the terms troublesome knowledge (Perkins, 1999) and threshold concepts, but explanations for 'troublesome' labels and the degree to which such concepts may incorporate learning thresholds are more difficult to formulate. A preliminary study in 2004

R. Land, J.H.F. Meyer & J. Smith (Eds.), Threshold Concepts within the Disciplines, 185-195.
© *2008 Sense Publishers. All rights reserved.*

(Taylor, 2006) asked biologists to identify troublesome areas in biology and to suggest possible examples of threshold concepts. Since biology is a very broad discipline, participants in the study came from research areas as diverse as plant physiology, neurobiology, marine biology, biochemistry, and animal ecology. An analysis of the interviews identified commonalities in perceptions of troublesome knowledge and threshold concepts across the discipline. *Complexity* is acknowledged as integral to biology, as is the concept of *change* and the *dynamic nature* of biology, and the concept of *scale*. Integrating these concepts into an understanding of any area of biology requires an acknowledgement of their central role and a constant re-building of knowledge. In a biological context these concepts appear to fit the definition inherent in traversing a learning threshold, since they are fundamental to developing a sophisticated understanding of biology and are transformative. However the extent to which the requirements for concepts to be integrative, and demonstrate boundedness (Meyer & Land, 2003, 2005) are satisfied becomes more complex. Likewise, the irreversible nature of the understanding proves more difficult to apply to the concepts identified above. Meanwhile most discussion of the teaching of biology did not necessarily focus on these more abstract concepts, and instead centred on biological processes, such as photosynthesis, as key attributes of living individuals and systems.

Such areas invariably become a focus of discussion when identifying topics which involve troublesome knowledge when teaching. This appears to relate to the fact that it is widely acknowledged that students tend to build up an arsenal of islands of such knowledge, which then sits in isolation as a collection of facts, unless connections are made which reveal the links across the discipline and its inherent complexity. Whether students make these links and cross thresholds, as they are more exposed to the topic, or the extent to which teachers focus on developing the links, is not clear. However, it is clear that the way in which these teachers perceived potential problems of troublesome knowledge and possible thresholds has implications for the approach they take to their teaching of these topics (Martin *et al.*, 2000; Trigwell *et al.*, 2005).

Identifying specific examples of threshold concepts in biology from these discussions, may be helped by applying the categories and definitions subsequently described by Davies and Mangan (2005). Their investigations in economics lead them to propose three types of conceptual change, namely basic concepts, discipline concepts, and modelling concepts. Thus many of the troublesome areas in biology teaching, discussed above, would fall into the basic concepts category, and the larger abstract areas, which certainly seem to incorporate discipline thresholds, would be described by the modeling concepts category. To further explore these ideas obviously requires further input from those involved in learning biology.

PERSPECTIVES OF BIOLOGY GRADUATES IN RELATION TO TROUBLESOME KNOWLEDGE AND POSSIBLE THRESHOLD CONCEPTS

During 2005-2006 biology students and graduates, all currently conducting individual research projects as part of their honours year, or working on a PhD project, participated in an extension of the aforementioned study.

The participants were recruited from different areas within biology, including plant and animal ecology, genetics, molecular biology, plant biochemistry and mycology to represent the range of fields within the discipline. Graduates were asked to provide examples of thresholds and troublesome knowledge given the Meyer and Land (2003) definitions of the two. After discussion of their experiences of problem areas in their degree, they were provided with the perceptions of the teachers, and asked in what way their experiences matched these views.

Overall, the graduates could also relate to the definitions, and had reflected on the questions and their experiences in biology or related disciplines in science. However, while general ideas were floated by each interviewee as possible threshold concepts or troublesome areas, they were not expanded on in the detail shown by teachers. Many concepts initially raised were from other branches of science eg mathematics or chemistry and sometimes related to experiences in school. An analysis of the topics covered from all interviews, indicated that senior students seemed to remember relatively few topics, from their early undergraduate years, that had been problematic to the extent that they would be classified as threshold concepts in biology.

> Third year molecular biology, I don't think I ever got it! I don't think I knew it at the time; I got through it, but couldn't teach it to someone else – that's the benchmark. (Interviewee 2)

> In molecular biology there were lots of difficult concepts far too much. Then lab classes would make sense of the topic, the tute would use analogies. They're incredibly useful for difficult abstract concepts, you can't see them. (Interviewee 5)

Many examples focused on the mass of theory covered in first year courses, but rationalised the necessity for this. It was agreed that the basic theory was necessary before you could embark on more detailed and relevant study in higher years. Graduates also identified the same dislocation of understanding in lower undergraduate years which had been discussed by the teachers. One interviewee referred to the 'island effect' of pieces of knowledge sitting in isolation.

> In lower years it's like a lot of jigsaw pieces, you can't do anything with them, you don't know enough. You see later and can make the links. Once you recognise they are linked that's what makes them useful. Once you've done it before you can see how it came together. (Interviewee 3)

The whole of first year was a blur, though the pracs were fun, they linked to the theory and things made sense. Biology was important though because it was about you. (Interviewee 7)

Teachers had discussed this problem at some length, to explain the difference between teaching and learning in first year courses and making links in higher level courses (Taylor, 2006). Graduates agreed that there has to be a grounding in theory, requiring a large amount of material being presented in the first year, and also that these concepts would be repeated in later years with a focus on more useful contexts.

There's a change comes in the third year, and your understanding evolves with the change. In first year I felt I had to learn what's required, learning towards the exam; that's a different way of learning. (Interviewee 2)

These reflections on the learning experiences of early undergraduate years would fit closely with the theories of difficulties discussed by Perkins (1999).

Graduates were less likely to mention the abstract nature of possible threshold concepts in biology, although there were some examples.

There are abstract concepts such as 'What is the scale at which you define something like species and population?' There are so many different scales, you have to keep redefining all the time because of these problems, and have to write with this context in mind. (Interviewee 1)

This may be due to the fact that teachers are generally covering a broader range of concepts in their courses and are more likely to see commonality across areas of biology. Graduates seemed to focus more on the areas related to specific theory, perhaps a reflection of their more recent learning experiences and involvement with learning for exams and assessment. When asked about other concept areas which had been raised by teachers they felt that few had been problems. For example, all interviewees were asked to give their views on the language of biology as a threshold concept, but most saw this as an example of troublesome knowledge in earlier years of the degree.

With language in biology I expected that to happen. I came here to find out about these things, to see what people were talking about. I wanted to be part of it so you learn the language. (Interviewee 2)

Here the interviewee takes responsibility for dealing with something troublesome, as a result of which they have the opportunity to become more like the biologists they meet in their courses. Hence, as students, these graduates appeared to recognize troublesome knowledge, and make a conscious effort to work with it, since it would allow them to cross a larger threshold to becoming a biologist.

As you go on you have to reevaluate new material – that's what's fun! (Interviewee 8)

This ability to acknowledge problems, and take responsibility for them in learning, is a key characteristic of all the graduates interviewed. Of course these graduates have been very successful in their undergraduate courses so may not have encountered significant problems in biology. In addition they have all embarked on a new stage of their education, which has provided them with more significant challenges, thus diminishing the effects of earlier problems. The extent to which they identified thresholds concepts at this higher level will be discussed later.

THE SIGNIFICANCE OF THE EXPERIENCE OF TEACHING IN THE IDENTIFICATION OF THRESHOLD CONCEPTS

A distinct facet of many interviews involved discussion of potential threshold concepts in the context both of being troublesome for students and for the graduates themselves when trying to teach. Further thoughts on the topic veered towards what might be improved in teaching, and how to approach these problem areas. Since most of the graduates were engaged in tutoring or demonstrating, particularly in first year classes, this proved an interesting development to the conversations. This area was a key section of interviews with teachers, who necessarily spent significant time in the classroom. Graduates however, unilaterally explored the way in which teaching required them to think about troublesome knowledge and thresholds (Vermunt & Verloop, 1999). All those involved in teaching agreed on the discontinuity in early years where didactic teaching, and cramming knowledge, led to a situation where material would not be understood by students and needed further work. There was much discussion about how they perceived students to be making links between different areas of knowledge to come to a new understanding, and how they were trying to do the same thing in their own teaching.

> I find I'm trying to think in a new way, explaining in more than one way, remembering things which may be problems and then work out how I'd explain it, I test myself before the labs ..... (Interviewee 1)

Since the graduate interviewees had been engaged in teaching first years for varying lengths of time, there was significant variation in the way in which they thought about how to engage with students and their problems.

> I can explain through the practicals, use drawing for examples, but students don't make the links and demonstrators can't do it for them. Students have to make their own links between labs and back to the theory in lectures (Interviewee 1)

> Teachers can show examples but students don't follow. You need to use it yourself and see how it works. (Interviewee 4)

> When you're teaching several ways of explaining, it's like charades, you try until one way works. It's about getting into the space in the other person's mind. (Interviewee 3)

In many cases the tutors and demonstrators form the main contact point for students having problems with biology. Lectures have been shown to be less useful as forum for discussion of problems, and the graduates are very aware of their responsibility to the students in labs or tutorials, where discussion and opportunities for further explanation occur. They also showed a keen interest in all aspects of the curriculum and provided interesting insights into thresholds in assessment, which may not have been obvious to lecturers and examiners. Graduates were very clear, in their discussions, that they had now *joined a community* in which they engaged with challenges inherent in biology (Becher, 2001). While they articulated this sense of belonging in a research culture, it is also important that we encourage them to be partners in all aspects of teaching and the curriculum. Such initiatives are crucial, since teaching approaches have a significant effect on learning and understanding in the discipline (Prosser *et al.*, 2005; Martin & Leuckenhausen, 2005).

> There's a problem with this for students in that they have exam questions which should be easy but students don't see it – they don't know what scale to answer on – There's more than one answer and they can't work it out (Interviewee 1)

> At the level of threshold concepts I think students see things as different blocks, and keep them separate. You develop knowledge only in terms of what you need to know to get through. There's also no connection between courses and the concepts of application loses the students. (Interviewee 6)

Each student differs in their interaction with the learning environment, depending on the context in which they find themselves (Prosser & Trigwell, 1999). If they are struggling with a concept which requires a certain focus to cross the threshold, some students *create* the environment or conditions in which they can surmount the challenge. Our graduates articulate their experiences of this at various stages in their degree, culminating in awareness of their ability to meet the challenges of post graduate projects where they have complete control over the context in which they operate.

Discussions with graduates to this point seem to have focused on areas encompassed by Davies and Mangan's (2005) basic concepts. Many responses seemed to be focusing on areas of biology which were certainly troublesome, but were also more complex than that expected of a fundamental threshold. This mirrored the same argument postulated when interviewing the teachers, namely that biology has a special level of complexity, and the more fundamental threshold concepts have already been dealt with at the school level. The graduates did however, give detailed accounts of the point at which they moved from complete misunderstanding of difficult material, by making links between areas of knowledge which allowed them to cross the threshold.

Osmosis is counter intuitive, it goes the opposite way. When does it click? When you study marine fish in 2nd or 3rd year, you see what would happen, it's in a relevant situation. In first year you do mechanisms in blocks and there's no relevance. (Interviewee 5)

A key threshold concept, or series of related concepts, identified by all graduates, was associated with experimental design, hypothesis development and data analysis.

The concept of a hypothesis, I hadn't ever put anything into a testable hypothesis. I still do that 'what is the question and how can it be answered.' You have to write it specifically, it needs to be unambiguous, and only testing one thing. (Interviewee 2)

Using statistics to analyse data – it helps to have a relevance, then you can apply it to biology. If you have seen it before then you think, what could I do with it? If not, it's too new to use. (Interviewee 4)

The use of statistical tests, how you apply to the data. The way it's limiting what you can do, it's definitely counter intuitive. (Interviewee 5)

Most saw an understanding of these concepts as a major change in the way *they thought* about these areas in biology, and such thinking required the integration of concepts. Thus the experiences of these graduates in grasping the significance of osmosis, experimental design, hypothesis testing and use of statistical tests certainly involved a change which was transformational, irreversible and integrational – the key characteristics of a discipline threshold concept (Meyer & Land, 2003; Davies & Mangan, 2005). A threshold concept has been described as 'a keystone bringing form and robustness where previously there was a collection of ideas' (Davies, 2006, p. 203) which describes an interesting parallel with the concept of a keystone in biology. A keystone species is defined a one which is part of an ecological community, and is involved in a web of interaction and interdependences, but has a disproportionately high influence on the functioning of the system. The species can thus be used as a focal point for conservation biology, since if the keystone species is 'happy' it is assumed that the whole system is 'happy'. Threshold concepts perform a similar function since they have a central role in combining a series of concepts which, to students, are not obviously related. Grasping the threshold concept thus has significant power in creating a new view of the disciplinary knowledge.

GRADUATES PERCEPTIONS OF CROSSING THRESHOLDS

As interviewees continued talking about the idea of challenges and thresholds, the discussions moved to their more recent experiences carrying out honours projects and starting a PhD. They recognized that they had been, or were currently, crossing thresholds, but now knew how to cope with them. This change in approach to the challenge of new thresholds was universally acknowledged as being mainly due to the training in the honours program.

Thus we move into more complex engagement with the discipline which is encapsulated both in Modelling Concepts (Davies & Mangan, 2005) and 'ways of thinking and practising' (McCune & Hounsell, 2005; Entwistle & McCune, 2001).

> You have to start applying the theory before it makes sense. In ecology you have to put your own interpretation onto things. First years don't know this, Second years have sessions which help you do this, Honours requires you to think and explain why you did what you did. As a postgrad you're your own boss, field work engenders this, and you create as you go, thinking dynamically, making new tools. You have to be challenged! (Interviewee 1)

Most graduates realised that they had been building towards this all the way through undergraduate study, such that they could now face challenges and know what to do. They expressed great confidence in their ability to work with what they perceived to be obvious thresholds. A similar area in which all graduates appeared to be working with a distinct threshold was associated with the complexity and dynamics of biology. Although these abstract concepts had been mentioned in a number of contexts, relating to particular fields of biology in which graduates were now working, it was clear that their ability to make the links necessary for crossing thresholds and understanding complex concepts now allowed a more detailed and holistic picture of biology to emerge. The graduates articulated this in a number of ways, demonstrating the bringing together of disparate areas of biology and trying out of concepts in new situations as their research projects demanded. The graduates articulated this in a number of ways, demonstrating the bringing together of disparate areas of biology and trying out of concepts in new situations as their research projects demanded.

> In honours you're independent, solving problems developing skills and it gives you a much better perspective on biology. (Interviewee 6)

> In honours you're doing more analyzing, you have time to make mistakes and things don't work, and you start to understand when you've screwed it up every way. It's about being a scientist. (Interviewee 7 and 8)

> Going to a conference, and at the end all the different bits were working together with a common theme – mammals. You can see how physiology, genetics, ecology, though you don't study them all, do different parts of the same story. (Interviewee 3)

This engagement with the complexity of biology, was particularly obvious for one graduate who had moved from a related discipline to carry out research in biology. This interview described a progression involving a constant focus on working with various thresholds.

You need to use one topic to understand another, 'You know this now apply it to this area'. You need practice but it's hard to test applying to new situations to some extent in exams, so when does it happen? (Interviewee 3)

The move to biology then required a change in approach to using knowledge in a very different context, and in adapting methodologies to fit different systems.

Can you recognize the change? There's a progression, with little things all fitting together. But then you can relate to different problems, you can change systems. I used dyes for reactions in Chemistry, but now I'm using them in living systems in biology, and seeing if it all fits together. It's a whole different perspective, as in biology it takes longer to develop working with living things it's longer and slower. (Interviewee 6)

Thus a new area can be identified where students have to work with concepts which present a distinct threshold. Graduates talked about these experiences as different to the necessity to grapple with troublesome knowledge in the early years of their degree. All the interviewees appeared to recognize topics as troublesome and described tactics for dealing with them. In some cases this involved shifting the focus of their degree to avoid the topic: aspects of molecular biology were mentioned as falling into this category. In general, the graduates were highly motivated to become biologists, and felt that the effort required to incorporate troublesome knowledge into their understanding of biology was justified. They then engaged with a series of distinct threshold concepts in their honours program. Success in crossing these thresholds was attributed to an ability to recognize them as such, being able to work with them in a relevant context, and the opportunity to take ownership of the situation through work on their projects. Students at this stage of their learning have clearly passed through a phase where they are engaged with the modeling conceptual changes described by Davies and Mangan (2006). It is also obvious that as part of this process they have acquired the more sophisticated levels of thinking and practising inherent in being a biologist.

HOW DO WE WORK WITH TROUBLESOME KNOWLEDGE, THRESHOLD CONCEPTS AND WAYS OF THINKING AND PRACTISING IN BIOLOGY?

The interviews with teachers and graduates provide clear evidence of the complexity of the discipline of biology, and build a distinct picture of key areas of troublesome knowledge and potential thresholds. Both groups identified a number of areas of biology which possessed the characteristics of threshold concepts, and most of these areas dealt with the complexity, dynamics and variability in biological systems. The area of molecular biology was seen by many as particularly troublesome as it involved concepts which are constantly changing as new discoveries are made. Graduates are keenly aware of their new position at the cutting edge in science, and the inherent problems and challenges in this area. The boundaries have to be constantly re-assessed and the new knowledge and thinking integrated into the view of the discipline.

> We have to decide what are the standard areas of biology, much of biology is new, biochemistry is still advancing, DNA becomes more complex with too many components. Biologists have to regulate what's 'in' and what's 'out', as we add in new areas and applications. (Interviewee 6)

A different perspective on molecular biology sees this constantly emerging area as fundamental to biology and the foundation for the disparate fields within the discipline. Interestingly, it also makes elegant use of the same analogy, expressed in an earlier interview with teachers, to explain students' experience of crossing thresholds.

> If you see molecular biology as the floor of a big sea, then all the different bits of biology are little islands sitting in it. Now the water levels are falling and we can understand what's on this seafloor, more and more is exposed. Once we can see the floor, we appreciate that it holds together all the islands, and shows how all biology is linked together (I. Hughes pers.comm.)

Clearly our graduates have successfully engaged with this rapidly evolving world of theory and investigation, as a result of their experiences during their undergraduate careers, to the extent that they have been transformed by their experience.

> Once you're a scientist, a biologist, you have to think differently, you can't go back. You can't watch something like Mythbusters any more, because you know they're not replicating, not enough samples, ignoring the inherent variability! (Interviewee 5)

An analysis of the interviews described above has further enhanced our understanding of threshold concepts by incorporating a new dimension into our view of problem areas in biology. This has involved following the progression of students through the degree program to their acceptance into the research community. The challenge for teachers in undergraduate biology is to incorporate ideas of conceptual change, and threshold concepts into a series of learning experiences which guide, model and demonstrate processes of integration of knowledge. This support for students will allow them to practice bringing together different understandings of a topic to cross conceptual thresholds. They are then in a position to take up the task of developing their integrative skills in research and enquiry such that they become productive members of this dynamic discipline.

ACKNOWLEDGMENTS

I would like to thank all the biology graduates who provided insights into their experiences as undergraduates and as part of the biology community. I am grateful to Noel Entwistle for spending time in very stimulating discussions on threshold concepts and ways of thinking and practising, and to Peter Davies and Jean Mangan for sharing their experiences of threshold concepts in Economics and discussing parallels in biology.

REFERENCES

Becher, T. & Trowler, P. R. (2001). *Academic tribes and territories: Intellectual enquiry and the culture of disciplines.* Philadelphia: Open University Press.

Davies, P. (2006). Threshold concepts: How can we recognize them? In J. H. F. Meyer & R. Land (Eds.), *Overcoming barriers to student understanding: threshold concepts and troublesome knowledge.* London and New York: Routledge.

Davies, P. & Mangan, J. (2005). Recognizing threshold concepts: An exploration of different approaches. Paper presented at the 11th biannual conference of the *European Association for Research on Learning and Instruction* (EARLI), Nicosia, Cyprus, August 23-27.

Entwistle, N. J. & McCune, V. (2001). Conceptions, styles and approaches within higher education: analytic abstractions and everyday experience. In R. Sternberg & L-F. Zhang (Eds.), *Perspectives on cognitive, learning, and thinking styles.* Mahwah, NJ: Lawrence Erlbaum.

Martin, E. & Leuckenhausen, G. (2005). How university teaching changes teachers: affective as well as cognitive challenges. *Higher Education, 49*(3), 389-412.

Martin, E., Prosser, M., Trigwell, K., Ramsden, P., & Benjamin, J. (2000). What university teachers teach, and how they teach it. *Instructional Science, 28*(5). 387-412.

McCune, V. & Hounsell, D. (2005). The development of students' ways of thinking and practising in three final-year biology courses. *Higher Education, 49*(3), 255-289.

Meyer, J. H. F. & Land, R. (2003). Threshold concepts and troublesome knowledge: linkages to ways of thinking and practising within the disciplines. In C. Rust (Ed.), *Improving student learning. Improving student learning theory and practice — 10 years on.* Oxford: OCSLD.

Meyer, J. H. F. & Land, R. (2005). Threshold concepts and troublesome knowledge (2): Epistemological considerations and a conceptual framework for teaching and learning. *Higher Education. 49*(3), 373-388.

Meyer, J. H. F. & Land R. (Eds.) (2006). *Overcoming barriers to student understanding: Threshold concepts and troublesome knowledge.* London and New York: Routledge.

Perkins, D. N. (1999). The many faces of constructivism. *Educational Leadership, 57*(3), 6-11.

Prosser, M. & Trigwell, K. (1999). Relational perspectives on higher education: Teaching and learning in the sciences. *Studies in Science Education, 33,* 31-60.

Prosser, M., Martin, E., Trigwell, K., Ramsden, P., & Luekenhausen, G. (2005). Academics' experiences of understanding their subject matter and the relationship of this to their experiences of teaching and learning. *Instructional Science, 33*(2), 137-157.

Taylor, C. E. (2006). Threshold concepts in biology: Do they fit the definition? In J. H. F. Meyer & R. Land (Eds.), *Overcoming barriers to student understanding: Threshold concepts and troublesome knowledge.* London and New York: Routledge.

Trigwell, K., Prosser, M., Martin, E. & Ramsden, P. (2005). University teachers' experiences of change in their understanding of the subject matter they have taught. *Teaching in Higher Education, 10*(2), 251-264.

Vermunt, J. D. & Verloop, N. (1999). Congruence and friction between learning and teaching. *Learning and Instruction, 9*(3), 257-280.

AFFILIATION

Charlotte E. Taylor
School of Biological Sciences
University of Sydney

MOYA COVE, JULIE MCADAM & JAMES MCGONIGAL

15. MENTORING, TEACHING AND PROFESSIONAL TRANSFORMATION

Knowledge and understanding are transformed in unpredictable ways for beginning teachers. Their first steps in teaching children are often a revelation about how other human beings learn, and about how they themselves need to re-frame their own prior knowledge of subjects and concepts to encourage learning in others. The process of learning to teach is itself a new discipline, freighted with professional discourse and practical procedures that they struggle to grasp during the brief, turbulent period of a Postgraduate Certificate of Education (PGCE) year of training.

Breakthroughs in teaching rarely take place in isolation. The struggle with professional understanding happens within social contexts that can sustain the young teacher through new experiences. But each teacher must, as an individual, make the breakthroughs that will transform his or her realisation of what children's learning can be. Such transformations are the subject of this chapter, which also explores the social capital that accrues for inexperienced teachers from their more experienced mentors within the school community; from the professional and inter-personal norms into which they are inducted; and from the networks of personal, professional and community relationships in which they must make their way. Methods of teacher induction attempt to achieve some combination of the necessary conceptual or propositional knowledge (knowing that, or about) together with the procedural or strategic knowledge (knowing how to, or when) and the dispositional knowledge of values and attitudes (knowing whether to, or why) that experienced teachers and professional bodies emphasise as central to classroom effectiveness and whole-school ethos (Billett, 1993; Mason, 2000).

The Scottish mentoring programme for beginning teachers offers the continuity of one guaranteed probation year of paid employment that also provides some 30% of non-contact time to engage in a range of staff development activities. It provides a radical alternative to the variability that pertains elsewhere in the UK system (Draper et al., 2004). Our project set out to examine the early professional develop-ment of a group of beginning teachers during the probation year in Scottish schools that is now guaranteed to PGCE students graduating from their one-year course in Faculties of Education in Scottish universities. In particular, it focused on continuities and developments between the mentoring that they receive from university tutors during initial teacher education and the subsequent school-based mentoring arrangements provided by Local Authorities during that probation year.

Our project used two main theories to illuminate the empirical data gained through focus groups, questionnaires and semi-structured interviews: *threshold*

R. Land, J.H.F. Meyer & J. Smith (Eds.), Threshold Concepts within the Disciplines, 197-211.

concepts as key conceptual gateways to confident progress in professional knowledge and skills (Meyer & Land, 2003, 2005); and *social capital*, which is just beginning to be applied in school contexts but still lacks sufficient empirical basis for its heuristic potential (McGonigal *et al.*, 2007). We wanted to explore the intersections between the threshold concepts discerned by beginning primary and secondary teachers (and their tutors) during their one-year pre-service PGCE course, and by their professional mentors during the school session immediately following. These are two linked but distinctive liminal spaces. We also wanted to examine those concepts through the professional contexts and social relationships in which troublesome knowledge emerges, and through the sorts of social capital which can engender and sustain, or else close down, a positive understanding of such transformative experience for beginning teachers. (Brief definitions of social capital terms are included in Appendix A, based on Catts & Ozga, 2005.)

CONTEXT OF RESEARCH

Using an initial cohort of 24 probationer teachers employed in 10 Local Authorities from Highlands and Islands in the far north of Scotland to Dumfries and Galloway on the border with England, and a cohort of 10 primary and secondary mentors from 6 of these authorities, we developed a methodology that included taped focus groups, discourse analysis of resulting transcripts, an on-line questionnaire, and semi-structured interviews of probationer teachers and mentors from their employing authorities (not their current mentors, for reasons of confidentiality). These authorities vary in size and topography, with Dumfries and Galloway and Highland being predominantly rural, and the others mainly urban.

We sought to answer the following key questions, which explore intersecting dimensions of troublesome knowledge and social capital:

- What are the key networks of professional support that are available to student and probationer teachers, and by what means are these sustained?
- At what points, and by whose induction, do beginning teachers adapt their academic 'subject discourse' to professional discourse, values and sense of identity?
- What crucially transformative or integrative 'threshold points' do students and probationer teachers recognise and cross in teaching a range of subjects, within both primary and secondary sectors?
- What social value do beginning teachers and their mentors place on such transformative experiences?
- To what extent might threshold concepts or troublesome knowledge be used to reconfigure the curriculum in PGCE and probationer years?

Two mixed focus groups of PGCE Primary and Secondary student teachers at the end of their pre-service training were used to clarify issues that had been, or continued to be, problematic for them. Structured around troublesome issues, events and terminology encountered during their pre-service year, as well as such social capital features as networks, norms, trust and reciprocity as they might have met on their course and school placements, these taped discussions furnished some three hours of transcripts. From them we were able to identify possible threshold concepts or troublesome knowledge, interleaved with social capital dimensions of the emotional and relational world of classroom and school that had impacted upon their student teacher experience. Of course, these were anecdotal and embedded within particular experiences, yet they seemed to resonate for the groups: (in)effective use of language to foster learning and engagement; class management and school discipline issues; lesson planning and pedagogy; the opacity of some the 'benchmark statements' of the Standard for Initial Teacher Education (already achieved, but without students knowing exactly what the statements really meant); social and professional relationships within schools; and a disconcerting lack of correlation between some teachers' seniority and their actual effectiveness in the classroom – all of these still figured as worrying dimensions of their professional lives to come.

Summarised, this furnished a draft of 9 possible threshold concepts, eventually used as a Likert Scale that was a final contribution to the semi-structured interviews for both probationers and mentors, but only after it had undergone refinement through anonymous comment and testing on the electronic network of participants, of which more will be said below.

1. Teaching is about learning, and about structuring/segmenting the content to meet pupils' needs, newly understood.
2. 'Less is more' in the classroom, or can be: it is useless to try to teach too much for children to take in or relate to.
3. Language controls relationships in the classroom, and beginning teachers need to learn how to talk in a way that children listen and respond to.
4. In matters of class management, an individual teacher is most effective when contributing to or helping to sustain community ethos and structures.
5. One comes to understand the place of reflection and careful observation in learning to teach more 'professionally'.
6. One comes to understand one's own role in the mentoring process and what the aim of mentoring is.
7. 'Professionalism' is seen as the freedom to make an informed and considered choice.
8. Taking advice and guidance from others is basically a matter of trust.
9. One comes to understand the point of professional language/jargon with more experience of working with others in schools and communities.

To permit limited ongoing contact with these beginning teachers, while allowing them autonomy to develop new professional relationships with mentors and other colleagues, we designed an online database and questionnaire (which could only be responded to anonymously) and used this to test out the possible threshold concepts already mentioned, and to invite comments on or descriptions of incidents, perceptions or experiences that seemed to match these. This provided us with some key insights to be probed in semi-structured interviews out in schools. It also prompted some of the probationers to keep reflecting on issues that they might otherwise have forgotten or internalised.

Troublesome knowledge on the one year PGCE course had typically involved class management and behaviour, teaching methodologies and assessment issues. To that extent, the experiences were typical of what Berliner (1994) terms the 'novice' stage, but also touching on what Meyer and Land (2003) term 'liminality' and 'mimicry'. Even at this early stage, however, it was clear to some at least of the participants that observing very young children's engagement in their own learning during the pre-service Nursery placement had opened a transformative conceptual gateway concerning the nature of learning and teaching. The online questionnaire gave clear evidence that working with children with additional learning needs can also enable beginning teachers to 'see' them as individuals, and to move through what appears to be an irreversible shift of pedagogic perspective.

The centrality of relationships and communication in classroom learning emerged clearly, and it was here that a social capital focus on the networks, norms, trust and reciprocity that marked their progress towards professional identity provided a useful perspective. A vignette of one young teacher's experience is included in Appendix A. Briefly, we found various kinds of social capital present in the beginning teacher's experience. *Bonding capital* was available, for example, through Local Authority support systems and identification with fellow probationers and recently qualified teachers: *'knowing they were in the same position last year'*. The more professionally useful *Bridging capital* came from beginning to make links with other professionals, such as the Area Learning Support Network staff: *'it's good when you're looking for a job, they know your skills, it's like having a friend'*. Mentors sometimes began early to position their mentees for future job interviews, giving advice on what questions to expect and experiences to highlight. Thus networks of all kinds are crucial in the Probation year: networks of knowledge, electronic networks with other probationers (used to share ideas and resources) and professional networks, as well as friendships carried forward from the PGCE year, based mainly on their professional tutorial group. Social capital was interleaved with the extended threshold concepts that were developed from our analysis of taped interviews with the beginning teachers and their mentors.

EXTENDED THRESHOLD CONCEPTS

The early establishment of classroom 'norms' of behaviour, organisation, and a 'learned effectiveness' within classroom life had, in prospect, seemed particularly troublesome. Learning to confidently walk the social and pedagogical boundaries between firmness, direction and supportive engagement with young learners may well be a threshold concept that eases the pursuit of many other classroom aims. Listening to these beginning teachers' experiences and reflections, we found a validation of the initial troublesome areas identified a year earlier, but a firmer sense of where threshold concepts had begun to alter their awareness of teaching and learning. This led to a more nuanced articulation of the original nine concepts, and the addition of a tenth, as outlined below.

1. Teaching is about learning, both the particular achievements of individual children (often those who have initially presented 'problems' for the beginning teacher) and also the progress made by the class as a whole.

Teaching had come to be seen as being crucially about structuring or segmenting or pacing the subject content appropriately, in order to meet pupils' needs, increasingly with greater relevance. This created a vertical dimension to learning: a sense of depth.

There was in some cases a discovery of what assessment really is, what its forms and purposes are, how it can shape future teaching and learning, and how it can clarify learning purposes and positively affect children's attitudes and awareness. Problems in planning in relation to assessment and how this skill might be developed had been noted in the initial focus groups, but it did not emerge as an ongoing problem within the interviews. Perhaps it might return as an issue at a later stage of teacher development, and what was registering now was their general early increase in confidence about standards of performance, or about children's potential. The various induction programmes run centrally by Local Authorities would also have focused on both summative assessment at national level and formative assessment techniques for classroom learning.

Whatever was the case, assessment as currently understood seemed to offer a humane dimension to their work, helping them to move beyond a judgemental approach. This concept often involved 'children who make teachers think' and the realisation that this is a better working description than 'difficult' or 'troublesome' children. They had begun to think more deeply about the impact of social and emotional background on such children's learning, and about more responsive and effective ways of teaching them. This new awareness was often combined with the realisation of concept two:

2. The same curriculum can be effectively taught in different ways by different teachers across different stretches of time.

These beginning teachers had realised from experience that it is useless to try to teach too much for children to absorb or retain (a common fault early in the PGCE year). A more confident awareness had emerged of the need to pace the curriculum and to estimate children's understanding over longer stretches of time. They now understood that the rhythm of learning involves peaks and troughs: a horizontal dimension that can offer breadth to the learning, and a more 'relaxed' yet alert sense of how to return to the same learning issues over these longer stretches, varying the teaching slightly each time. This moved significantly beyond the 'one-off lesson' that had featured in PGCE school placements.

A third key conceptual shift was a more confident understanding that:

3. Language creates ethos, atmosphere and positive working relationships in the classroom, and beginning teachers can learn how to talk in a way that children listen and respond to.

This involved a realisation of the impact of tone, pitch, pace, emphasis and volume, varied empathetically according to the age, stage, needs and norms of the children being taught. The part played by modulation, rather than volume, was noted as a breakthrough in classroom communication. Learning to talk in a way for which recent degree studies had not at all prepared the beginning teacher, particularly with very young learners (and which actually sounds 'odd' or 'out of (social) character') was seen as particularly effective in gaining children's attention and trust. The impact extended to, and varied within, different contexts beyond the classroom: corridor, playground, sports field, outside the school gates and into the local community. Issues of dialect, accent and solidarity with the community impinge here. There was a growing awareness that the teacher's language needs to model for children (and sometimes for parents) helpful patterns of effective thinking and social relationships.

Our probationers were beginning to explore the tensions between Standard English precision in classroom language (with its potential to provide bridging capital to the language of literacy and formal registers of social discourse) and the local dialect of their pupils (with its bonding capital of community identity). Some were teaching in towns where they themselves had gone to school, rendering this negotiation of linguistic identity even more complex. Exploring social class boundaries, and the relationship between one's own emerging professional discourse and a (possible) identification or empathy with the social class background of pupils, seems potentially a site of troublesome knowledge, and perhaps a threshold concept. Sport or other after-school activities provided occasions to reflect less problematically upon these tensions of relationship or identity, since strands of language, emotion, teamwork and trust were intuitively interwoven there.

All of this impacted on issues of class management and discipline, which had concerned these beginning teachers before probation, seeing it mainly as a test of their individual professional success, rather than as a shared community endeavour. Now they revealed a much more confident and committed sense of the crucial effect of the establishment of classroom 'norms' of behaviour, organisation, and learned effectiveness (for both probationer teachers and pupils):

4. In class and behaviour management, an individual teacher is most effective when contributing to and helping to sustain whole-school ethos and structures.

They were learning to define more precisely for their pupils and themselves the emotional boundaries between firmness, direction and supportive engagement with learning. Similarly now, school disciplinary systems appeared generally supportive to beginners. There was every appearance of them learning confidence in employing discipline strategies effectively and consistently, and discovering how this can assist effective teaching and learning. In marked contrast to the PGCE experience, discipline matters now became more '*mundane*', and part of normal classroom functioning. This in itself may be part of the social capital of teacher-pupil relationships, as trust and awareness build the sort of positive 'bonding' over the course of a consistent year of daily contact which is, of course, impossible to achieve during the brief and varied periods of school experience (in up to five different establishments in the Primary PGCE, and three in the Secondary) during initial training.

Pupils' response (which can be gradual) to the beginning teacher's intentions, and positive whole-class teacher-pupil relationships generally, appear as the keys to conceptual gateways for both parties. It is noteworthy how often breakthroughs are embodied in dealing with more challenging pupils. Learning how to deal with emotional and behavioural problems more effectively, with an increasing awareness of the complexity of individuals and their backgrounds, seemed to signal threshold experiences for several of our cohort.

5. One realises what makes reflection work, and its importance in learning to teach more insightfully and effectively.

The ideal of 'the reflective practitioner' has been a shaping influence on course design and assessment in initial teacher education during recent times (Banks & Shelton Mayes, 2001; Moon, 2003). Reflection is often a troublesome concept for beginning teachers, sitting as it does at an unforeseen angle to the sorts of performative and content-based learning of their degree studies. Faculty tutors often struggle, with variable success, to convey the purpose of evaluation of teaching and learning, and of broader reflection on professional progress, and to provide methods or 'targets' that might enable this particular 'benchmark' or 'competence' (the jargon varies) to be understood.

In contrast, we found among the probationers that there was now a more personalised approach to reflection and to where it happened most effectively for individuals, and a new awareness of what aids or sustains it. Possible sources of reflection included careful observation, conversations about classroom incidents, ideas encountered in current or previous reading, and (in one case) journalling continued from ITE models. More formal dialogue with colleagues, electronic and social networks of professional friends, and effective use of thinking time between a mentor's observation of their teaching and receiving feedback upon it were also helpful.

Some interviewees contrasted their earlier PGCE awareness with a newly confident accuracy of classroom observation of other teachers and pupils. Mentors encouraged such opportunities for reflection. Learning to discriminate between effective teaching and a 'merely' authoritative or experienced classroom persona had become possible. Several expressed this in terms of being able to transform or transpose what they had seen others do into the context of their own classroom style or pupil stage, moving on from earlier mimicry.

Apart from critical incidents and colleagues' advice, prompts on key developmental issues can promote and support reflection. Our on-line questionnaire functioned for some probationers in this way. But broadly, there was a realisation that effective teachers are thinking much of the time about effective teaching and learning, and planning for this. Part of any mentor's role is to prompt and support reflection, helping beginners to articulate the significance of this sort of thinking, listening out for areas of puzzlement and giving advice on new or alternative directions. Effectively done, this leads towards a sixth dimension of professional awareness, although not all probationers may be fortunate in moving through it.

6. One comes to understand one's own role in the mentoring process and what the aim of the mentoring process is.

There appeared in some beginning teachers to be a conceptual movement from a basic acceptance of being judged on classroom performance to becoming an active and interactive partner in a developing professional project. This involved a basic trust in the mentoring system, generally enhanced by a layering of networks of support and advice, at varying levels of formality. There was a realisation, achieved through observation, anecdote or the attitude of more experienced colleagues, that success in teaching is subject to many variables but that commitment and a positive outlook are nevertheless sustainable and vital.

Features of positive mentoring, as articulated by mentors and mentees, included planned opportunities for shadowing and observation of colleagues (which in secondary also focused on subjects beyond the probationers' own specialisms), targeted visits to external agencies and special schools to extend their professional knowledge and help them serve the more particular needs of their pupils, and the shadowing of colleagues on the first Parents Evening of the year to reduce predicted anxiety. Both mentors and mentees were largely positive about the support for probationers provided by their local authority, and the needs of the mentors themselves were recognised through the facilitation of area mentor meetings.

Mentors themselves were found to be helpful and supportive, and mentoring offered beginning teachers both social capital and a way of handling troublesome knowledge. Learning to negotiate the complexity of the mentoring relationship, particularly as it is connected with current success and future employment prospects, proved difficult, however, when the mentor was '*too powerful*' or there was a clash of roles, such as in one case where the mentor was also the probationer's line manager, and early problems with classroom discipline made communication and trust difficult.

How mentors create and sustain trust, or embody professionalism for others, is a critical area and one which involves developing a mutually respectful relationship which moves beyond the level of assessor and assessed. Mentors felt this was often achieved through a growing appreciation that the mentoring partnership brought about learning for both parties. Recognising and valuing the talents and skills which new teachers brought into the school helped to validate them as professionals and to enhance their trust in the mentoring process. Mentors recognised that trust came through an openness to sharing vulnerabilities as well as professional strengths, and that emotional support was indeed intrinsic to mentoring.

7. 'Professionalism' comes to be seen as attaining the confidence and 'earning' the freedom to make an informed and considered choice about how the curriculum might most effectively be paced and taught by an individual teacher with the group of learners for whom s/he is most closely responsible.

This is a complex area of professional learning, and, as originally articulated on the Likert scale, it was the threshold concept that gave rise to widest range of responses. Effective mentoring can model this combination of flexibility and responsibility, but because the mentor's role here includes a gate-keeping responsibility for professional progress that will impact on both the mentee and his or her future colleagues, it remains a troublesome threshold. From our interviews, it was clear that beginning teachers come to understand the point of professional language/jargon with more experience of working with others in schools and communities. There may have been some cases of early over-confidence here: they were surer about what the benchmark statements were meant to mean, but not perhaps of the extent of the implications of their meaning.

Many changes take place in professional confidence and self-awareness during the Probation year. Learning to define 'professionalism' in a way that is complex, personal and consonant with experience of teaching and children may be a threshold concept for some. We certainly found a changed attitude to, and confidence with the Benchmark statements in the Standard for Initial Teacher Education completed at the end of the PGCE year, and in the Standard for Full Registration completed in two stages during Probation.

What was clear was the role of relationships in teaching: the eighth threshold. Learning to trust the judgement of school colleagues, and being trusted by them, again signalled a social reciprocity that clearly meant a great deal to our probationers.

8. Relationships matter in teaching and learning: recognising the social dimensions of professional life can make a major difference to a teacher's individual effectiveness in the classroom.

Taking advice and guidance seriously from others is basically a matter of trust in their judgement. The mentoring system, as well as the basic magnanimity that other teachers had shown towards these beginners in terms of time, attention and advice (particularly their 'stage partners' in primaries, working with children at about the same level of attainment) provided grounds for such trust. There can be negative as well as positive dimensions of teacher networks, however, especially where there is a lack of active bridging and linking to wider social and professional experience. There was some evidence of the 'dark side' of bonding, where negativity and distrust of leadership initiatives led to a culture of public compliance and private complaint. Occasionally, staffroom cynicism and weariness of a much altered and continually demanding professional role provided probationers with depressing models of what teachers might become.

What were the true rewards of teaching, whether over the longer or shorter term? Some of our questions probed the 'reciprocity' that is one marker of social capital. Rewards for the beginning teacher were expressed as coming from successful teaching ('*like opening a door*'), recognition or affirmative feedback from colleagues and pupils, parental trust in the work they were doing, and respect from the community (expressed as sustaining '*the good name of the school*'). Beginners probably see these things with greater clarity and keener appreciation. Reciprocity and generosity clearly matter in the creation of satisfying professional development: making a contribution and appreciating its recognition within the community was a source of satisfaction to all concerned.

Varieties and layering of networks can support the beginning teacher: we found that electronic, social, professional and familial networks can all help extend the range of professional life beyond the narrower negativity and cliquishness that they occasionally encountered. Some considered the effect of their social and personal networks to be more positive than the sometimes constrained or contrived Local Authority networks of probationers, although there was some benefit recognised in these.

There was clear evidence of the beginning teacher's place in the local community, carrying professional norms beyond the classroom and in some sense acting as '*a role model*' for pupils and their parents. This is recognised in the ninth, perhaps most surprising, concept.

9. There is a realisation that teaching and learning take place in 'communities' that overlap and affect each other, positively and negatively: home, school and locality can assist or hinder each other's efforts for children.

Feedback from parents can be a revelation both about children and about oneself. Parents often validated the beginning teachers' effectiveness, to their surprise and delight. There was evidence of conceptual breakthroughs and social capital combining to impact upon beginning teachers' awareness through Parents Evenings, parental observation of classroom teaching, and parental presence at school concerts and seasonal celebrations. Teacher participation in extra-curricular or sports activity also seemed to offer a rich source of social capital, with a positive effect on classroom learning for some pupils, or on class management skills for beginning teachers. Indeed, coming to appreciate the balance of intellectual, emotional, physical and team learning within the school curriculum seemed to have made a breakthrough for several probationers. Within this nexus of effects, we wondered whether social capital's 'trust' might best be seen within school contexts as an alignment of social capital and threshold concepts. The questions of what it means to trust pupils, and of how trust is gained and lost, seemed worthy of further consideration.

The impact of whole-school social, celebratory, creative and sporting events appeared to symbolise for beginning teachers the worth of their individual efforts in teaching and learning. Social capital dimensions of networks, reciprocity and positive bonding and bridging capital seemed to have an influence here. The teacher's place within the communities of school and locality was realised more forcefully on such occasions, with a heightened awareness of the social norms of dress, speech, and behaviour expected by parents and colleagues.

10. There emerges an energising sense of 'owning' or 'earning' a professional identity, confidently and realistically understood.

This involved integration of many particular classroom insights or experiences encountered during the probation year. It was often evidenced by reference to a positive skill in the efficient orchestration of a range of educational factors, and it seems likely that the memory and competence of this period will rarely be lost thereafter. To that extent, this was a transformative awareness, although doubtless it might be tested by challenging pupils or fragmented schools or communities in a professional career. It was clearly felt by probationers to mark a transition, at least for this stage of development, and it was recognised as such by mentors and other colleagues as well as themselves.

USING THRESHOLD CONCEPTS IN TEACHER EDUCATION

One would note initially that there is probably a chronological element to crossing some of these thresholds. Clearly, concepts 5, 9 and 10 can only emerge over time. This may in itself be useful in clarifying for beginners the trajectory of their understandings of a teacher's work. It might also enable a continuity or progression from PGCE to Probation in terms of thresholds. Some of these thresholds may be crossed in the pre-service year (for example, 3) but most will not.

Our original ordering of nine possible threshold concepts reflected the formulation of professionalism in the General Teaching Council for Scotland's Standard for Initial Teacher Education (GTCS, 2006): *Professional knowledge and understanding, Professional skills and abilities,* and *Professional values and personal commitment.* These are then articulated into twenty-two benchmark statements and ten transferable skills. This is a reduction from the almost 50 'teaching competences' that the benchmarks sought to replace, but are still complex for beginners to comprehend. It may be that the ten threshold concepts here could help student teachers to conceptualise the distinct emphases of the above formulation, especially of the third element, which both university tutors and student teachers find difficult to discuss or assess on a confidently evidential basis, since the initial school experience is so fragmented in the PGCE year. Threshold concepts might therefore assist in developing student teachers' confidence about their progression through the teacher education experience, and its often puzzling jargon.

Other questions emerge from this formulation of our evidence. To what extent do these concepts need to be varied for university and school mentors? What other thresholds emerge from the experience of mentoring within different professional contexts? The mentoring needs of newly-seconded university tutors have also emerged as a significant issue. The whole process of networks, including the use of electronic networks, in promoting reflective learning and teaching seems important to explore. The relative effectiveness of various mentoring practices and structures across local authorities also require closer attention.

Overall, however, there is clear evidence that the quality of the Probation experience has been remarkably enhanced by the new arrangements, compared with the formerly unstructured and variable experience of too many young teachers. Schools and classrooms too have been rejuvenated by the energy and positive qualities of almost all the teachers we have been fortunate to interview. What emerges is a clearer understanding of the rewards or reciprocity that teachers expect from and give to others (colleagues, children, community). It is here that the social capital perspective that ran alongside our focus on threshold concepts has proved helpful.

> True professionalism depends on a continued commitment to hold up knowledge to public collaborative scrutiny. It also depends on the commitment to create and maintain those spaces within professional life where critical discourse can flourish. (Furlong *et al.*, 2000, p. 27)

This view would reflect our hopes for the current Scottish system, as evidenced by the experience of both mentors and mentees. Social capital's emphasis on the collaborative role of networks, norms, trust and reciprocity is responsive to the values and emotional commitment that young teachers bring to their new profession. But teaching, despite its reliance on partnerships, is also, and always, an individual pursuit of positive learning in others. To that extent the place of threshold concepts is vital, and frequently troubling, for beginning teachers, and we need to balance social insights with conceptual ones, and the sense of belonging to a professional community with the energising sense of new horizons that threshold concept theory can reveal. Mentoring can help them to walk with a certain balance (if not yet complete poise) along the unmarked borderlines and liminal spaces they must learn to negotiate if they are to be of lasting service to their pupils and school communities. Threshold concepts are encountered and crossed individually, but their fullest realisation often depends upon the insights and empathy of those who accompany us on the professional journey towards them.

APPENDIX A

Social Capital in Teachers' Early Professional Development

Social Capital is understood to be a resource that may help in *bonding* fragmented social life. It may also support the *bridging* of communities to their external environments, and the *linking* of people to formal structures and agencies. It is important to distinguish between these different forms of social capital, and to appreciate that social capital may open or limit opportunities.

BONDING Social Capital is characterised by strong bonds among group members: this variety of SC can help people to 'get by'. It is valuable in building a sense of shared identity and security. Families and school staffs may create strong bonds, and these may have supportive or restrictive effects. Bonding social capital may affect different groups in a school in different ways, or be produced in undesirable locations, for example in gangs;

BRIDGING Social Capital is a resource that helps people to build relationships with a wider, more varied set of people than those in the immediate family or school environment, for example between students and employers, or teachers and community workers. Bridging SC helps people to 'get on' and not just 'get by'. Bridging SC is understood as important in helping employment and career advancement;

LINKING Social Capital enables connections between people across differences in status, for example links between parents of children attending the same school, but from different backgrounds, or between their children. It may help teachers link with parents or children from different social, religious or ethnic backgrounds from their own. Linking social capital connects individuals and agencies or services that they would not otherwise access easily. Linking social capital may help people 'get around'.

The key words in social capital are *Networks, Norms, Trust* and *Forms of Reciprocity*. The above definitions were developed for the Schools and Social Capital Network of the Applied Educational Research Scheme [aers.org.uk].

Social Capital in the Probation Year: A Vignette

David has a PGCE in Primary Education and is more than midway through his probation year, teaching seven year olds in a Scottish denominational primary school. He experiences *Bonding SC* with parents in the local community (near where he grew up) and with pupils through taking a football team and through his earlier drama involvement with the school's Christmas show. He has a sense of identity with a colleague who teaches another class at the same age/stage: she has helped him plan and pace the curriculum more confidently. A fellow Probationer whose initial training was through a 4 year BEd course co-teaches with him, and they have developed a cohesive team approach to decision-making and class management.

Bridging SC has come from discussions with a social worker and two members of the Area Learning Support team concerning three of David's pupils. The Head and Depute of the school have introduced him to the 'wider picture' of Local Authority policies and personalities. His very helpful mentor has facilitated observation of experienced colleagues at other school stages, as well as a visit to a nearby primary school to look at their new mathematics resources. She also arranged for David to take drama lessons across the upper stages.

Linking SC has come from engaging with Local Authority advisory staff at monthly meetings for primary and secondary probationer teachers, and from membership of a school planning group on workload (as young teacher representative). As a member of his local church, David has met teachers of other faiths through an ecumenical group.

Networks both social and professional have sustained him in his work. Socially, his girlfriend (also a trainee teacher) and her mother (a teacher in a different authority) have provided a sounding board for ideas, while his father (who does not work in education) provides a sense of perspective. Professional networks include his Early Stages school colleagues and other probationers within local authority schools. Blending social and professional dimensions is the network of five friends from his education tutor group at university, who continue to meet monthly. David now has a surer sense of the *norms* of classroom interaction and of relationships with both parents and children. He has made himself familiar with expectations in local authority policy documents, and has attended two staff development courses on current issues. *Trust* has developed strongly with his pupils through a consistent, firm but good-humoured approach to classroom management. The relationship with his mentor is clearly based on trust in her advice, maturity and sense of vision. Rewards and *reciprocity* come from David's desire to make a difference in children's lives and be a 'cornerstone' for their futures. That his pupils and their parents respect his work means a great deal to him, and he has a growing awareness of providing an example of professional values and commitment within the wider community. He also believes that as a new teacher he can offer a 'fresh perspective' and new approaches even to experienced colleagues, and thus repay to some extent the efforts made by them on his behalf.

REFERENCES

Banks, F. and Shelton Mayes, A. (Eds.) (2001). *Early professional development for teachers.* London: David Fulton Publishers.

Berliner, D. (1994). Teacher expertise. In Moon, B. & Shelton Mayes, A. (Eds.), *Teaching and learning in the secondary school* (pp. 107-113) London: Routledge.

Billett, S. (1993). Authenticity and a culture of practice. *Australian and New Zealand Journal of Vocational Education Research, 2,* 1-29.

Catts, R. & Ozga, J. (2005) *What is Social Capital and how might it be used in Scotland's Schools?* CES Briefing Paper 36, December. Centre for Educational Sociology: University of Edinburgh.

Draper, J., O'Brien, J., & Christie, F. (2004). First impressions: The new teacher induction arrangements in Scotland. *Journal of Inservice Education, 30*(2), 201-223.

Furlong, J., Barton, L., Miles, S., Whiting, C., & Whitty, G. (2000). *Teacher education in transition.* Buckingham: Open University Press.

General Teaching Council for Scotland (GTCS). (2006). Standard for initial teacher education. Available from http://www.gtcs.org.uk/Publications/StandardsandRegulations [last accessed 12 June 2007].

Mason, M. (2000). Teachers as critical mediators of knowledge. *Journal of Philosophy of Education, 34*(2), 343-352.

McGonigal J., Doherty R., Allan, J. *et al.* (2007). Social capital, social inclusion and changing school contexts: A Scottish perspective. *British Journal of Educational Studies, 55* (1), 77-94.

Meyer, J. & Land, R. (2003). Threshold concepts and troublesome knowledge: Linkages to ways of thinking and practising in the disciplines. In Rust, C. (Ed.), *Improving student learning: Improving student learning theory and practice – Ten years on*. Oxford: Oxford Centre for Staff and Learning Development.

Meyer, J. & Land, R. (2005). Threshold concepts and troublesome knowledge (2): Epistemological considerations and a conceptual framework for teaching and learning. *Higher Education, 49*, 373-388.

Moon, J. A. (2003) *Reflection in learning and professional development*. London, Kogan Page.

AFFILIATION

Moya Cove
Julie McAdam
James McGonigal
Faculty of Education
University of Glasgow

MARINA ORSINI-JONES

16. TROUBLESOME LANGUAGE KNOWLEDGE: IDENTIFYING THRESHOLD CONCEPTS IN GRAMMAR LEARNING

INTRODUCTION

Nel mezzo del cammin di nostra vita
mi ritrovai per una selva oscura,
che la diritta via era smarrita.[1]
(Dante, Divina Commedia, Inferno, Canto Primo:31)

The discussion about threshold concepts in Meyer and Land (2003, 2005) has reverberations that bring to mind Medieval studies and Medieval literature, namely Dante's *La Divina Commedia* and the troubled state in which the author/narrator finds himself at the beginning of his allegorical journey, the latter being both personal ('mi ritrovai' – I found myself) and collective ('nostra vita' – our life). In fact, Dante's journey could be seen as a reflection of the four modes of variation proposed by Meyer, Land and Davies (this volume) i.e. *subliminal* (his prior knowledge, his 'baggage' before the journey), *pre-liminal* (*Inferno*/Hell), *liminal* (*Purgatorio*/Purgatory) and *post-liminal (Paradiso/*Paradise). At the beginning of the journey there is darkness, there is a dark forest, it is difficult to find the way.

It could be argued that students embark on a similar troublesome voyage when faced with concepts so challenging that they feel lost. Like Dante's allegorical journey, learning is both a personal and a collective affair. Ackermann points out that 'Without connection people cannot grow, yet without separation they cannot relate' (1996, p. 32).

It is proposed here that to help students with crossing threshold concepts it is necessary to devise student-centred activities that allow them to engage both in individual and collective reflection on the troublesome knowledge encountered. The overcoming of stumbling blocks will be greatly helped by the opening up of a dialogue between students and tutors and amongst students themselves, and by activities that foster this dialogue, as well as by encouraging students to engage in 'metareflection' on the difficulties encountered.[2]

This chapter will focus on the troublesome knowledge experienced by students in the module *Academic and Professional Skills for Language Learning* when carrying out an assessed grammar project in groups. Between 2002-2006 this

R. Land, J.H.F. Meyer & J. Smith (Eds.), Threshold Concepts within the Disciplines, 213–226.

module was compulsory for all year 1 undergraduates reading a language (or two) as a major or joint degree subject at Coventry University.

The data reproduced here refer to two cohorts of students participating in this study, those in academic years 2003-2004 and 2004-2005 with 128 students in total. In order to evaluate the students' learning experience following the introduction of a grammar project, both quantitative and qualitative data were gathered. The marks received by each student for their project, their feedback in individual reports and portfolios and WebCT tracking data were analysed. Roughly 30% of all students (self-selected) participated in semi-structured group interviews in each of the two academic years studied.

The findings of this research showed that the stumbling blocks encountered by students reading languages while engaging in reflection on how they learn a language are both of a subject specific nature (specific grammar concepts) and of a more generic skills nature (independent learning, reflection on personal development planning). Here the focus will be on the identification of the subject specific issues encountered by students while engaging in an assessed grammar group project. It will illustrate how this task was created to provide languages students with the basic tools necessary to understand how grammar works. As part of the project, students had to analyse sentences according to principles of functional grammar (using the Hallidayan *rank scale* – Halliday, 1985). The analysis of the data collected on this showed that students found the grammar analysis troublesome. It is proposed here that the functional grammar's *rank scale* is a threshold concept, as defined by Meyer and Land (2003, 2005).

The distinguishing feature of this study in comparison with the majority of the other literature on threshold concepts (Meyer and Land 2003; 2005; 2006), is that its outcomes are based entirely upon interviews carried out with students – not staff – and upon students' 'metareflections' – both individual and in groups – about their learning experience. The identification of the threshold concept has therefore been entirely based upon the students' voices and underpinned by a student-centred constructionist and dialogic approach (Laurillard, 1993; Kafai & Resnick, 1996; Perkins, 2006; Orsini-Jones & Jones, 2007).

IDENTIFYING ISSUES AND SOLVING THEM – THE GRAMMAR PROJECT TASK

A wider variety of students, with a range of different backgrounds and needs, is entering UK higher education due to government measures to widen participation (Warren, 2002). A typical first-year cohort of undergraduate languages students at Coventry University presents the following characteristics:[3]

– Age range 18-70;
– Variety of degree titles under study (International Relations and German, Tourism and French, Marketing and Russian, Business and Italian, IT and Spanish, French and German, etc.);
– Different levels of prior knowledge;

- Different expectations from the learning experience at university (part-time/full-time, mature/18-year-olds);
- A-level grades varying from 'E' to 'A';
- Different levels of ICT proficiency;
- 12% of students with a declared disability;
- 13 different nationalities (and, as a consequence, many non-native speakers of English).

This diversity appears to be reflected in the students' previous levels of grammatical knowledge. Focus group research, carried out between 2000-2002, and the analysis of students' work showed that many were challenged by grammar analysis and had difficulties in grasping fundamental grammar concepts, such as word classifications (noun, adjective, verb, etc.) and the structure of a sentence.

In addition, the Subject Benchmark Statements for Languages and Related Studies (LRS) were published in 2002. Under the heading '4.2 Language related skills' it is stated that by the end of their course:

> Students of LRS will have developed appropriate linguistic tools and metalanguage to describe and analyse the main features of the language(s) studied. They will thus be able to make effective use of language reference materials, such as grammars, standard and specialised dictionaries and corpora, to refine knowledge and understanding of register, nuances of meaning and language use. Students of LRS will be effective and self-aware independent language learners. (QAA, 2002, p. 9)

It was therefore important to foster the development of the above-mentioned skills, particularly in view of the students' weaknesses in grammatical analysis as identified in the focus group research. A team of linguists and educational developers designed an ICT (Information and Communication Technology)-based collaborative grammar project task. This became the major assessment component for the module *Academic and Professional Skills for Language Learning* (Orsini-Jones & Jones, 2007, pp. 92-93):

> Working in groups, students were required to create a website containing linked web pages (minimum of three/maximum of five). In each page they had to analyse a sentence. At least one of the three sentences had to be in one of the target languages studied, and the other(s) in English. Students chose three sentences from a list given to them, and each group had to create the relevant analysis and website. The latter had to be uploaded into the Virtual Learning Environment (WebCT)'s collaborative group area, and was available for all students and staff to view and use. Each website had to be presented to the rest of the class by the group which had created it, with the support of a PowerPoint slide presentation to highlight the major issues encountered while completing the project.

Both the websites and the PowerPoint slides were available in WebCT for all students until the end of the academic year following the completion of the project. WebCT was also used to enable students to exchange files and ideas in dedicated discussion forums created for each group. After the presentation had taken place, students had to write an individual reflective report on the project.

The assessed grammar task was revised yearly according to a cycle of action research (Kemmis & McTaggart, 1990). A phase of 'reconnaissance' (or identification of an issue or issues) normally precedes the start of the cycle, followed by planning, implementation/action(s), observation, reflection and re-planning (Orsini-Jones, 2004, p. 192):

- An issue is identified;
- Change is planned collaboratively (staff and students) to address the issue;
- The change process is implemented - 'acted out';
- All agents involved in the change process reflect upon its outcomes, both while it is happening and at the end of the first phase of implementation;
- Actions are taken to re-plan the changes and the second phase of the action-research cycle starts (Carr & Kemmis, 1986; McNiff, 1988; McKernan, 1992; Kember, 2000).

The aim of the grammatical part of the task was to provide students with some elementary tools and a basic framework for analysis, which could be applied to any of the languages they studied, while encouraging them to reflect both as a team and individually on the metacognitive aspects of their learning experience. In line with current trends in the teaching of language and linguistics, the Hallidayan *rank scale* (Halliday, 1985) was used to explain the basic structure of these languages. As suggested in Perkins (2006, pp. 42-43) the aim of the grammar analysis task was to equip the students with the 'conceptual arsenal' of linguistic analysis, to make them fluent in the 'foreign' epistemic game of linguistics. Coulthard (1985, p. 121) summarises the *rank scale* concept:

> A first assumption of a 'categories' description is that the analytic units can be arranged on a *rank-scale* which implies that units are related in a 'consists of' relationship with smaller units combining with other units of the same size to form larger ones. Thus a sentence consists of one or more clauses, each of which in turn consists of one or more groups, and so on. The *structure* of each unit is expressed in terms of permissible combinations of units from the rank below, the structure of a clause for example being described in terms of nominal, verbal, adverbial and prepositional groups.

For the purpose of the grammar project it was decided to use 'phrase' instead of 'group', as the two terms can be used interchangeably in functional grammar, even if some scholars like to underline the finer points of the fuzzy boundaries between them (Quereda, 2006).

Students were provided with examples in class and an example on paper of the type of analysis required. Essentially this involved an analysis of the structure of sentences, clauses, phrases and words in terms of the item immediately below each one on the *rank scale,* and a taxonomy of clauses, phrases, words and morphemes. All the examples used were of formal written language; some were invented by the teaching staff in the relevant languages while others were taken from authentic sources, though often adapted to remove difficulties which went beyond the scope of this particular exercise (see Appendix A for a sample analysis of a sentence).

TROUBLESOME GRAMMAR KNOWLEDGE

The analysis of the interview transcripts, and of the students' reflections in their learning journals and on WebCT's discussion forums showed that students felt challenged mostly by the grammatical categories of morpheme, phrase and clause. Students also found some of the word classifications challenging, e.g. 'adverbs' and the difference between possessive adjectives and possessive pronouns. This confusion could be partially ascribed to what Meyer and Land (2005) define as "tensions arising from the use of competing discourses and existing identities"; the students' 'tacit' knowledge (Meyer and Land, 2003) was proving to be part of the troublesome aspect of their approach to the understanding of the structure of a sentence. Many students had, in fact, been taught grammar formally in their previous educational experience and the new functional grammar terminology displaced these earlier terms and challenged their (false) sense of security about grammar:

There were certain aspects of the grammar lectures that were being taught in a new way. I'd never learnt about morphemes before and phrases were different. I think we all thought phrases were different to what we were being taught. (Written feedback 2003-2004)

Phrases were perceived as particularly troublesome:

Interviewer: Now, if I ask you, what is difficult about phrases, what is difficult in grasping how to break down a noun phrase, a prepositional phrase, a verb phrase, what is difficult about it?

Student 1: Probably, erm, probably recognising which is the controlling word within the phrase, well first of all obviously breaking the phrase down, breaking the whole sentence down into phrases, but also knowing whether it's prepositional or if it's a verb phrase, which one controls the type of phrase that it is. I think my interpretation of it is that anything with a preposition is a prepositional phrase. But I wasn't sure how, you know (...) I understood it in class, it was when we went away, and I just seemed to have completely forgotten everything that we did on it, and I think that was when I struggled because when we were sat in here, we'd obviously got help if we had questions, but I did grasp the concept of breaking it down, but when it came to applying it to the project (...) I couldn't. I understood the lectures and everything that we did on it but couldn't actually apply it, I think that was the difficulty

Interviewer: Right. Did you feel the same as student 1?

Student 2: Yeah I felt lost.

Interviewer: In lecture times as well?

Student 2: In lecture times as well. You know, I understood the concept for about, lets say 10 seconds, yes yes, I got that and then suddenly, no no, I didn't get that, you know, suddenly, like this.

Because of the complexities of functional grammar, students appeared to grasp some of its components in isolation, but many failed to see the full picture. This proved to be particularly frustrating for students who were fluent speakers of foreign languages. They could unconsciously handle both their native language and the foreign language at the spoken level, but found grammar analysis challenging. Perkins highlights this phenomenon when he points out that 'the Chomskian machine keeps us speaking grammatically in our mother tongues, although we cannot directly introspect its mechanism or rules' (2006, p. 40). A competent linguist must however be able to understand the concept underpinning the hidden architecture of a sentence to function effectively. It can be argued that the discussion about the different meanings of the same words in different contexts is a 'meta' threshold concept for linguists, particularly those who intend to specialise in translation. Interestingly enough, Meyer, Land and Davies (this volume) highlighted the links between variation theory and Ferdinand De Saussure's linguistic theory:

> Variation theory in the phenomenographic tradition seems to constitute an educational application of Saussurian structuralism in linguistics ... in terms of the way in which individual words (*parole*) come to have operational meaning within a language *(langue)*. More specifically this comes about through the way in which words come to have specific meaning by not meaning what every other word in a language means, that is through variability of definition...When some new situation arises, which is almost constantly in the use of a language, the structure of awareness and hence the meaning can change dramatically, so the state of variation is again always dynamic.

Although many students admitted they were still struggling with the *rank scale* concept by the end of the academic year, both the assignments that they carried out and the interview data showed that some rays of light (and understanding) were filtering through the metaphorical dark forest. However, the 'opening' sometimes closed down again before they had fully grasped the concept. This would appear to confirm the oscillation between states reported in Meyer and Land (2005, p. 384). What was puzzling was the fact that some students had grasped the concept for the grammatical analysis of one language but not for that of another. So, for example, some students appeared to have grasped the threshold concept for English, or German, but not both. The fact that British students generally carried out the grammar analysis more accurately for the sentences in the target language studied than for those in English (their native language) provides evidence to support the hypothesis that the threshold concept identified might not be transferable. Could this be due to having first encountered the formal teaching of grammar categories (and related grammatical metacognition) when studying foreign languages rather than English? Or is it due to the different way in which the two languages are processed in the brain? The students themselves appeared to favour the first suggestion, as illustrated in this extract, from the semi-structured interviews recorded in December 2004 (Orsini-Jones & Jones, 2007, p. 100): 'We all contributed to the English sentence. Perhaps we just don't understand English grammar as much as German grammar as we have done so much German grammar during A-level'. It appeared that the majority of British students, who had not been exposed to the formal teaching of grammar categories as much as international students, were struggling more with the 'meta' level of grammar analysis in English. This highlights the importance of pre-liminal variation (Meyer & Land, 2005, p. 12).

In view of both the above definitions of threshold concept and the students' feedback and performance, it could be argued that each of the individual grammar components – morphemes, words, clauses, phrases – were perceived as troublesome even if with different degrees of perceived troublesomeness. There would appear to be some similarities, therefore, between the individual components of the underlying threshold concept and the 'knowledge objects' described by Entwistle and Marton (1994). Some students appeared to be at ease with these concepts when analysed individually, but then struggled when carrying out the grammar analysis of the whole sentence and failed to see the connections amongst them. Others, on the other hand, could see the individual components eventually fit together, like the pieces in a puzzle once it is completed. It could, therefore, be suggested that each of these individual grammar categories is a self-standing threshold concept, which, once mastered, opens up a new door into the next one. Or, as suggested here, it could be argued that the *rank scale* concept underpinning functional grammar is the overarching threshold concept identified here and that it is in turn composed of what could be defined as *the rank scale threshold concept's components*, each of which needed to be crossed in order to grasp the overarching concept.

The interview data helped the tutors in creating activities that would make it easier for students to understand the individual component of the concept. The identification of the stumbling blocks was helped by the analysis of the transcripts. The following are extracts from the semi-structured interviews carried out in December 2004:

The clauses and morphemes are difficult for me I think, because I can't find a correct definition of these two grammar terms, and I have to analyse them in the sentence. [They were difficult] for the group, because everybody has a different idea about clauses. (Student 1)

(...) the morphemes in particular I hadn't really encountered before, so they were the ones that were most difficult to get our heads round really. (Student 2)

The biggest problem we had was trying to work out what the clauses were; the phrases weren't too bad, and the word classification, the nouns, adjectives, that was all right, morphemes were fine. It was just the clauses that are slightly more complex. (Student 3)

We had problems analysing phrases, and then we would bring up the doubts and the questions to the group, and then, when we were stuck, we went to the lecturer to get help about phrases again, looked at grammar books, but it wasn't very helpful. (Student 4)

Interviewer: Did you have any problems with grammar, any areas where you had difficulties, got stuck?

Student 5: Yeah, with distinguishing the phrases and the clauses.

Interviewer: Right, and do you think you've cracked it now?

Student 5: No.

Interestingly, as previously noted (Orsini-Jones & Jones, 2007, p. 100), the initial perception of a new concept as problematic to learn did not always match the reality of what students really found difficult to understand. And vice-versa, there were worrying levels of confidence amongst students who declared in the interviews that they had grasped the principles of the *rank scale* concept but subsequently analysed their sentences incorrectly. This ties in with research carried out by Wenden (1991) on learners' beliefs, which also highlights a weakness in qualitative research, i.e. that sometimes students think that they have learned a concept when they have not,, as beliefs are sometimes held more tenaciously than knowledge. It also ties in with the concept of tacit knowledge (Meyer & Land, 2003). As highlighted by Perkins, 'learners' tacit presumptions can miss the target by miles' (2006, p. 40).

On the whole, it appeared that many students were struggling to see the connections amongst the various components that form the scaffolding that holds a sentence together. Some were also struggling to understand the function of each grammatical 'brick'. The quotes above also confirm that some students – either consciously or unconsciously - were in a state of liminality with reference to grammar analysis. Although they were attempting to carry out the analysis required, these attempts came through as random guesses and betrayed a lack of true understanding, as reported on the literature on thresholds: 'mimicry (...) seems to involve both attempts at understanding *and* troubled misunderstanding, or limited understanding.' (Meyer & Land, 2005, p. 377).

Motivation and attitudes towards the subject matter studied also impacted upon students' oscillation. The students who struggled most with the grammar analysis were, in some cases, those who did not value the learning experience on the module. Skills and research methodology modules can be perceived as a 'waste of time' by some students, even if they are fully integrated with the subject specific curriculum, like the one described here (for further details on this, see Orsini-Jones, 2004).

To summarise, amongst the factors that appeared to hinder the process of crossing the threshold were:

- 'new to me' terminology (students opposed to change, refusing new type of analysis, refusing its semantics);
- prior (mis)knowledge of terms such as 'phrase' or 'clause' - lecturers had to 'undo' their pre-conceived definitions of the grammar categories involved
- the cohort's composition and the variety of nationalities present in it (e.g. 14 different ones in academic year 2003-2004);
- 'pre-liminal variation' - background and previous grammar learning experience;
- reliance in group work upon peers who found the grammatical categories 'troublesome' but decided nevertheless to take a lead in the analysis of the sentences;
- misunderstanding of the concepts and lack of ability to ask lecturers for help;
- lack of motivation towards the module.

In view of the data collected, it would appear that only a few students crossed the overarching grammar threshold concept identified (the rank scale). Most students could, however, grasp at least some of its components. It is enlightening to analyse student feedback to see how the mastering of individual components was achieved in their view:

> I found the first assessment the most challenging. This was to create a web page, breaking up the grammar of a particular sentence in one of the target languages and in English. I think that this was because it was the first assessment and the fact that I was still settling at university. I had never really studied grammar in this depth and found it quite difficult to grasp at first. *However, as we worked as a group, I began to understand more....*I have learnt a lot of grammar and now know all the different aspects of grammar, such as clauses, morphemes, etc. *This has helped me with my two languages a lot.* (Written anonymous feedback, May 2004, emphasis added). (Orsini-Jones & Jones, 2007, p. 101).

The above quotes appear to confirm the results of previous research (Orsini-Jones & Cousin, 2001; Orsini-Jones, 2004; Orsini-Jones & Jones, 2007), i.e. that a combination of student-centred activities, integrated and effective use of technology and constructivist teaching methods can create a 'safe' and 'powerful' learning environment, within which students thrive. Despite the difficulties encountered with the grammar analysis, the perception that the grammar project had greatly enhanced their learning experience was also reflected in the individual reports on the task.

Curriculum design also appeared to help students to overcome 'knowledge blocks'. The data collected in the academic year 2003-2004 informed changes to the grammar task following an action research cycle (McNiff, 1988; McKernan, 1992). In 2004-2005, for example, more time was allocated to explaining the concept of the morpheme, as this had proved troublesome for the students in the previous cohort. Subsequently, most students stated that they were confident they had understood this concept despite their initial difficulties with it, and their marks confirmed their confidence. Ten grammar projects were completed in 2004-2005: in seven groups students had made some mistakes – mostly minor ones – in identifying morphemes correctly, but they had at least demonstrated an understanding of what a morpheme is. This was pleasing to the lecturers involved, as these results compared favourably with those from the previous year and showed that a change in the syllabus can help students to understand troublesome knowledge. The major changes implemented to achieve this result were:

– doubling the time allocated to explaining grammar in general (increased from two to four face-to-face sessions) and morphemes in particular, and changing the assessment of the module to better reflect this increase in grammar input;
– provision of more samples of grammatical analysis;
– provision of more collaborative practice/workshops on morphemes following the lecture on grammar;
– uploading of all the grammatical explanations and exercises onto WebCT for those students who had not been able to attend;
– creation of a dedicated grammar forum in WebCT's discussion area, enabling students to air their concerns. (Orsini-Jones & Jones, 2007, p. 97).

Students' learning journals, the individual reports compiled by students after the completion of the grammar task and the reflective postings in WebCT's discussion forums provided evidence that metareflection can also help with troublesome knowledge. There was evidence that students were acknowledging that they were undergoing change. The acknowledgement of the transformative impact of the learning experience upon an individual with reference to the module *Academic and Professional Skills for Language Learning* can be seen in this extract:

I believe I have changed as a learner. This module has introduced new ideas, methods and programmes which was not covered as much in A-Levels and GCSEs. I heave learnt more about key skills for languages, listening, reading, writing and speaking. It has helped me for work in other subjects like coursework, presentations both group and individually and exams. I have also learnt more about grammar ideas and skills and identifying parts of speech. I feel this module has helped me very much this year.

There were students whose work demonstrated that they had crossed the threshold concept identified by the end of the year and many commented on the beneficial and transferable nature of the knowledge acquired (Orsini-Jones & Jones, 2007, p. 102):

From doing this project I have definitely learned a lot more about grammar. Initially English grammar such as morphemes and derivation and inflection. This has in turn helped my understanding of foreign grammar. I think English people would benefit if we were taught grammar at a younger age, as people are in foreign countries. ...Learning some terms for certain words (nouns, adjectives, adverbs, prepositions) was also helpful as it is helping me with understanding both English and the target languages I am studying. (Portfolio reflective entry about the grammar project, May 2004).

CONCLUSION

The evidence collected shows that the grammar project task has somewhat helped students in making gradual steps towards understanding the threshold concept identified – the *rank scale* – as well as grammatical analysis in general. Collaborative work on the tasks set and metareflection also proved to help with overcoming knowledge blocks and helped students to develop a professional approach to their work. However, as proposed by Perkins, a constructivist approach like the one adopted for the development of the grammar project described here, does not suit all learners as it requires a high level of cognitive engagement 'and not all learners respond well to the challenge' (2006, p. 36).

The student feedback and performance informed changes in the way the grammar task was delivered in 2003-2004 and 2004-2005. Such changes have made some elements of the scaffolding supporting the hierarchical structure of a sentence like morphemes and words less troublesome for students than in previous academic years. However, the overarching threshold concept identified here is closely linked to the way language is processed and can be influenced by a variety of factors, such as affective, personality and motivation factors (Chomsky, 1968; Krashen, 1981; Krashen & Terrell, 1983). This might add an extra layer of difficulty, as whenever language is the focus of analysis, the 'discursive reconfiguration' (Meyer & Land, 2005) and the repositioning necessary to bring a threshold concept into view require an extra 'meta' level of analysis.

However, by the end of the year, some of the students who had managed to grasp the *rank scale* concept became very aware that there was an extra dimension to grammar analysis which was new to them and that had opened new doors of linguistic understanding. The realisation that the *rank scale* unlocked the hidden architecture of a sentence *transformed* their perception of language learning and language analysis. Some students also stated that grasping the *rank scale* concept had helped them in analysing sentences in all the languages they were studying. They were now able to transfer the concept and this was enabling them to see grammar links that they had not seen before. However, both the *integrative* nature of this concept and its *irreversibility* came under discussion when, in some cases, students were able to understand the concept and apply it to the analysis of sentences in one language (e.g. German) but not another (e.g. English). Could it be possible that the *rank scale* concept is a threshold concept that can only be transferred within the same language, not across different languages? Or does it require more time – and the crossing of more thresholds – for some students to see the connections between languages?

More research is needed to answer the above questions and to investigate further the integrative and irreversible nature of the rank scale threshold concept.

APPENDIX

Table 1. Sample analysis of a sentence according to the rank scale concept

Bundling his black cassock around himself, the bishop climbed into the back seat and settled in for the infuriatingly long drive to the country retreat (adapted from Brown 2003, p. 205)

Bundling	verb	verb phrase - verb	Reduced
his	adjective	noun phrase - d object	clause
black	adjective		
cassock	noun		
around	preposition	preposition phrase -	
himself	pronoun	adjunct	
the	article	noun phrase - subject	Main clause
bishop	noun		
climbed	verb	verb phrase - verb	
into	preposition	preposition phrase -	
the	article	adjunct	
back	adjective		
seat	noun		
and	conjunction		Main clause
(the bishop)		*noun phrase - subject*	
settled	verb	verb phrase - verb	
in	adverb		
for	preposition	preposition phrase -	
the	article	adjunct	
infuriatingly	adverb		
long	adjective		

drive	noun
to	preposition
the	article
country	noun
retreat	noun

Sample Morphemes:

bundl(e)-	free (root)
-ing	bound (inflection)
infuriat(e)-	free (root)
-ing-	bound (inflection)
-ly	bound (derivation)

NOTES

[1] 'In the middle of our life's journey, I found myself in a dark forest, as the right way had been lost'.

[2] Please note that some of the data reported has been published in a forthcoming article by Orsini Jones and Jones (forthcoming, 2007).

[3] These characteristics were those of the students in academic year 2002-2003 as reported in Orsini-Jones (2004).

REFERENCES

Ackermann, E. (1996). Perspective-taking and object construction. In Y. Kasai & M. Resnick (Eds.), *Constructionism in practice: Designing, thinking and learning in a digital world* (pp. 25-35). Mahwah, NJ: Lawrence Erlbaum.

Alighieri, D. (2005). *Divina commedia*. Roma, Newton Compton.

Brown, D. (2003). *The da Vinci code*. New York: Bantam/Random House.

Carr, W. & Kemmis, S. (1986). *Becoming critical*. Brighton: Falmer Press.

Chomsky, N. (1968). *Language and mind*. New York: Harcourt, Brace and World.

Coulthard, M. (1985). *An introduction to discourse analysis*. Harlow: Longman.

Entwistle, N. J. & Marton, F. (1994). Knowledge objects: Understandings constituted through intensive academic study. *British Journal of Educational Psychology, 64,* 161-178.

Halliday, M. (1985). *An introduction to functional grammar*. London: Edward Arnold.

Kafai, Y. & Resnick, M. (1996). *Constructionism in practice*. Mahwah, NJ: Lawrence Erlbaum.

Kember, D. (2000). *Action learning and action research: Improving the quality of teaching and learning*. London: Kogan Page.

Kemmis, S. & McTaggart, R. (Eds.) (1990). *The action research reader*. Victoria: Deakin University.

Krashen, S. D. (1981). *Second language acquisition and second language learning*. Oxford: Pergamon.

Krashen, S. D. & Terrell, T. D. (1983). *The natural approach: Language acquisition in the classroom*. Oxford: Pergamon Press.

Laurillard, D. (1993). *Rethinking university teaching*. London: Routledge

McKernan, J. (1992) *Curriculum action research*. London: Kogan Page.

McNiff, J. (1988). *Action research: Principles and practices*. London: Routledge.

Meyer, J. H. F. & Land, R. (2003). Threshold concepts and troublesome knowledge (1). Linkages to ways of thinking and practising within the disciplines. In C. Rust (Ed.), *Improving student learning*

– *Ten years on* (pp. 412-424). Proceedings of the 2002 10th International Symposium, the Oxford Centre for Staff and Learning Development. Oxford: OCSLD.

Meyer, J. H. F. & Land, R. (2005). Threshold concepts and troublesome knowledge (2): Epistemological considerations and a conceptual framework for teaching and learning. *Higher Education, 49*, 373-388.

Meyer, J. H. F. & Land, R. (2006). *Overcoming barriers to student understanding: Threshold concepts and troublesome knowledge.* London: RoutledgeFalmer.

Meyer, J. H. F., Land, R. & Davies, P. (2006). Threshold concepts and troublesome knowledge (4): Issues of variation and variability. Paper presented at the *Threshold Concepts within the Disciplines* Symposium, University of Strathclyde, Glasgow, 30th Aug.-1st Sept.

Orsini-Jones, M. & Cousin, G. (2001). Focus research in modern languages: Creating a 'powerful learning environment' for students with students'. In J. A. Coleman, D. Ferney, D. Head, & R. Rix (Eds.), *Language-learning futures: Issues and strategies for modern languages provision in higher education* (pp. 71-82). London: Central Books/CILT.

Orsini-Jones, M. (2004). Supporting a course in new literacies and skills for linguists with a Virtual Learning Environment: Results from a staff/student collaborative action-research project at Coventry University, *ReCALL, 16* (1), 189-209.

Orsini-Jones, M. & Jones, D. (2007). Supporting collaborative grammar learning via a Virtual Learning Environment (VLE): A case study from Coventry University. *Arts and Humanities in Higher Education: An International Journal of Theory, Research and Practice, 6* (1), 90-106

Perkins, D. (2006). Constructivism and troublesome knowledge. In J. H. F. Meyer & R. Land *Overcoming barriers to student understanding: Threshold concepts and troublesome knowledge* (pp. 33-47). London: RoutledgeFalmer.

Quality Assurance Agency (QAA) for Higher Education (2002). *Languages and related studies, subject benchmark statement.* Gloucester: QAA.

Quereda, L. (2006). The unit "*group*" in Halliday's *An introduction to functional grammar,* available online at http://www.ugr.es/~lquereda/the_unit_group.htm (last accessed 29/07/06).

Warren, D. (2002). Curriculum design in a context of widening participation in higher education. *Arts and Humanities in Higher Education, 1*(1), 85-99.

Wenden, A. L. (1991). *Learner strategies for learner autonomy.* New York: Prentice Hall.

AFFILIATION

Marina Orsini-Jones
Coventry University

CARYL SIBBETT & WILLIAM THOMPSON

NETTLESOME KNOWLEDGE, LIMINALITY AND THE TABOO IN CANCER AND ART THERAPY EXPERIENCES

Implications for Teaching and Learning

INTRODUCTION

This chapter draws on our experiences of teaching, practice and research across a number of areas: art psychotherapy and cancer care (first author), counselling, medical education and organisational dynamics (both authors). These experiences raised our awareness that healthcare practitioner/learners experience 'troublesome' (Perkins, 1999) or 'difficult knowledge' (Britzman, 1998, p. 2), as do 'their clients. Various types of knowledge can be 'troublesome' for learners, such as 'inert, ritual, conceptually difficult, and foreign' (Perkins, 1999, p. 8) and tacit knowledge (Meyer & Land, 2003). Knowledge can be troublesome not just cognitively, but also emotionally, attitudinally, bodily and inter-personally or institutionally and socially.

Particularly over the past seven years, our teaching, practice and research indicated that the concept of 'liminality' (Turner, 1995; van Gennep, 1960) was relevant to understanding troublesome knowledge. Liminality (Latin: *limen*, threshold) is an anthropological term that relates to the 'betwixt and between' limbo state in a transition (Turner, 1995, p. 95; van Gennep, 1960). Prior to 2000 the first author's professional learning about liminality was in its early stages and she was virtually unaware that something else was in its early stages. Then she was plunged into deeper personal experiential learning when she was diagnosed as having a rare form of cancer. This further developed her awareness of the relevance of liminality and also her motivation for additional research into liminality in cancer care and art therapy.

BACKGROUND: RESEARCH STUDY

The broad concept of liminality has been described as a 'major category' of cancer experience (Little *et al.*, 1998) and an inherent dimension of therapy experience (Schwartz-Salant & Stein, 1991). However, wishing to explore in depth, the first author examined the source literature on liminality (van Gennep, 1960; Turner, 1995) and its emerging key facets all seemed relevant: *limbo, powerlessness/*

R. Land, J.H.F. Meyer & J. Smith (Eds.), Threshold Concepts within the Disciplines, 227–242.

power, symbolic expression, playing, reflexivity, communitas and *embodied experience*.

The first author hypothesised a good fit between these facets of liminality and experiences of cancer and art therapy and undertook arts-based autoethnographic research (Sibbett, 2005a-c, 2006a-b) that aimed to explore this further. The methodology was a variant of a/r/tography (Irwin & de Cosson, 2004) as 'an inquiring process that lingers in the liminal spaces between a(artist) and r(researcher) and t(teacher)' (Springgay, Irwin, & Kind, 2005, p. 902) that was relevant to my roles of a(artist), r(researcher) and t(teacher)/t(therapist).

Congruent with autoethnography (Hayano, 1979; Ellis & Bochner, 2000) and reflective practitioner approaches (Schön, 1995) the research reflexively explored my art therapy clients' and my own cancer and art-making experiences in the context of the wider culture. Non-random, purposive sampling (Mays & Pope, 1995) (n=20) and multi-modal data collection procedures were used until 'saturation' was reached (Morse, 1999). Data analysis was guided by 'framework analysis' (Ritchie & Spencer, 2002), chosen because it allows inclusion of *a priori* and emergent concepts and is relevant in healthcare contexts (Lacey & Luff, 2001). Informed consent and relevant organisational ethical permission were obtained for the research (BAAT, 2005). Data was checked with participants and professional peers where possible. The results found a good fit between the liminality framework and experiences of cancer and art therapy. Art therapy seemed particularly relevant in dealing with transitional experience because liminality generates symbolic expression (Turner, 1995, p. 128) and also the creative liminality and rites inherent in art therapy could foster management of liminal situations.

IMPLICATIONS FOR LEARNING

Psychotherapy has been deemed a form of learning (Rose, Loewenthal, & Greenwood, 2005) or education (Freud, 1917/1973, p. 504) for *clients*. However, by making analogous speculations from the research, this chapter contemplates possible implications of using liminal arts-based approaches to assist *healthcare practitioner/learners* to manage troublesome knowledge. It will also explore the reciprocal relationship between liminality, learning, 'troublesome knowledge' (Perkins, 1999) and 'threshold concepts' (Meyer & Land, 2003, 2005). A threshold concept is 'akin to a portal, opening up a new and previously inaccessible way of thinking about something' and 'the transition to understanding' can prove 'troublesome' (Meyer & Land, 2003, p. 1).

This chapter argues that *designing* appropriate liminal experiences into professional courses is important for several reasons. Firstly, it can help learners deal with the transitions they experience. Secondly, it can help them deal with troublesome knowledge and resulting liminality encountered during learning experiences and thereafter.

Entry into a profession, such as healthcare, involves a number of transitions as learners proceed from novice to expert (Benner, 1984, cited in Neary, 2000, p. 38). All transitions involve experiencing liminality and societies create rites of passage that both mark the transition and potentially promote passage through it (Turner, 1995). These rites of passage provide a microcosmic structure of separation, liminality and re-incorporation that develops the person to be able to take on the new status (Turner, 1988, p. 25). It has been recommended that social work training should clear a transformational space in which students and faculty can explore issues of identity and 'perpetual liminality' (Irving & Young, 2004).

Liminality evokes symbolic expression (Turner, 1995, p. 128) and we speculate that appropriately facilitated arts-based approaches can utilise this symbolic expression in rites that offer navigable and potentially transformative experiential learning. Such liminal experience involves risk and needs to be contained and supported to help learners navigate through to genuine understanding, rather than leaving them stuck in liminality not understanding, or stuck and mimicking understanding.

Using designed liminal experiences and associated symbolic 'rites' is perhaps especially valuable for professions in which liminality is inherent in the troublesome knowledge encountered. Such knowledge can also evoke liminality leaving learners in 'a suspended state in which understanding approximates to a kind of mimicry or lack of authenticity' (Meyer & Land, 2003, p. 10). This chapter will explore some issues relevant to Meyer and Land's proposal that the connections between liminality, creativity and problem-solving (2005) and liminality and power dynamics (2003, p. 10) need further enquiry.

NETTLESOME KNOWLEDGE

The idea of 'nettlesome knowledge' (Sibbett, 2006b) is proposed. This comprises elements of knowledge that are deemed taboo in that they are defended against, repressed or ignored because if they were grasped they might 'sting' and thus evoke a feared intense emotional and *embodied* response. The sting of nettlesome knowledge can make us uncomfortable and so it can be stigmatised.

Nettlesome knowledge can be defended against at *social* levels because of a collective collusion to deny it, to maintain the status quo, as when, for example, a healthcare practitioner/learner becomes aware that a colleague is unfit to practice, but the professional culture stigmatises whistle-blowers. Sometimes the holder and declarer of such knowledge can be left holding the 'nettle'. Such a person can be split off from the organisation and be perceived as the problem. They can be scapegoated as a dysfunctional way of attempting to dispose of the problem. Object relations theories are thus relevant to these dynamics (Sibbett, 2006).

Nettlesome knowledge can be defended against at *individual* levels because of a feared response by others or because it contradicts the learner's own cherished beliefs or assumptions. For instance, if a healthcare practitioner/learner denies their own vulnerability out of a belief that 'they' (patients) get sick, but 'we' don't (Thompson *et al.*, 2001).

However, just as nettles when used appropriately can be nutritional and medicinal, such nettlesome knowledge can, if approached safely, be a threshold concept that offers openings to new understandings of self and others at individual and cultural levels. Nevertheless, dealing with nettlesome knowledge involves risk and discomfort, perhaps particularly in organisational contexts, and so support is needed.

LIMINALITY AND ARTS-BASED LEARNING: INCLUSION OF NETTLESOME KNOWLEDGE

Some of the above ideas will now be explored in the context of the research into liminality in cancer care and art therapy (Sibbett, 2006). Relevant to nettlesome knowledge, a trans-thematic aspect of the research indicated that liminal material, and those in liminal states, can be regarded as taboo or stigmatised (Turner, 1967, p. 97; van Gennep, 1960, p. 114). Having cancer and its treatment can be a stigmatising experience (Lawton, 1998, p. 127; Muzzin et al., 1994). Cancer patients can experience *sustained liminality* (Little et al., 1998, p. 1490). Liminality features ambiguity and being 'betwixt and between' (Turner, 1995, p. 95). Ambiguous issues can be difficult to classify. Thus they seem to threaten order, are frightening and can be designated as taboo (Douglas, 1966).

The research analysis suggested that cancer experiences can comprise nettlesome aspects that may be excluded in that they are deemed taboo and thus *unthinkable, unspeakable, unhearable, unseeable* and *untouchable*. The dynamics involved in this can feature protective defence mechanisms, but they can also be a form of 'symbolic violence' (Bourdieu, 1990) or impose a belief that some issues are, for example, unspeakable.

In addition to finding that liminality is a 'fundamental category of the experience' of cancer illness (Little et al., 1998, p. 1490), the research analysis was also consistent with Turner's (1995, p. 128) assertion that liminality is a condition in which there is frequently an urge to generate 'symbols, rituals ... and works of art'. The research also indicated that, during liminality in cancer experiences, one purpose of this urge to generate art is to reveal. Jaspers (1931, p. 716) suggests that 'the basic meaning of art is its revealing function.' Arts-based expression and learning offers the potential for revelatory inclusion of that which otherwise might be excluded as taboo.

It is therefore speculated that when facilitating learning about threshold concepts which evoke liminality, and particularly when the discipline inherently involves liminality, it is important to take advantage of the reflexive symbolic and art expression generated by liminality as a means of navigating it. Indeed, at the higher levels of experiential learning, 'manipulative and tactile activities will result in creative written works, in art expression, in construction, and in many other ways' and help achieve the learner's identification with and internalization of the learning (Steinaker & Bell, 1979, p. 123).

An important part of arts-based learning is playing, a key facet of liminality (Turner, 1995). The research found that playing was associated with the power/powerlessness dynamics inherent in liminality (Turner, 1995) and cancer experiences. Appropriately facilitated arts-based learning could foster a shift from compliant play (*ludus*), at one end of the play spectrum, to the spontaneous improvisational play (*paidia*) at the other end (Caillois, 1962). Improvisational play fosters personal development (Rogers, 1996). In creative liminality, one can experience absorption and 'flow' (Csikszentmihalyi, 2002) that is similar to the 'reverie' that art-making offers (Milner, 1977 p.163) and the relaxed state that generates creative play (Winnicott, 1996). The creative potential in liminality has relevance for personal development that underpins, parallels and promotes professional development.

Liminal states can be characterised by *powerlessness* and inferiority (Turner, 1995). Creative play in liminality can help express and process some of the power dynamics experienced and promote 'egalitarianism' (Turner, 1995, pp. 95-96). Turner (1995) notes that Caillois (1962), a surrealist, identified four types of play. These are relevant to cancer and art therapy experiences and potentially to healthcare learning as they help us see the relationship between play, power and liminality.

Firstly, *'vertigo'* (*ilinx*) is panic-related play that evokes a sense of reeling. Little *et al* (1998 p.1491) quote Jaspers (1986, p. 112) to link this to cancer experience: 'The movement of fright, expressed as vertigo and shuddering ... I become conscious that I can be annihilated.' Learners and teachers can experience panic when faced with troublesome and nettlesome knowledge. Even the prospect of such knowledge can evoke a state of 'anticipanic'. Measures to acknowledge and support such feelings are needed.

Secondly, 'competition' (*agôn*), such as typified by battle and win-lose scenarios. With cancer patients, 'Putting up a good fight is socially endorsed' (Little *et al*, 1998 p.1491). In learning, constructive uses of competition need to be adopted and destructive agonistic dynamics avoided.

Thirdly, 'chance'/'fate' (*alea*): the play that involves probability and feeling 'played with'. Cancer experiences feature survival probability yet actually, as the first author's oncologist said, 'It will either be 0% or 100%, life or death!' Understanding of probability and risk is important and so is 'learner empowerment' (Cranton, 1994, p. 72).

Fourthly, 'role-play' (*mimicry*) can involve playing a part, hiding, disguising. Cancer patients can feel they have to act as a 'good patient' and healthcare practitioners can play the part of the expert who does not get emotionally involved or sick. Learners can find inappropriate ways of mimicking understanding, playing the game, but missing the 'underlying game' or 'underlying episteme' (Perkins, 2006, p. 43). Constructive ways need to be used to develop authentic understanding and congruent practice.

Professional training needs to have a reflexive liminal dimension, because otherwise it may only develop knowledge, skills and perhaps what might be called 'surface professionalism', but have little impact on deeper motivations and attitudes. An individual, system or professional culture may be conceived of as having various layers that exert reciprocal influence on each other. Systemic models have been developed (Hawkins, 1997, p. 426, figs. 2-3; Hofstede, 1991; Purnell, 2005; Trompenaars & Hampden-Turner, 1997) that suggest that such layers include:

- unconscious motivations, values and basic assumptions;
- practice (behaving and expressing, or not);
- created artefacts.

In integrated professionalism there is congruence between these layers and they act to reinforce one another. However, in surface professionalism there is, within and across the layers, incongruence that produces mimicry which may approximate appropriate professional behaviour, but there can also be *eruptions of incompetence* and/or inappropriate behaviour. There are discrepancies between professional beliefs and underlying lay beliefs and, particularly at times of stress, the latter can override the former thus adversely affecting behaviour. These aspects may relate to role play (*mimicry*) (Caillois, 1962) and thus to a tendency toward having a professional mask. Such practitioners may have a professional looking-glass self (Cooley, 1922) and, because of an assumption of expected perfectionism, be less likely to disclose weakness or error. They may be more vulnerable to other negative influences of play such as having a tendency towards agonistic thinking (*agôn*) and being compliant and convention-bound (*ludus*) and thus having difficulties with risk-taking (*alea*), the panic of unboundedness (*ilinx*) and handling uncertainty and improvisation (*paidia*).

The research indicated that in cancer experiences, amidst frightening, competitive, chance-driven and mimicry forms of play, art therapy offers play with symbolic transitional objects (Winnicott, 1996), thus stimulating flow experience, promoting empowerment and fostering a both/and rather than an either/or perspective. Arts-based approaches might offer similar experiences in learning. Unequal power dynamics inherent in cancer and learning experiences can demand compliant play. However, arts-based learning based on art therapy principles would aim to foster spontaneous improvisational play that enables the generation of *communitas*, 'egalitarianism' and 'communion' (Turner, 1995, pp. 95-96). This also has implications in healthcare training for the building of collegiality within communities of practice (Wenger, 2000).

Language can be another 'source of conceptual troublesomeness' (Meyer & Land, 2003, p. 9). The inclusion of arts-based and non-verbal learning might help address language issues. In addition, arts-based approaches can help move material towards language in various ways.

The research found that taboo material that is unthinkable, if contained (Bion, 1959) by the art and the facilitator, can be 'modified', 'digested', tolerated, owned (Bovensiepen, 2002, p. 245) and it can thus become 'food for thought' (Glover, 1998), or literally thinkable. If uncontained, material can remain at the feeling level as 'a nameless dread' (Bion, 1993, p. 116) leaving learners stuck in *limbo*.

Taboo material perceived as unspeakable can be expressed in arts-based ways which can also help it to be speakable, hearable and witnessed. The unspeakable can relate to times when 'language "collapses"' (Little *et al.*, 1998, pp. 1486-1488). It can also relate to tacit truth that is known by everyone but there is an implicit agreement not to speak of it (*mokita*) (Hunt & Agnoli, 1991, p. 377), particularly formally, for instance, knowledge of unethical or unsafe practice that is perceived as unspeakable or unactionable. Penson *et al.* (2001) assert that medical errors can have 'a disastrous effect on patients, staff, and institutions' and will 'always be a taboo subject.'

A theme in cancer narratives is denial, both by patients and doctors (Aronson, 2000, p. 1601). Liminality is associated with silence and marginalisation (Turner, 1995, pp. 103, 128). Material can also be unhearable in that even when spoken it is not acknowledged by healthcare staff (Beach *et al.*, 2005; White, 2003, p. 24), such as a conspiracy of silence about dying (Stanley, 2000). This leads to a breakdown of communication and prohibits empathy. Consequential silencing could be a form of 'symbolic violence' (Bourdieu, 1990).

Social role valorisation theory (Race, Boxall, & Carson, 2005) and 'sick role' theory (Parsons, 1951) may be relevant here in terms of rendering as taboo certain aspects perceived as deviating from the role expected by society. Research participants reported that art enabled the creation of multi-sensory products and metaphors thus enabling expression of material otherwise verbally difficult to express. Participants could also approach such material gradually, initially as an 'it', then as 'he/she' and then as 'I' (Wadeson, 1980, p. 10). Art can thus be helpful in addressing the 'silence of the limits' and the 'silence of oppression' (Lynch, 1997, p. 128).

Taboo material perceived as unseeable can become seeable through symbolic expression of that which cannot be seen. A revelatory function of artwork is that it offers an imaginary visual knowledge of the body's interior and otherwise invisible mind-body experiences. Artwork also offers a time-space in which to view the self, the social self and intersubjective and socially imposed dynamics. Issues of shame, gaze and power (Foucault, 1977, 1991) can be symbolised and processed, possibly facilitating a positive movement along the shame/pride axis (Cooley, 1922, p. 184). This could help develop professional esteem.

Taboo material that is untouchable can become touchable through multi-sensory art which has 'corporeality' and capacity to metaphorise the body and contain (Connell, 1998, p. 44; Glover, 1998). This can enable re-processing of taboo *embodied* experiences such as unbounded leaky bodies which can be sequestered in hospices (Lawton, 1998).

All of the above creative processes can lead to a form of social inclusion of material that otherwise might remain taboo and therefore unlearnable. Exposure through 'various sensory stimuli' and reproducing learning physically as well as mentally are important parts of experiential learning (Steinaker & Bell, 1979, p. 10). Perceptions and assumptions about such material can be re-evaluated, making use of the reflexivity inherent in liminality (Turner, 1988, pp. 24-25). Therefore artworks can be 'reclassifications of reality' (Turner, 1995, p. 128) and issues can be re-conceived and included. Thus material can be revealed and included in three intra- and inter-personal ways: to awareness, to understanding and to others through being shared and witnessed.

In healthcare training, these taboo issues may be threshold concepts and they include mortality, death, bodily needs, disruption of bodily boundaries, suffering, impact on sexuality and the practitioner's empathy with and witnessing of these. Clouder (2005) argues that caring is a threshold concept in healthcare.

Arts-based learning based on art therapy principles can be a liminal 'potential space' (Winnicott, 1996) and time that can act as a mirror and is potentially expressive, playful and transformative. Utilising the creative potential in liminality means that it can be accompanied by 'processes of growth, transformation, and the formulation of old elements in new patterns' (Turner, 1967, p. 99). Perhaps the inclusion of liminality and its associated symbolic processing into learning, teaching and professional development might help learners find positive ways of processing troublesome and nettlesome knowledge and forming a more congruent professional identity.

LIMINALITY IN PROFESSIONAL IDENTITY DEVELOPMENT

In the development of professional identity and culture there is a reciprocal shaping influence between the systemic layers. Professional development training hopes to change behaviours and it must be acknowledged that these are grounded in and emerge from basic assumptions, beliefs, lay theories and values and therefore training needs to foster personal development at these deeper levels. Liminal time space is inherently reflexive (Turner, 1988, p. 25) and thus, if created and used in professional development, it offers opportunities for such change at foundation levels where individual and culture interact so that motivations, assumptions, attitudes and intersubjective influences can be questioned and re-evaluated.

Training, therefore, might be said to be about the development of identity at personal and professional levels. This might be informed by literature on the phases of psychosocial or ego identity development (Erikson, 1994; Marcia, 2002) where 'identity' refers to 'the central organising principle of the personality system' that accounts for 'the persistence of the pattern' in the life history of an individual and in interaction with their community (Paranjpe, 1975, p. 36). Erikson and Marcia suggest that such identity development requires successful negotiation of a number of crises, each accompanied by positive ritualisations or negative stereotyped ritualisms.

In discussing a parallel of professional identity development, a crucial phase would be the equivalent of 'adolescence' in which various identity statuses might be experienced. A vital one is a 'moratorium' status featuring the delay and exploration of options needed for forging identity and working toward commitment. This might be viewed as a type of liminality. Successful negotiation of this engenders the virtue of 'fidelity' (Erikson, 1994), an ethical principle required in psychotherapy (BACP, 2002) and medicine (Beauchamp & Childress, 1994). Successful negotiation may lead to a status of 'identity achievement' in which identity and commitment initiated during the moratorium are consolidated (Patterson, Sochting, & Marcia, 1992). This can enable the professional to develop intimate, caring, supportive and mentoring relationships, an engagement with life in the face of death, and an authentic wisdom. Therefore, it might be speculated that a moratorium or liminality phase is needed in professional cultures and training.

However, in an unsuccessful negotiation of the crucial phase, a professional may experience either a status of 'identity foreclosure' or mimicry in which there is little commitment or exploration, or a status of 'identity diffusion' that features a lack of integration. Erikson suggests that an identity that is foreclosed or diffused, and therefore not initiated or integrated, can be less likely to be able to develop relationships and wisdom and may be more likely to develop towards burnout, elitism, authoritism[1] and a pretence of wisdom. Those with such an identity can experience 'a sense of over-all ashamedness' (Erikson, 1994, p. 135) and at some level a desire to 'be a suicide' can be an 'inescapable identity choice' (Erikson, 1994. p. 137). There may be some link here with the fact that the healthcare professions report high levels of distress (Williams, Michie, & Pattani, 1998; Tillett, 2003) and comparatively high suicide rates (BMA Board of Science and Education, 1993).

Practitioners who face the suffering and mortality of patients and who work at the raw interface of tenderness and compassion (Thorne, 1991) may be especially vulnerable and so in need of such positive professional identity development. Therefore, training in healthcare professions has a responsibility to patients and practitioners to assist constructive professional identity development that aids the negotiation of thresholds and crises and fosters more authentic and integrated professionals. This can only be built on the foundations of personal development incorporated into professional development.

Such professional development could incorporate liminality across a number of dimensions. Firstly, professional development training could aim to *create and use liminal time spaces*. Rather than being heterotopias of crisis or deviation (Foucault, 1986), these would aim to be 'heterotopias of transformation' (Foucault, 1986) and transformative threshold chronotopes[2] (Bakhtin, 2000, p. 248). Appropriate contained time space needs to be considered, perhaps such as weekend and residential contexts. Secondly, professional development training would aim to *incorporate liminal methods* that use ritual, embodied performance and play using arts- and narrative-based approaches, all of which foster a reflexive subjunctive mood.

Thirdly, the curriculum would aim to *include and address problematic liminal issues*. Such issues are associated with liminality in several ways. One association is that they tend to be inherently liminal because they can relate to culturally taboo, frightening or embarrassing areas and so they may have been marginalised or even neglected due to their difficulty. Examples might include those pertaining to limbo and uncertainty, powerlessness, power, various types of playing, communion and spirituality, embodied experience such as suffering, unboundedness, sex, gender identity and mortality. Even issues that may not be culturally taboo but which are just difficult can still be marginalised in professional development training. The uncertainty such issues can engender when approached also tends to evoke liminality in learners and, indeed, in trainers, perhaps as a form of secondary liminality.

The Platonic concept of *aporia* is associated with doubt, uncertainty and non-passage. It is relevant in experiences of illness such as when seemingly contradictory illness narratives are present (Rimmon-Kenan, 2002). Derrida (1993) associates aporia with cases where the crossing of the border of death becomes a problem and he explores the personal question 'My death – is it possible?' When conceived of, not as a barrier, but as connecting passages in which one can sometimes get lost and make discoveries, the concept of *aporia* is also relevant in learning and teaching (Burbules, 2000). *Aporia* [*a*: lacking; *poros*: a passage] is a 'state of conceptual puzzlement' (Burbules, 1997) and Plato uses corporeal metaphors to describe its sensation as one of feeling 'benumbed' during an experience as a necessary stage out of which learning can begin (Plato, 1964, p. 91). This can be the sting of the nettlesome knowledge. It is a state in which 'a learner must be exposed, stripped of misconceptions, before true learning can occur' (Burbules, 1997). The aporia is thus a transitional time of potential for learning (Burbules, 1997).

CONCLUSION

Liminality can have a potential as a place or state in which to get held or stuck (Turner, 1974), but it also has a potential for 'processes of growth, transformation, and the formulation of old elements in new patterns' (Turner, 1967, p. 99) and a *kairotic* 'opening' or 'opportunity' (White, 1987, p. 13). Consistent with Meyer and Land's (2005) notion of threshold concepts, perhaps taboo and liminal material might be 'nettlesome knowledge' in that it is difficult to grasp but if processed, like grit in an oyster, it can be transformed into something valuable. To follow Bion's (1959) digestion metaphor, perhaps the 'nettle' can be used to make something that can become 'food for thought' (Glover, 1998) by means of, for example, arts-based processes that contain and transform the liminality.

When addressed, a 'threshold concept' is 'transformative' in that it brings about a 'significant shift in the perception' and possibly a 'transformation of personal identity', a 'shift in values, feeling or attitude' and may involve a 'performative element' (Meyer & Land, 2003, p. 4). The 'transformative' potential inherent in liminality, ritual performance (Turner, 1967, p. 95) and arts-based (Eisner, 2002) approaches and their capacity to bring reflexive insight might be used in professional development to address relevant threshold concepts. Art therapy-based approaches particularly could accommodate the value of 'serious play' for learning (Rieber, Smith, & Noah, 1998) and offer a postmodern embodied paradigm valuable in exploring a holistic model of health (Corker & Shakespeare, 2002).

A threshold concept is 'irreversible'; it involves deep long-lasting learning (Meyer & Land 2003, p. 4). If such concepts are addressed, potentially through such liminal experiential means, then deeper personal and emotional development and more authentic professionalism may be developed that is more likely to be a congruent way of being. Liminal experiences tend to generate commitment (Turner, 1974).

A threshold concept is 'integrative' in that 'it exposes the previously hidden interrelatedness of something' (Meyer & Land, 2003, p. 4). The revelatory and inclusive potential of arts-based approaches may be useful in this and some necessary areas of the curriculum may be included that otherwise might be excluded due to their problematic nature, such as threshold concepts that are otherwise unthinkable, unspeakable, unhearable, unseeable and untouchable. Writing of arts-based research, Weber and Mitchell (2004) summarise how 'Eisner (1995) views the aesthetic as inherent to our need to make sense of experience.'

In healthcare and wider caring work, some of the unconscious and conscious basic assumptions and motivations attracting people to the profession may be pathological, anti-therapeutic or even masochistic (Sussman, 1992). These might include having a repressed need for therapy oneself, wanting to be a rescuer and being attracted to power that can include the power of life and death. Writing of healthcare, Seale (1998, p. 3) warns: 'The killing of other people, both in actuality and in acts of symbolic violence, exclusion and stigma, is also a means for sustaining personal security about being in the world.' The use of liminality in professional development thus has an important role in trying to minimise 'symbolic violence' (Bourdieu, 1990) and maximise non-maleficence (Beauchamp & Childress, 1994, p. 189) in healthcare.

It is speculated here that liminality, if used in professional development, can have a reflexive and transformative potential in which spontaneous play with new ideas and identity development can occur. This might enable change to occur at deeper levels and ripple out to behaviour and products so that congruent ways of being are fostered. Discrepancies between what is espoused and what is enacted may be minimised by such professional development.

The use of liminality in professional development would not be without problems, however, and so further debate and research on such matters is needed. Meyer and Land (2003, p. 10) highlight the power dimension in training in relation to who determines the threshold concepts to be addressed. In order for professional development training to incorporate constructive, reflexive, liminality time-spaces that are safely facilitated, there are also time and cost implications. All these factors pose challenges for higher education institutions as to how to design such training and give appropriate resources to support and nurture it. The wider system would also need to support and deal appropriately with difficulties highlighted during such professional development training so that it too would be congruent across its layers.

However, such professional training may engender fidelity and foster the development of practitioners who have greater capacities to be more authentic, develop constructive relationships and have a deeper understanding of troublesome knowledge, threshold concepts and liminal areas. Such attributes are especially vital in healthcare disciplines. Appropriately facilitated arts-based learning can offer positive liminal experience that features spontaneous play, flow and multi-

237

sensory, metaphorical, and reflexive ways of approaching and processing troublesome and nettlesome experience. Using liminality and reflexive arts-based approaches in professional development training can also help to facilitate learners towards the higher levels of Steinaker and Bell's (1979) experiential taxonomy. This aids the development of cultural competency necessary for healthcare practitioners (Lister, 1999) and art psychotherapists (BAAT, 2005). Therefore the incorporation of liminality into training seems applicable to various healthcare trainings at entry and continuing development levels. Indeed it may have value if included more in wider education and training in a range of areas across the lifespan.

NOTES

[1] 'Authoritism' refers to 'ritualism that can occur during Erikson's seventh stage of development. This involves using power for selfish gains instead of helping others'. (Source: http://psychology-lexicon.com/lexikon/authoritism.htm)

[2] Bakhtin (2000 p.84) uses the term "chronotope", literally meaning "time space", to refer to "the intrinsic connectedness of temporal and spatial relationships that are artistically expressed ..." Bakhtin (2000, p. 248) identifies various types of chronotope including "the chronotope of threshold" which he regards as "highly charged with emotion and value" and "always metaphorical and symbolic" Bakhtin (2000, p. 258) argues that "every entry into the sphere of meaning is accomplished only through the gates of the chronotope."

REFERENCES

Aronson, Jeffrey K. (2000). Autopathography: The patient's tale. *British Medical Journal, 321,* 1599-1602. http://bmj.bmjjournals.com/cgi/reprint/321/7276/1599.pdf (accessed 13 October 2006).

BAAT (2005). *Code of ethics and principles of professional practice for art therapists.* London: British Association for Art Therapists (BAAT).

BACP (2002). *Ethical framework for good practice in counselling and psychotherapy.* Rugby: British Association for Counselling & Psychotherapy.

Bakhtin, M. M. (2000). *The dialogic imagination.* (Ed. Michael Holquist. Trans. Michael Holquist & Caryl Emerson). Austin, TX: University of Texas Press.

Beach, W. A., Easter, D. W., Good, J. S., & Pigeron, E. (2005). Disclosing and responding to cancer 'fears' during oncology interviews. *Social Science & Medicine, 60*(4), 893-910.

Beauchamp, T. L. & Childress, J. F. (1994). *Principles of biomedical ethics,* 4th edition. Oxford: Oxford University Press.

Benner P. (1984). *From novice to expert: Excellence and power in clinical nursing practice.* California, Addison Wesley.

Bion, W. R. (1959). Attacks on linking. *International Journal of Psychoanalysis, XL,* 308-315. Reprinted in Bion (1987) chapter 8.

Bion, W. R. (1993). *Second thoughts: Selected papers on psychoanalysis.* London: Maresfield Library.

BMA Board of Science and Education (1993) *The morbidity and mortality of the medical profession.* London: British Medical Association.

Bourdieu, P. (1990). *The logic of practice.* Cambridge: Polity Press.

Bovensiepen, Gustav (2002). Symbolic attitude and reverie: Problems of symbolization in children and adolescents. *Journal of Analytical Psychology, 47,* 241-257.

Britzman, D.P. (1998). *Lost subjects, contested objects: Toward a psychoanalytic inquiry of learning.* Albany, NY: State University of New York Press.

Burbules, Nicholas C. (1997). Aporia: Webs, passages, getting lost, and learning to go on. *Philosophy of education yearbook*. http://www.ed.uiuc.edu/EPS/PES-yearbook/97_docs/burbules.html (accessed 13 Oct. 2006).

Caillois, Roger (1962). *Man, play and games*. London: Thames and Hudson.

Clouder, Lynn (2005). Caring as a 'threshold concept': Transforming students in higher education into health(care) professionals. *Teaching in Higher Education, 10*(4), 505-517.

Connell, C. (1998). *Something understood. Art therapy in cancer care*. London: Wrexham Pub.

Cooley, Charles H. (1922). *Human nature and the social order*. New York: Scribner's.

Corker, Mairian & Shakespeare, Tom (Eds.) (2002). *Disability/postmodernity: Embodying disability theory*. London/New York: Continuum International Publishing Group.

Cranton, P. (1994). *Understanding and promoting transformative learning: A guide for educators of adults*. San Francisco, CA: Jossey-Bass Inc.

Csikszentmihalyi, M. (2002). *Flow*. London: Rider.

Derrida, Jacques (1993). *Aporias*. (Trans. Thomas Dutoit.) Stanford: Stanford University Press.

Douglas, Mary (1966). *Purity and danger: An analysis of concepts of pollution and taboo*. New York: Frederick A Praeger, Inc.

Eisner, E. (2002). *The arts and the creation of mind*. New Haven: Yale University Press.

Ellis, C. & Bochner, P. A. (2000). Autoethnography, personal narrative, reflexivity: Researcher as subject. In Denzin, N. K. & Lincoln, Y. S. (Eds.), *Handbook of qualitative research* (pp. 733-768). Thousand Oaks: Sage.

Erikson, Erik H. (1994). *Identity and the life cycle*. New York: W.W. Norton & Co. Inc.

Foucault, Michel (1977). The eye of power. In Gordon, C. (Ed.), *Power/knowledge*. New York, NY: Pantheon Books.

Foucault, Michel (1986). Of other spaces. *Diacritics 16*, Spring, 22-27.

Foucault, Michel (1991). *Discipline and punish: The birth of the prison*. London: Penguin.

Freud, S. ([1917] 1973). Analytic therapy. In: *Introductory lectures on psychoanalysis. Volume one*. Harmondsworth: Penguin.

Glover, N. (1998). *Psychoanalytic aesthetics: The British school*. On-line book. Human-Nature.Com, Robert M. Young & Ian Pitchford. http://www.human-nature.com/free-associations/glover/index.html (accessed 13 October 2006).

Hawkins, P. (1997). Organizational culture: Sailing between evangelism and complexity. *Human Relations, 50*(4), 417-440.

Hayano, David M. (1979). Auto-ethnography: Paradigms, problems, and prospects. *Human Organization, 38*(1), 99-104.

Hofstede, G. H. (1991). *Cultures and organizations*. London: McGraw-Hill.

Hunt, E. & Agnoli, F. (1991). The Whorfian hypothesis: A cognitive psychology perspective. *Psychological Review, 98*, 377-389.

Irving, A. & Young, T. (2004). 'Perpetual liminality': Re-readings of subjectivity and diversity in clinical social work classrooms. *Smith College Studies in Social Work, 74*(2), 213-227.

Irwin, R. L. & de Cosson, A. ((2004). (Eds) *A/r/tography: Rendering self through arts-based living inquiry*. Vancouver, BC: Pacific Educational Press.

Jaspers, K. (1931). *Philosophie*. Berlin. Cited in Macquarrie, J. (1973) *Existentialism: An introduction, guide and assessment*. London: Penguin.

Jaspers, K. (1986). *Karl Jaspers: Basic philosophical writings*. New Jersey: Humanities Press.

Lacey, Anne & Luff, Donna (2001). *Trent focus for research and development in primary health care: An introduction to qualitative data analysis*. Trent Focus. http://www.trentrdsu.org.uk/cms/uploads/Qualitative%20Research.pdf (accessed 13 October 2006).

Lawton, Julia (1998). Contemporary hospice care: The sequestration of the unbounded body and 'dirty dying.' *Sociology of Health & Illness, 20*(2), 121-143.

Lister, P. (1999). A taxonomy for developing cultural competence. *Nurse Education Today, 19*(4), 313-318.

Little, M., Jordens, C.F., Paul, K., Montgomery, K., & Philipson, B. (1998). Liminality: A major category of the experience of cancer illness. *Social Science & Medicine*, *47*(10), 1485-1494.

Lynch, Gordon (1997). Words and silence: Counselling and psychotherapy after Wittgenstein. *Counselling*, *8*(2), 126-128.

Marcia, J.E. (2002). Identity and psychosocial development in adulthood. *Identity*, *2*(1), 7-28.

Mays, N. & Pope, C. (1995). Rigour and qualitative research. *British Medical Journal*, *311*(6997), 109-112. http://www.bmj.com/cgi/content/full/311/6997/109 (accessed 13 October 2006).

Meyer, J. H. F. & Land, R. (2003). Threshold concepts and troublesome knowledge: Linkages to ways of thinking and practising within the disciplines. *ETL project, Occasional report 4*. http://www.ed.ac.uk/etl/docs/ETLreport4.pdf (accessed 13 October 2006).

Meyer, J. H. F. & Land, R. (2005). Threshold concepts and troublesome knowledge (2): Epistemological considerations and a conceptual framework for teaching and learning. *Higher Education*, *49*(3), 373-388.

Milner, Marion (1977). *On not being able to paint*. Oxford: Heinemann Educational Books.

Morse, Janice (2000). Qualitative generalizability. *Qualitative Health Research*, *9*(1), 5-6.

Muzzin, L. J., Anderson, N. J., Figueredo, A. T. & Gudelis, S. O. (1994). The experience of cancer. *Social Science & Medicine*, *38*(9), 1201-1208.

Neary, M. (2000). Responsive assessment of clinical competence: Part 2. *Nursing Standard*, *15*(10), 35-40. http://www.nursing-standard.co.uk/archives/ns/vol15-10/pdfs/p3540v10w10.pdf (accessed 13 October 2006).

Paranjpe, A. C. (1975). *In search of identity*. New York: John Wiley & Sons Inc.

Parsons, T. (1951). *The social system*. London: The Free Press.

Patterson, S. J., Sochting, I., & Marcia, J. E. (1992). The inner space and beyond: Women and identity. In Adams, G. R., Gullota, T. P., & Montemayor, R. (Eds.), *Adolescent identity formation*. Los Angeles, CA: Sage Publications.

Penson, R. T., Svendsen, S. S., Chabner, B. A., Lynch, T. J., & Levinson, W. (2001). Medical mistakes: A workshop on personal perspectives. *The Oncologist*, *6*(1), 92-99. http://theoncologist.alphamedpress.org/cgi/content/full/6/1/92 (accessed 13 October 2006).

Perkins, D. (1999). The many faces of constructivism. *Educational Leadership*, *57*(3), 6-11.

Perkins, D. (2006). Constructivism and troublesome knowledge. In Meyer, J. H. F. & Land, R. (Eds.), *Overcoming barriers to student understanding: Threshold concepts and troublesome knowledge*. New York and London: RoutledgeFalmer.

Plato (1964). *The symposium and other dialogues*. London: J.M. Dent & Sons Ltd.

Purnell, L. (2003). Transcultural diversity and health care. In Purnell, L. & Paulanka, B. (Eds.), *Transcultural health care: A culturally competent approach*, 2nd edition (pp. 1-7). Philadelphia: E.A. Davis.

Race, D., Boxall, K., & Carson, I. (2005). Towards a dialogue for practice: Reconciling social role valorization and the social model of disability. *Disability & Society*, *20*(5), 507-521.

Rieber, L. P., Smith, L., & Noah, D. (1998). The value of serious play. *Educational Technology*, *38*(6), 29-37. http://it.coe.uga.edu/~lrieber/valueofplay.html (accessed 13 October 2006).

Rimmon-Kenan, Shlomith (2002). The story of "I": Illness and narrative identity. *Narrative*, *10*(1), 9-27. http://muse.jhu.edu/demo/narrative/v010/10.1rimmon-kenan.pdf (accessed 13 October 2006).

Ritchie, Jane & Spencer, Liz (2002). Qualitative data analysis for applied policy research. In Huberman, A. M. & Miles, M. B. (Eds.), *The qualitative researcher's companion*, (pp. 305-330). London: Sage.

Rogers, Carl R. (1996). *On becoming a person*. London: Constable.

Rose, T., Loewenthal, D., & Greenwood, D. (2005). Counselling and psychotherapy as a form of learning: some implications for practice. *British Journal of Guidance and Counselling*, *33*(4), 441-456.

Schön, Donald (1995). *The reflective practitioner: How professionals think in action*. New York: Basic Books.

Schwartz-Salant, N. & Stein, M. (Eds.) (1991). *Liminality and transitional phenomena*. Wilmette, IL: Chiron Publications.

Seale, Clive (1998). *Constructing death: The sociology of dying and bereavement.* Cambridge: Cambridge University Press.

Sibbett, C. H. (2005a). 'Betwixt and between': Crossing thresholds. In Waller, D. & Sibbett, C. H. (Eds.), *Art therapy and cancer care*, chapter 2. Maidenhead: Open University Press.

Sibbett, C. H. (2005b). Liminal embodiment: Embodied and sensory experience in cancer care and art therapy. In Waller, D. and Sibbett, C. H. (Eds.), *Art therapy and cancer care*, chapter 4. Maidenhead: Open University Press.

Sibbett, C. H. (2005c). An art therapist's experience of having cancer. Liminality: Living and dying with the tiger. In Waller, D. & Sibbett, C. H. (Eds.), *Art therapy and cancer care*, chapter 16. Maidenhead: Open University Press.

Sibbett, C. H. (2006a). *Liminality, cancer and art therapy: An autoethnographic exploration – Living with the tiger.* Unpublished PhD thesis. Belfast: Queen's University Belfast.

Sibbett, C. H. (2006b). Art therapy in cancer care: revelatory expression and inclusion of liminal and taboo issues. In Spring, D. (Ed.), *Art in treatment: Transatlantic dialogue*, chapter 7. Springfield, IL: Charles C. Thomas Publisher Ltd.

Springgay, S., Irwin, R. L., & Kind, S. W. (2005). A/r/tography as living inquiry through art and text. *Qualitative Inquiry, 11*(6), 897-912. Accessed 11 Oct. 2006. http://qix.sagepub.com/cgi/reprint/11/6/897.

Stanley, K. J. (2000). Silence is not golden: Conversations with the dying. *Clinical Journal of Oncology Nursing, 4*(1), 34-40.

Steinaker, N. & Bell, M. (1979). *The experiential taxonomy: A new approach to teaching and learning.* New York: Academic Press.

Sussman, Michael B. (Ed.) (1992). *A curious calling: Unconscious motivations for practicing psychotherapy.* Northvale, NJ: Jason Aronson.

Thompson, W. T., Cupples, M. E., Sibbett, C. H., Skan, D. I., & Bradley, T. (2001). Challenge of culture, conscience, and contract to general practitioners' care of their own health: Qualitative study. *British Medical Journal, 323*(7315), 728-731.

Thorne, B. (1991). The quality of tenderness. In Thorne, B. (Ed.), *Person-centred counselling: Therapeutic and spiritual dimensions* (chapter 5, pp. 73-81). London: Whurr Publishers.

Tillett, R. (2003). The patient within – Psychopathology in the helping professions. *Advances in Psychiatric Treatment, 9*(4), 272-279. http://apt.rcpsych.org/cgi/reprint/9/4/272.pdf (accessed 13 October 2006).

Trompenaars, F. & Hampden-Turner, C. (1997). *Riding the waves of culture.* London: McGraw-Hill.

Turner, Victor W. (1967). *The forest of symbols: Aspects of Ndembu ritual.* Ithaca: Cornell University Press.

Turner, Victor W. (1974). Liminal to liminoid in play, flow and ritual: An essay in comparative symbology. *Rice University Studies, 60*(3), 53-92.

Turner, Victor W. (1988). *The anthropology of performance.* New York: Performing Arts Journal Publications.

Turner, V. W. (1995). *The ritual process: Structure and antisStructure.* New York: Aldine de Gruyter.

van Gennep, A. (1960). *The rites of passage.* London: Routledge & Kegan Paul.

Wadeson, H. (1980). *Art psychotherapy.* New York: Wiley-Interscience, John Wiley & Sons.

Weber, S. & Mitchell, C. (2004). Visual artistic modes of representation for self-study. In Loughran, J., Hamilton, M., LaBoskey, V., & Russell, T. (Eds.), *International handbook of self-study of teaching and teacher education practices* (chapter 10). New York, NY: Kluwer Press. Excerpt at www.iirc.mcgill.ca/static/methodology/artbased.html (accessed 13 October 2006).

Wenger, E. (2000). *Communities of practice.* Cambridge: Cambridge University Press.

White, E. C. (1987). *Kaironomia: On the will-to-invent.* Ithaca: Cornell University Press.

White, Susan (2003). Autoethnography – An appropriate methodology? *Qualitative Research Journal, 3*(2), 22-32. www.latrobe.edu.au/aqr/journal/2AQR2003.pdf (accessed 13 October 2006).

Williams, S., Michie, S., & Pattani, S. (1998). *Improving the health of the NHS workforce: Report on the Partnership on the Health of the NHS Workforce*. London: Nuffield Trust.
Winnicott, D. W. (1996). *Playing and reality*. London: Routledge.

AFFILIATIONS

Caryl Sibbett
School of Education
Queen's University Belfast

William Thompson
dpo consultants UK

JANE OSMOND, ANDREW TURNER & RAY LAND

18. THRESHOLD CONCEPTS AND SPATIAL AWARENESS IN TRANSPORT AND PRODUCT DESIGN

INTRODUCTION

The second assessment was more that you had to design something and that is when I struggled. And surprisingly – even though it is a design course – maybe I am more suited to a modelling background. (1st year Transport and Product Design student)

In 2005, Coventry University was successful in obtaining funding from the Higher Education Funding Council for England for the Centre of Excellence for Transport and Product Design (CETPD) under the CETL initiative. The CETL initiative has two main aims: to reward excellent teaching practice, and to invest further in that practice so that the funding delivers substantial benefits to students, teachers and institutions. The pedagogical research activity undertaken within the CETPD has three inter-related strands of enquiry: threshold concepts in design, the nature of spatial awareness and internationalisation of the design curriculum. In terms of threshold concepts in design, the pedagogical research programme is investigating ways in which students, like the student quoted at the outset, acquire, or face difficulty in acquiring, transformative threshold design concepts that are crucial for the levels of design practice required by the global transport design community. The research draws upon the continuing work of Meyer and Land (2003, 2005, 2006) into threshold concepts and troublesome knowledge.

Transport and Product Design at Coventry University is acknowledged as a centre of national excellence with claims to international prominence. The underlying philosophy of the course at Coventry is to bring students to a point where they are eligible to enter the transport design and other international product design industries. This philosophy is informed by a conceptual framework of learning drawing on notions of situated cognition and the theory of communities of practice (Wenger, 1998). Because learning within a community of practice transforms who a student is, and what a student can do, teaching staff consider participation within the programme as an experience of identity formation. The course offers more than the accumulation of skills and information, and is viewed as a process of becoming – in this case becoming a certain kind of creative and critically minded design practitioner. Through this transformative practice a

R. Land, J.H.F. Meyer & J. Smith (Eds.), Threshold Concepts within the Disciplines, 243–258.

professional identity is formed, and, through the desire to become accepted within the community of creative design practitioners, learning can become a source of motivation, meaningfulness and personal and social energy. At the heart of this process is the development of spatial awareness and access to a set of knowledge practices that are necessary to visual design.

USING THRESHOLD CONCEPTS AS AN ANALYTICAL FRAMEWORK

Outcome-led approaches, in which student learning is expressed in terms of measurable cognitive outcomes, have dominated curriculum design in recent years. Davies (2003, p. 2), however, considers that the creative arts are challenging with respect to outcome-led learning because 'we work with rather more ambiguous terms such as 'creativity', 'imagination', 'originality'. Creative art subjects have long been regarded as somewhat problematic in this regard, and particularly in terms of assessment, as they contain what Gordon calls the 'wow' factor – 'creativity, originality, inventiveness, inspiration, ingenuity, freshness and vision' (2004, p. 61).

Approaches to teaching used by the Transport and Product Design staff at Coventry are underpinned, in the words of one respondent, by a tacit 'underlying agenda of things the students need to have'. A large proportion of the work the students are involved in is carried out in studio conditions. As such, the working environment tends to resemble the *atelier* method of teaching which 'involves a group of students ... working with one or two tutors ... through a year-long cycle of design' (Caddick & O'Reilly, 2002, p. 190). Further, members of staff feel that the environment the students become part of is important in terms of feeling comfortable. This is facilitated through the enthusiasm of the staff who pass on their knowledge in the manner of an 'apprenticeship' coupled with 'respect for the creative mind' (Design Tutor).

Within the context of the Transport and Product Design course, we chose to apply the threshold concepts framework (Meyer & Land, 2006) as a lens for identifying or surfacing this 'underlying agenda of things the students need to have'. Through clarification of the knowledge practices that students must acquire, our longer term aim is then to identify pedagogic strategies for enhancing the student learning experience. Given the difficulties in expressing measurable outcomes of learning within the discipline, and the comparatively lesser degree of consensus on what constitutes the working body of knowledge, it was recognised that identifying threshold concepts could be difficult. However, according to Meyer and Land (2003, p. 11), even 'where there is not such a clearly identified body of knowledge it might still be the case that what [we]have come to encapsulate in the term *ways of thinking and practising* (*WTP*) also constitutes a crucial threshold function in leading to a transformed understanding.'

Given the salience of spatial awareness in the process of becoming a creative and critically minded design practitioner, the CETPD research team decided to investigate perceptions of spatial understanding with both staff and students. This enabled us to open up these ways of thinking and practising in Transport and

Product Design, and, through the analysis of empirical data, to help identify threshold concepts that lead to a transformed understanding. Staff and student perceptions of what constitutes the development of spatial awareness were explored through interviews with staff and ten first-year Transport and Product Design students together with a questionnaire circulated to the whole first year intake.

SPATIAL UNDERSTANDING

A search of the literature revealed that the concept of spatial awareness has long been debated, and a number of terms are offered, including Spatial Awareness (Karnath et al., 2001), Spatial Functioning (Temple & Carney, 1995), Spatial Ability (Garg et al., 1999), Spatial Orientation (Bodner & Guay, 1997), Spatial Visualisation Ability (McGee, 1979, cited in Alias et al., 2002) and Spatial Intelligence (Eliot, 2002; Gardner, 1983; Shearer, 2004). In this instance, we draw on Gardner:

> Central to spatial intelligence are the capacities to perceive the visual world accurately, to perform transformations and modifications upon one's initial perceptions, and to be able to re-create aspects of one's visual experience, even in the absence of relevant physical stimuli ... spatial intelligence emerges as an amalgam of abilities. The most elementary operation, upon which other aspects of spatial intelligence rest, is the ability to perceive a form or an object ... appreciating how it will be apprehended for another viewing angle, or how it would look (or feel) were it turned around ... Such tasks of transformation can be demanding. The ability to solve these problems efficiently is special. (Gardner, 1983, pp. 173-174)

Staff Perceptions

It soon became apparent that a definitive staff view of the meaning of the term 'spatial awareness' had not yet emerged even within the context of the course. This debate over meaning was reflected during a meeting with all members of the teaching staff present, and during individual staff interviews. It was possible to group indicative responses into the following categories:

Table 1. Staff perceptions of spatial awareness

Category	Indicative response
All around awareness	'I don't think there is any area of conscious thought about anything that the design business doesn't touch on in a way that few others do: it is this business of this incredible all-round awareness.'

	'Holistic approach: cloud of information with polarised areas.'
	'I think spatial awareness is one of the mechanisms of this wider consciousness that people need to tap into to become a designer.'
	'Awareness of where things are - boundaries where you cut off your understanding.'
	'Holistic integrity.'
Co-ordination	'Hand/eye/brain co-ordination.'
Design sensitivity	'Sensitivity: being able to 'see' design; some see it as a picture, others see it as presenting and manipulating information.'
	'Seeing things as a whole, but having an instinct to knowing which bit to highlight to achieve certain purposes.'
	'Aesthetic understanding.'
Space	'Displacement of space.'
	'Relationship between form and spaces.'
	'Form-space-intelligence.'
'Intuitive/6th sense.'	'Intuitive/6th sense.'
Looking at an object from the outside	'I think it really has to be looking at an object.'
	'Awareness of an object at a distance.'
	Looking at an object from the outside rather than being in an object.'
Mental rotation	'2D to 3D translation.'
	'Looking at an object at a distance, but able to perceive it in the round in detail.'
	'Read views and put together in their heads.'
	'Manipulation and holding things in their head.'
Positioning system	'Is about navigation and urban environments.'
	'An awareness of space from what is occupying that space already.'
	'Associated with moving through space, retaining a memory of navigation?'
	'Mental markers of space that allow you to judge big or smaller spaces.'
	'Spatial positioning system working on several planes.'
	'Natural navigation.'
	'Dead reckoning: awareness of where we are in relation to things.'
	'I see it as a kind of navigational positioning where you are relative to other things…like a positioning system.'

Time	'Relates to time especially when orienting through large spaces.'
Visualisation	'Somebody being able to sit in a chair and visualise what the space around them is and look at that on drawings and have a concept of what that means.'
	'Understand what that means in terms of space around a product, car, phone etc.'
	'Looking at space required around or within something.'
Volume	'Relates to the ability to transform volume.'

Student Perceptions

This lack of clarity regarding the characteristics of spatial awareness was similarly reflected during ten one-to-one interviews with students which took place in their first term. It became clear that student responses were relatively untheorised and that students did not use a disciplinary language to describe the concept. Responses to a question asking about their understanding of the term 'spatial awareness' ranged from total lack of knowledge:

- 'I can't say I do. I would like to guess but I might be wrong.'
- 'Never heard of it before.'
- 'Not a lot really.'

to a recognition of the phrase:

- 'No, I have heard the term but I am not aware of it.'
- 'I've heard of it before …'

to an approximate guess:

- 'Like distance from things and if something will fit into a certain space or if it doesn't?'
- 'In what sense – when you walk into a room and feel a lot of space?'
- 'It depends on what context you mean it in: driving a car – do you know where the other cars are or being able to rotate things in your head.'
- 'Being aware of people and things around you – taking careful look at things and understanding them.'

During the second term, a questionnaire was circulated which included a question about spatial awareness. From the noticeably more sophisticated responses to this question it appeared that the students had made some progress in their understanding:

Table 2. Student perceptions of spatial awareness

Category	Indicative response
User needs	Being aware of design for the needs of others
Scale	Building of scale models accurately
Perspective	Helps understand dimensions and perspective for any angle
Relation of object to space	How well a product looks within the space its placed, e.g. you wouldn't put a dolls chair in a concert hall because it would be unnoticeable
Proportion	I like to look at an object and realise the proportions and why they are like that
Design sensibility	Making something look 'right' transitional form helped me with this
Observation	Noticing and constantly analysing objects around you. Shoe project − analyzed the 'make-up'
Use of space	Spatial awareness − designing the space around you
3D awareness	Spatial awareness is your ability to perceive and interpret 3D objects
Visualisation	Spatial awareness: could be described as the ability to 'imagine' how your proposed design would look, before actually representing it on paper
Ability to design from 2D into 3D	The ability to translate two dimensional sketches into three dimensional forms, i.e. models
Fit	The layout of my work − making each piece flow and work together
Drawing techniques	Through lectures, I have learnt how to draw an object from different angles from the same position

Relation of object to environment	Understanding the space around you on a particular environment and designing and modifying the components in that environment. This awareness is important when dividing perspective models

More research is to be undertaken, in particular the piloting of a test to assess students' skills in this area as they enter the course. It is hoped that findings from this test will allow the development of skills to be benchmarked and possibly to enable a greater degree of consensus on spatial awareness to be reached as it relates to this context. If this greater consensus can be reached it has been suggested that a new phrase be coined to distinguish the meaning of visual-spatial understanding in the design context when compared to phrases used by other disciplines. Suggestions have included 'Generative 3D ability', '3D creativity', 'Form-space intelligence'.

IDENTIFICATION OF THRESHOLD CONCEPTS WITHIN THE PROGRAMME

Through the discussions surrounding the notion of spatial awareness, some possible components were identified by the staff, which could be considered as threshold concepts (see below). These, it could be argued, underpin the tacit 'underlying agenda of things the students need to have':

Table 3. An articulation of candidate threshold concepts in Transport & Product Design

Possible threshold concept /practice	Students need to be able to:	Threshold Concept Characteristic(s)
Confidence to challenge/expand design clichés	inculcate design conventions and expand upon them using information from a variety of sources and experiences	Transformative Irreversible Troublesome
Empathy	to think outside of themselves and think of other people	Transformative Irreversible Troublesome
Group work	accept that designing is a team effort	Transformative Irreversible Troublesome
Language of design/designer identity	communicate using the recognised language of the design community of practice	Irreversible

Touching	understand the link between the physicality of the subject – feeling, touching, stroking, arms and bodies moving; clay, paper, resistance, different materials – enhances design skills	Transformative
Observation /perspective/ proportion/ colour	understand where they are and what they are looking at in order to draw objects in a representative manner and how colour can alter the shape of a design	Integrative
3D Visualisation to 2D representation	create a drawing and link that together as a 3D space and think about where things would be	Integrative

Some of these components were explored during the student interviews and the most troublesome appeared to be the confidence to challenge/expand design clichés. This related to the first module to be assessed, in particular to a task called the 'Thought Receptacle'. This was a reflective exercise which involved producing a diary-like item that outlined designs and objects that the students particularly liked, backed up by information as to why that was so. The task is designed to develop students' confidence to challenge existing style and practice and to foster a degree of conceptual transgression. Several students failed this task and had to re-submit. Their typical comments in relation to staff feedback included: 'really thought I had understood [the thought receptacle] – but from the feedback I hadn't. Apparently it was too planned'. Another reflected that: '[the thought receptacle] should reflect your personality and music I liked and sometimes poems and wrote down a lot of ... but it wasn't much so then later on [the lecturer] said relate to design as well ... the creative thing wasn't really set in.'. This was echoed by staff comments in relation to this assessment, which identified a 'limited sense of personal point of view, ... distance from being a designer, lack of confidence.' As well as the fact that there was 'not much personal stuff coming through.' On the other hand one felt there was evidence of a 'Good mix of work, confident, having a go, not afraid to go into areas where she hasn't been before, confident in herself or staff to play, will find a niche eventually.'

Empathy was a problem for some of the students, particularly during the ergonomic module, which puts a high emphasis on the link between design and user needs. Some students had difficulty seeing the link. One said 'I enjoy the designing side of things but some of the other bits they are getting us to do I really don't understand the relevance of it.' Another commented: 'I came in mind to do auto design and I think the first year was designing landscapes and development plans – not only with me but I guess with most of the students. It [the assignment] should have a bit of car in it. I suppose it might make sense later.'

Group work also proved troublesome, with some of students expressing their frustration when group members didn't turn up or pull their weight. One complained that 'we have had a lot of trouble with our first group work assignment. We were all given a user to focus on in the group work but when the day of the assessment came, two of the user groups did not turn up to set up their stuff in the morning. So out of the five user groups we only had three displays for three user groups.' Another said of a fellow group member 'when we needed the assessment in he never turned up and I had rung him and texted him and all things like that and after our assessment was over – later in the day he sent me a text saying who was this even though he knew perfectly well who it was, so that made me very cross.' One expressed dislike of the group process as a whole: 'I don't really like working as a group – I don't like relying on other people – because I don't work like most others and people don't work like me and you end up with clashes.'

On the other hand, some students found that they unexpectedly enjoyed their group work: 'We had a really good group – one of the best groups I have worked in over the course of the year and everyone sort of clicked. There would be some who wouldn't turn up to the group meetings but we left them to their own devices. We bonded together and got everything sorted – actually had fun in that module'. Another, in similar vein, commented That ' the group work I enjoyed. We had a group discussion, worked out our strengths and what we felt we did best – and we went off and did that. I enjoyed that. Not everyone turned up but we did the best that we could and passed it. We just kind of discussed it [who would do what in the group] and it seemed like the best thing to do.'

The most significant progression in the students was evidenced in the development of a language of design. In order to ascertain this, the students were asked if they had to explain themselves when discussing the course with people who were not part of it:

– 'Another thing about the design language – we use it because it is a lot easier to use than – we say rendering rather than saying we did our drawing and then coloured it in, because it is a lot easier to say rendering.'
– 'It's funny you should say that because I tell people I am on the auto and product course and some people don't know what automotive is … I don't think many people would understand rendering – drawing maybe but not rendering.'
– 'I do yes … often when I am talking to my brothers about what I am doing I talk about rendering, ellipses and they are like what? I am picking it up as I go along.'
– 'Yes, people do ask me to explain – if I am talking to people who I have gone to school with and done technology with they do know what I am talking about – but say my parents or my sisters or something they don't really know what I am

talking about sometimes. It was always like that but it has got worse since I have been on the course.'

– 'Yes, they do all the time. When I am talking to my family I sometimes wander into the design world and maybe name an artist or piece of work, and I tell them about a particular technique and they are like are you speaking alien? It is really hard work to try and explain what you are projecting onto someone who doesn't understand it.'

THE UNDERLYING EPISTEME AND CONCEPTUAL GAMES

From the staff responses in relation to the concept of spatial awareness it became clear that the skills and knowledge practices that staff impart to the students in order for them to complete the course and become successful designers remain, in the main, relatively untheorised and tacit. The lack of clarity in relation to a definitive meaning of spatial understanding in this context is perhaps because spatial awareness is, in the words of one teacher on the programme, 'Not something that designers acknowledge or talk about because it is the natural world they inhabit.' Another commented that 'it is an intuitive skill you develop, especially through experience.' Significantly the staff felt that '*is not a single threshold concept: there are components that result in this.*' This was possibly attributed to the fact that the course does 'not explicitly explore spatial awareness'.

These latter responses provide an interesting illustration of the important distinction David Perkins has made between threshold *concept* and underlying *episteme*. He points out that 'Although some of what is troublesome about knowledge squarely concerns the categorical function of concepts, much concerns the larger conceptual games around them' (2006, p. 41). He cites as an example the difference a history student might experience between coming to understand, on a conceptual level, the notion of bias when examining historical sources, and actually having to consult and use historical sources whilst keeping her critical antennae alert to the possibility of bias, and making appropriate allowance for the effects of bias when it is encountered. The former might remain at the level of inert knowledge whilst the latter most definitely would constitute an active knowledge practice. 'As with inert knowledge,' he argues, 'so with ritual, conceptually difficult, foreign, and tacit knowledge – these troubles have as much to do with the activity systems that animate concepts as they do with concepts in their basic categorical functions' (p.41). Besides recognising what he terms 'the games of enquiry we play' with particular concepts, it is, he argues, important to look beyond the particular. 'The disciplines', he states, 'are more than bundles of concepts. They have their own characteristic *epistemes*' (Perkins, 2006, pp. 41-42). Perkins provides a helpful definition of an episteme as:

a system of ideas or way of understanding that allows us to establish knowledge. Schwab (1978) and Bruner (1973) among others have emphasised the importance of students understanding the structure of the disciplines they are studying. 'Ways of knowing' is another phrase in the same spirit. As used here, epistemes are manners of justifying, explaining, solving problems, conducting enquiries, and designing and validating various kinds of products or outcomes. (Perkins 2006, p. 42)

Each discipline brings with it its own distinctive episteme and distinctive form of validation. Perkins points out that in various sub-disciplines of Engineering, for example, 'effective designs find their validation in not just sets of principles but practical performance from prototypes to wide-scale field tests' (p. 42). The design tutors we interviewed often indicated their sense that what design students required to enter the design community of practice, and to think and practice like a designer, was 'not a single threshold concept' but 'components that result in this'. What characterises the 'this' that is referred to seems to be primarily a nexus of attributes that are *integrated*. 'It is this business of this incredible all-round awareness' one respondent remarked. Another felt it was a 'holistic approach', a 'cloud of information with polarised areas.' Yet another felt the designer needed a capacity for 'holistic integrity.' Spatial awareness, some tutors felt, was an important 'component' – 'Awareness of where things are, boundaries where you cut off your understanding.' – but only one component of this broader epistemic fluency. 'I think spatial awareness is one of the mechanisms of this wider consciousness that people need to tap into to become a designer.' This underlying episteme of design appears to be a powerful and ever-present determinant of subjectivity: 'I don't think there is any area of conscious thought about anything that the design business doesn't touch on in a way that few others do'. This, too, resonates with Perkins' (2006) observation that 'threshold concepts certainly include more than particularly tough conceptual nuts in the content of a discipline. There are threshold epistemes that shape one's sense of entire disciplines' (p. 44).

The empirical data from our interviews with Design staff and students highlighted the troublesome nature of *tacit* understandings in the teaching of spatial awareness in design contexts. This seems to concur with Perkins' own findings.

Perhaps tacit knowledge is the most pervasive trouble with epistemes. Many teachers play the epistemic games of their professional disciplines fluently and automatically, and successful students ultimately need to do so as well. The problem is, many students never get the hang of it, or only slowly, because the epistemes receive little direct attention. For [students], surfacing the game through analytic discussion and deliberative practice could make a big difference. (2006, p. 43)

Davies (2006), researching into the learning of Economics, comes to similar conclusions. He points out that a threshold concept is very likely to be troublesome because 'it not only operates at a deep integrating way in a subject, but it is also taken for granted by practitioners in a subject and therefore rarely made explicit' (p. 74). He, too, rejects the reductivist notion that the knowledge practices of a disciplinary community can be represented in terms of a skill set or 'bundle of concepts' in Perkins' phrase. He cites Mitchell (2001) who emphasises 'ideologies' as they relate to disciplinary thinking:

It is the way in which such concepts are related, the deep-level structure of the subject which gives it coherence and creates a shared way of perceiving that can be left unspoken. This shared way of perceiving is the ideology of a subject, 'the invisible structures and beliefs by which we operate and which appear as natural unchallengeable ways of doing things'. (Mitchell, 2001, p. 2, cited in Davies, 2006, p. 71)

So in addition to their categorical functions, threshold concepts seem to be entangled with a much wider pattern of practice and enquiry, a set of games that are played with the concepts, and which in turn can provide a further source of troublesomeness for the novitiate. Within transport and product design, students seem to be required, *inter alia*, to gain sophisticated three-dimensional spatial understanding, and to nest this within a streetwise and sophisticated cultural sensitivity to prevailing taste, style and fashion. At the same time their designs draw on these spatial understandings and cultural antennae, they must also on the one hand conform to the material, cost, efficiency, environmental and safety constraint, of the industry (referred to within the community's discourse as 'packaging') *and* surprise and pleasantly shock their tutors through a degree of conceptual transgression which ensures that their creative work does not replicate the styles and norms of the older generation of their tutors. Where the expected or permissible boundaries of such transgression lie remains tacit and implicit. The shock of the new, yes, but they still need to pass. And the examiners are the older generation. This is something of a tall order and entails a complex process of enculturation if the students are to eventually make it in the design world. These necessary disciplinary understandings and attributes might be presented diagrammatically as in Figure 1.

ENTERING THE COMMUNITY OF DESIGN

So how might design students gain sufficient understanding of the 'underlying agenda of things the students need to have'? The Coventry programme draws these students into a state of 'liminality' (Meyer and Land, 2005), an in-between state of uncertainty and insecurity in which they do not enjoy full community membership status and struggle both to make sense of the underlying episteme and also to find their own creative identities as design practitioners. Perkins draws attention to 'the toolkit fallacy' which maintains that 'providing the students with the toolkit of explicit heuristics would enable their effective use'. He argues that this is insufficient:

instead, it was found that students also needed a self-management strategy to monitor their deployment of heuristics and their progress. Moreover, it was not enough for teachers to work model problems, they had to comment directly on the heuristics as they were deployed so students gained a situated sense of their utility. The combination of a self management strategy and explicit modelling yielded a dramatic improvement in students' ... problem solving. (2006, p. 43)

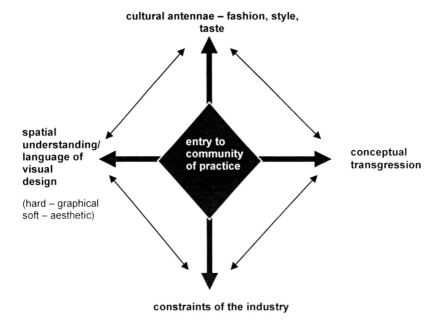

Figure 1. A conceptualisation of the transport & product design student's disciplinary enculturation.

The threshold concepts framework (Meyer and Land, 2006) also emphasises that the act of learning is an act of identity formation, and that entrance to a particular discourse community and the ways of thinking and practising particular to that community involves integrated transformations in language, identity and conceptual structure. But as Davies maintains, immersion in the ways of the community is necessary but insufficient.

> A student can accumulate knowledge about a community and the ideas that are commonly accepted in that community, but this falls short of acquiring the way in which members of that community see the world. When asked to explain a given theory, or to cite extracts from a body of received knowledge, they may be able to do this perfectly well. But when asked to look around them they do not see the world as viewed by a member of a subject community. (Davies, 2006, p. 71)

Seeing the world as viewed by a member of a subject community also requires an affective transformation, or the gaining of what Cousin (2006) has termed 'emotional capital'. The liminal state encountered within the Transport and Product Design programme provides space for the development of a self-management

255

strategy in the terms Perkins speaks of. The liminal state, a place of transition, uncertainty and hybridity, can also be a space for resistance and the assertion of difference (Bhabha 1998). In terms of identifying threshold concepts, it is possible that the problem with the thought receptacle task discussed earlier, which relates to the possible threshold concept of 'confidence to challenge' (conceptual transgression), was that the students were not yet confident in their own abilities and had not yet reached the stage where they felt confident in expressing their own ideas. One member of staff identified students who 'reach the point where being creative is not possible, can't think beyond the box'. This proved troublesome for one student who performed well in the first assignment but not in the second, and expressed her uncertainty about carrying on with the course because:

> the second assessment was more you had to design something and that is when I struggled. And surprisingly – even though it is a design course – maybe I am more suited to a modelling background. (1st year design student)

Here the conceptual barrier prevents access to an identity that is desired by the student (designer) and brings into view an alternative subjectivity which seems less desired and less satisfying (modelling). It is also possible that the problem with the group work was that the students who did not turn up for their meetings were not willing to accept that designing is a team effort, and therefore had not reached the possible threshold concept stage of the maturity (emotional capital) to accept such a constraint. In both instances, the troubled transition to a particular conceptual structure inhibits transformation to a more developed identity and access to the community of practice. What is particularly troublesome in these instances is that the underlying episteme necessary for these students to move on does not even come into view. This argues strongly for a mode of pedagogy which can render these less accessible knowledge practices more visible and explicit so that they can become the focus of discussion and exploration between deign students and their tutors. 'Without this openness' suggests Davies, 'the interaction between teachers and learners is shrouded in a mystery that ultimately deprives many learners of an opportunity to experience the way of thinking and practising that is apparently being offered to them. They just cannot see it' (Davies, 2006 p.71).

CONCLUSION

Using the threshold concept framework has enabled the research team to open up a dialogue with teaching staff in a discipline that appears, in the main, to be relatively undertheorised. The usefulness of this dialogue was evidenced – during the whole-staff meeting and in individual interviews – by the enthusiasm of staff to participate. The Design tutors, as reported earlier, felt that there was an underlying agenda of things the students needed to experience before they could become successful designers, but our initial investigations found that this underlying agenda had previously not been articulated clearly. This could speak to the nature of the subject, in that creative arts subjects are not easily quantifiable, with regard to learning outcomes and especially in assessment terms.

In addressing the original research question relating to spatial awareness, the first year of research by the CETPD team has found considerable variation in first year Design students' understanding of spatial issues. As the course progressed, the students were beginning to formulate more sophisticated understandings of spatial matters, but the variation in their understanding at this stage did not appear to be particularly influenced by age, gender or culture. Further research to address patterns of variation will take place in the form of a longitudinal study following the original group of ten student interviewees through their four-year programme. A research methodology is planned that intends to gain insights into variation in the pre-liminal, liminal, post-liminal and sub-liminal (epistemic) dimensions of their development of spatial awareness in line with the model proposed by Meyer, Land and Davies (2006). Throughout this continuing study the research will focus on the following issues:

– what is the student understanding of spatial awareness (and other relevant threshold concepts) in the first year of entry?
– how might factors such as age, gender and culture influence this understanding?
– what patterns of variation in the development of conceptual understanding relating to spatial design issues are discernible across subsequent years of the programme?

Findings from the data analysis will be used to explore, with the Design staff, the relative advantages and limitations of the *atelier* method as a learning environment for the development of spatial awareness and other related concepts necessary for the successful education of automotive design practitioners.

REFERENCES

Alias, M., Black, T., & Gray, D. (2002). Effects of instructions on spatial visualisation ability in civil engineering students. *International Education Journal, 3*(1).

Bhabha, H. (1998). Culture's in between. In Bennet, D. (Ed.), *Multicultural states: Rethinking difference and identity* (pp 29-26). London: Routledge.

Bodner, G. & Guay, R. (1997). The Purdue visualization of rotations test. *The Chemical Educator, 2*(4), 1-17.

Caddick, M. & O'Reilly, D. (2002). Structures for facilitating play and creativity in learning: A psychoanalytical perspective. In Wisdom, J., *Academic and educational development: Research, evaluation and changing practice in higher education*. London: Kogan Page.

Cousin, G. (2006). Threshold concepts, troublesome knowledge and emotional capital: An exploration into learning about others. In Meyer, J. H. F. & Land, R. (Eds.), *Overcoming barriers to student understanding: Threshold concepts and troublesome knowledge*. London and New York: Routledge.

Davies, A. (2003). Writing learning outcomes and assessment criteria in art and design. Report for the Art, Design and Communication Learning and Teaching Support Network (ADM Subject Centre) 2000/2001. http://www.brighton.ac.uk/adm-hea/projects/adm-projects/effect-assess-ad.html. Accessed: August 14th 2006.

Davies, P. (2006). Threshold concepts: How can we recognise them? In Meyer, J. H. F. & Land R. (Eds.), *Overcoming barriers to student understanding: Threshold concepts and troublesome knowledge* (pp. 70-84). London and New York: Routledge..

Eliot, J. (2002). About spatial intelligence: I [1,2]. *Perceptual and Motor Skills, 94,* 479-186.

Gardner, H. (1983). *Frames of mind: The theory of multiple intelligences.* New York: Basic Books.

Garg, A., Norman, G., Spero, L., & Taylor, I. (1999). Learning anatomy: Do new computer models improve spatial understanding? *Medical Teacher, 21*(5).

Gordon, J. (2004). The 'wow' factors: The assessment of practical media and creative arts subjects. *Art Design & Communication in Higher Education, 3*(1).

Karnath, H., Ferber, S., & Himmelbach, M. (2001). Spatial awareness is a function of the temporal not the posterior parietal lobe. *Nature, 411* (6840), 950-953.

McGee, M. (1979). *Human spatial abilities: Sources of sex differences.* New York: Praeger.

Meyer, J. H. F. & Land, R. (2003). Threshold concepts and troublesome knowledge: Linkages to ways of thinking and practising within the disciplines. In C. Rust (Ed.), *Improving student learning. Improving student learning theory and practice − 10 years on,* (412-424) OCSLD, Oxford.

Meyer, J. H. F. & Land, R. (2005). Threshold concepts and troublesome knowledge (2): Epistemological considerations and a conceptual framework for teaching and learning. *Higher Education, 49*(3), 373-388.

Meyer, J. H. F. & Land R. (Eds.) (2006). *Overcoming barriers to student understanding: Threshold concepts and troublesome knowledge.* London and New York: Routledge.

Meyer, J. H. F., Land R., & Davies, P. (2006). Threshold concepts and troublesome knowledge (4): Issues of variation and variability. Paper delivered at the *Threshold Concepts within the Disciplines Symposium,* Glasgow UK. 1 September.

Mitchell, S. (2001). Some key concepts in argument. In Andrews, R. & Mitchell, S. (Eds.), *Essays in argument.* London: Middlesex University Press.

Perkins, D. (2006). Constructivism and troublesome knowledge. In Meyer, J. H. F. & Land R. (Eds.), *Overcoming barriers to student understanding: Threshold concepts and troublesome knowledge* (pp. 33-47). London and New York: Routledge.

Shearer, B. (2004). Multiple intelligences theory after 20 tears. *Teachers College Record. 106*(1), 2-16.

Temple. C. & Carney, R. (1995). Patterns of spatial functioning in Turner's syndrome. *Cortex, 31*(1), 109-118.

Wenger, E. (1998). *Communities of practice: Learning, meaning and identity.* Cambridge: Cambridge University Press.

AFFILIATIONS

Jane Osmond
Andrew Turner
Coventry University

Ray Land
Strathclyde University, Glasgow

PART III: PEDAGOGIC DIRECTIONS

GLYNIS COUSIN

19. THRESHOLD CONCEPTS: OLD WINE IN NEW BOTTLES OR NEW FORMS OF TRANSACTIONAL CURRICULUM INQUIRY?

INTRODUCTION

This chapter is in two parts: the first examines perspectives with which threshold concepts has affinities; the second discusses the distinctiveness of threshold concept research in relation to its break from student-centred perspectives. In particular, I argue that it is timely to disturb the binary of student/teacher-centredness for a relational model of educational research and development in which key actors (e.g. students, teachers, researchers) work within a framework of co-inquiry. I propose that threshold concept research offers a valuable way of generating such a framework.

At a recent conference at which I presented a paper on threshold concepts and curriculum design, a participant handed me a note as I sat down. The note said that all I had done was to rehash ideas from known educational theories. To some extent, he was right, of course. As I elaborate below, there are clear overlaps and affinities with a number of the ideas shared by the theory of threshold concepts and other perspectives in education; as well as briefly discussing these, my aim is to draw out some of the particular features of threshold concept research against the notion that it is simply old wine in new bottles. I will start with an acknowledgement that threshold concept theory shares with Gestalt perspectives (Curzon, 2001) a notion that a grasp of the whole allows the learner to see the constituent parts.

THE ROLE OF INTEGRATION IN LEARNING THEORIES

At one level, Gestalt learning theorists might read the notion of a threshold concept as one which fragments the learning and structure of a subject by privileging one or two concepts over others, apparently refusing the principle that the total is more than the sum of the parts. But like Gestalt theories, the idea of mastering a threshold concept incorporates the likelihood of the slow gestation of understanding and a 'penny dropping' moment in which once a difficulty is grasped, other things fall into place. As Meyer and Land (2006, p. 7) write, threshold concept mastery 'exposes the previously hidden interrelatedness of something'. An illustration of how students search for this interrelatedness is provided by Entwistle (2006).

R. Land, J.H.F. Meyer & J. Smith (Eds.), Threshold Concepts within the Disciplines, 261–272.
© 2008 Sense Publishers. All rights reserved.

In their recent research, Entwistle and Entwistle's interviews with students revealed that 'different facets of a topic come together simultaneously – "click into place" – to create a satisfyingly complete picture' (in Entwistle, 2006, p. 216; see also Entwistle & Entwistle 1992, 2003). Entwistle and Marton (1994) have advanced the idea of *knowledge objects* to capture ways in which this eventual clicking into place is facilitated by the students themselves, through representing the deep linking of their personal experience and knowledge to 'understanding targets'. In indicating a promising line of inquiry for threshold concept research, Entwistle (2006, p. 217) concludes that 'it would be surprising if some of the experiences of the transformations in thinking about the subject created by grasping threshold concepts were not similar to those found in the studies of knowledge objects'. Similarly, Perkins (2006) suggests that students need to grasp the 'underlying game' to their subject if they are to master it fully. The disciplines, writes Perkins (2006, pp. 41-42) 'are more than bundles of concepts. They have their own characteristic epistemes ... epistemes are manners of justifying, explaining, solving problems, conducting inquiries, and designing and validating various kinds of products or outcomes.'

This notion of epistemes proved fruitful for the investigations carried out by Osmond *et al.* (2006) who found that the threshold concept of 'spatial awareness' in transport and product design cannot be grasped without learners having a handle on a 'set of knowledge practices that are necessary to visual design'.

A further area of overlap between threshold concepts and other theories concerns the intertwining of affective and cognitive journeys for mastery. Arguably, one of the most influential engagements with these journeys at undergraduate level has been provided by Perry (1970).

LEARNER JOURNEYS

While the learner journeys described through states of liminality (Meyer & Land, 2006) might have some parallels with Perry's five epistemological states (from dualism through to relativism), there are some important differences. Though his writings remain insightful in many ways, Perry's (1970) research is rather outdated, particularly concerning his characterisation of an ideal epistemological stance, namely that of a relativism which is held to be guided by the light of objective evidence. In Perry's view, a learner eventually appreciates the provisional nature of knowledge and, as such, learns to judge the worth of a discovery by evaluating the 'objective' evidence on its side. There are two difficulties with this: firstly, we can never know the extent to which the epistemological stages a student journeys through are a reflection of how he or she is taught, rather than a natural orientation towards knowledge. Secondly, the ideal epistemological stance of a 'detached observer' is far from ideal from the viewpoint of the growing number of critics of an objectivist perspective. Indeed, in some academic perspectives, identification with researcher detachment would be taken to be a pre-liminal state in relation to the mastery of the threshold concept of, say, 'representation' (Booth, 2006). A general idea of learner maturation through increasingly sophisticated epistemological understandings is of some help to curriculum designers. The idea of threshold concepts will support a disciplinary sensitive view of this maturation. In either case, however, it will be hard to unravel processes of intellectual maturation from those of disciplinary enculturation.

WAYS OF COMING TO KNOW

The very useful efforts to characterise 'ways of teaching and practising (WTP)' in the disciplines by McCune and Hounsell, (2005) need to include an appreciation that these ways will never be stable or uncontested; the risk is of representing hegemonic WTPs as *the* WTPs and it should be acknowledged fully that this risk is not absent from the inquiry into threshold concepts. Threshold concepts are always epistemologically informed, which is why they are theorised as provisional, contestable and culturally situated. For instance, a Keynesian economist and a Marxist one may propose different threshold concepts for the economics they respectively teach because they have quite different views about what is central to their subject. As Knights (2005) has argued for the case of English, the subject they teach is always overladen with the teacher's epistemological stance. No-one actually teaches 'English', rather they teach, for instance, poststructuralist or structuralist English, and are thus inducting their students into a school of thought as much as they are inducting them into the subject.

We must keep reminding ourselves that we are characterising what some people hold to be threshold concepts in given situations at given moments. We need to remember too that for learners grasping a threshold concept may require knowing about rival concepts, and that, for researchers into this area, a degree of reflexivity about such rival concepts and their own investments in their selection and representation of threshold concepts is important. The troublesomeness of a threshold concept may include its own inherent instability. One of the insights we gain from Perry (1970) concerns students' yearnings for clear and safe explanations, but of course such clarity and safeness is often unavailable.

LEARNER SAFETY

A key dimension to the threshold concept literature centres on learner safety and the need to create something akin to a 'holding environment' (Winnicott, 1971) while students struggle with comprehension. In arguing that learning often involves encounters with troublesome knowledge (Perkins, 1999) or a sense of immobility in 'stuck places' (Ellsworth, 1997), threshold concept theorists have suggested that we need to convey to learners that discomfort and uncertainty are normal dimensions to learning. This emphasis differs a little from the humanist psychology represented by Maslow (1970) or Rogers and Freiberg (1993). Whereas these writers urge teachers to create safe environments as a prerequisite to learning, the idea of threshold concept mastery is tied into seeing unsafety as an unavoidable part of the learner's journey and the concept of liminal states offers an explanatory framework for this journey which links up learning with identity processes. Not 'getting it' can be associated with a learner not *feeling* comfortable, ready or able enough to master a concept. This is particularly so where a student cannot identify with a successful learner position for whatever reason.

Of course, some aspects of classroom unsafety can be avoided, particularly those concerned with inclusion and respect for others, but evidence from a number of researchers suggests that mastery of threshold concepts involves unavoidable learner anxiety. For example, Caryl Sibbett (2008) proposes the notion of 'nettlesome' knowledge which refers to 'elements of knowledge that are taboo in that they are defended against, repressed or ignored because if they were grasped they might "sting" and thus evoke a feared intense emotional and *embodied* response'. McGonigal, Cove and McAdam (2006) talk usefully of 'learner optimism' and 'learner pessimism' in the mentoring of probationer teachers. Flanagan and Smith (2008) refer to 'the confused and the bemused' in their research into learning to programme. Booth (2006) stresses the affective dimension to learning philosophical threshold concepts. See also my own work (Cousin, 2006) where I offer the idea of emotional capital to support our sense-making of dimensions of learner anxiety concerning threshold concept mastery.

The curriculum design principle of constructing a 'supportive liminal environment' in threshold concept theory addresses the kind of complicated learner transitions learners undergo. Generating such an environment involves a deep appreciation of a dialectic between knowing and being, as the tale of the desirée potato's journey to roastedness in the Editors' Preface of this volume vividly exposes. In this playful narrative Land, Meyer and Smith illustrate how mastery simultaneously changes what we know and who we are. Learning is a form of identity work. An acknowledgement of this and thus the focus on the affective aspects of learning threshold concepts offers a welcome departure from investigations which centre on that very abstract and purely cognitive concept of 'ability'. In this regard, attention to the liminal is particularly important in the exploration of facilitative learning environments for those who are the first in their family to enter university or for those who are different from a majority of students in other respects – perhaps female students in the sciences, international students or ethnic minority students. Before getting to two theorists who have written much on the connectedness of the affective and the cognitive, namely Lave and Wenger (1991), I first want to acknowledge the similarities between Vygotsky's (1978) concept of the zone of proximal development and that of states of liminality proposed by Meyer and Land.

THRESHOLD CONCEPTS AND VYGOTSKY'S ZONE OF
PROXIMAL DEVELOPMENT

Teaching for Vygotsky is about coaching students from what they know towards what they can know and he famously described this space between actual and potential ability as the zone of proximal development (ZPD). Appropriately stretching learners within this zone, argued Vygotsky, will help them to access fresh understandings, and will lead them eventually to share a common epistemological space (a perceptual mass as Vygotsky called it) with their tutors. They are then ready to move on to the next 'just out of reach' sphere of knowledge.

There are clear affinities with the metaphors of the zone of proximal development and that of a liminal space advanced by Meyer and Land (2006). Each metaphor invites a view of learners who go through journeys that involve insecure, transitional states before mastery. In Vygotsky's perspective, this journey requires careful scaffolding and the skilled facilitation from a more knowledgeable Other who can take the learner from the realm of what they know to new fields of experience and knowledge. Learning in the ZPD is not linear and incremental but involves recursive movements (this was transported into curriculum design principles through Bruner's spiral curriculum). Similarly, as Meyer and Land (2006) put it, threshold concept mastery involves oscillating states (see Orsini-Jones' chapter in this book for a fine discussion of this in relation to language students). Incidentally, Land *et al.* (2005) have argued that the nature of learner oscillation creates challenges for the learning outcomes movement in the UK where there does tend to be an emphasis on linear, incremental progression.

Despite Vygotsky's constructivist insistence on the social nature of learning and the place of experience in learners' sense-making activities, we tend to see the journey in the ZPD as resulting largely from 'transfigured thought'. While learners are held to move from the lower to the upper end of their zone of proximal development as they gain increased mastery there is little sense that this movement involves the 'transfiguration of identity' to use Meyer and Land's words (2006, p.21). The interlinking of these transfigurations – of thought and identity – have been very well theorised by Lave and Wenger.

LAVE AND WENGER – PERIPHERAL PARTICIPATION AND LIMINALITY

The situated learning principles offered by Lave and Wenger (1991) and later Wenger (1998) are that: a) participation in communities of practice enables learning; b) that learning inextricably includes processes of enculturation; and c) as such, it changes who we are as much as it changes what we know. Lave and Wenger share with theorists of threshold concepts the use of an anthropological lens through which to view how the ontological and the epistemological connect.

A significant strength of Lave and Wenger's work lies in their insistence that learning always involves a process of becoming; it is never a completed state. There are rites of passage at different points of this becoming (e.g. examinations, graduation ceremonies and the granting of a license to practice) which are as important for acquiring the 'ways of thinking and practising' of a subject (McCune & Hounsell, 2005) as is the cognitive grasp of its intrinsic concepts. The emphasis in Lave and Wenger's writings is on the informal learning that takes place in work-based communities rather than in the formal curriculum provided by universities. While we get much to think about from Lave and Wenger (1991) in terms of the social difficulties that attend initiation and the maintenance of learner and subject/professional identities, there is less on the linkage of these difficulties with specific conceptual ones. In Lave and Wenger (1991) learning largely rests on successful degrees of participation and the availability of 'facilities for engagement' for this. Indeed in Wenger (1998) there is a lot about creating the conditions for learning, about the need to 'be there' (in a community of practice) but not so much detail on 'doing there'. In my view, where we can most fruitfully cross-fertilise the concept of peripheral participation with that of liminality is in the encouragement in universities of generating what Brew (2006) has called inclusive 'communities of scholars', that is communities of students and academics researching together. Threshold concept research can lend itself to this kind of inclusive research as I later discuss.

I now turn to what has been over the past thirty years the most influential perspective in higher education research, namely phenomenography. I first discuss its affinities with threshold concept theory as 'action poetry' and secondly explore the student-centredness this perspective has encouraged. I conclude with the suggestion that threshold concept curriculum inquiry lends itself to an inclusive, negotiated form of such inquiry.

ACTION POETRY

Recently various writers have pointed to a range of difficulties with the phenomenographic tradition which has dominated higher education research for some thirty years. This range has included: the implied hierarchy of the binaries of deep/surface learning; their classificatory limits and analytical closure (Webb, 1996); the erasure of learner particularities and of researcher presence in the interpretation (Conrad et al., 1997); the failure of phenomenographic methods to engage with paradox or complexity (Haggis, 2006) and the tendency of phenomenographers to see language as a transparent, unproblematic tool which can be placed in the service of dispassionate explanation (Bayne, 2004). These are interesting challenges but they are incomplete without an appreciation of the ways in which phenomenographers succeeded in speaking to academics about higher education learning and teaching at a particular historical point. The notions of deep and surface learning and of orientations to learning accessibly theorised variation in students' experiences and performance.

The explanatory power of the deep and surface metaphors that emerged from phenomenographic research (Marton et al., 1984) has been enormously important to curriculum research and design in many universities across the world. These metaphors have helped teachers to organize their thinking about how to provide the best kind of learning experiences for their students. Beaty (2006) points to the resonance this binary created with the academic teachers attending teacher development programmes. Describing the deep and surface binary as 'action poetry' (Perkins' term for facilitative language) which has 'enhanced the development of learning and teaching for the past 25 years', Beaty adds that:

> Recently our focus of attention has become more sensitive to differences
> between individual learners and in the different pedagogies within

disciplines. Thus threshold concepts is action poetry for our time. (Beaty, 2006, p. xii)

In my view, Beaty is quite right to locate the appeal of threshold concepts in its disciplinary focus. I am not sure that this is because pedagogies need to be distinctive for each of the disciplines, and it is important to avoid the reading of cultural differences as essential differences. That said, the view that each subject area has its own difficulties and that curriculum inquiry can fruitfully explore these is a message that threshold concept proponents have very successfully conveyed. Like that of deep and surface learning, this simple proposition has resonance with subject specialists who are exploring the best ways of teaching their students.

There are some interesting differences between the research framework for deep and surface learning (phenomenography) and that of threshold concepts research (which does not have a settled methodological framework). Phenomenography explores student experiences for the discovery of variation in learners' reported ways of experiencing a given phenomenon. Although phenomenographic research is often based on dialogic interviews with students, there is a sense in which it is also research *on* the students because once extracted from them, the data becomes the researcher's text to analyse in decontextualised form. The phenomenographer is not interested in biographic or singular features of an interview because she collapses all interview data into one text in order to discover what variations inhere in the presently understood world rather than in individuals. One difficulty with this approach is that, inescapably, this form of student experience research can be read as the researcher's experience of the students' experience. It seems to me that there is an emergent trend in the research into threshold concepts that is apace with contemporary concerns about this kind of interpretive dilemma. Firstly, I think threshold concept research offers a form of transactional curriculum inquiry in which all the key players (academics, students, educationalists) work iteratively together to explore the difficulty of the subject. Secondly, I think that this emergence decentres student-centredness in higher education research and development and that we have reached the right point of maturity for this to happen.

STUDENT-CENTREDNESS

Firstly, I wish to stress that most academics who have been exposed to the insights offered by student-centred perspectives have largely benefited from them. O'Neill and McMahon (2007) show in their very useful summary of the literature on student-centredness that it is best understood in counterposition to teacher-centredness, with the latter characterised by: a) low level of student choice; b) student passivity; and c) power resting primarily with the teacher, and the former as the reverse of these characteristics. Another common way of representing the difference between teacher- and student-centredness is to characterise the first as content transmission-based and the second as process-based. While this dualistic logic is easy prey for those with a postmodern bent, it would be arrogant as well as inaccurate to deny the immense contribution to the quality of student and teacher experiences that student-centred perspectives (much of which is inspired by phenomenographic research) have provided. The move from thinking about what they are going to do as teachers to a consideration of what will prompt the best learning activities and outcomes from their students marks a transformative shift in practice for academics. Indeed many teachers find it liberating when they realise that they need not relentlessly occupy centre stage for the delivery of a didactic performance.

With the above qualification in mind, we need to recognize also that some academics continue to express hostility about student-centred approaches. This hostility can be defensively packaged by developers as academic conservativism. For instance, Land's (2004, p. 132) research into UK educational developers shows how some members of this tribe engage in an unhelpful 'otherising' of academic 'resisters and obstructers' who do not want to make the changes requested of them. In my experience, there is the mirror opposite problem of the 'convert'. This is the academic colleague who produces a narrative of reflective practice in which he or she demonstrates the taking of a Damascene path to student-centredness. I am sure I am not alone in having read many assessed portfolios from teacher development courses which offer this narrative. It is sometimes difficult to know whether it is a heartfelt or a dutiful conversion. Either way, the adoption of student-centred approaches appears to require the symbolic shedding of the self as teacher. Perhaps this is a step too far for some academics.

I wonder whether those academics who deride student-centredness are worried that getting students to break out into small groups in seminars, or to talk to their neighbours in lectures, will somehow profane their subject and their academic status. Educational developers have not always trod carefully on territory which is held to be sacred by academics. Is there a fear from academics that student-centred techniques rob the teaching and learning event of its ceremonial, ritual content, its theatrical dimension? Lectures may not be effective in linear, aligned ways, but perhaps it debases their purpose to worry about this because they have a symbolic function. Arguably, lectures perform identity work for both teachers and students, enabling each to feel part of the university and of the subject community. Moreover, the lecture theatre *is* a sacred place in the sense that it delineates a space where academics hope to exercise their freedom, and where radical, interesting, contentious ideas are tested and voiced from behind a lectern.

My suggestion then is that an unintended outcome of the student experience tradition has been what one writer describes as 'the mortification of the teacherly self' (McShane, 2006, p. 59). This Goffmanesque melodramatic notion aids an exploration into how some educational developers have viewed their task as that of dismantling and outlawing 'teacher-centredness' in favour of 'student-centredness'. Has a counter-position meant as a heuristic device been turned into a source of moralising? Is it time to swing the pendulum back to teachers, not as lone sages on the stage but to strongly position them with their students and educational researchers/developers as partners in an inquiry into disciplinary concerns? Threshold concept research can do this because it squarely places subject specialists at the centre of an inquiry into the difficulty of their subject. In this way there is a restoration of dignity for academics and a promising reconfiguration of the research relationships between students, academics, educational researchers and developers.

TOWARDS TRANSACTIONAL CURRICULUM INQUIRY

An important dimension in the threshold concepts perspective, then, lies in the ways in which it places subject specialists at the centre of inquiry. I am not suggesting that phenomenographic research never did this – such a suggestion would ignore the many studies by subject specialists themselves. But, arguably, threshold concept research starts from the authority of the subject specialist rather than that of the educational research specialist. Moreover – and this is my central point – characteristic of a number of research projects into threshold concepts is the dialogue they have generated among subject specialists, students and educationalists. The following quote from Osmond, Turner and Land (2006, p. 120) illustrates:

> Using threshold concepts as a framework has enabled the research team to *open up a dialogue* with the staff in a discipline that appears, in the main, to be relatively undertheorised. This usefulness of the dialogue was evidenced during the whole-staff meeting and individual interviews by the enthusiasm of the staff to participate. (My emphasis)

Another good example of this 'opening up of a dialogue' is in Orsini-Jones' (2006) research on 'crossing grammar thresholds' – here are some illustrative quotes from students and the tutor:

> *Student*: You know, I understood the concept for about lets say 10 seconds, yes yes, I got that and then suddenly, no no, I didn't get that, you know, suddenly, like this.
> *Tutor*: Did you have any problems with grammar, any areas where you had difficulties, got stuck?
> *Student*: Yeah, with distinguishing the phrases and the clauses.
> *Tutor*: Right, and do you think you've cracked it now?
> *Student*: No.

These extracts illustrate two key points. Firstly, the interview itself forms a relation of care between teacher and student in that the former is clearly listening carefully to the students to know more about what is troublesome and difficult for them. I think that this in itself lays the basis for the 'supportive liminal environment' referred to by Land *et al.* (2006). Secondly, the teacher returns to the scene of the difficulty *with* the students to check ongoing problems with mastery. This dynamic involves both learners and teachers in shared reflections. The research and the pedagogy overlap. The overwhelming strength of threshold concepts is precisely in the opportunities for co-inquiry it presents between subject experts, students and educational researchers; I have called this *transactional curriculum inquiry* to capture the negotiations between these key actors in pursuit of shared understandings of difficulties and shared ways of mastering them. It follows that this idea of a transactional approach spills into the pedagogic posture of teachers which becomes neither student-centred nor teacher-centred but something more active, dynamic and in-between.

To conclude, in exploring the theoretical affinities threshold concepts shares with other educational perspectives, I have acknowledged its overlap with them. At the same time I have attempted to draw out the distinctive characteristics of threshold concept research: firstly, this concerns its theorisation of how the affective and cognitive are inextricably bound with respect to mastery; secondly, I have suggested that threshold concept theory has struck a chord with the increasing number of subject specialists who are exploring the pedagogy of their discipline, rendering it 'action poetry for our times'; thirdly, because of its emphasis on the difficulty of the subject and thus its need to work both from the authority of subject specialists and to work with students and educationalists to explore this, I have called threshold concept research 'transactional curriculum inquiry'. Further, I have suggested that a transactional approach offers a pedagogic posture that defeats the binary opposition of teacher-centred/student centredness. In short, the ideas of transactional curriculum inquiry and pedagogy aim to capture a new, inclusive paradigm for higher education research, teaching and learning.

REFERENCES

Bayne, S. (2004). *Learning cultures in cyberspace*. Unpublished PhD thesis, University of Edinburgh.

Booth, J. (2006). On the mastery of philosophical concepts: Socratic discourse and the unexpected 'affect'. In Meyer, J. H. F. & Land, R. (Eds.), *Overcoming barriers to student understanding: Threshold concepts and troublesome knowledge*. London and New York: Routledge.

Beaty, L. (2006). Foreword. In Meyer, J. H. F. & Land, R. (Eds.), *Overcoming barriers to student understanding: Threshold concepts and troublesome knowledge*. Routledge: London and New York.

Brew, A. (2006). *Research and teaching: Beyond the divide*. London: Palgrave.

Conrad, L., Hazel, E., & Martin, E. (1997). Issues in gender and phenomenography. *Higher Education Research & Development, 16*(2), 213-226.

Cousin, G. (2006). Threshold concepts, troublesome knowledge and emotional capital: An exploration into learning about others. In Meyer, J. H. F. & Land, R. (Eds.), *Overcoming barriers to student understanding: Threshold concepts and troublesome knowledge*. London and New York: Routledge.

Curzon, L. (2001). *Teaching in further education*. London: Continuum.

Ellsworth, E. (1997). *Teaching positions: Difference pedagogy and the power of address*. New York: Teachers College Press.

Entwistle, A. C. & Entwistle, N. J. (1992). Experiences of understanding in revising for degree examinations. *Learning and Instruction, 2*, 1-22.

Entwistle, N. J. (2006). Threshold concepts within research into higher education. Paper presented at the *Threshold Concepts within the Disciplines* Symposium, University of Strathclyde, Glasgow, 30th Aug.-1st Sept.

Entwistle, N. J. & Entwistle, D. M. (2003). Preparing for examinations: The interplay of memorising and understanding, and the development of knowledge objects. *Higher Education Research and Development, 22*, 19-42.

Entwistle, N. J. & Marton, F. (1994). Knowledge objects: Understandings constituted through intensive academic study. *British Journal of Educational Psychology, 64*, 161-178.

Flanagan, M. T. & Smith, J. (2008). From playing to understanding: the transformative potential of discourse versus syntax in learning to program. In Land, R., Meyer, J. H. F. & Smith, J., *Threshold concepts within the disciplines*. Rotterdam and Taipei: Sense Publishers.

Haggis, T. (2006). Problems and paradoxes in fine-grained qualitative research: An exploration of 'context' from the perspective of complexity and dynamic systems theory. Paper presented at *Higher Education Close Up 3*, University of Lancaster, July 2006. Available at: http://www.lancs.ac.uk/fss/events/hecu3/documents/tamsin_haggis.doc.

Knights, B. (2005). Intelligence and interrogation: The identity of the English student. *Arts and Humanities in Higher Education, 4*(1).

Land, R., Cousin, G., Meyer, J. H. F. & Davies, P. (2005). Threshold concepts and troublesome knowledge (3): Implications for course design and evaluation. In C. Rust (Ed.), *Improving Student Learning – Equality and Diversity*. Oxford: CSLD.

Land, R. (2004). *Educational development: Discourse, identity and practice*. Maidenhead: Open University Press/SRHE.

Lave, J. & Wenger, E. (1991). *Situated learning: Legitimate peripheral participation*. Cambridge: Cambridge University Press.

Marton, F., Hounsell D. J., & Entwistle, N. J. (Eds.) (1984). *The experience of learning*. Edinburgh: Scottish Academic Press.

Maslow, A. H. (1970). *Motivation and personality*, 2nd edition. New York: Harper & Row.

McCune, V. & Hounsell, D. (2005). The development of students' ways of thinking and practising in three final-year biology courses. *Higher Education, 49*, 255-289.

McGonigal, J., Cove, M., & McAdam, J. (2006). On the threshold of teaching: Troublesome knowledge in the mentoring of probationer teachers. Paper presented at the *Threshold Concepts within the Disciplines* Symposium, University of Strathclyde, Glasgow, 30th Aug.-1st Sept.

McShane, K. (2006). *Technologies transforming academics: Academic identity and online teaching*. University of Technology Sydney, Accessed May 18, 2007 from: http://www.itl.usyd.edu.au/aboutus/mcshane06_thesis.pdf

Meyer, J. H. F., Land, R., & Davies, P. (2006). Threshold concepts and troublesome knowledge (4): Issues of variation and variability. Paper presented at the *Threshold Concepts within the Disciplines* Symposium, University of Strathclyde, Glasgow, 30th Aug.-1st Sept.

Meyer, J. H. F. & Land, R. (2003). Threshold concepts and troublesome knowledge (1): Linkages to ways of thinking and practising. In C. Rust (Ed.), *Improving student learning – Ten years on*. Oxford: OCSLD.

O'Neill, G. & McMahon, T. (2007). Student-centred learning: What does it mean for students and lecturers? Retrieved May, 2007: http://www.aishe.org/readings/2005-1/oneill-mcmahon-Tues_19th_ Oct_SCL.html

Orsini-Jones, M. (2006). Identifying troublesome concepts and helping undergraduates with crossing grammar thresholds via assessed collaborative group work. Paper presented at the *Threshold Concepts within the Disciplines* Symposium, University of Strathclyde, Glasgow, 30th Aug.-1st Sept.

Osmond, J., Turner, A., & Land, R. (2006). Threshold concepts and spatial awareness in transport and product design. Paper presented at the *Threshold Concepts within the Disciplines* Symposium, University of Strathclyde, Glasgow, 30th Aug.-1st Sept.

Perkins, D. (1999). The many faces of constructivism. *Educational Leadership, 57*(3), 6-11.

Perkins, D. (2006). Constructivism and troublesome knowledge. In Meyer, J. H. F. & Land, R. (Eds.), *Overcoming barriers to student understanding: Threshold concepts and troublesome knowledge*, London and New York: Routledge.

Perry, W.G. (1970). *Forms of intellectual and ethical development in the college years: A scheme*. New York: Holt, Rinehart and Winston.

Rogers, C. & Freiberg, H. J. (1993). *Freedom to learn*, 3rd edition. New York: Merrill.

Sibbett, C. (2008). 'Nettlesome' knowledge, liminality and the taboo in cancer and art therapy experiences. In Land, R., Meyer, J. H. F., & Smith, J. (Eds.), *Threshold concepts within the disciplines*. Rotterdam and Taipei: Sense Publishers.

Vygotsky, L. S. (1978). *Mind and society: The development of higher mental processes*. Cambridge, MA: Harvard University Press.

Wenger, E. (1998). *Communities of practice: Learning, meaning and identity*. Cambridge: Cambridge University Press.

Webb, G. (1996). Deconstructing deep and surface: Towards a critique of phenomenography for staff developers (1). In *Proceedings HERDSA Conference* (pp. 8-12). Perth, Western Australia.

Winnicott, D. H. (1971). *Playing and reality*. New York: Basic Books.

AFFILIATION

Glynis Cousin
Higher Education Academy
York

VERNON TRAFFORD

20. CONCEPTUAL FRAMEWORKS AS A THRESHOLD CONCEPT IN DOCTORATENESS

INTRODUCTION

I was a few months into my research, thinking that a doctorate wasn't all that hard after all when I realised that I had missed the point. I could not understand or explain what was happening with my research or with the conceptual tools that I had at my disposal. I then realised that the doctorate was not a big Masters dissertation. My ability to conceptualise was clearly inadequate for my (doctoral) journey. I then read extensively to build a foundation and framework of concepts that allowed me to understand and, more importantly, to interpret facts. Then I was OK, and could make real progress with my thesis.

This account by a doctoral graduate contains many insights on the research process. He recognised the difference between his previous and current studies and that he now had to develop new intellectual capabilities. He identified his deficiencies plus some desirable learning outcomes which he then addressed. He also acknowledged the transformation that had occurred once he had overcome his inadequacies. He appreciated that he was on an educational journey that was different from what he had expected. He resolved his inadequacies through his own efforts. He knew exactly what he needed to learn and he did this on his own. He had identified his inability to conceptualise as his inadequacy, which represents a sophisticated way of thinking about research. It suggests that he saw this as unlocking his understanding of doctoral level research. He did not mention his research topic or its various boundaries, or any concerns over the mechanics of research methods, which are each relatively low-risk research issues. Thus he perceived an ability to conceptualise as a strategic necessity in order to proceed with his doctoral research.

This account captures the position for most supervisors as they start supervising another doctoral candidate. You might well consider what type of learning difficulties your new candidates will encounter and how you will assist their intellectual development on their journey to completing the thesis. You might wonder how their experiences will compare with those of others as they tackle their own doctoral research. Finally you could ask yourself, how they will cope with the need to conceptualise. Doctoral supervisors and examiners will recognise such issues as they start to read another thesis. These issues reflect the expectation that

R. Land, J.H.F. Meyer & J. Smith (Eds.), Threshold Concepts within the Disciplines, 273–288.

doctoral study contains challenges which candidates may not have met in previous studies or research.

The doctoral degree poses special intellectual demands on those who seek it. The Quality Assurance Agency (QAA, 2001, p. 2) outlines these parameters as follows: 'A doctorate is awarded for the creation and interpretation of knowledge which extends the forefront of a discipline, usually through original research. Holders of doctorates will be able to conceptualise, design and implement projects for the generation of significant new knowledge or understanding'. A composite view of how British universities express this intent would be: 'A doctoral degree may be awarded to a person who has made an original and independent contribution to knowledge and thereby demonstrated critical capabilities of scholarship and appropriate modes of investigation'. These statements emphasise scholarship and conceptualisation as essential components of doctoral research.

This chapter focuses on how doctoral candidates encounter difficulties in learning about and using conceptualisation. It illustrates how they cope with that learning need and the consequences for them after they have acquired that new knowledge and understanding. Since confidence in handling conceptual frameworks is an integral component of doctorateness, such frameworks jointly represent a potential threshold concept for doctoral candidates as they undertake their research and write their thesis.[1]

A FREQUENT ISSUE OF CONCERN

The notion of threshold concepts has been an unrecognised part of my supervisory experience for many years. Alongside this, I have been involved in designing and presenting workshops for doctoral candidates and supervisors, nationally and internationally. Workshop participants and those I have supervised are drawn from over twenty disciplines, with about 60% coming from the social sciences. As an active participant in these activities I had 'observed myself into the core of the research' (Sanger, 1996, p. 25). As a consequence, the chapter portrays actions, opinions and experiences accumulated by me as 'unobtrusive research' (Robson, 2002, p. 349).

The issue that appears to cause candidates difficulty and even intellectual distress is the conceptual framework. Questions always arise about its role, significance, design, presentation and location in a thesis during workshops. This view accords with Burton and Steane (2005, p. 53) who accept that 'the notion of a conceptual framework often causes concern amongst those new to research because of uncertainty as to what it means.' Candidates frequently admit to knowing what it means but then being unable to create a framework for use in their own research.

The term 'conceptual framework' is defined by Miles and Huberman (1984, p. 33) as 'the current version of the researcher's map of the territory being investigated.' Whilst this may be self-explanatory, Weaver-Hart (1988) introduces a subtle contradiction by arguing that 'concepts are abstract whereas frameworks are concrete.' More positively, Rudestam and Newton propose that conceptual frameworks are 'simply a less developed form of a theory (consisting of) statements that link abstract concepts to empirical data.' They see this being 'a network (and) a graph displaying the independent and dependent variables' as 'the basis for a conceptual framework' (Rudestam & Newton 1992, pp. 6 and 118). Punch simplifies this by suggesting as a template for conceptual frameworks 'the conceptual status of the things being studied and their relationship to each other' (2000, p. 54). These explanations are consolidated in Leshem and Trafford's (2007) observation that 'The practicality of conceptual frameworks is their capacity to introduce order in candidates' thinking about the conceptual background and context of their research'.

Explaining the conceptual framework illustrates its features in doctoral research and theses. Explicit conceptualisation is therefore necessary to give coherence to ideas, clarify relationships between research components and provide shape to research conclusions. By connecting theory with practice, conceptual frameworks integrate linkages between ideas and so clarify the issues under investigation. Those linkages exhibit differing levels of abstraction which often represent intellectual challenges and potential difficulties for candidates. Although the literature may use other words as surrogates for 'conceptual framework,' there is no alternative to the functions that they all provide in doctoral research.

Candidates frequently ask where conceptual frameworks come from. Figure 1 shows three origins. Firstly, reading gives access to theoretical perspectives on the research topic where abstractions provide deeper understandings of issues and clarify relationships between ideas. Secondly, the personal experiences and assumptions which candidates have in relation to their topic form impressionistic perspectives which can modify interpretations of what the literature contains. Thirdly, reflecting on the topic and how to conceptualise it provide potentially deeper understandings of that topic and how it might be investigated (Schön, 1983). This represents 'thinking with a purpose' (Dewey, 1933) since it 'moves thinking on' (Moon, 1999, p. 23). Where the three origins overlap concepts tend to appear as new interpretations of the issue. The three origins would normally meld to produce a conceptual framework which offers 'some sort of meaning on the world' in which 'reality is given sense, order and coherence' (Cohen, Manion, & Morrison, 2000, p. 13).

However, candidates' enthusiasm for their topic becomes tempered when they are faced with reviewing the literature. Its purpose is to analyse and synthesise the writings of others, justify their own theoretical approach to the topic and demonstrate that their intended research can contribute something to their field (Hart, 1998: 1-2). It also enables candidates to associate theories as 'pragmatically useful concepts' (Bruner, Goodnow and Austin, 1999:122) with their real-world research context. This process of converting what they have read as abstracts into conceptualisation is not easy for many candidates. But conceptualisation is integral to doctorateness. That too presents learning difficulties for many candidates – and they are usually the same individuals.

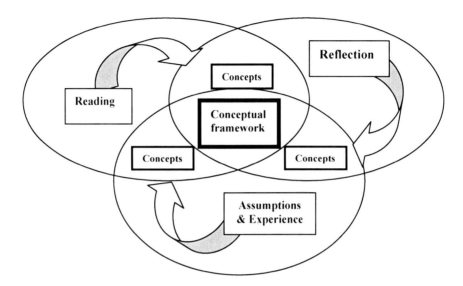

Figure 1. Sources of conceptual frameworks

SEEKING DOCTORATENESS

Candidates appear to adopt different viewpoints on producing doctoral theses. Firstly, as a continuation of previous studies, some believe that 'It will follow the same pattern and basic structure that I used in my Masters' dissertation. That was successful.' These candidates interpret the research and writing of a doctoral thesis as a technical exercise but containing more words than a dissertation. These candidates therefore display pre-conceptual innocence where the significance of conceptualisation has yet to be recognized (Bruner, Goodnow, & Austin, 1999, p. 101). The second viewpoint is when candidates announce 'I don't understand what a conceptual framework is or how it comes into my research.' This view shows a lack of developed understanding regarding the framing of research in appropriate theoretical perspectives which are drawn from the literature as abstractions. These candidates do, however, recognise their need to learn. Thus, although they possess 'a mental category of issues' (Armstrong, Gleitman, & Gleitman, 1999, p. 226) nonetheless their vision is restricted by underdeveloped conceptual thinking about the nature of doctoral research.

The third viewpoint is typified by candidates saying 'I am looking forward to the intellectual challenge of thinking and learning that will allow me to make a contribution in this area of (knowledge).' They appreciate that a doctorate is a sophisticated, conceptually coherent and complex piece of research and writing that has to meet exacting standards of rigour and theorising. Thus, these candidates have projected their academic intentions through 'the underlying realities of subject matter to seek deeper understandings of the immediately non-obvious' (Gelman & Wellman, 1999, p. 613).

Evidence from examiners' reports and their questions in vivas confirm that the doctoral process is expected to contain explicit conceptualisation of research issues and structural coherence in theses, and that these are explored in vivas (Trafford & Leshem, 2002a; Denicolo, 2003; Tinkler & Jackson, 2004, p. 113; Pearce, 2005; Leshem & Trafford, 2007). If this is the 'end-state' that candidates should aspire to, then it is a goal which, if met, should indicate successful completion of the doctorate. Table 1 presents examples from examiner reports illustrating how the significance of conceptualisation is characterised in theses that were judged as either successful or unsuccessful. They show that conceptualisation is critical in determining the scholarly quality of the thesis, and that, in turn, theses reflect the research that the candidate has undertaken.

Table 1. Extracts from examiners' reports

Those which were successful

- 'There was a self-evident intellectual grasp of the topic, plus a genuine engagement with the literature and its respective concepts.'
- 'A careful and explicit explanation of research design and research methodology enabled me to follow the theoretical framework throughout the thesis.'
- 'The candidate challenged the received orthodoxy of certain authors, with reasoned argument and evidence to develop a focal theory.'
- 'The thesis was conceptually quite exciting and convincingly argued in each chapter.'

Those which were not successful

- 'The text omitted any acknowledgement of accepted primary sources, the wider literature on the topic or the developmental processes during th research itself.'
- 'The lack of concepts to explain the literature that was used and how the research was designed was a major weakness in this thesis.'
- 'The final chapter did not distinguish between factual and conceptual conclusions which could easily have been drawn from the findings and this has sub-optimised the potential of the research itself.'
- 'The thesis lacked intellectual conviction and insight.'

Displaying doctorateness results from candidates being able to demonstrate capability in four areas that have an ascending order of importance (Trafford & Leshem, 2002b):

1. Technology of the thesis
2. Theoretical perspectives
3. Practice of research
4. Doctorateness

This shows that the constituent elements of doctorateness which need to be explicit in doctoral research and theses are: establishing links between the components of differing research processes; synthesising the concepts used in the research; developing and advancing conceptual conclusions; critiquing research conceptually rather than through descriptive methods of analysis; advancing a modest contribution to knowledge that is supported by evidence and reasoned argument.

Then, of course, these features should be defended plausibly and successfully by candidates in their viva when other elements of doctorateness will be explored, as shown in Figure 2.

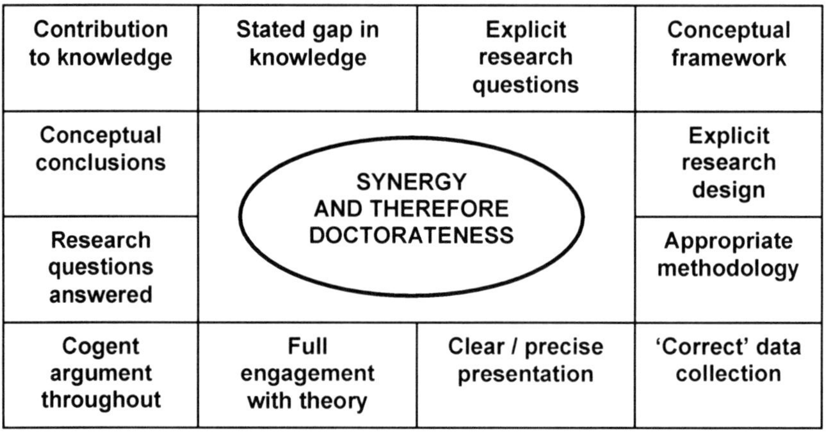

Contribution to knowledge	Stated gap in knowledge	Explicit research questions	Conceptual framework
Conceptual conclusions	SYNERGY AND THEREFORE DOCTORATENESS		Explicit research design
Research questions answered			Appropriate methodology
Cogent argument throughout	Full engagement with theory	Clear / precise presentation	'Correct' data collection

Figure 2. Technical components of doctorateness

These individual features are not, of themselves, 'a research mystery' (Burnham, 1994) since they are familiar items in serious texts on research methodologies. Collectively, though, they seem to present doctoral candidates with genuine appreciative blocks to their thinking. This may originate in how many candidates initially describe their research topic, e.g.: 'I want to investigate the relevance of

XY ...' or, 'My research will develop a questionnaire to be used in ...'. Here, descriptive language is used to outline the topic as a surrogate for thoughtful explanation. Learning how to use more sophisticated modes of explaining research are essential to the doctoral process (Quality Assurance Agency, 2004, p. 8; Green & Powell, 2005, p. 152). Not surprisingly, at some point during their doctoral journey these candidates will experience blockages to their learning.

TWO THRESHOLD CONCEPTS

Successful completion of the doctoral degree requires candidates to make an original contribution to knowledge and this obliges them to create and use conceptual frameworks. When that occurs they will then also display doctorateness in their thesis. However, if they are unable to conceptualize then, consequentially, they cannot demonstrate doctorateness either. Since the doctorate degree exemplifies high quality thinking and research, the emergence of a learnable element that prevents a candidate from progressing constitutes, for that candidate, an intellectual threshold. This would manifest itself particularly when that candidate seeks to progress from description into 'conceptually coherent accounts of the theories being used' (Murphy & Medin, 1999, p. 427). If that progress is interrupted by learning difficulties then it would constitute what Meyer and Land (2003) term 'a portal of understanding.' A candidate who does not understand the nature of conceptualisation would not understand the notion of doctorateness either. That candidate would then have encountered two associated portals of understanding, with each being a potential restriction to their intellectual progress and both being a threshold concept.

In the Editors' Preface to this volume, the primary tenets of threshold concepts were shown as explaining the consequences for learners of approaching, and then passing through, a portal of understanding and personal development. The core notions of irreversibility, transformation, integration, boundedness and troublesomeness are interrelated as they apply to individual learners progressing beyond the portal and seeing things differently than 'before.' Their new lens on the world is therefore a paradigm shift in perception (Kuhn, 1996) since it 're-positions the individual in relation to the community of scholars who have developed this way of thinking and in relation to all others who adopt one standpoint or another in relation to the thinking of these scholars' (Davies & Mangan, 2006).

Integral to threshold concepts are three further characteristics. The first is when learners progress from knowing about, in a descriptive sense, to understanding as a 'thought-demanding' process. This progress extends learning beyond what the learner already knows (Perkins, 1993). The second is that of *epistemes* which Perkins defines as 'the system of ideas or ways of understanding that allows us to establish knowledge' (2006, p. 42). He outlines epistemes from a discipline-specific viewpoint and explains how they encapsulate the accepted ways of thinking about that discipline by members of that discipline. These views accord with similar academic beliefs about research. Arguing that 'research (demands) the development of understanding ... to grasp the conceptual underpinnings...within particular ways of doing social science research', Salmon implies that certain presumed modus operandi exist among social science communities (1992, pp. 16-17). This process of professional maturation in research processes are how candidates start to think like serious researchers and 'come to terms with their (conceptual) experience' (Cohen, Manion, & Morrison, 2000, p. 13).

The third characteristic is the state of liminality that learners encounter as they approach the portal. This is a period when they are 'uncertain about the identity of self and purpose' (Meyer & Land, 2006, p. 22). It includes the transformation from not knowing to knowing, but for learners it is akin to being in the neutral zone. Here candidates would recognise the void of understanding facing them, seek to renew their enthusiasm to learn and yet feel (potentially) 'frightened, confused and assailed by self-doubt' (Bridges, 1991, p. 37). This is also when disenchantment becomes a prelude to transition in what van Gennep (1909) termed liminality when moving from one status to another as a rite of passage. For doctoral candidates being in a liminal state is when genuine intellectual progress is severely restricted.

CAMEO ACCOUNTS OF THRESHOLD CONCEPT ENCOUNTERS

These recent (2006) accounts by doctoral candidates and graduands were their responses to the following open-ended questions:

1. How did you acquire an understanding of conceptualizing?
2. What difficulties did you meet in the process of acquiring that understanding?
3. How did you overcome those difficulties?
4. Once you had understood the nature of conceptualizing, how did this help you to undertake your research?

These cameo accounts have been clustered according to whether the respondent is approaching, at or beyond the portal. Responses relating to being 'at' the portal were divided into social and cognitive to distinguish between significantly different actions or experiences.

A   Approaching the Portal: Difficulties with Conceptualising

It was all so clear when my supervisor explained it, but left to my own devices I doubted my understanding of conceptualisation and how it fitted into my research or thesis.

There is the fear when doing a doctorate of things being too simple. I believed that doctoral research is hard and is supposed to be so. Therefore it can't be something straightforward or easily understandable. I had created my own barriers to understanding and only I could demolish it. I was genuinely looking for difficulties and I found them.

Nobody had ever before made me sit down and think about what conceptualizing was and why it was needed in a thesis. I was unsure what was wanted, what to include or why it was wanted. I was indeed ignorant of this part of research.

I had to look for a long time before finding theories that developed my understanding of my topic. Until it was found I was wondering whether such ideas even existed and if I had chosen a non-issue for my doctoral topic. It was very worrying.

I believed everything that I read and found it difficult to deconstruct arguments, raise alternative explanations or overcome my implicit knowledge. I could not escape my academic comfort zone.

It took me a long time to understand the term, even though I knew all the words that explained what it was and what everyone said it all meant. However the links between concepts were not clear to me.

Each new concept looked interesting and provided insights on my data. I felt like using it to analyse my data, but a week later a different theory seemed just as promising. I was conceptually lost.

One cannot conceptualize what one cannot see or grasp. I felt lost since I could not grasp the significance of conceptualisation. I needed the right language to express myself and I did not have it to use.

I had read the books and attended the workshops but still didn't understand how to produce a conceptual framework. I was mixing together descriptions of my topic with all sorts of other things and not getting anywhere. I needed help to sort out what it meant for me and my topic.

B   At the Portal: Social Actions

I developed an understanding of conceptualizing through discussions with my supervisor. Initially I was concerned with the implications for social work, education and practice. I was so enthusiastic about my results but had not really conceptualised their contribution to knowledge.

My supervisor asked me: 'Can you sum up in a few words exactly what you are looking for and what you think about it?' That was it! At that moment I understood the direction of my research in those few words. Why had I not thought in that very focussed way previously?

I just kept asking questions of other researchers and seeing how they explained what I was trying to do. I saw how others had described their work and that gave me ideas which I then adapted to my topic. It took me a long time and I had to ask many questions.

My understanding of conceptual frameworks came from attending workshops and tutorials. It was a slow process that was hastened by discussion groups that we (candidates) organized ourselves outside these formal meetings.

I did ask for help. I sat with my colleagues and asked them about their conceptual frameworks. Everybody was talking about 'IT,' but most of them were looking at an illusion. They thought that they knew what IT was but gradually I doubted it. I then felt at peace when I realised that most of them were still looking for their conceptual frameworks. But it was still sort of useful to listen as they described what they were doing.

Three of us met fortnightly as a self-help group. We helped each other to think about conceptual frameworks and create them. Because we were at different stages in our research that was good because we could see how we dealt with these problems in turn.

C   At the Portal: Cognitive Actions

I really got into conceptualisation through philosophical and conceptual analysis during my Masters studies. These skills, although relatively primitive and simple as I now see them, gave me a basic understanding. They were invaluable for my doctoral research and study.

I stumbled and groped my way towards it, always learning and quite clear where I wanted to go.

I adopted a 'drift-net' exercise, reading anything that I could find with the slightest bearing on my topic. Gradually I began to build up a picture that contributed to my understanding and that became, later, my conceptual framework.

I read and re-read the works of the major authors in my area trying to focus what they said and how it fitted in with what I wanted to say. This really focussed my work. It was a form of using theory for grounded theory I suppose.

A throwaway remark at a conference indicated another, simpler, approach to my topic. When I applied it to my own research a whole new landscape appeared! So, my entire research changed from a straightforward content-based investigation to the far more fascinating implication of methodology on theory in that field.

I created a diagrammatic representation that explained the relationships between the important aspects of the concept in my area. This clarified the model that I used throughout my research. It was a visual solution and this is how I prefer to solve these sorts of problems.

Drawing the concepts visually which I encountered enabled me to reflect on the findings differently – conceptually. I could not do that when just words were used. This showed me what the texts had failed to do.

I stopped using words and moved to graphics to liberate me from the limitation that words had bound me with. I closed my eyes and the entire (conceptual) diagram was in front of me. It made sense then and finally I understood what conceptualisation meant at last!

D   *Beyond the Portal: Understanding the Nature and Use of Conceptual Frameworks*

It was like a light coming on! Everything seemed clearer and I felt more in control of my research than I was before.

Cohesion of thinking was possibly the most crucial outcome of conceptualisation for me. This gave me the academic confidence that I needed to complete my research successfully.

It helped me to understand the contribution of my research to knowledge and it also gave me an analytical framework that I could use to critique my research.

After understanding the nature of conceptualisation, I was in a position to appreciate what was happening in my research, and so interpret issues both conceptually and practically.

After grasping the nature of conceptualisation the rest of my research was a matter of mechanics.

Understanding conceptualisation shaped and focussed all my subsequent work.

Once I recognised what my research was about (conceptually) I realised what I wanted to discover, what it was possible for me to do and what I could accomplish. Great!

I could now engage with the work of other writers, and so writing non-descriptive text became much easier. Maslow would have been proud of me since now I felt less of an outsider with hints even of starting to belong!

Afterwards the literature that I then read was done with a much clearer idea of what I was seeking. It started to make sense, with most of the meanings becoming recognizable and I could actually now work with them.

Concepts often evolve from other concepts and I have now been able to see the connections and so easily relate my research to that in other fields.

Over the years most candidates will have voiced similar sentiments. Those hearing them will have sympathized with the difficulties of many and applauded the progress of others.

THRESHOLD CONCEPTS IN PRACTICE

These cameos may confirm what candidates, supervisors and examiners have suspected always happened. The evidence, though, indicates that there are two practical implications from these accounts. The first concerns social mediation via engagement with various others through explanations by supervisors, discussions with other researchers and membership of communities of practice. In these instances, intervention by others provided coping strategies, scaffolding support, and encouragement once candidates had recognised their deficiencies and accepted the need to learn. The assistance of others was therefore instrumental in overcoming learning blockages and moving candidates through their respective liminal states. This corresponds with the phenomenon of the 'zone of proximal development'. Vygotsky (1978, p. 86) described this as 'the distance between the actual development level as determined by independent problem-solving and the level of potential development through problem-solving under adult guidance or in collaboration with more capable peers.' Vygotsky claimed that learning occurred in this zone which bridges the gap between what is known and what can be known – the liminal state.

The second practical implication concerns cognitive action that was self-initiated and acted on without help from others. This comes about through: reading, thinking and reflecting; thinking at a deeper and higher level; visualisation of concepts and relationships; drawing on prior professional conceptualisation which was then applied and used; being acquisitive to gain skills and knowledge that were absent or low. This self-motivated behaviour was directed at understanding abstraction, engaging with conceptual aspects of their research that had previously been difficult and developing higher-order thinking. Research into student learning based upon models of conceptual change processes support this cognitivist perspective of their learning (Postner, Strike, Hewson, & Gertzog, 1992).

Although examples of troublesome knowledge were not explicit in the cameos, received wisdom from supervisors suggests that it is encountered. The most frequently appearing example of troublesome knowledge is disciplinary boundaries. Newly acquired conceptual insights often challenge unidisciplinary approaches to designing conceptual frameworks especially when the potential explanatory relevance found in other disciplines, or fields of study, becomes apparent. For instance, a hospice matron investigated the coping strategies of the terminally ill using traditional nursing practices and models. She had not anticipated drawing upon the applied disciplines of marketing (planned projection of messages to influence others), business practices (continuous evolution of self-image) and cosmetics (make-up and hair styling).

This example fits Perkins' framing of troublesome knowledge (2006). Before starting her doctorate, she had witnessed patients adopting each of these coping tactics, but this became part of her tacit knowledge. However, she had not *de-ritualised* them, overlooking too the *inertness* of those experiences and not recognising the actions themselves as deeply significant communicative symbols. When she gained her conceptual lens she extended the disciplinary scope of her research, but only, as she admitted, 'after some agonising over how to combine marketing, business studies and cosmetics with death and dying.' This example illustrates quite starkly the potential difficulties awaiting those who pass through their threshold to conceptual learning.

The cameos also illustrate the connection between doctoral issues that have their roots in research processes and achieving developments in levels of thinking. Figure 3 shows this connection in which doctoral candidates are expected by examiners to progress from description to conceptualisation and similarly from micro- to meta-levels of thinking. The outcome from these shifts in candidates' thinking would be conceptual understanding.

SOME CONCLUSIONS

This chapter focussed on how candidates develop and use conceptual frameworks both in their research and theses. The importance of this process has been shown as a major determinant of how examiners assess the scholarship submitted by candidates. It shows too that many candidates encounter learning difficulties in realising its research potential. In this respect the conceptual framework represents a threshold concept. As they approach and pass beyond it, doctoral candidates exhibit the associated phenomena of liminality and troublesome knowledge

The cameos exemplify threshold concepts that were not discipline-specific but displayed generic relevance within a defined research process. This was located in a distinctive forum of individualised learning – the doctoral degree – where candidates' scholarly development is often limited by 'knowing about' but not necessarily 'understanding' the interconnectedness and utility of concepts. Threshold concepts, therefore, have both theoretical and practical explanatory relevance to a research process that is transdisciplinary and generic.

Occasionally candidates possess conceptual capability prior to their doctoral registration and do not encounter such limiting experiences. However, viewing conceptual frameworks as a threshold concept explains why candidates make slow

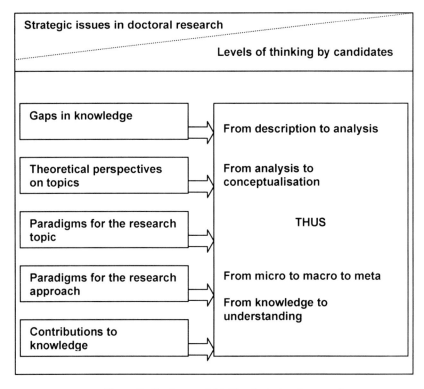

Figure 3. Strategy and thinking in doctoral research

progress with their studies. An ideographic explanation of their situation could possibly be that conceptualisation had not been explained to help them understand and use it. As a result they did not associate theory with intellectual problem-solving. Thus, they had no first-hand acquaintance with concepts and were intellectually distant from the notion (Burrell & Morgan, 1979, p. 6).

The conceptual capability of candidates determines their ability to make a contribution to knowledge. However, achieving this outcome is usually the consequence of extended collaboration between candidate, their supervisor(s) and selective others. So, perhaps approaching and passing through the threshold concept to understanding conceptualisation and doctorateness is an ontological perspective hitherto underemphasised by supervisors and their candidates.

NOTES

[1] The words Conceptual Framework include other research terms with similar meanings, such as core concept, focal theory, mapping the research territory, theoretical framework, etc. (Leshem & Trafford, 2007).

REFERENCES

Armstrong, S. L., Gleitman, L. R., & Gleitman, H. (1999). What concepts might not be. In Margolis, E. & Laurence, S. (Eds.), *Concepts*. Cambridge, MA: MIT press.

Bridges, W. (1991). *Managing transitions: Making the most of change*. Reading, MA: Addison-Wesley.

Bruner, J., Goodnow, J., & Austin, G. (1999). The process of concept attainment. In Margolis, E. & Laurence, S. (Eds.), *Concepts*. Cambridge, MA: MIT press.

Burnham, P. (1994). Surviving the viva: Unravelling the mystery of the PhD oral. *Journal of Graduate Education, 1,* 30-34.

Burrell, G. & Morgan, G. (1979). *Sociological paradigms and organisational analysis*. Aldershot: Gower.

Burton, S. & Steane, P. (Eds.) (2005). *Surviving your thesis*. London: Routledge.

Cohen, L., Manion, L., & Morrison, K. (2000). *Research methods in education*, 5th edition. London: Routledge Falmer.

Davies, P. & Mangan, J. (2006). Embedding threshold concepts: from theory to pedagogical principles to learning activities. Paper presented at the *Threshold Concepts within the Disciplines* Symposium, Glasgow, 30th August-September 1st.

Denicolo, P. (2003_. Assessing the PhD: A constructive view of criteria. *Quality Assurance in Education, 11*(2), 84-91.

Dewey, B. (1933). *How we think*. Boston, MA: DC Heath.

Gelman, S. A. & Wellman, H. M. (1999). Insides and essences: Early understandings of the non-obvious. In Margolis, E. & Laurence, S. (Eds.), *Concepts*. Cambridge, MA: MIT press.

Van Gennep, A. (1909). *The rites of passage*. Reprint 1960. London: Routledge and Kegan Paul.

Green, H. & Powell, S. (2005). *Doctoral study in contemporary higher education*. Maidenhead: Society for Research into Higher Education/Open University Press.

Hart, C. (1998). *Doing a literature review: Releasing social science research imagination*. London: Sage.

Kuhn, T. (1996). *The structure of scientific revolutions*, 3rd edition. Chicago: Chicago University Press.

Leshem, S. & Trafford, V. N. (2007). Overlooking the conceptual framework. *Innovations and Education Training International, 44*(1), 93-105.

Meyer, J. H. F. & Land, R. (2003). Threshold concepts and troublesome knowledge: Linking to ways of thinking and practising within the disciplines. ETL Project Occasional Report 4. TLRP/ESRC.

Meyer, J. H. F. & Land, R. (Eds.) (2006). *Overcoming barriers to student understanding: Threshold concepts and troublesome knowledge*. London and New York: Routledge.

Miles, M. B. & Huberman, A. M. (1984). *Qualitative data analysis: A sourcebook of new methods*. London: Sage.

Moon, J. (1999). *Learning journals*. London: Kogan Page.

Murphy, G. L. & Medin, D. L. (1999). The role of theories in conceptual coherence. In Margolis, E. & Laurence, S. (Eds.), *Concepts*. Cambridge, MA: MIT press.

Pearce, L. (2005). *How to examine a thesis*. Maidenhead: Open University Press.

Perkins, D. (1993). Teaching for understanding. *American Educator: The Professional Journal of the American Federation of Teachers, 17*(3), 28-35.

Perkins, D. (2006). Constructivism and troublesome knowledge. In Meyer, J. H. F. & Land, R. (Eds.), *Overcoming barriers to student understanding: Threshold concepts and troublesome knowledge*. London: Routledge.

Postner, G., Strike, I., Hewson, P., & Gertzog, W. (1992). Accommodation of a scientific concept: Toward a theory of conceptual change. *Science Education, 66*, 211-227.

Punch, K. F. (2000). *Developing effective research proposals*. London: Sage.

Quality Assurance Agency (2001). *The framework for higher education qualifications in England, Wales and Northern Ireland*. London: Quality Assurance Agency.

Quality Assurance Agency (2004). *Code of practice for the assurance of academic quality and standards in higher education: Section 1*, 2nd Edition. Gloucester: Quality Assurance Agency.

Robson, C. (2002). *Real world research*, 2nd Edition. Oxford: Blackwell.

Rudestam, K. E. & Newton, R. R. (1992). *Surviving your dissertation*. London: Sage.

Salmon, P. (1992). *Achieving a PhD – Ten students' experience*. Stoke on Trent: Trentham.

Sanger, J. (1996). *The compleat observer? A field guide to observation*. London: Falmer Press.

Schön, D. A. (1983). *The reflective practitioner: how professionals think in action*. Cambridge: Maurice Temple Smith.

Tinkler, P. & Jackson, C. (2004). *The doctoral examination process*. Maidenhead: Open University Press.

Trafford, V. N. (2003). Questions in a doctoral viva: views from the inside. *Quality Assurance in Education, 11* (2), 114-122.

Trafford, V. N. & Leshem, S. (2002a). Starting at the end to undertake doctoral research: Predictable questions as stepping stones to doctorateness. *Higher Education Review, 34*(4), 43-61.

Trafford, V. N. & Leshem, S. (2002b). Anatomy of a doctoral viva. *Journal of Graduate Education, 3*, 25-37.

Vygotsky, L. S. (1978). *Mind and society: the development of higher mental processes*. Cambridge, MA: Harvard University Press.

Weaver-Hart, A. (1988). Framing an innocent concept and getting away with it. *UCEA Review, 24*(2), 11-12.

AFFILIATION

Vernon Trafford
Anglia Ruskin University

MIA O'BRIEN

21. THRESHOLD CONCEPTS FOR UNIVERSITY
TEACHING AND LEARNING

A Study of Troublesome Knowledge and Transformative Thinking in the Teaching of Threshold Concepts

INTRODUCTION

The importance of threshold concepts in the design and facilitation of effective learning has been clearly signalled (see Meyer & Land, 2003, 2006a) and there is widespread and enthusiastic uptake of this notion across the disciplines (Davies, 2006; Meyer & Land, 2006a). However, the *teaching* of threshold concepts implies pedagogical knowledge and thinking that is itself threshold in nature and potentially troublesome. At present research on the kinds of pedagogical thinking teachers of threshold concepts undertake is limited, as is our empirical understanding of the transformative nature of this practice for teacher knowledge and expertise.

Since threshold concepts can be considered fundamental to successful learning within all disciplines and fields of study (Davies, 2006), and since they prove challenging for learning and teaching (Meyer & Land, 2003, 2006b; Perkins, 2006), they are a point of interest when considering the quality of teaching practice, and in particular for understanding the knowledge-base and expertise of university teachers (Land, Cousin, Meyer, & Davies, 2006).

The introduction of *threshold concepts* through Meyer and Land's work has drawn attention to the importance of significant concepts for university teaching and learning. Their construct delves more deeply into the nature of such concepts in that there is a foregrounding of their epistemological nature and ontological characteristics (Meyer & Land, 2005) or the ways of thinking and knowing they may represent (Entwistle, 2005). In doing so, Meyer and Land have succeeded in bringing to light an aspect of pedagogy that is often overlooked – the importance of enabling a *transformation of viewpoint or worldview* – and the epistemological nuances and ontological shifts this entails on the part of students (Davies, 2006; Meyer & Land, 2005, 2006b; Perkins, 2006).

Because threshold concepts draw attention to the need for substantial transformation in existing ways of thinking, and since their learning may entail comprehension of knowledge that may appear to be counter-intuitive or absurd to students (and hence *troublesome* to learn, and in turn challenging to teach), a closer examination of teachers' thinking and knowledge related to the teaching and

R. Land, J.H.F. Meyer & J. Smith (Eds.), Threshold Concepts within the Disciplines, 289-305.

learning of threshold concepts can expand our understandings of pedagogy in threshold concepts, and of pedagogical content knowledge. The expectation is that, following Shulman's model (Shulman, 1987; Wilson *et al.*, 1987), the teaching of threshold concepts would embody rich formulations of teachers' knowledge and understandings about subject matter, student learning, and useful ways to attend to the *troublesome* aspects these comprise.

ACCESSING AND EXAMINING TEACHER THINKING ABOUT THRESHOLD CONCEPTS

Pedagogical knowledge and thinking refer to rich understandings about *particular components* of subject matter (Gess-Newsome & Lederman, 1999; Meyer & Land, 2003; Wilson *et al.*, 1987). Applied to threshold concepts in a university context, these understandings and their related pedagogical intentions are likely to be implicit and tightly bound to teachers' disciplinary knowledge and epistemological points of view (Malcolm & Zukas, 2001). Access requires some form of disciplinary-based prompting which, for the work reported in this chapter, relied on conversations between pairs of disciplinary colleagues on how threshold concepts within their discipline might be taught. An advantage of this approach is that such conversations are likely to produce deeper engagement with subject-related pedagogical issues (Healey & Jenkins, 2003).

The study reported in this chapter was informed by the work of Rubin and Rubin (2005) and Seidman (1991) on semi-structured interview methods, and the prompting process:

- Entailed in-depth discussion between two university teachers from the same discipline or teaching contexts.
- Used one teacher as the focus of the interview, in that their thinking, intentions and reasoning related to the teaching and learning of a threshold concept was the primary point of analysis; this teacher selected a threshold concept for discussion, and nominated a disciplinary colleague to act as 'peer'.
- Used the nominated peer as both interviewer and provocateur. Their brief was to use their disciplinary knowledge (and own experiences or views of the selected threshold concept) as a means by which to dig deeply, challenge and probe their colleague to facilitate disciplinary-specific conversations about the teaching and learning of the threshold concept.

All the teachers involved possessed a postgraduate qualification in university teaching, and most had won teaching awards of various kinds. Three simple, open and thematic questions guided the discussions: What is the threshold concept and why is it important for students to learn it? What is difficult, challenging or problematic about learning this threshold concept? What do you do to support students to learn this concept and why?

Case Studies of University Teacher's Engagement with the Teaching and Learning of Threshold Concepts

Specific threshold concepts considered within particular disciplines were: Deconstruction and binary oppositions within contemporary studies (Arts), nursing as a psychosocial practice requiring the integration of interdisciplinary knowledge and understandings applied to healthcare contexts (Health Sciences), Asian studies and 'Asia' as a phenomena reflexive of social, economic, cultural and political trends over time place and space (Business studies), inertia and the related laws of physics that explain and describe the forces at play during motion (Physical Sciences), egocentrism, conservation within Piaget's stage theory of psychological development (Psychology) and Mendelian genetics and the process of genetic inheritance (Biological Sciences).

Aspects of teacher thinking, knowledge and reasoning that appear significant in this study can be framed within two distinct interrelated points of reference. The first refers to the suite of categories, subcategories and variable dimensions that comprise teachers' accounts of the threshold concept selected, what must be learned, and what is difficult or challenging for students. The second point of reference comprises the way in which teacher's construe and rationalise their pedagogical approach and activities.

CATEGORIES OF TEACHER THINKING RELATED TO THE TEACHING AND LEARNING OF THRESHOLD CONCEPTS

Categories of teachers' thinking related to the teaching and learning of threshold concepts are: (a) how the teacher construes the threshold concept as an object of knowledge, (b) what the teacher explicitly articulates or describes as the learning agenda, in terms of what the students must learn in order to understand the threshold concept and, (c) attendant challenges to learning and teaching considered to be significant.

Teachers' thinking varied within each of these categories in ways that reflect the qualitatively different emphases individuals bring to this task. Variation is captured in two ways. Firstly, thematic subcategories are established to identify clusters of conceptually similar thinking (for example descriptions about the nature of 'worldview' inherent within the threshold concept). Secondly, dimensions were established within each subcategory to further illustrate and distinguish variation of qualitative properties within the subcategories (such as the distinction between 'disciplinary-oriented' and 'philosophically-driven' worldviews).

To provide a sense of the grounded nature of the data, and of the way in which this analytic lens provides insights into individual teacher thinking and reasoning, the categories, subcategories and dimensions are explicated through three examples (Asian studies, Derrida, inertia) from the original study. Each example represents a distinct pattern of pedagogical thinking, knowledge and reasoning and collectively they provide an overview of the variation exhibited across the study.

291

Category 1: The Threshold Concept as an Object of Knowledge

All teachers provided articulate and descriptive overviews of their selected threshold concepts, yet striking differences appeared in the ways in which teachers construed threshold concepts as 'objects of knowledge'. This category exemplifies the distinctive and variable nature of teachers' pedagogical thinking and knowledge (summarised in Table 1).

Table 1. Teacher's accounts of their pedagogical knowledge and thinking related to the threshold concept as an object of knowledge (category one)

Subcategory	Subcategory properties	Variable dimensions
1A	Specific worldview	*The threshold concept as an explicit position, perspective or philosophically values-based approach*
		The threshold concept as a discipline-oriented, principled and/or theoretically informed lens
1B	Significance of knowledge	*The threshold concept as foundational to other concepts or ways of thinking within the discipline (as in inertia and genetics)*
		The threshold concept as reflective of the direction/approach of the discipline or field
		The significance of the threshold concept as of general and diverse importance to people/society
		The significance of the threshold concept as the work of the original theorist
1C	Substantive structure and epistemological characteristics	*The threshold concept as a set of concepts, principles, laws, formula, skills and processes of application*
		The threshold concept as a web of related ideas and concepts
		The threshold concept as a suite of concepts that together comprise a theoretical and analytical framework (single theorist/disciplinary-centric)
		The threshold concept as a suite of concepts that together comprise a theoretical and analytical framework (multi-disciplinary)

Subcategory	Subcategory properties	Variable dimensions
		The threshold concept as an objective and analytic process or way of thinking
1D	Ontological dimensions	*Clear and explicit ontological position*

The way in which a threshold concept facilitates or is connected to *a specific worldview* or way of thinking about, apprehending or perceiving phenomena or events was a common and defining feature of teachers' descriptions. The qualities of the particular worldview or way of thinking articulated by teachers are furthermore reflective of disciplinary (or professional) epistemologies and ontologies. Asian studies was viewed as a '*framework from which to develop an enthusiasm and way of thinking about events in Asia*'. Deconstruction was seen by the Arts teacher as the basis for developing '*a kind of scepticism towards the building blocks of western thought*' and a '*way of working against that way of phrasing things*'. And in the assertion of a clear ontological position the understanding of inertia was seen to both enable and reflect what it means to '*think like a physicist*'.

Note that not all subcategories were evident within every teacher's account. However, patterns of dimensionality within individual accounts indicated variation in epistemological detail within teacher's thinking. Comparatively little more was said for example about the nature of the selected threshold concept in Asian studies, the account being limited to the 'way of thinking' (worldview) and 'informative' (significance) dimensions. Similarly, the Arts teacher had little to say about the significance, substantive qualities or ontological dimensions of deconstruction.

In contrast, the view of inertia as a threshold concept was multidimensional extending into each of the subcategories to cover descriptions of (a) the significance of 'inertia', both to the field and to the world, (b) the epistemological and substantive structure of inertia as part of a web of interrelated concepts and, (c) the ontological position that such a way of viewing would entail. From individual perspectives there thus appeared to be a more complex and multifaceted view of a threshold concept as an object of knowledge in Physics compared to Asian studies and Arts.

Category 2: What Must Be Learned in Order to Master the Threshold Concept?

Descriptions of threshold concepts in terms of *what must be learned* were often tied to perceptions of the threshold concept *as an object of knowledge*. This obvious relationship should not be taken for granted however because inconsistencies and gaps across these categories proliferated within individual cases. Teachers provided detailed accounts of threshold concepts as an object of knowledge, but did not include equally detailed (or parallel) descriptions within accounts of what *must be learned*. The sub-categories and variable dimensions are detailed in Table 2.

Table 2. Teacher's accounts of their thinking and knowledge about what must be learned (category two)

Subcategory	Subcategory properties	Variable dimensions
2A	Adoption and enactment of a worldview	*Apprehension emphasis (to apprehend and view phenomena via the lens of the adopted worldview/stance/perspective) Enactment emphasis (to enact the adopted worldview/stance/perspective within forms of practice or action)*
2B	Conceptual understanding of 'big picture'	*Inductive Deductive*
2C	Substantive knowledge and procedural capability	*Variable combinations of substantive/procedural or what/how: Principles, laws formula to analyse phenomena Theoretical concepts/principles to explain phenomena Theoretical concepts/principles used to analyse phenomena and to interact with, be interpretative of, phenomena; Deliberate combination of knowledge and worldview to enact practice/devise action; Skills relevant to achieving or enacting concepts*
2D	Appreciation of theory/theorist	*Value inherent - theorist as original and valuable thinker Value empirically evident - contribution of the theory and therefore the theorist*
2E	Sense of mastery, achievement, enthusiasm and interest	*No variation exhibited in this sample*

In Asian studies the threshold concept was essentially described as a 'way of thinking' about people, events, affairs, culture and change within Asia, but the 'worldview' dimension did not transfer explicitly into descriptions of what must be learned. Neither was there a detailed account of what this interpretatively oriented concept might demand in terms of learning processes or substantive conceptual undertakings. Instead description emphasised learning as a process in which the student must 'focus on the big picture'; and grasp the deductive application of learned theories (for example, modernisation) to contexts and examples provided. While there were some elements of the third subcategory (students use theoretical concepts to explain phenomena), the account generally remained anchored to relatively fuzzy descriptions of 'be enthusiastic' and 'get the big picture'.

The Arts teacher offered a more detailed explication. In her view students needed to cultivate the scepticism inherent within deconstruction, and her description emphasised the capacity to *apprehend* phenomena through this lens (worldview). Her account included acknowledgement of the *deductive* nature of the bigger picture (conceptual understanding), and the *interpretative use* of binary opposition in the identification of hierarchies within text (substantive knowledge and procedural capability). The importance of learning *about* the theorist and his work (appreciation) was also emphasised.

The inertia teacher provided the most detailed account of substantive knowledge and procedural capabilities, touching on three dimensions as interrelated aspects of learning. This multidimensional account included an emphasis on the need to develop both an *inductive and deductive* way of viewing phenomena (conceptual understanding) and to cultivate both *apprehension* and *enactment* aspects of thinking like a physicist.

Category 3: What Seems Ttroublesome or Challenging for Learning and Teaching?

This category documents teachers' views of what seems troublesome and reveals variation in thinking about the challenges students encounter (see Table 3). The first two subcategories relate to substantive knowledge and knowing, and the *challenges this poses for students' cognitive or affective processes.* In the third and fourth subcategories teachers couched troublesomeness as *'gaps' students faced in learning* subject matter. Distinct from this focus in the final two categories is the emphasis on the challenge within the *inherent complexity of the threshold concepts.* Descriptions and comments centred on issues or challenges the threshold concept posed *for teachers* are identified in the last subcategory.

Table 3. Teacher thinking and knowledge about the nature of problematic knowledge/challenges for teaching and learning in the teaching of threshold concepts (category three)

Subcategory	Subcategory properties	Variable dimensions
3A	Threshold concept elicits discontinuity or disequilibrium in students' cognitive or intellectual status	*Counter-intuitive concepts* *Counter-intuitive processes* *Mismatch between concept and preconceptions* *Occurrence or evidence of concepts within concrete phenomena or contexts appears opaque or confounded* *Relevance ambiguous* *Disciplinary terms/language similar to, but different in meaning to, familiar common usage language*
3B	Threshold concept elicits discontinuity or disequilibrium in	*Existing bias or scepticism toward the concept or way of thinking* *Resistance or rejection of new*

Subcategory	Subcategory properties	Variable dimensions
	students' affective status	*epistemological/ontological position or perspective*
3C	Student approximations of learning do not match cognitive or affective processes required to master threshold concepts	*Focus on surface features of threshold concept Conflation of conceptual distinctions between informing concepts Focus on surface features of contexts for application or interpretation Oversimplified interpretation/application of threshold concept*
3D	Gap between existing knowledge and what students need to learn/know	*Incomplete or unconsolidated prerequisite knowledge of foundational or related subject matter New knowledge not making cumulative sense/fitting with existing knowledge Comprehension of new knowledge in terms of lived experience or concrete phenomena difficult New knowledge is abstract, opaque and presents new ways of thinking*
3E	Complexity of subject matter/processes that comprise threshold concepts	*Threshold concept comprises a web of related ideas, principles and concepts presenting a part-whole-part dilemma Informing concepts, principles and ideas need to make sense (as an integrated mutually-informing set) of in the context of practice or application*
3F	Threshold concepts challenge teachers' knowledge and/or expertise	*Challenge to depth of teacher knowledge and understanding of subject matter Challenge to teachers' capacity to scope, structure and sequence the curriculum 'content' Avoiding overly theoretical, abstract or text-based approaches and/or the limitations of traditional pedagogical canons*

Of particular interest is the degree to which teachers construed the depth and complexity of troublesomeness their threshold concept potentially presented. At one end of this continuum troublesomeness was construed within singular and simple dimensional terms, despite the quite complex or potentially multifaceted nature of the threshold concept. The Asian studies teacher felt the primary challenges stemmed from student's propensity to attend to superficial aspects of subject matter, and (mis)perceptions of the relevance of key concepts to the course and/or their lives (hence the teacher's emphasis on interesting, exciting examples).

The Arts teacher acknowledged that the *density* of Derrida's original works and the *abstract nature* of the related concepts could prove difficult for students to access (complexity of subject matter). However in her mind, these were easily overcome by the provision of teacher-constructed summaries and teacher-led modelling. She emphasised challenges *for her teaching*, and her need to maintain an explicit 'expert and authority' stance in the classroom. While both teachers described conceptually complex and multidimensional threshold concepts, neither engaged in a comprehensive analysis of challenges for learning.

At the other end of the scale, the inertia teacher provided a detailed and multifaceted account of the range of difficulties students encountered, again touching on most of the subcategories. He documented examples from previous teaching experiences, particular anecdotes and (with his colleague) shared a range of recurringly 'troublesome' themes. Together they speculated on underlying issues (counter-intuitive nature of informal experiences, abstract nature of physics principles learned in pre-tertiary studies, limited opportunities to encounter phenomena formally, and so on). The account demonstrates how one threshold concept entails a wide range of potentially troublesome aspects that students can (and do) encounter.

Across the cases, the depth with which troublesomeness was considered signalled substantial variation in pedagogical thinking and understanding. Within each case, interrelated dimensions of pedagogical thinking emerged as distinctive qualities within individual teacher's intentions and reasoning.

DIMENSIONS OF TEACHER THINKING RELATED TO SUPPORTING THE LEARNING OF THRESHOLD CONCEPTS

The focus here is on what teachers do to facilitate learning and to support students in overcoming troublesome knowledge. These accounts reveal how pedagogical intentions and reasoning comprise a suite of related dimensions: (a) intention, comprising a focus, action and rationale, (b) reasoning, in which teachers described the role of the student as learner, the positioning of the student to the threshold concept, the role of the teacher, and the positioning of the teacher to the threshold concept.

Dimensions of Pedagogical Intentions and Reasoning (Focus, Action and Rationale)

Pedagogical intentions could be discerned through three related dimensions: *focus, action, and rationale.*

The *focus dimension* refers to the aspect of the teaching and learning agenda that is foremost in the teacher's mind, or of uppermost concern within pedagogical intention. The Asian studies teacher was concerned with imbuing high levels of interest and enthusiasm within students. The Arts teacher was highly focused on offsetting potential resistance to the sceptical perspective (she felt students often considered analysis of the structure and framing of a message to be 'silly'). The inertia teacher grounded his intentions in a focus on the nature of everyday 'physics' experiences that appeared to students to be counter to the formal physics principles and concepts needed for learning. Each focus is based on a genuine concern for students, but they are qualitatively different when *troublesome knowledge* is the point of reference. Only the Arts teacher and the inertia teacher are explicitly concerned with what is troublesome for students.

Closely related to the focus dimension is the *action dimension*, the particular actions or activities the teacher *intends* (or intended) to undertake or facilitate within pedagogical interactions. The Asian studies teacher described highly detailed, multimedia presentations, each carefully selected by himself or his colleagues to engender a passion and interest in all things Asian. The Arts teacher also related her use of media representations and current events she hoped provided a connection or sense of relevance for students. This emphasis on the *presentation* of materials or contexts comprised the mainstay of both teachers' intended actions. Moreover, both teachers indicated that much of their planning and teaching energies were allocated to the collection and presentation of such materials, viewed as central to their pedagogical role and expertise.

In contrast, the inertia teacher described his attempts and intentions to *engage students in looking at phenomena differently* by highlighting particular phenomenological aspects and posing questions he hoped would put into doubt the informal assumptions about inertia students may have constructed based on everyday, but counter-intuitive, experiences (such as standing up in a bus as it brakes or turns a corner).

The contrast is sharper still as we examine the *rationale dimension* of each teacher's stated intentions and reasoning. The Asian studies teacher is committed to generating widespread interest and enthusiasm; he wants students to '*see just how interesting Asia is*'. He likes to think that the theoretical concepts within the threshold concept (a reflexive integration of concepts such as modernisation, globalisation, cultural convergence) *come in through the back door*, since they are apparent within the many examples and events 'presented' in seminars and lectures (provided students read the textbook). Similarly, the Arts teacher hopes to change the way her students view the nature and purpose of deconstructive work. By providing interesting and topical examples of text and media, she feels students will more readily engage in the process. This, together with her emphasis on '*modelling how to do*' deconstruction, comprises her pedagogical rationale, which she couches as 'providing access to' materials and concepts.

The inertia teacher is also concerned with shifting student's existing ways of thinking, but seeks to do so through deliberate collaborative engagement in the *re-examination* of these assumptions and guided *analysis* of physics phenomena. He argues that by bringing the phenomena of inertia into view from various angles students are more able to question, modify and rebuild their thinking appropriately. Moreover, he feels that by doing so students will gain first hand experience in the process of *thinking like a scientist;* a process he feels is better learned through collaborative questioning, analysis, and inquiry, than by direct explanation.

In summary, the inertia teacher places student's existing *ways of apprehending* the threshold concept, and his detailed understanding of what may prove *troublesome for learning*, as central to his pedagogical agenda. The Asian studies teacher appears to place a premium on how students *feel* about the topics or themes that engender the threshold concept, while the Arts teacher is primarily concerned with *presenting a particular way of 'doing' deconstruction* that she expects will be directly taken up by students.

Within each of these examples, and in others within this study, questions of who does what and why emerge: within teachers' pedagogical intentions, and most explicitly within teacher's pedagogical reasoning, there are distinct views about the role of the student, what needs to be done to learn, and how the student is positioned (by the teacher) in relation to the threshold concept. There are similar views about the role and positioning of the teacher.

Dimensions of Pedagogical Reasoning (Roles and Positioning of Students and Teachers)

As teachers described their approaches, and reasoned through and elaborated on their pedagogical activities with their colleagues, four salient themes or dimensions emerged. These dimensions proved useful in representing further variation of teacher's ways of thinking about their students within the act of learning, and how they view themselves as teachers within this interaction. Since teachers' accounts are directed at the teaching and learning of a particular threshold concept, they entail a reference to the relatedness of both the student and the teacher to the threshold concept in question. The role of the participants in the pedagogical act, together with the positioning of the participants to the pedagogical focus, comprise potent aspects of teacher's pedagogical thinking.

Briefly put, dimensions of pedagogical reasoning include: (a) the role of the student as learner positioned in relation to the threshold concept, and (b) the role of the self as teacher and positioning to the threshold concept.

The Role of the Student in Position to the Threshold Concept

Throughout the Asian studies teacher's account students are positioned as 'audience' to a sequence of detailed highly visual presentations. The teacher assumes students will make sense of the course by making connections between what they read in a textbook and the examples, events, and visual anecdotes provided in lectures and seminars. Since the connections are not made explicitly, nor the concepts within the textbook attended to directly in teacher-student interactions, the role of the student seems to entail the identification of concepts within presentations. However the integration and composition of the concepts as a coherent whole, and indeed the threshold concept of 'Asia' itself, are not discussed nor explicitly invited within the teaching and learning agenda. Students may play 'spot the concept' whilst sidestepping an integrated understanding of 'Asia'.

The Arts teacher describes clear expectations of the student's role in learning, which entail learning the process of deconstruction *as she has demonstrated it*, and taking on the stance, processes, and understanding *by virtue of the access she has provided.* Foremost for her is the student's undertaking to apprehend this object of learning. Given her emphasis on providing examples of how this may be done (which are evident in her focus, action and rationale dimensions) her view of students appears to be that of *naïve and uncritical learner* as she discounts the need to acknowledge existing ways of thinking. Like the Asian studies teacher, she overlooks the need of students to navigate a *deliberate shift in existing ways of knowing*, despite the distinctly sceptical positional stance deconstruction requires. As a result, students appear positioned towards *unquestioning acceptance* of a threshold concept that is *construed and represented by the teacher.*

The inertia teacher again differs in comparison. By his account, students must undertake the role of learner by *engaging in constant analysis* of their existing ways of thinking. By his direction, they are required to continually assess the degree to which their evolving understanding usefully explains the phenomena of inertia within a range of contexts. This continuous inquiry means the threshold concept is introduced and reintroduced to students, not as a 'pre-packaged object of knowledge' but as a phenomenon that requires careful apprehension and deliberate redevelopment of individual understanding. In this account, students are involved in the continuous *reconstitution* of the threshold concept as an internally, personally constructed phenomena, vetted through further engagement with their peers and the teacher.

The Role of the Teacher and Positioning to the Threshold Concept

For both the Asian studies and Arts teachers, the question *'what do you do to support students in learning this threshold concept?'* garnered responses grounded firmly in presentation-oriented approaches. Each saw their role as entailing the formulation of the threshold concept and the context in which it would be best presented. Each enjoyed hunting down particularly salient representations of the object they had in mind, albeit with a focus on what they felt students would find interesting, relevant, and accessible. The Arts teacher placed particular emphasis on her capacity to 'repackage' the threshold concept for students.

In each of these two cases, the teachers viewed themselves as 'experts' in both the discipline and the threshold concept, where the status of the threshold concept wavered towards being teachers' constructs rather than vetted disciplinary thinking and knowing. Returning to troublesomeness as a filter, this emphasis is problematic. What may be difficult or challenging for students conceptually, epistemologically, or procedurally is easily overlooked, and the potential for mimicry seems high.

On the other hand, the inertia teacher casts his role as one of pedagogic inquirer, where he as teacher is focused on unearthing the many possible issues students may face in learning. He details the various ways in which students construe inertia, and plans to engage in these directly from a range of angles.

CONCLUDING DISCUSSION: THRESHOLD CONCEPTS FOR UNIVERSITY TEACHING AND LEARNING

There are three threshold concepts central to university teaching and learning: *threshold concepts as subject matter, as learning, as teaching.* These simple labels run the risk of appearing derivative or obvious. While these terms are well known and soundly articulated within the literature, an argument supported by the data presented earlier is that a deep and transformative understanding of these concepts *cannot be taken for granted* within university teaching.

Exploration, discussion and evidence for each proposed threshold concept are considered within the original Meyer and Land (2003) framework, except here reference to 'particular discipline' refers to the *discipline of teaching and learning in higher education*):

–   How is this threshold concept *fundamental* to how members of this discipline or field of study 'think' or view knowledge?
–   What entails effective and *transformative learning* for students/new members in this discipline? What are the existing ways in which they may view this concept, the subject matter, and the subject landscape, in order to develop sound comprehension of (a) the threshold concept, and in turn, (b) the discipline and its subject matter?
–   What may be *problematic* about this threshold concept (and in what way)?
–   What is the consequent *transformation of worldview* that is evoked by an understanding of this threshold concept?

Threshold Concept 1: As Subject Matter for Learning and Teaching

This threshold concept draws from the findings in this study, which point directly to the need to recast what we think we teach (and students learn). Disciplinary threshold concepts should provide the basis for considering *what to teach* and *what must be learned.* That is, *threshold concepts comprise the subject matter for learning and teaching.*

How Is Threshold Concept Fundamental to Disciplinary Ways of Thinking and Viewing Knowledge?

Expanding our view of the 'what' in learning to include transformative concepts – a particular philosophical stance, a values-based position, an affectively-oriented approach, evidence-based decision-making and practice, creative abstraction and conceptualisation of phenomena, interpretative analysis and commentary – changes the way *we think* about subject matter. Each of these concepts represents the *threshold nature* of the concepts described in this study, yet few teachers demonstrated the concrete presence of such concepts within the courses they were actually teaching. Despite the best pedagogical intentions, subject matter often remains limited to disparate substantive components, concepts, principles, laws and processes, while the transformative and integral aspects remain largely implicit.

What May Be Troublesome about This Threshold Concept?

The troublesome aspect of this threshold concept for new (and perhaps not so new) teachers is complex and multi-faceted. Few academics have taken time to examine and identify threshold concepts or the challenging but essential knowledge that comprises their discipline, and less have mapped out the transformational learning that must occur, and when. That science assumes an epistemology and set of social characteristics that are strikingly different (and to an extent counter to) social science has been documented. The ways in which these epistemological differences play out within teaching and learning – and in *learning to be* a university teacher are under examined.

What Is the Consequent Transformation That Is Needed/Evoked by This Threshold Concept?

Within the university context, subject matter has been shown to be highly problematic and teaching heavily critiqued as a forum for content-heavy curriculum that gives too little significance to deeper endeavours. The enhancement of learning is not simply a matter of embedding critical thinking or deep learning. Rather, it entails the more difficult task of engaging students in, and inducting them into, disciplinary ways of thinking and practising (Entwistle, 2005), discourses, canons, values and philosophies (Parker, 2002, 2003), and the *ways of being* within a profession or field of research and practice entails (Barnett, 2004). The epistemological nature of this endeavour invites significant transformation of our existing view of pedagogical knowledge and expertise.

Threshold Concept 2: Learning (as an Ongoing Process of Mastery and Transformation, of Particular Ways of Knowing, Viewing and Doing)

Learning is perhaps the most taken-for-granted concept related to teaching – yet remains widely under-examined as a *disciplinary-based phenomenon.* The descriptor 'an ongoing process of mastery and transformation, of particular ways of knowing, viewing and doing' recasts learning as a threshold concept, and asks 'what counts as transformational learning, and what manifests as troublesome, within the discipline, and why?'

How Is This Threshold Concept Fundamental to Disciplinary Ways of Thinking and Viewing Knowledge?

Every teacher in this study articulated an apparently student-centred approach. Each account included details of rich multimedia resources, modules and scenarios of immense currency and interest to students, and activities of a social, scaffolded and inquiry-oriented nature. No doubt each task appeared constructively 'aligned' and complete.

What remained absent was a focus on *learning* that was comprehensively informed by explicit articulations of *what must be learned: cognitively, affectively, philosophically, procedurally, and ontologically,* and understandings of *what proves troublesome, challenging, and recurringly difficult* for students. To this add the knowledge that learning requires opportunities for constant reconstitution of an individual's experience of phenomena. This is not a new idea but a perspective that, if embraced, could shift the propensity within university teaching from the need to 'pre-package' objects for learning.

What May Be Troublesome about This Threshold Concept?

This study revealed consistent mismatches between teacher's descriptions of threshold concepts as objects of knowledge and anticipated forms of learning and learning outcomes. The deficit appeared anchored within unexamined questions about what entails learning within specific concepts. As one example, the nursing teacher in this study provided a comprehensive and compelling description of 'psychosocial nursing' as a threshold concept comprising advocacy, mediation, and enactment of an integrative interdisciplinary knowledge base from which to construe healthcare contexts. Yet these concepts were barely present within her descriptions of her teaching or how/what her students might learn. The same could be said of many teachers in this study: the *aspect of self* that requires *transformation* on the part of the student seems absent from the pedagogical agenda.

Threshold concept 3: Teaching (as the facilitation of transformative learning and the induction of students into disciplinary ways of thinking, knowing and viewing)

The pedagogical act of teaching remains variably interpreted and enacted within higher education despite decades of praxis. For teaching to become practice directed at both the facilitation of *transformative* learning, as well as the *induction* of students into disciplinary ways of thinking, knowing and viewing, more is required of the average academic.

How Is This Threshold Concept Fundamental to Disciplinary Ways of Thinking and Viewing Knowledge?

Academic work involves a complex set of specialised knowledge, skills and understandings that together comprise the basis of expertise within a particular discipline or field of practice. Meyer and Land have deftly reminded us that teaching involves the translation of such understandings into experiences that enable others to learn. This *process of translation* is a complex one, the quality of which directly impacts upon the quality of learning. An academic who teaches by presenting 'relevant knowledge and information' provides a vastly different

303

learning experience for students to the academic who engages students in inquiry-oriented immersion of the discipline's ways of thinking and practice. This process of translation and the epistemological and ontological orientations that underpin it establishes a fresh view of pedagogical knowledge and expertise.

What May Be Troublesome about This Threshold Concept?

This question presents two related gaps for university teachers to traverse: (a) the gap between the assumed and taken for granted epistemological and ontological foundation from which an academic currently views the world, and the capacity to speak objectively about this view from a critical perspective, and (b) the necessity for pedagogical thinking, reasoning and action to be grounded within disciplinary epistemologies and ontology and to locate these centrally within the learning experience of students (often in the absence of a critical curriculum philosophy) (O'Brien, 2006).

The first gap challenges both teachers and development staff as they find themselves wedged between disciplinary epistemologies and critical curriculum discourse. The reflexivity and willingness to accept uncertainty and contestability, and to undertake the kind of evaluativist epistemological stance this requires cannot be taken for granted; yet is an essential precursor to the second challenge – the *translation* of disciplinary knowledge, thinking and practice into experiences of learning, being and acting for students. The second gap invites a reframing of current practices and discourse used by academic developers to engage disciplinary academics in pedagogical endeavours.

Herein lies the work to be done, for both pedagogical research and academic development. If we embrace these threshold concepts for university teaching and learning, and engage directly in the troubles they pose for pedagogical knowledge and reasoning, teaching may be more effectively directed towards student learning.

ACKNOWLEDGEMENTS

The author wishes to acknowledge the valuable contributions of Professor John D. Bain and Dr Linda Conrad in the design of the peer-to-peer discussion method used in the original study.

REFERENCES

Barnett, R. (2004). Learning for an unknown future. *Higher Education Research & Development, 23*(3), 247-260.

Davies, P. (2006). Threshold concepts: how can we recognise them? In J. H. F. Meyer, & R. Land (Eds.), *Overcoming barriers to student understanding: Threshold concepts and troublesome knowledge.* London and New York: Routledge.

Entwistle, N. (2005). Learning outcomes and ways of thinking across contrasting disciplines and settings in higher education. *The Curriculum Journal, 16*(1), 67-82.

Gess-Newsome, J. & Lederman, N. G. (Eds.) (1999). *Examining pedagogical content knowledge.* Dordrecht: Kluwer Academic Publishers.

Healey, M., & Jenkins, A. (2003). Discipline-based educational development. In H. Eggins & R. Macdonald (Eds.), *The scholarship of academic development*. Buckingham, United Kingdom: The Society for Research into Higher Education & Open University Press.

Land, R., Cousin, G., Meyer, J. H. F., & Davies, P. (2006). Implications of threshold concepts for course design and evaluation. In J. H. F. Meyer, & R. Land (Eds.), *Overcoming barriers to student understanding: Threshold concepts and troublesome knowledge*. London and New York: Routledge.

Malcolm, J. & Zukas, M. (2001). Bridging pedagogic gaps: Conceptual discontinuities in higher education. *Teaching in Higher Education, 6*(1), 33-42.

Meyer, J. H. F. & Land, R. (2003). Threshold concepts and troublesome knowledge: linkages to ways of thinking and practising within the disciplines. In C. Rust (Ed.), *Improving student learning: Improving student learning theory and practice − 10 years on*. Oxford: OCSLD.

Meyer, J. H. F. & Land, R. (2005). Threshold concepts and troublesome knowledge (2): Epistemological considerations and a conceptual framework for teaching and learning. *Higher Education, 49*(3), 373-388.

Meyer, J. H. F. & Land, R. (Eds.) (2006a). *Overcoming barriers to student understanding. Threshold concepts and troublesome knowledge*. London and New York: Routledge

Meyer, J. H. F. & Land, R. (2006b). Threshold concepts and troublesome knowledge: Issues of liminality. In J. H. F. Meyer & R. Land (Eds.), *Overcoming barriers to student understanding: Threshold concepts and troublesome knowledge*. London and New York: Routledge.

O'Brien, M. (2006). Threshold concepts for university teaching. Paper presented to the Inaugural International Conference for the International Society for Scholarship in Teaching and Learning (ISSoTL), Washington DC, United States, 9th to 11th November.

Parker, J. (2002). A new disciplinarity: Communities of knowledge, learning and practice. *Teaching in Higher Education, 7*(4), 373-386.

Parker, J. (2003). Reconceptualising the curriculum: From commodification to transformation. *Teaching in Higher Education, 8*(4), 529-543.

Perkins, D. (2006). Constructivism and troublesome knowledge. In J. H. F. Meyer & R. Land (Eds.), *Overcoming barriers to student understanding: Threshold concepts and troublesome knowledge*. London and New York: Routledge.

Rubin H. J. & Rubin I. (2005). *Qualitative interviewing: The art of hearing data* (2nd edition). Thousand Oaks, CA: Sage Publications.

Seidman, I. E. (1991). *Interviewing as qualitative research: A guide for researchers in education and the social sciences*. New York: US: Teachers College Press.

Shulman, L. S. (1987). Knowledge and teaching: Foundations of the new reform. *Educational Researcher, 15*(2), 1-22.

Wilson, S. M., Shulman, L. S., & Richert, E. (1987). 150 different ways of knowing: Representations of knowlege in teaching. In J. Calderhead (Ed.), *Exploring teachers' thinking*. Wiltshire: Cassell Education Limited.

AFFILIATIONS

Mia O'Brien
Teaching and Educational Development Institute
The University of Queensland

LIST OF CONTRIBUTORS

Andrew Ashwin has a background in Economics education and currently works as Content Developer at Biz/ed, a free online service for students, teachers and lecturers of business, economics, accounting, leisure and recreation and travel and tourism. Biz/ed, part of Thomson Learning, is targeted at students and teachers in the post-16 education sector, covering schools, further education colleges, universities and beyond. The site offers support for economics, business, accounting, leisure and recreation and travel and tourism at many different levels from A Levels to MBA.

Caroline Baillie is the Dupont Canada Chair of Engineering Education Research and Development at Queens University, Kingston, Ontario. Her role is to enhance the learning experience of engineering students across the Faculty whilst maintaining her research and teaching interests in materials science and engineering She has over 100 publications, papers and books in materials science and education. Her most recent books include a Routledge publication 'Effective learning and teaching in engineering' and an edited Campus volume 'Travelling facts: the social construction, distribution and accumulation of knowledge'.

Jonte Bernhard is an associate professor in experimental physics, especially electronics, at Linköping University, Campus Norrköping, Sweden. His research is presently focused on engineering and physics education, and he has initiated the Engineering Education Research Group in the School of Engineering at Linköping University. Dr Bernhard is/has been responsible for several projects in Engineering and Physics Education Research and Development funded by either the Swedish Research Council or the Swedish National Agency for Higher Education. Previously Dr Bernhard has an extensive record of research in magnetic materials with a Ph.D. in Solid State Physics and a M.Sc. (Eng.) degree in Engineering Physics from Uppsala University. Presently he is the chairman of the Physics Working Group of the European Society for Engineering Education (SEFI) and the chairman for the Swedish Science Education Research Association.

Jonas Boustedt has a University Diploma in Electronics and Computer Engineering from University of Gävle, a Master of Education in Mathematics and Computer Science from Uppsala University, a Master of Science in Computer Science from Uppsala University, and a Licentiate of Philosophy in Computer Science with specialization in Computer Science Education from Uppsala University. He holds a tenure position as lecturer at the Computer Science Department at University of Gävle (Sweden) and is currently working on the second part of his Ph.D. He started his working carreer as a developer of embedded systems for tele and radio communications in the rescue industry.

Anna-Karin Carstensen, M. Sc. (Eng.), is a lecturer at the School of Engineering at Jönköping University, Sweden. She is also a doctoral student in Engineering education research within the Swedish National Graduate School in Science and Technology Education at Linköping University. Mrs Carstensen will defend her thesis with the preliminary title 'Connect: Models and the Real World Connected through Lab-Work in Electric Circuit Theory' in 2007. She has an M.Sc. degree in Engineering Physics and Electronics from Linköping University.

Glynis Cousin has a background in the sociology of educationand has worked in teacher training across the school, adult, community and higher education sectors. Her publications are on issues of diversity, e-learning and higher education research and evaluation methods. She is Senior Adviser at the Higher Education Academy in York, UK.

Moya Cove is a lecturer in the Faculty of Education at the University of Glasgow where she teaches on a range of undergraduate and postgraduate literacy courses in teacher education. Her background in primary teaching has included working in mainstream and special schools and she has retained an interest in inclusive education. Her research interests include early literacy development, formative assessment of reading, the development of 'new' literacies and teacher education. She has worked in partnership with a number of Scottish education authorities to support national and local literacy initiatives and with the Scottish curriculum body (Learning and Teaching Scotland) to develop national curriculum support materials in pre-school education.

Peter Davies is Professor of Education Policy and Director of the Institute for Educational Policy Research (IEPR) at Staffordshire University, Stoke on Trent, UK. His current research focuses on economic and access issues in education policy and disciplinary contexts for assessment for learning. He is co-editor of the International Review of Economics Education and is currently directing a project on 'Embedding threshold concepts in undergraduate Economics' funded by the Higher Education Funding Council for England.

Anna Eckerdal has an M.Sc. in Scientific Subjects Education including Mathematics and Physics, and a Licentiate of Philosophy in Computer Science with specialization in Computer Science Education from Uppsala University. After many years of teaching high school mathematics, physics and programming, she currently holds a tenure position as lecturer at the Department of Information Technology at Uppsala University. She is finishing up the second part of her Ph.D., studying how students learn object-oriented programming. From this research she has published a number of empirical-computer-science-education papers.

Noel Entwistle is Professor Emeritus of Education at the University of Edinburgh and has been an Editor of the *British Journal of Educational Psychology* and of the international journal, *Higher Education*. He has honorary degrees from the Universities of Gothenburg and Turku, and holds an Oeuvre Award from the European Association for Research in Learning and Instruction. His main research interests have been in the identification and measurement of approaches to studying in higher education, and influences on these, and in exploring the nature of academic understanding. Between 2001 and 2005 he was co-director of a four-year ESRC research project, within the Teaching and Learning Research Programme, on 'Enhancing teaching-learning environments in undergraduate degree courses' within the Teaching and Learning Research Programme, and he has recently edited *Student Learning and University Teaching* for the British Psychological Society.

Mick Flanagan is a Senior Lecturer in the Department of Electronic and Electrical Engineering, University College London (UCL). He started his research career as a biochemist and then crossed disciplines to electronic engineering, specialising in the overlap of electronics and biology. He initially carried out this research in a large industrial laboratory later moving to UCL. In common with many engineers who have moved from industry to academe he became concerned with many aspects of the conventional training of engineers. As much of his teaching has been in interdisciplinary areas, such as nanotechnology and the teaching of aspects of computer science to engineers, he has also developed pedagogic interests in the problems of teaching interdisciplinary subjects to classes of students with mixed disciplinary backgrounds.

Gigi Foster is a Senior Lecturer in Applied Microeconomics & Econometrics based in the Centre for Regulation and Market Analysis at the University of South Australia. She has a Bachelor's degree in Ethics, Politics and Economics from Yale University and a Ph.D in Economics from the University of Maryland. Her teaching interests range across labour economics, applied microeconomics/ econometrics, health economics and public finance and evaluation. Her research interests include social effects in education, health, and the workplace, human sorting processes, labour and health economics and applied microeconomics

Anne Johnson holds undergraduate degrees in Art History with a minor in English Literature, Education and Computing and Information Science. She is currently working on a master's thesis in the Faculty of Education at Queens University, Kingston, where her focus is on Engineering Education. Her professional experience includes several years as Documentation Editor for Queen's Information Technology Services. Since completing her Computing Science degree, she has worked as a technical writer specializing in software documentation for the rail and mining industries. She taught computer programming and communications within the Computer Engineering-Technology-Software Developer and Electronics Engineering Technology programmes at St. Lawrence College for seven years before returning to Queen's.

Ray Land is Professor of Higher Education and Director of the Centre for Academic Practice and Learning Enhancement (CAPLE) at the University of Strathclyde, Glasgow. His research interests include educational development, threshold concepts and troublesome knowledge, and theoretical aspects of digital learning. He is the author of *Educational Development: Discourse, Identity and Practice* (Open University Press 2004) and co-editor of *Education in Cyberspace* (RoutledgeFalmer, 2005), and *Overcoming Barriers to Student Learning: Threshold Concepts and Troublesome Knowledge* (Routledge, 2006).

Jean Mangan is a Principal Lecturer at Staffordshire University and has taught a wide range of economics courses. In recent years she has specialised in econometrics, business decision making and risk management, and the economics of the arts. Currently her research is in the area of the Economics of Education, where she has published widely in leading international journals. Since 2004 she has been Manager of the *Embedding Threshold Concepts* Project funded by the Higher Education Funding Council for England. This project aims to improve students' understanding in economics by developing first year undergraduates' acquisition of threshold concepts, to extend the identification of these concepts and to assess ways of embedding these in the first year curriculum.

Julie McAdam is a University Teacher in English Language in the Department of Curriculum Studies at the University of Glasgow. She is engaged in teaching Language on the Bachelor of Education Programme and the Post Graduate Diploma in Education. She also supervises students on the Masters in Education (English Language pathway). She is currently involved in research on threshold concepts in the formation of beginning teachers and in the mentoring of teachers.

Robert McCartney earned his B.S. and M.S. degrees in Natural Resources from the University of Michigan. After a number of years working in a photobiology lab at the Smithsonian Institution, he returned to school at Brown University, where he earned his Sc.M. and Ph.D. degrees in Computer Science. He has published papers in artificial intelligence (planning, robotics, and diagrammatic reasoning) and computer science education. He is currently a faculty member of the Computer Science and Engineering Department at the University of Connecticut, and co-editor-in-chief of the ACM Journal on Educational Resources in Computing.

Robert McCormick is Professor in the Centre for Curriculum and Teaching Studies, Faculty of Education and Language Studies, The Open University (OU) UK. In almost 35 years at the OU he has worked on many courses on curriculum, assessment and learning, and more recently on the use of ICT in the classroom. He has directed several research projects in technology education: a UK Economic and Social Research Council (ESRC) funded study of problem solving, a UK Design Council funded study on the use of mathematics in Design and Technology, co-directed an evaluation of a project to encourage electronics in the curriculum. In the last few years he has completed a series of projects (ERNIST, CELEBRATE, P2P) co-ordinated by European Schoolnet. He was until recently co-director of the ESRC Teaching and Learning Programme research project *Learning how to learn – in classrooms, schools and networks* (almost £1 million), and directed an evaluation of the UK National College for School Leadership online environment. He has also worked in China, Pakistan and Tanzania on distance learning projects.

James McGonigal is Professor of English in Education in the Department of Curriculum Studies at the University of Glasgow. His work involves teaching, research, editing and supervision in the learning and teaching of children's language and literacy. His research interests include knowledge about language, children's literature, classroom interaction, teacher formation, Scots-Irish literary and cultural relations, and creative writing. He is co-editor of *Ethically Speaking: Voice and Values in Modern Scottish Writing* (Rodopi, 2006). His poetry in English and Scots has won literary prizes in Scotland and Ireland, and a bursary in 2002 from the Scottish Arts Council.

Jan Meyer is a Professor of Education and the Director of the Centre for Learning, Teaching, and Research in Higher Education at the University of Durham in the United Kingdom. Much of his research career has been devoted to exploring mechanisms for developing metalearning capacity in students, to the modelling of individual differences in student learning, and to the construction of discipline centred models of student learning. He has more recently developed with Ray Land and others the conceptual framework of *threshold concepts* – a framework that provides a new lens through which to focus on critical aspects of variation in student learning and the acquisition or not of disciplinary-specific ways of thinking, reasoning and explanation.

Jan Erik Moström has an M.Sc. in Computer Science from Luleå Technical University, Sweden and a Technical Licentiate from Umeå University, Sweden. He currently holds a tenure position as lecturer at the Department of Computing Science at Umeå University and has extensive experience in teaching a wide range of computer science related subjects, ranging from software development and operating systems to human computer interaction to computer architecture. He has also been teaching software courses for several companies. He has published a number of computer science education articles.

Mia O'Brien is an academic at the Teaching and Educational Development Institute, University of Queensland, where she frequently sips coffee in an outdoor cafe whilst consulting with disciplinary colleagues on the nature of threshold concepts. Her research is driven by an insatiable interest in the nature of knowledge and practice within disciplinary communities, and the implications for theorising learning and the curriculum. She has a passion for investigating teachers' pedagogical content knowledge and reasoning, and continues to seek creative ways to research students' experiences of troublesome knowledge. In

311

each of these pursuits, Mia aims to collaborate with like-minded souls who share an enthusiasm for good coffee and great jazz.

Marina Orsini-Jones is Subject Co-ordinator for Italian and employability tutor for the Department of International Studies and Social Science at Coventry University. Marina is seconded as Teaching Fellow for 50% of her time to the Centre for the Study of Higher Education (CSHE) and is involved in staff development both within the Faculty of Business, Environment and Society and in the CSHE. She researches mainly in the field of Education and Educational Technology. She has been involved in action research investigating the impact of WebCT-based collaborative learning environments into teaching and learning, and in 2004 founded the UK-wide 'Virtual Learning Environments Languages User Group'. She is also the co-ordinator for the CITLL (Centre for Information Technology in Language Learning). Since 2003, she has also been involved in researching 'troublesome knowledge' encountered by first year students at University, with particular reference to reflective learning, personal development planning and portfolio writing.

Jane Osmond has a strong interest in issues of equality and diversity in higher education, in particular equal access to the curriculum. She is currently a researcher for the Centre of Excellence for Transport and Product Design (CETPD) at Coventry University and is involved in researching Transport and Design students' spatial awareness skills, threshold concepts in design and internationalisation of the curriculum. Previous projects include 'Improving Retention, Supporting Students'; 'Same but different: working effectively with student diversity in HE'; 'Mapping Equality and Diversity Initiatives in HE' and 'Meeting the Challenge: Managing Equality and Diversity in Higher Education'.

David Perkins is a Senior Professor of Education at the Harvard Graduate School of Education. He is a founding member of the well-known research and development group Harvard Project Zero, co-directed it for almost 30 years, and now serves as senior co-director. He has conducted long-term programs of research and development in the areas of creativity and reasoning in the sciences and arts, learning for understanding, organizational development, and online learning. He is the author of *Archimedes' Bathtub, Smart Schools, Outsmarting IQ, Knowledge as Design,* and several other books, as well as many articles. He has helped develop instructional programs and approaches for teaching for thinking and understanding, including initiatives in South Africa, Sweden, Australia, Israel, and Latin America.

Mark Ratcliffe received the B.Eng. and Ph.D. degrees from the University of Wales, Aberystwyth. He taught computer science for 14 years, most recently as a Senior Lecturer in Aberystwyth. In recent years he has developed research interests in computer science education and in particular, has worked on two distinct areas: VorteX and Tweek. He is a member of the British Computer Society and currently has taken a position as a software engineer at Valtech UK in London.

312

Kate Sanders has an A.B. in classics from Brown University, a J.D. from Harvard Law School, and Sc.M. and Ph.D. degrees in computer science from Brown University, with a dissertation on artificial intelligence and law. She is Associate Professor and Chair of the Mathematcs and Computer Science Department at Rhode Island College, in Providence, Rhode Island (USA). In addition to her work in artificial intelligence, she has published numerous empirical-computer-science-education papers and an introductory programming textbook, Object-Oriented Programming in Java: a graphical approach (with A. van Dam).

Maggi Savin-Baden is Professor of Higher Education Research at Coventry University and Director of the Learning Innovation Group. Maggi's current research is exploring the impact of innovative forms of learning in new spaces such as Second Life and new distance spaces. To date she has published six books on problem-based learning. Her seventh book entitled *Learning Spaces* was published in December 2007. In her spare time she is doing an MSc in digital technology and learning to snowboard both in real life and Second Life.

Martin Shanahan is Associate Professor in Economics at the University of South Australia. He researches in a variety of fields including economics education. Economic history, wealth and income distribution, and applied cost-benefit analysis. He is currently co-editor of the *Australian Economic History Review.* He has worked for a number of years wit professor Jan H. F. Meyer modelling variation in undergraduate students' approaches to learning and postgraduate students' conceptions of research. The practical applications of their research – Learning to Learn in Economics – recently received a University of South Australia Vice-Chancellor's Award for Innovation

Dermot Shinners-Kennedy works in the Computer Science and Information Systems (CSIS) department of the University of Limerick, Ireland. He is a programmer who tries to teach programming to novices and anyone else prepared to listen. He is influenced by the constructivist approach and his main interests relate to the conceptions and misconceptions of novices and exploiting the analogical and metaphorical basis of everyday examples *à la* Papert and others. He is not a member of a programming language sect and therefore has no evangelical baggage for a particular programming language .He is a member of the language of programming sect, which currently has a membership of one!

Caryl Sibbett is a lecturer in the School of Education, Queen's University Belfast, and she lectures in art therapy, counselling and education. She is an Art Therapist (HPC Reg.), a BACP Accredited Counsellor/Psychotherapist and a supervisor, working in private practice and a Health and Social Care Trust. Current research projects include research supervision in one of four sites in a large scale national three-arm, parallel, randomised controlled trial of art therapy groups for people with schizophrenia. International connections include teaching on a Masters in Art

Therapy programme in Europe. Publications include a co-edited book on *Art Therapy and Cancer Care*, book chapters and papers in various journals including the *British Medical Journal*. She is Chair of the Northern Ireland Allied Health Professions Research Forum. Research interests are diverse and include "nettlesome knowledge", liminality, art therapy, arts-based learning and research, medical culture and education.

Jan Smith is a lecturer in the Centre for Academic Practice and Learning Enhancement at the University of Strathclyde where she teaches on the Postgraduate Certificate in Advanced Academic Studies. Her research interests are in the history, policy and communicative aspects of e-learning and the theories and practices of educational development work. Her doctoral research focuses on the socialisation experiences of new academic staff. Prior to her current role, she worked on a range of curriculum development projects at University College London, the University of London's External Programme and in the Learning Technology Research Institute at the University of North London. Before educational development work in higher education, she taught aspects of computing in further education.

Charlotte Taylor is a Senior Lecturer in the School of Biological Sciences, and Associate Dean for Learning and Teaching in the Faculty of Science, at the University of Sydney. As deputy director in the First Year Biology Unit, Charlotte had 15 years' experience in course design, assessment and online learning for large classes of over 1,500 students, and received a University of Sydney Teaching Excellence Award in 2000 for this work. She is the Chair of the Science Faculty Education Research Group (SciFER) and has published collaborative papers in areas of learning through writing, teaching large classes, giving feedback and the use of online discussions in development of academic writing skills. Her research on threshold concepts in Biology encompasses investigations into teachers' and students' conceptions of troublesome knowledge.

William Thompson began his professional career as a secondary school teacher, after this he worked as an educational psychologist before joining the staff of Queens University Belfast where he taught Guidance and Counselling in the School of Education for 24 years. For the past 8 years he has been self-employed working as a consultant in both public and private sector organisations. His research interests include exploring the relationships between organisational and professional cultures and personal and professional development. He is particularly interested in the shadow cast within organisations on both culture and individual development by the suboptimal resolution of dilemmas with an ethical dimension.

Vernon Trafford is Research Professor in the Faculty of Education and in the Research and Development Services at Anglia Ruskin University. Since 2001 his research, with Dr Shosh Leshem, of Oranim Academic College and Haifa University, has been into the nature of doctorateness and the doctoral viva. Their work into under-researched aspects of the doctoral experience generates theoretical insights on practice for candidates, supervisors and examiners. Their research findings will appear in Trafford and Leshem, *Achieving your Doctorate: by focusing on your viva from the start*, Open University Press 2008. Their presentations at IATEFL, EARLI, ECER and their consultancies have drawn upon threshold concepts to explain blockages in doctoral learning. Vernon is currently Consultant/Researcher in a 3-year Higher Education Academy project entitled 'Supporting and enhancing postgraduate students' research and related skills development through research-evidence based practices'. This project incorporates threshold concepts as a diagnostic tool to assess doctoral learning.

Andrew Turner is Principal Lecturer in Education Research and Development in the Centre for the Study of Higher Education (CSHE) at Coventry University where he leads the iPED Pedagogical Research Network and the team of Teaching Development Fellows. In addition, he co-ordinates the University's Personal Development Planning strategy and is Research Fellow at the Centre of Excellence for Transport and Product Design. Andrew has a background as an environmental biologist and made the move to education research and development around 3 years ago although he still maintains an interest in science communication and education. His main research interests are in the student experience of Higher Education and the scholarship of educational development.

Carol Zander has an A.B. in Mathematics from San Diego State University and an M.S. in Mathematics from the University of Colorado. After a short hiatus working at IBM, she received an M.S. and Ph.D. in Computer Science from Colorado State University, with a dissertation in Distributed Artificial Intelligence. She has taught at the University of Maine, Colorado State University, Seattle University, and is currently on the faculty at the University of Washington, Bothell. Her current primary research interests lie in computer science education, in particular object-oriented design and issues relating to software development in general.

INDEX

Lightning Source UK Ltd
Milton Keynes UK
06 November 2009

145910UK00001B/54/P